W9-DGG-879

The
PRACTICE of
QUALITATIVE
RESEARCH

Second Edition

Dedicated with love to Sarah Alexandra, Julia Ariel, and Madeline Claire

The PRACTICE of QUALITATIVE RESEARCH

Second Edition

Sharlene Nagy Hesse-Biber

Boston College

Patricia Leavy

Stonehill College

Los Angeles | London | New Delhi
Singapore | Washington DC

Copyright © 2011 by SAGE Publications, Inc.

All rights reserved. No part of this book may be reproduced or utilized in any form or by any means, electronic or mechanical, including photocopying, recording, or by any information storage and retrieval system, without permission in writing from the publisher.

For information:

SAGE Publications, Inc.
2455 Teller Road
Thousand Oaks, California 91320
E-mail: order@sagepub.com

SAGE Publications India Pvt. Ltd.
B 1/I 1 Mohan Cooperative Industrial Area
Mathura Road, New Delhi 110 044
India

SAGE Publications Ltd.
1 Oliver's Yard
55 City Road
London EC1Y 1SP
United Kingdom

SAGE Publications Asia-Pacific Pte. Ltd.
33 Pekin Street #02-01
Far East Square
Singapore 048763

Printed in the United States of America

Library of Congress Cataloging-in-Publication Data

Hesse-Biber, Sharlene Nagy.
The practice of qualitative research/Sharlene Nagy Hesse-Biber, Patricia Leavy.—2nd ed.
   p. cm.
Includes bibliographical references and index.
ISBN 978-1-4129-7457-8 (pbk.)
  1. Social sciences—Research. 2. Qualitative research. I. Leavy, Patricia, 1975– II. Title.

H62.H478 2011
001.4′2—dc22   2009047929

This book is printed on acid-free paper.

10 11 12 13 14   10 9 8 7 6 5 4 3 2 1

Acquisitions Editor:	Vicki Knight
Associate Editor:	Lauren Habib
Editorial Assistant:	Ashley Dodd
Production Editor:	Astrid Virding
Copy Editor:	Jacqueline Tasch
Typesetter:	C&M Digitals (P) Ltd.
Proofreader:	Scott Oney
Indexer:	Kathleen Paparchontis
Cover Designer:	Candice Harman
Marketing Manager:	Stephanie Adams

Brief Contents

Detailed Contents

Preface

When we wrote the first edition of *The Practice of Qualitative Research,* our goal was to provide students and teachers with *a practice model* of qualitative research. Unlike authors of other qualitative methods texts, we wanted to present students with *a problem-centric approach* to qualitative research. In other words, instead of offering a laundry list of research methods, we wanted to link the practice of any research method to specific research questions. We stress the importance of having a "tight fit" between the specific research question and the method or set of methods chosen to get at any research problem. Another goal was for students to practice research reflexively by becoming aware of their own researcher standpoint, that is, the set of values and attitudes they bring to any given research project, as well their assumptions about the nature of the social world.

The Practice of Qualitative Research presents a practice model of qualitative research. This means several things. First, we present qualitative research as a process. By emphasizing process, students are shown how researchers make decisions along the way that impact the research findings. We offer a *holistic approach* to research, which emphasizes the interconnections between ontology, epistemology, methodology, and methods. Inspired by Erving Goffman's notion of "back stage" and "front stage," we present "behind-the-scenes" boxes written by leading qualitative researchers. Each behind-the-scenes piece offers students a window into the real-world practice of qualitative research, which at times is messy and unpredictable.

Finally, *The Practice of Qualitative Research* was meant to be an engaging and user-friendly book. In this regard, we included several features. First, each chapter contains a glossary of key terms. Second, each methods chapter ends with discussion questions. Last, each chapter has an annotated list of Web sites so students can further explore areas of particular interest.

Major Themes and Features of the Second Edition

Our second edition has retained all of the key features that distinguish our approach to teaching qualitative research: a practice model, a holistic approach to research as a process, and user-friendly source material meant to engage students. However, we also bring a wealth of new information from the lessons we continue to garner from our own research practice, as well as those pedagogical ideas learned within the classroom setting. These experiences have informed the major themes, reorganization, and content of our new edition. One of the major challenges in writing the second edition was to retain the unique features of the first edition, such as the emphasis on practice, while adding new and diverse material, such as more interdisciplinary research examples (from communications, criminology, education, health studies, social work, sociology, and psychology). We hope we have done this well.

The Practice of Qualitative Research, second edition, presents a truly comprehensive review of qualitative and mixed methods research. We have made four important changes across all chapters in the book. First, we have added more diverse research examples in every chapter so that a broad cross-section of students can relate to the research topics covered. Second, we have provided a more balanced mix of theoretical perspectives. For ease of teaching and learning, we have categorized theoretical perspectives under two umbrella categories: the interpretive tradition and critical perspectives. Third, we have edited and streamlined the writing of each chapter. The chapters are more concise. Fourth, we have updated the citations throughout the book.

We have also clarified the four major themes of this book, which has informed the reorganization of the chapters in a consistent manner. The four themes of this book are (1) the pedagogy of engagement, (2) a practice model, (3) ethical decision making, and (4) resource material and live research methods.

The Pedagogy of Engagement

We have written the second edition bearing in mind how students learn and how teachers teach. As such, this book is predicated on the *pedagogy of engagement*. Each book chapter presents a set of key concepts as posed questions; as readers uncover the answers or a set of answers, they will participate in the social research process. The idea of each chapter is to place students and teacher in a dialogue with a set of critical questions that are meant to engage them. We can think of this type of pedagogy of engagement as compared with what is often thought of as a pedagogy of discussion.

Pedagogy of Engagement	Versus	Pedagogy of Discussion
Creation of ideas		Taking a specific action
Tracing reasoning		Convergence of ideas
Discovery		Arguing or debating
Seeking multiple understandings		Holding a position, defending a position
Playful		Needing to win/persuade
Relies on power of the group for input		Individualistic thinking
Iterative		Linear

The new edition also provides students with the opportunity for practicing reflexivity in the research process by providing them with a set of examples of research projects that range along a continuum from exemplary research to research that "needs improvement." Through engagement with different levels of research quality, this revised version will provide students with the opportunity to reflect on how the choices researchers make during the research process can impact the effectiveness of their projects. Students are encouraged to brainstorm about how less effective research projects can be made more effective. Students are presented with case studies that contain some of the most common mistakes researchers run into as their research projects proceed (for example, when the research problem and method are mismatched) and are offered an opportunity to benefit by developing on-the-fly research strategies for each of these less effective case studies. This serves to empower them with research strategy tools they can use when they encounter research issues in their own projects.

An Enhanced Practice Model

We have added more information about research design as a means of showing students how research is a process. We have clarified the relationships between ontology, epistemology, methodology, and methods through streamlined writing and tables that visually display the research process. The second edition also emphasizes the integration of theory and methods through clear examples that illustrate the linkage that we term the *research nexus.*

Expanded Ethical Decision-Making Focus

A strength of our first edition was an in-depth chapter on research ethics as an important part of the research process. In our second edition, we give ethics an even more central place by also weaving ethical decision making into individual methods chapters as well. In addition, we have revised the chapter on ethics so that it also presents students with more examples of types of ethical issues that are most likely to arise in their experiences, as well as the more notorious examples of ethical misconduct reviewed in the first edition. In addition, the world students live in is rapidly changing due to technological advances. Accordingly, we address the ethical issues that emerge as a result of Internet research and personal networking sites such as Facebook and MySpace.

Resource Material: Live Research Methods

We have added activities as well as more discussion questions that can be worked on in class or assigned as homework. We have reordered the end of each chapter, creating a Resources section that includes an annotated list of suggested Web sites as well as relevant journals. Most significant, we have created an in-depth resource for professors and students on our book's Web site. Our user-friendly Web site contains many additional resources including printable flashcards for glossary terms, hotlinks to relevant articles, and other ancillary materials that make the second edition of

The Practice of Qualitative Research a truly comprehensive textbook. Our Web site links make the research experience come alive by introducing student researchers to a wider research community with which they can readily interact.

New in the Second Edition: Chapter-by-Chapter Changes

Whereas our original edition was 11 chapters, we have expanded to 14 streamlined chapters divided into three parts.

Part I is titled "Qualitative Practice." Chapter 1 presents a student-friendly invitation to qualitative research. Chapter 2 focuses on approaches to qualitative research. For reader ease, we have categorized various theoretical approaches under three umbrella categories: post-positivist, interpretive, and critical. Under the interpretive umbrella, we review symbolic interaction, dramaturgy, the Chicago School, phenomenology, and ethnomethodology. Under the critical umbrella, we review postmodernism, post-structuralism, feminism, critical race theory, and queer theory. Using clear tables for visual learners, we illustrate the differences between these approaches. In this way, we also demonstrate a larger theme interwoven throughout the book: the integration of theory and methods. Chapter 3 provides a step-by-step analysis of the research process with specific examples and many tips for conducting research. Chapter 4 contains a review of ethical practice drawing on new technology-based examples. This chapter is geared toward the specific ethical problems student researchers may face as they embark on their first research project. We provide in-depth tips and strategies for navigating the sometimes thorny ethical issues involved throughout the research process.

Part II focuses on specific qualitative research methods. We have retained all of the methods chapters from the first edition and have added a new chapter on case study research. Chapter 5 on in-depth interviewing contains a wealth of examples and tips on conducting an interview as well as strategies student researchers may find useful as they hone their interviewing skills. Chapter 6 on oral history has been streamlined, and new research examples have been added on contemporary events and issues such as the September 11th terrorist attacks, Hurricane Katrina, developments in Iraq during and after the war, and the long-term aftermath of the Columbine High School shootings. We have also added a section about the impact of emergent technologies, such as digitization, on the oral history process, including data collection, analysis, and archiving. Chapter 7 on focus groups provides new research examples, such as the use of focus groups to study gay youth. We expand our discussion of the use of focus groups for accessing disenfranchised groups. We have also expanded our discussion of focus groups as a part of multimethod research, adding a section on combining focus groups with diary research. We have added three new sections on the following topics: the new practice of "concept mapping"; cross-cultural and international focus groups; and the impact of new technologies on focus group practice. Chapter 8 on ethnography provides student researchers with guideposts for conducting an ethnographic study. The chapter contains a number of exemplary ethnographic projects as well as strategies for analyzing ethnographic data. Chapter 9 on content analysis and unobtrusive methods includes a range of interdisciplinary and current media topics such as the 2008 presidential election, "green" advertising, and changing portrayals of race in media. Chapter 10 on case study research is entirely new. We provide an extensive case study for students to follow as well as a template for writing up their case study project. Chapter 11 on mixed methods research is written for the novice researcher and contains exemplary mixed methods research studies to guide student researchers through the variety of mixed methods designs that they might employ in their research projects. We stress the importance of the research question in deciding on a mixed methods research design. We present some tips on analyzing mixed methods data and introduce a range of analysis options students might consider.

We have restructured Part III, moving from two to three chapters. First, we have separated analysis and interpretation from the writing and representation phase. Chapter 12 now focuses entirely on analysis and interpretation. In this chapter, we have added additional information about computer-driven data analysis. We have provided a step-by-step guide to computer-assisted software for qualitative data analysis. We have also added a meaningful discussion of how a literature review and theory inform the analysis and interpretation of qualitative data. Finally, we provide a rich discussion of assessment issues, showing students how to assess qualitative research. Chapter 13 focuses on the writing and representation process. In this chapter, we provide a "hands-on" or "how-to" approach to conducting a literature review and show how to organize and present a research project. Chapter 14 focuses on the future of qualitative research. In this unique concluding chapter, we provide a prospective review of cutting-edge qualitative research practices especially with respect to digital multimedia data. We believe students will draw from these new data sources as they develop thesis projects. In this review, we discuss our concept of emergent methods, which are interdisciplinary innovative methods. These methods develop in response to new research questions, new theoretical perspectives, globalizing forces, and other changes that impact the work of social scientists. In particular, we briefly review technology-based emergent methods, arts-based research practices, new trends in narrative inquiry, and critical indigenous approaches to research.

We hope that these changes will make the second edition more comprehensive, engaging, user-friendly, and practice focused.

Sharlene Hesse-Biber and Patricia Leavy

Acknowledgments

We appreciate the help of a number of people who supported the project. First and foremost, we wish to acknowledge the support from the staff at SAGE Publications. We extend a spirited thank-you to our editor, Vicki Knight, for all of her wisdom, support, encouragement, and expert advice. We also thank the reviewers, who have aided us enormously with the revision process. We want to extend our thanks to Astrid Virding and Jacqueline Tasch, our SAGE editorial staff, as well as Stephanie Adams, SAGE'S marketing manager. Our gratitude also goes to the many scholars who let us "behind the scenes" with them, sharing their personal stories about the qualitative research process. We are deeply grateful to our students at Boston College and Stonehill College, particularly those in our qualitative methods courses, for their questions and inspiration.

Sharlene Nagy Hesse-Biber wishes to send a heartfelt thanks to her husband, neurologist Michael Peter Biber, M.D., and her two children, Sarah Alexandra Biber who is obtaining her PhD in genetics at Brandei University, and Julia Ariel Biber, who is obtaining her PhD in cello performance at CUNY graduate center. She is extremely grateful to her Boston College undergraduate research assistants, Natalie Horbachevsky (2009), Alicia Johnson (2011), and Lauren Kraics (2009), for their invaluable research skills and editorial advice, as well as their sense of humor and grace.

Patricia Leavy thanks her family and friends for their help, support, patience, inspiration, and humor during the preparation of this book. She is especially grateful to Mark for all of the conversations and laughs. Patricia dedicates her work on this book to Madeline for all of the magical hugs and giggles. She is deeply grateful to her Stonehill College undergraduate research assistants Jennifer Errante (2010) and Meaghan Stiman (2010) for their outstanding research assistance.

Finally, thanks to our reviewers:

Adia Harvey Wingfield, Georgia State University

Michelle L. Jay, University of South Carolina

Deborah Piatelli, Boston College

Susan B. Twombly, University of Kansas

About the Authors

Sharlene Nagy Hesse-Biber, PhD, is Professor of Sociology and the Director of Women's Studies at Boston College in Chestnut Hill, Massachusetts. She has published widely on the impact of sociocultural factors on women's body image, including her book, *Am I Thin Enough Yet? The Cult of Thinness and the Commercialization of Identity*, which was selected as one of *Choice* magazine's best academic books for 1996. In 2007, she published *The Cult of Thinness*. She is the coauthor of *Working Women in America: Split Dreams* and coeditor of *Feminist Approaches to Theory and Methodology: An Interdisciplinary Reader, Approaches to Qualitative Research: A Reader on Theory and Practice*, and *Emergent Methods in Social Research*. She recently edited the *Handbook of Feminist Research: Theory and Praxis*, which was selected as one of the Critics' Choice Award winners by the American Education Studies Association and was also chosen as one of *Choice* magazine's Outstanding Academic Titles for 2007. She is coeditor of the *Handbook of Emergent Methods*, and she contributed to the *Handbook of Grounded Theory* and *The Handbook of Mixed Methods Research* and editor of the forthcoming *Handbook of Emergent Technologies for Social Research*. She is author of *Mixed Methods Research: Merging Theory With Practice*. She is co-developer of the software program HyperRESEARCH, a computer-assisted program for analyzing qualitative data (www.researchware.com), and the new transcription tool, HyperTRANSCRIBE. A fully functional free demonstration of these programs is available at www.researchware.com. You can also find a free teaching edition for the programs at this Web site.

Patricia Leavy is Associate Professor of Sociology and was the founding Director of the Gender Studies Program (2004–2008) at Stonehill College in Easton, Massachusetts. She was the president (in 2009) of the New England Sociological Association. Patricia is the author of *Understanding Qualitative Research: Oral History, Method Meets Art: Arts-Based Research Practice*, and *Iconic Events* and coauthor of *Feminist Research Practice: A Primer* and *The Practice of Qualitative Research*. She is the coeditor of *Hybrid Identities: Theoretical and Empirical Examinations, Handbook of Emergent Methods, Emergent Methods in Social Research*, and *Approaches to Qualitative Research: A Reader on Theory and Practice*. She is the editor of a forthcoming book series, tentatively titled Understanding

Qualitative Research. She has published numerous scholarly articles and op-ed essays in the areas of collective memory, gender, popular culture, and research methodology. She is also a published poet. She has appeared on CNN's Glenn Beck show, Lou Dobbs Tonight, and Boston's Channel 5 news, and she is routinely quoted in newspapers for her expertise in gender and popular culture.

PART I

Qualitative Practice

CHAPTER 1

An Invitation to Qualitative Research

I n recent years, binge drinking has caused considerable concern among administrators at colleges and universities, compelled by statistics that show marked increases in such behavior. A qualitative researcher studying this topic would seek to go behind the statistics to *understand* the issue. Recently, we attended a faculty meeting that addressed the problem of binge drinking and heard concerned faculty and administrators suggest some of the following solutions:

- stricter campus policies with enforced consequences
- more faculty-student socials with alcohol for those over 21 years old
- more bus trips into the city to local sites such as major museums to get students interested in other pastimes

Although well-intentioned, these folks were grasping at straws. This is because although they were armed with statistics indicating binge drinking was prevalent and thus could identify a problem, they had no information about *why* this trend was occurring. Without understanding this issue on a meaningful level, it is difficult to remedy. At this point, we invite you to spend 5 to 10 minutes jotting down a list of questions you think are important to investigate as we try to better understand the phenomenon of binge drinking at college.

What Is Qualitative Research?

The qualitative approach to research is a unique grounding—the position from which to conduct research—that fosters particular ways of asking questions and particular ways of thinking through problems. As noted in the opening discussion of binge drinking in college, the questions asked in this type of research usually begin with words like *how, why,* or *what.* Look at the list of questions you generated—what words do they begin with? As we asked you to think about understanding this topic, you likely framed your questions from a qualitative perspective or approach. Qualitative researchers are after meaning. The social meaning people attribute to their experiences, circumstances, and situations, as well as the meanings people embed into texts and other objects, are the focus of qualitative research. Therefore, at the heart of their work, qualitative researchers try to extract meaning from their data. The focus of research is generally words and texts as opposed to numbers (as is the case in quantitative/statistical research). More than a concept or a series of techniques that can simply be employed, qualitative research is an intellectual, creative, and rigorous craft that the practitioner not only learns but also develops through practice.

Qualitative research is an exciting interdisciplinary landscape comprising diverse perspectives and practices for generating knowledge. Researchers across departments in the social and behavioral sciences use qualitative methods. In addition, the research process itself, also referred to in this book as the knowledge-building process, takes center stage in qualitative research. This means that researchers are very attentive to all aspects of the research process, including the conceptualization of the project, the interconnections between each phase of the research process, and the effect the researcher has on the process. Therefore, we advocate a *holistic approach* to qualitative research, which uses a process-oriented approach to knowledge-building. To understand what we mean by a holistic approach, it is necessary to first understand the major dimensions of research.

Dimensions of Qualitative Research

There are many important aspects of research aside from methods, although college-level courses are often misleadingly called "research methods" instead of "research practice." The major dimensions of research are ontology, epistemology, methodology, and methods. Each dimension impacts how a research question is formulated, how a project is conceptualized, and how a study is carried out. Furthermore, ontological and epistemological positions invariably inform methodological and methods choices.

Ontology: An **ontology** is a philosophical belief system about the nature of social reality—what can be known and how. For example, is the social world patterned and predictable, or is the social world continually being constructed through human interactions and rituals? These assumptions represent two very different ontological perspectives. A researcher's ontological assumptions impact topic selection, the formulation of research questions, and strategies for conducting the research.

Epistemology: An **epistemology** is a philosophical belief system about who can be a knower (Guba & Lincoln, 1998; Harding, 1987; Hesse-Biber & Leavy, 2004). The researcher's ontological and epistemological positions form the *philosophical basis of a research project*. This philosophical foundation impacts every aspect of the research process, including topic selection, question formulation, method selection, sampling, and research design.

Methodology (theoretical perspective) is an account of social reality or some component of it that extends further than what has been empirically investigated. Our methodological perspective is always a part of the research process.

There are three major methodological approaches in qualitative research: (1) post-positivist, (2) interpretive, and (3) critical. Post-positivism posits that the social world is patterned and that causal relationships can be discovered and tested via reliable strategies. The interpretive position assumes the social world is constantly being constructed through group interactions, and thus, social reality can be understood via the perspectives of social actors enmeshed in meaning-making activities. Critical perspectives also view social reality as an ongoing construction but go further to suggest that discourses created in shifting fields of social power shape social reality and our study of it. These approaches are reviewed in-depth in Chapter 2.

There are two primary approaches to using theory: deductive and inductive. A **deductive approach**, which is emphasized in post-positivism, tests theory or a hypothesis against data. An **inductive approach,** which is usually emphasized in interpretive and critical belief systems, generates theory directly out of the data. These approaches can also be linked and are discussed further in Chapter 3.

Methods: Methods are the tools that researchers use to collect data. These techniques for learning about social reality allow us to gather data from individuals, groups, and texts in any medium. Sandra Harding (1987) defines research methods in the following way:

> A **research method** is a technique for . . . gathering evidence. One could reasonably argue that all evidence-gathering techniques fall into one of the three categories: listening to (or interrogating) informants, observing behavior, or examining historical traces and records. (p. 2)

Qualitative researchers often use one or more of the following methods (although this is not an exhaustive list): ethnography or field research, interview, oral history, autoethnography, focus group interview, case study, discourse analysis, grounded theory, content or textual analysis, visual or audiovisual analysis, evaluation, historical comparative method, ethnodrama, and narrative inquiry. The diversity of the methods with which qualitative researchers work is one of the distinguishing features of the qualitative landscape, which makes for a vast range of possible research topics and questions. Put differently, qualitative researchers have a lot of tools in their toolboxes. So, how does a researcher select a research method?

When selecting a research method or methods for a particular project, it is most important to have a tight fit between the purpose or question and the method selected. Different tools are better suited to different projects, just as in life. For example, it is advisable to have a hammer, screwdriver, and wrench in one's toolbox. It is also advisable to know when to use them, which depends entirely on the particular problem at hand. Some researchers tend to become comfortable with a particular method or set of methods, and this can lead to a misalignment of research goals and the methods selected to achieve those goals. To select a method arbitrarily without considering carefully what kind of data you are seeking is to the put the cart before the horse, so to speak. We encourage new researchers to work with a variety of methods so that they will feel comfortable selecting appropriate methods for future projects.

The researcher's methodological (theoretical) and method choices form the *design framework* for a research project. The combining of theory and methods determines the methodology for a given study.

A Holistic Approach to Research

Methodology is the bridge that brings our philosophical standpoint (on ontology and epistemology) and method (perspective and tool) together. It is important to remember that the researcher travels this bridge throughout the research process.

Our methodology serves as a strategic but malleable guide throughout the research experience. In terms of malleability, methodology can be altered during research to the extent to which a researcher's ontological and epistemological beliefs allow for modifications. Researchers' conception of subjectivity and objectivity within the research process is likely to influence whether or not they will be open to revising their methodology once data gathering has commenced.

You may be wondering: why would researchers need to be open to changing their methodology once a project has begun? Sometimes no matter how much forethought we put into our research design plans, *the practice of research* gets complicated, and one of the following scenarios occurs: Unforeseen issues arise that make the strategy difficult to work with; we may realize our methodology needs to be revised—as well as our methods design. For example, we may find that once our study is put into practice; we are not eliciting the data we are interested in; or the data we are gathering suggest something unexpected that prompts a reexamination of our study. A qualitative grounding allows for the revision of a methodology as warranted if the researcher's philosophical belief system promotes this kind of fluidity. For example, Botting (2000) used oral history as a way to understand the experiences of a particular group of working women in the 1920s and 1930s. Specifically, she was interested in domestic servants who had migrated from coastal communities to a mill town in Newfoundland for employment purposes. She used oral history as a way to understand the experiences of both migration and domestic work for that group of female workers, who at the time represented a large proportion of women workers in that area. This kind of research is essential in filling gaps in our current knowledge base of what it means to be a woman from a particular social class in a given time, place, and industry, from the woman's own perspective. In this way, previously excluded groups can share their valuable knowledge with us. Botting twice modified her project based on the accessibility of data as well as insights garnered from her early findings, which prompted a reconfiguration. Botting's experience illustrates how important reflexivity is within the research process as well as the process-driven nature of qualitative inquiry (her study combined oral histories and census data). Through a rigorous process of reflection, Botting was able to "listen to the data," as we say, and follow it so that in the end, she, like many qualitative researchers, was able to create a research design that best allowed significant data to emerge.

Figure 1.1   Methodology: A Bridge Between Philosophical Framework and Methods Design

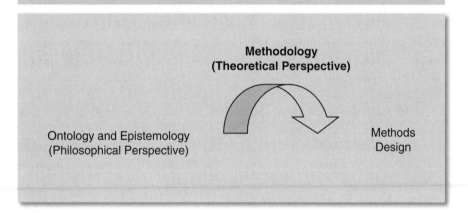

**Methodology
(Theoretical Perspective)**

Ontology and Epistemology
(Philosophical Perspective)

Methods
Design

Our approach to the qualitative endeavor is **holistic.** A holistic approach is attentive to the important connections between the philosophical framework and method(s) employed (see of Figure 1.1). A holistic approach explicitly integrates ontology, epistemology, methodology, and method, and can be thought of as a nexus—the research nexus. In other words, a holistic approach requires researchers not to disavow their underlying belief systems but rather to examine how their ontological and epistemological perspectives impact methodology. Therefore, a holistic approach views research as a process rather than an event. In this regard, adopting a holistic approach means the researcher views all research choices, from topic selection to final representation, as interrelated. This differs from an event-oriented approach, which views choices as a set of sequential steps. Throughout this book you will learn that this kind of holistic approach is successful in diverse research contexts and provides rewarding experiences for researchers who craft their own projects. In addition, it is not just the resulting information or research findings that we learn; the process itself becomes a part of the learning experience. In this regard and others, qualitative approaches to social inquiry foster personal satisfaction and growth.

Quantitative Research and Positivism

Qualitative research approaches represent one of the two major paradigms (worldviews) from which social research is conducted. Quantitative research represents the other paradigm. Although we hope the research community is moving past polarizing views of qualitative and quantitative approaches to research, comparisons are frequently drawn.

The epistemology through which quantitative practice developed as "the model of science" is important to understand. Positivist science holds several basic beliefs about the nature of knowledge, which together form *positivist epistemology,* the cornerstone of the quantitative paradigm. Positivism holds that there is a knowable reality that exists independent of the research process. The social world, like the natural world, is governed by rules, which result in patterns. Accordingly, causal relationships between variables exist and can even be identified, proven, and explained. Thus, patterned social reality is predictable and can potentially be controlled. This describes the nature of social reality from the positivist perspective (see Table 1.1).

For example, the quantitative approach to the study of binge drinking can be understood as a manifestation of these assumptions: A knowable, predictable reality exists "out there," constituted by clear causal relationships, such as patterned and predictable relationships between the enforcement of campus drinking policies and students' binge drinking patterns; this exists regardless of the research process and can be subsequently "tested." So far, we have been describing the nature of social reality according to positivism, but we must go further to examine assumptions about the relationship between that reality and the researcher who aims at explaining it. It should be noted that quantitative approaches can also employ qualitative methods.

Positivism's methods practices place the researcher and researched, or knower and what is knowable, on different planes within the research process. The researcher and researched, or subject and object, are conceptualized in a dichotomous model. Not only is there a rigid division between the subject and the object, but it is also a *hierarchical* division in which the researcher is privileged as the knower. This is particularly important in the social sciences, where data are largely derived from human subjects who, under this framework, become viewed as objects for research processes: They are acted on by others—the knowers.

Table 1.1   A Comparison of Qualitative and Quantitative Models of Research

Qualitative "Inductive" Methods Model	Quantitative "Deductive" Methods Model
Topical area	Formulate a research question
Analyze subset of data	Develop a hypothesis
Generate codes (literal to abstract)	Define variables
Reanalyze data; analyze additional data	Construct measurement instrument
Memo notes	Coding
Analyze additional data	Sampling (random sampling)
Refine codes; generate meta-codes	Reliability and validity checks
Analyze additional data	Statistical check (if necessary)
Embodied interpretation	Calculate results
Representation	Represent results (typically on charts or graphs)

What Kinds of Questions and Problems Can Be Addressed With Qualitative Methods?

Qualitative approaches to research typically use qualitative "inductive" methods (see Table 1.1). This means projects frequently begin with the accumulation of specific data, the analysis of which leads to a more general understanding of the topic. Therefore, guiding research questions are generally open-ended, allowing for a multiplicity of findings to emerge. Research questions typically begin with words like *why, how* and *what*. For example, consider the following sample questions:

- How might some people with a racial minority status experience prejudice in their workplace? In what ways does this occur? How does this make people feel? How does this impact work productivity? How does this impact professional identity?

- Why do many working women experience struggles to balance work and family? What is the nature of these struggles? How do working women cope with these challenges? What are the differences between working fathers' experiences and those of working mothers? What, if any, are the differences between white and minority women?

- How do people experience divorce? What does the process entail on an emotional level? What does it mean to uncouple? How does this impact self-concept?

- Why do students binge-drink? In what contexts do they binge-drink? What kinds of atmospheres promote binge drinking? How is binge drinking experienced differently by male and female students? What is the relationship between self-esteem and binge drinking in college-age students?

The framing of research questions is linked to the research purpose in a particular study. There are three primary research purposes: (1) exploratory, (2) descriptive, and (3) explanatory. *Exploratory research* seeks to investigate an area that has been underresearched. The data garnered is preliminary data that helps shape the direction of future research. *Descriptive research* seeks to describe the aspect of social reality under investigation. Qualitative researchers conducting descriptive research are typically after what Clifford Geertz (1973) termed "thick descriptions" of social life from the perspective of those being studied. *Explanatory research* seeks to explain social phenomena and the relationship between different components of a topic. This kind of research addresses the "why" of social life.

Table 1.2   Research Purposes

Exploratory[a]	Descriptive	Explanatory
Seeks to investigate an underresearched aspect of social life	Seeks to richly describe an aspect of social life	Seeks to explain an aspect of social life

a. Some qualitative researchers refer to this as Discovery.

Illustrations of Qualitative Studies

Here we provide qualitative research examples that seek to explore, describe, and explain, respectively. These are meant only as illustrations to get you thinking about how a research purpose is linked to the formulation of research questions, which then informs our methods choices. The researcher standpoint also informs the formulation of research questions, which is discussed in Chapters 2 and 3.

Exploratory

As noted in the opening of this chapter, binge drinking has recently become a topic of considerable conversation at U.S. colleges and universities and, accordingly, studies on this behavior have been conducted. Let's say we are interested in the experience of binge drinking specifically by minority students at predominantly white colleges. This is an underresearched topic so our study seeks to explore this topic and gain some preliminary insights into the key issues to help shape future research. These might be some of our research questions: Where do minority students "party" at predominantly white colleges? Do minority students attend predominantly white parties? If so, what is this experience like? What is the drinking environment like? In what contexts do the minority students engage in drinking? In what contexts do the minority students engage in excessive drinking? Is this a strategy of fitting in or coping with the pressures of being a minority in that context? If yes, how so? How does the minority students' drinking compare with the drinking of white students?

The best way to answer these questions is to gather data directly from the student population we seek to understand. We might, therefore, gather data through focus group interviews where multiple students are interviewed together. This provides responses to our initial questions, and the group dynamic is likely to bring the conversation into areas that we might otherwise not consider. Moreover, the participants can help guide us to select language that is appropriate to "get at" their experiences, about which we, at this point, know very little. Put differently, because there isn't much existing scholarship available about this topic that can help shape our research questions, we need to be open to learning unexpected information from our research participants. Alternatively, we might conduct an ethnographic study observing students in their social environments. This would allow us to observe people in their natural setting while we take in-depth notes based on our direct observations, and we could informally interview research participants.

Descriptive

Now let's say we are interested in understanding the experiences of military spouses coping with having their spouse serving in a war. For this study, we are interested in describing the experiences of military spouses, developing "thick descriptions" of the reality of the lives of people in this situation. These might be some of our research questions: How did you feel when your spouse was called to war? What did you do as a family to prepare for him/her to leave? What did you do individually to prepare? What are the hardest aspects of this experience? How has your daily life changed with your partner away? Describe the details of a typical day now. How has your parenting role changed with your partner away? What coping strategies do you use to deal with the worry, tensions, or pressure?

The best way to gather this kind of data is directly from the population in which we are interested. Given the sensitive nature of the topic as well as the in-depth data we are after, we might be interested in conducting in-depth interviews or oral history interviews that will lead to "thick descriptions."

Explanatory

Now let's say we are interested in explaining the relationship between college-age women's media consumption and their body image (the ways in which they think about their appearance, as well as their satisfaction or dissatisfaction). Based on our prior knowledge and assumptions, we are specifically interested in associations between media consumption, such as regular reading of women's fashion magazines, and poor body image. For this kind of project, we might choose a more structured approach to interviewing, where participants are asked a range of specific questions such as these: How do you feel about the way you look? What do you like about your appearance? What do you dislike? Why? How does that make you feel? What television programs do you watch? What do you like about them? Do you read magazines? Which ones? What do you think about the images you see?

How do they make you feel? Do you wish you looked more like the models? How so? If they make you feel bad, why do you continue to read them? Do you hang clips from magazines in your dorm? If so, why? How do you decide which clips to hang? How do you feel when you look at them?

As an alternative to structured interviews, we might be interested in a multi-methods approach to this research. One way to do this would be to combine survey research designed to get a breadth of responses from college-age women with in-depth interviews aimed at getting a depth of data from fewer participants. Another approach would be to combine structured interviews with a content analysis of the images in a representative sample of women's magazines. This approach would allow us to examine both the images themselves and how our participants internalize those images.

In each of the three preceding examples, the general research purpose (to explore, describe, or explain) helped us to formulate specific research questions. The specific research questions, in turn, led us to select an appropriate method or methods—those that are best suited to address our questions. This illustrates the importance of having a "tight fit" between the research purpose, questions, and methods. Moreover, this is the beginning of research design in qualitative practice, which is reviewed at length in Chapter 3.

- What do these studies have in common?

Whether seeking to explore, describe, or explain, all of the preceding research examples share a commonality: They seek to unearth and understand meaning. Moreover, they are after social meaning from the perspectives of research participants who are enmeshed in their context. Qualitative research approaches can investigate how people assign meaning to their experiences as well as social events and topics. Furthermore, qualitative research examines how the meanings we assign to our experiences, situations, and social events shape our attitudes, experiences, and social realities.

What Do We Want You to Learn From This Book?

This book serves as a comprehensive introduction to the practice of qualitative research. In this vein, after reading the book, you should have answers to the following research issues: How do you conceptualize a problem? How do you formulate a research strategy and research design? How do you execute the plan, and what issues may arise? How do you make sense out of your findings? How do you write-up the findings? We hope that after reading this book, you will have a firm understanding of a qualitative research approach as a holistic process. We present a practice model of research that goes behind the scenes to show you the complexities that can occur when we seek to better understand the human condition. A practice model encourages the doing of research, understanding that even the best-laid plans may not hold up during the practice of research. In this vein, we are delighted to present behind-the-scenes boxes throughout the book. These boxes were written by leading researchers and take us behind the curtain to the real world of qualitative research, with its messiness, disappointments, ethical dilemmas, and unique joys. We hope that the book encourages critical questions along the way.

Glossary

Deductive approach: This approach begins with theories that are tested against new data.

Epistemology: An epistemology is a philosophical belief system about who can be a knower. An epistemology includes how the relationship between the researcher and research participant(s) is understood.

Holistic: By holistic, we mean that researchers must continually be cognizant of the relationship between epistemology, theory, and methods and look at research as a process.

Inductive approach: This approach begins with specific data out of which more general ideas or theories are generated.

Methodology: Methodology is a theory of how knowledge building should ensue. Methodology is the bridge that brings our philosophical framework together with our methods practice.

Ontology: An ontology is a philosophical belief system about the nature of social reality—what can be known and how. The conscious and unconscious questions, assumptions, and beliefs that the researcher brings to the research endeavor serve as the initial basis for an ontological position.

Reflexivity: The ongoing questioning of one's place and power relations within the research process.

Research method: Methods are the tools that researchers use to gather data. A research method is a technique for gathering evidence.

Theory: Theory is an account of social reality or some component of it that extends further than what has been empirically investigated.

Discussion Questions and Activities

1. What is a qualitative approach to research? How are qualitative approaches different from quantitative?

2. Compare and contrast a qualitative "inductive" methods model with a quantitative "deductive" methods model.

3. What kinds of problems can qualitative research address?

4. Select a possible research topic (perhaps using an example from this chapter such as binge drinking among college-age students). Next, create sample research questions in order to conduct exploratory, descriptive, and explanatory research on your topic.

Resources

Suggested Web Sites

Qualitative Research

http://carbon.cudenver.edu/~mryder/itc_data/pract_res.html

This Web site, produced by the University of Colorado (Denver), contains links to resources that explain the art of qualitative educational research: critiques, literature reviews, research design methodologies, and other articles.

The Qualitative Report (online journal)

http://www.nova.edu/ssss/QR/index.html

Publishes qualitative research articles and book reviews across the disciplines. Also features "The Weekly Qualitative Report," which highlights current research articles, reviews resources, and includes relevant job postings, conferences, links, and so forth.

Relevant Journals

International Journal of Qualitative Research

International Review of Qualitative Research

Qualitative Health Research Journal

Qualitative Inquiry

Qualitative Sociology Review

The Qualitative Report (online journal)

CHAPTER 2

Approaches to Qualitative Research

Qualitative research doesn't occur in only one way. Qualitative studies are conducted from various methodological (theoretical) points of view. We think of these viewpoints as *approaches to research*. The major methodological approaches to qualitative research developed out of the confluence of differing ontological, epistemological, and theoretical perspectives. The qualitative landscape is robust with research conducted from diverse approaches. Different approaches lead researchers to different kinds of topics and questions. Therefore, researchers may adopt different approaches for different projects. This is a vital part of a problem-centric way of conducting research. A problem-centric way of doing research means that the research questions are at the center of research design choices. Methods are selected in light of their ability to address specific questions. This is an integral part of holistic practice.

What Are the Major Methodological (Theoretical) Approaches to Qualitative Research?

For the sake of simplicity, we are classifying the primary approaches to qualitative research under three umbrella categories that exist on a continuum: (1) post-positivist, (2) interpretive, and (3) critical. Post-positivism has evolved from positivism, a philosophy that usually supports quantitative research but can be employed in qualitative research, too. Interpretive approaches include symbolic interactionism, the Chicago School, dramaturgy, phenomenology, and ethnomethodology. **Interpretive approaches** focuses on subjective experience, small-scale interactions, and understanding (seeking meaning). Each interpretive approach developed within a specific discipline (although all are now also used in interdisciplinary contexts). Critical approaches include postmodernism, post-structuralism, feminism, critical race theory, and queer theory. The critical strand similarly values experience, understanding, and subjectivity, but it also critiques these categories. **Critical approaches** suggest that we live in a power-laden context. Moreover, critical approaches have a social justice orientation. Critical approaches look at how power and hegemonic discourses shape experience and understanding. Critical approaches developed across disciplines, in multidisciplinary and interdisciplinary contexts. These power-attentive approaches also directly challenge binary thinking. There is great variation within and across all of these interpretive and critical perspectives, which is explicated in this chapter. However, our discussion of these theoretical approaches is meant to serve as a broad overview, not an in-depth treatment.

Table 2.1   Comparing Post-positivism, the Interpretive Strand, and the Critical Strand

	Post-positivism	**The Interpretive Strand**	**The Critical Strand**
Developed:	Natural sciences	Disciplinary contexts	Interdisciplinary contexts
Focus:	Scientific objectivity	Subjective experience	Power-laden environments
	Reliability, verification, replication	Small-scale interactions	Hegemonic/dominant discourses
		Seek understanding	Resist binary categories
		Meaning-making	Social justice

Post-positivism

Typically, qualitative research is associated with interpretive and critical perspectives and not the positivist and post-positivist perspectives from which quantitative researchers operate; however, some researchers work from positivist and post-positivist approaches in qualitative practice. We have already discussed the tenets of positivism, so now we will briefly discuss post-positivism as an atypical approach for qualitative researchers.

Post-positivism is very similar to positivism, the difference being that when studying social reality, post-positivism recognizes that researchers cannot be absolutely positive about their knowledge claims (Creswell, 2008). Post-positivism asserts that social research can only approximate reality (Guba, 1990). Getting away from the positivist idea of *proving* causal relationships that constitute the social world, post-positivists *build evidence* to support a preexisting theory. In other words, relying on deductive logic and hypothesis testing, just as positivists do, post-positivists attempt to create evidence that will confirm or refute a theory, although not in absolute terms. Post-positivism focuses on questions such as this one: What evidence is there to support the hypothesis that Variable A is associated with Variable B? A post-positivist researcher might ask:

- What evidence is there to support the hypothesis that stricter gun legislation reduces violent crime?

- What evidence is there to support the hypothesis that small class sizes in elementary school increase student learning?

Post-positivist researchers often employ quantitative "deductive" methods practices in their research, such as statistics, within a qualitative or multimethod project (Denzin & Lincoln, 2007). In sum, post-positivism assumes that there is an objective reality "out there" constituted by testable cause-and-effect relationships. Social reality thus exists independent of the researcher and research project. Relying on deductive logic, these researchers engage in measurement and hypothesis testing to create evidence in support of, or against, an existing theory. You can see, given the assumptions about reality and knowledge construction, that this perspective is more congruent with quantitative analysis; however, some qualitative researchers may also choose to work from this kind of methodological (theoretical) framework.

The Interpretive Strand

This set of diverse approaches to research focuses on understanding, interpretation, and social meaning. Furthermore, interpretive approaches presuppose meaning is constructed via the interaction between humans or between humans and objects. Therefore, meaning does not exist independent of the human interpretive process. Researchers working from interpretive traditions value experience and perspective as important sources of knowledge.

Interpretive approaches are associated with the **hermeneutic tradition,** which is about seeking deep understanding by interpreting the meaning that interactions, actions, and objects have for people. This perspective posits that the only way to understand social reality is from the perspective of those enmeshed within it. Heidegger (1927/1962, 1975/1982) asserted that understanding is inseparable from the human condition. This philosophical stance informs interpretive approaches to research.

Symbolic Interactionism and the Chicago School

Symbolic interactionism was pioneered by George Herbert Mead (1934/1967) and Herbert Blumer (1969). **Symbolic interactionism** examines the interaction between individuals and small groups; between individuals and objects; and between individuals and small groups, on the one hand, and objects on the other. This approach suggests this interaction process is an interpretive and meaning-making endeavor where shared symbols are used to communicate meaning (i.e., shared language, gestures). Symbolic interactionism posits that people act differently with different people in different situations. People also act differently toward the different objects that they encounter. The source of these differential actions/reactions is the meaning we attach to particular people, interactions, and objects, as well as our perception of that interaction. For example, religious adherents respond differently to a necklace with a symbol of their religion, such as a Cross or Star of David, as compared to a purely decorative necklace. The difference in reaction results from the meaning people assign to the object. According to symbolic interactionists, these meanings develop out of ongoing social interactions. Social meanings are therefore created and re-created through an interpretive process. In turn, these meanings shape attitudes and influence behaviors and help people determine how to act "appropriately" in different situations. Symbolic interactionists are interested in questions such as the following:

- What meaning do people place on objects?

- How do people interpret facial expressions and gestures as a part of meaning-making?

An important extension of symbolic interactionism is referred to as "the Chicago School." From the 1920s through the 1940s, faculty and students in the social science and anthropology departments at the University of Chicago drew on the work of Mead and Blumer to understand the complex social dynamics beyond the academic gates of the university setting. Robert Park, W. I. Thomas, Ernest Burgess, and Everett C. Hughes were among the pioneers of the Chicago School. They conducted diverse ethnographic field research to understand social life by observing and interviewing people.

Dramaturgy

Erving Goffman (1959) developed dramaturgy as a theoretical approach to research; it focuses on people's presentation of self in everyday life. Building on the famous quote "all the world's a stage, and all the men and women merely players," dramaturgy uses the metaphor of theater to understand social life. **Dramaturgy** examines individual social experiences as a process of performance. Under this conception, social reality is conceived in terms of "front stage" and "back stage." Front stage is what occurs in front of others. Put differently, it is the public self. The back stage is all of the behind-the-scenes stuff of life that others do not see. Moreover, dramaturgy views social actors as constantly engaged in processes of "impression management" and "facework." This means that people are routinely trying to manage how they are perceived by others. For example, when people are embarrassed, they may try to "save face" to cover their embarrassment. Researchers working from this perspective might use observational techniques to address questions such as these:

- How does context impact people's behavior?
- How do people act in embarrassing situations?
- How do people publicly/privately cope with disappointment?

Goffman's notion of dramaturgy serves as the basis for the "behind-the-scenes" boxes throughout this book.

Phenomenology

Phenomenology had its early roots in the 18th century. Phenomenologists were critical of the natural sciences for assuming an objective reality independent of individual consciousness. **Phenomenology** is closely associated with European philosophy in the early 1900s, most notably in the works of German philosopher Edmund Husserl (1913/1963; see also Heidegger 1927/1962, 1975/1982) and French phenomenologist Maurice Merleau-Ponty (1945/1996).

Husserl was interested in human consciousness as the way to understand social reality, particularly how one "thinks" about experience; in other words, *how consciousness is experienced.* For Husserl, consciousness is always intentional, that is, it is directed at some phenomenon. To understand how consciousness operates enables us to capture how individuals create an understanding of social life. Husserl was especially interested in how individuals consciously experience their experience. How is it that we become aware of these experiences? Alfred Schutz (1967), a colleague of Husserl, brought the phenomenological perspective to American sociology; he was particularly interested in how individuals process experience in their everyday lives. Phenomenology is not only a philosophy but also a research method for capturing the lived experiences of individuals. Phenomenologists are interested in questions such as the following:

- How do individuals experience dying? (Kübler-Ross, 1969)

- How does one experience depression? (Karp, 1997)

- How does one experience divorce? (Kohler Riessman, 1987)

- How does one experience the bodily aspects of pregnancy? (Pillow, 2000)

For phenomenologists, there is not "one reality" in how each of these events is experienced. Experience is perceived along a variety of dimensions: how the experience is lived in time, space, and vis-à-vis our relationships to others, as well as a bodily experience. Phenomenologists use a variety of methods such as observations and in-depth interviewing, as well as looking at written accounts of experiences such as diaries. The following might be the type of question that could come up in an interview situation:

- Please tell me what it is like to live with depression (terminal illness, an eating disorder)? What are your daily experiences like? How does this make you feel?

In sum, phenomenology is a methodological (theoretical) perspective aimed at generating knowledge about how people experience.

Ethnomethodology

Ethnomethodology was popularized as a perspective in the field of sociology in the 1960s through the work of Harold Garfinkel (1967). **Ethnomethodology** draws on the phenomenological perspective: Both focus on the process whereby individuals understand and give a sense of order to the world in which they live. Ethno-methodologists are particularly interested in how meaning is negotiated in a social context through the process of interaction with others. Ethnomethodologists ask such questions as these:

- How do people go about making sense of their everyday lives?

- What are the specific strategies, especially those that appear to be common-sensical, that individuals use to go about the meaning-making process?

To the ethnomethodologist, social life itself is created and re-created based on the micro-understanding individuals bring to their everyday social contexts. Ethnomethodologists use a range of methods to go about capturing this process of meaning-making, from observing individuals in natural settings as they go about their daily routines to participant observations and interviews. Ethnomethodologists are especially interested in how individuals engaged in interaction talk about their experiences, asking,

- How is meaning created in everyday conversations individuals have with each other?

The main tenets of ethnomethodology are congruent with the methods of observation and interview that dominate qualitative practice.

The Critical Strand

Critical is an umbrella term for a large set of diverse methodological (theoreti-cal) and epistemological positions. *Critical approaches* developed in an interdisci-plinary and multidisciplinary context.

There are two main strands within the critical umbrella. The first group emerged largely out of theoretical work (postmodern and post-structural). The second are approaches that developed out of the social justice movements of the 1960s and 1970s including the women's movement, civil rights, and gay rights. These approaches—feminism, critical race theory, queer theory—all have a social justice or activist component.

Critical approaches assert that we live in a power-laden context. Things don't just happen to be the way they are; they have been constructed and reconstructed by people within evolving power-laden environments. Critical theorists are weary of notions of absolute truth and base their concerns on the historical inequities produced by this rigid view of knowledge (espoused in positivism). Therefore, crit-ical approaches reject and challenge binary categories that seek to polarize and essentialize difference. For example, categorizations such as male-female do two things: (1) they oppose two groups, and (2) they imply a similarity or sameness among all the members of one group. This could lead to ideas like "women's expe-riences," which assumes that all women, regardless of race, social class, sexuality, religion, or nationality, have the same experiences. In the critical theory view, the traditional positivist scientific process ultimately creates knowledge that is used to maintain (justify, fortify, reconstruct) the status quo in which minorities are oppressed through the reproduction of dominant ideology. Dominant ideology refers to the set of ideas and values put forth by those in power, which maintain the structures on which that power rests (through creating a "commonsense" set of ideas that everyone is exposed to although they may actually only benefit those in power). For example, critical theorists might challenge the binary categories heterosexual-homosexual, suggesting that these categories "naturalize" heterosexuality as "normal" and keep these two terms in opposition to each other. Critical theory seeks to reflexively step outside of the dominant ideology (insofar as possible) to create a space for resistive (counter-dominant) knowledge production that destabilizes oppressive material and symbolic relations of dominance. Critical theorists seek to access "subjugated knowledges"—the unique viewpoints of oppressed groups. To do this, critical theorists often examine the "micro-politics of power" (Foucault, 1976), which is how power operates on a day-to-day basis in people's lives. For example, if a homosexual college student doesn't feel able to talk about his or her partner openly in class discussion, the way a heterosexual student would, this is a part of what "naturalizes" heterosexuality and maintains inequality. In other words, the student is operating within a power-laden environment. As noted earlier, there are many variations within the larger umbrella of critical theory.

Postmodernism

Postmodernism focuses on the prominence of dominant ideology and the discourses of power that normalize this ideology to maintain a dominant world order—locally, nationally, and globally. Antonio Gramsci (1929) explained that people partly consent to their own oppression through the internalization of dominant ideology. In other words, power is maintained because, as Foucault (1976) explains, our ideas become the chains that bind us best. Being social creatures, our ideas are not simply created in our minds but are rather a part of a larger social, political, symbolic, and discursive context with its own materiality. When we talk about symbolic and discursive contexts, we are referring to images, objects, language, phrasing, and so forth. For example, postmodern researchers might ask questions like the following:

- How was the post-9/11 "United We Stand" politicized slogan normalized in Americans' daily lives? How did this discourse normalize dominant nationalistic views and responses to the events of 9/11?

- How do the images and narratives in advertising impact consumerism? How do ads reinforce dominant capitalist ideology? How does this impact the public?

The project of postmodern scholarship thus becomes accessing "subjugated knowledges" to transform these oppressive power relations.

Generally speaking, postmodern researchers aim at creating partial truths that are situated in historical material reality. In this way, knowledge produced from a postmodern approach is grounded in ongoing historical processes and the power-knowledge relations in which it is enmeshed. So, for example, stereotypes about femininity change over time. These stereotypes circulate in part via media images (symbolic context) and phrases such as "girly girls" or "tomboys" (discursive context). Postmodern approaches consider how these stereotypes are created, how they reinforce a dominant ideology that benefits those in power, and also how any research claims can be only partial perspectives and must be situated in their proper historical context.

Post-structuralism

Like postmodernism, **post-structuralism** is also concerned with challenging dominant ideology through an *engaged* research process. One strategy used is **critical deconstruction**. Jacques Derrida (1966), who has been at the forefront of changing how researchers think about knowledge production, urges critical deconstruction in which that which has been marginalized is transformed into the locus of investigation. Derrida also advocates breaking down unities to expose what has been rendered invisible in dominant discourse.

During a discussion of the oppression of women within the symbolic and material realms, Luce Irigaray explains deconstruction as follows:

> The issue is not one of elaborating a new theory . . . but of *jamming the theoretical machinery itself*, of suspending its pretension to the production of a truth and of a meaning that are excessively univocal. (Irigaray, 1985, p. 78; italics added for emphasis)

In other words, researchers take something that is whole and break it down to investigate its constituent parts and to note what is missing. For example, a researcher could critically deconstruct a presidential State of the Union address to reveal how pieces of information are revealed and juxtaposed, how rhetoric is used, and what perspectives are not put forward. Deconstruction, therefore, aims to break down unified narratives to expose the inner workings of dominant ideology in particular venues (speeches, newspapers, television, textbooks, etc.). Post-structural researchers might ask questions like the following:

• What are the components of the overall narrative of American history found in a sample of American history textbooks? What are the messages within the various components? How is dominant ideology distributed in this medium? Whose perspectives are rendered invisible, incorrect, or marginal?

Feminism

Feminist perspectives developed out of the second wave of the women's movement as a way to address the concerns and life experiences of women and girls, who, due to widespread androcentric bias, had long been excluded from knowledge construction, both as researchers and as research subjects. Feminism is a political project, which means it is an engaged position. Feminists seek to create a more just world for women. Feminist researchers value women's experiences and unearth women's subjugated knowledges.

A guiding understanding within feminism is that gender is a historically and socially constructed category. In general terms, feminism also challenges binary thinking and provides alternative ways of thinking about social reality and, correspondingly, the research process. Feminists critique the subject-object split that polarizes researchers and research subjects as a false binary that is inherently flawed, artificial, and ultimately undesirable. The feminist critique of the subject-object split has its roots in earlier feminist efforts to expose and correct the exclusion of women from research in the social and natural sciences. Halpin (1989) makes an important link between traditional scientific objectivity and a general process of "othering" in which women, people of color, and sexual minorities have been deemed "other" and have correspondingly been treated as inferior to the traditional white heterosexual male scientist. This process has resulted in systematic "scientific oppression," she says. A key dimension to this historical routinized exclusion/distortion has been the placing of the researcher on a higher plane than the research participants, because the researcher is viewed as the authoritative party (Sprague & Zimmerman, 1993). Feminism itself has been produced out of historical struggle and seeks to create contextualized and partial truths and avoid the absolute knowledge claims that have historically oppressed women and other marginalized peoples. Feminism seeks to answer questions such as these:

- What educational and occupational choices do women make? Why?

- How do women experience their various relationships?

- How do women negotiate their various roles?

Although there are many feminist perspectives, we briefly recount **feminist standpoint epistemology**, which is a touchstone for many feminist researchers. Dorothy Smith (1974) and Nancy Hartsock (1983) pioneered feminist standpoint epistemology, which is based on the assumption that in a hierarchically structured social world, different standpoints are necessarily produced. For example, the United States has a long history of gender inequality in politics, economics, and so forth. This constitutes an environment that is hierarchically structured along economic, social, and political lines based on gender. In such an environment, people develop different visions of the world based on the gender categorization that they embody and their corresponding space in the social structure.

Feminist standpoint theorists have primarily focused on the position that women occupy within a social context characterized by a patriarchal sex-gender system. Women, men, intersexuals, and transgendered individuals occupy different social positions, which produce different life experiences, differential access to the economic, cultural, and political reward system, and thus ultimately different standpoints. Some standpoint theorists argue that women's vision is not only different but in fact more complete and less distorted because they occupy a position of oppression in which they must come to understand their own social position as well as that of the dominant group (Hartsock, 1983; Jaggar, 1989) to survive.

Patricia Hill-Collins (1990) has increased our understanding of standpoint as an epistemology and critical methodology by introducing the idea of an **Afrocentric feminist epistemology** that begins with the unique standpoint of black women. In essence, Hill-Collins theorizes that we live in a "matrix of domination" where race and gender are overdetermined in relation to each other, producing a unique standpoint fostered by these "interlocking systems of oppression." By accessing the different standpoints within our social world, researchers are able to address new questions and to resist and even challenge former conceptions of truth and the ways of knowing from which they flow. This is referred to as an **intersectionality theory**.

Critical Race Theory

Critical race theory is an umbrella term for diverse research that developed in a multidisciplinary and interdisciplinary context. Critical race theory emerged out of the intersections of feminism, post-structuralism, and legal studies (Ritzer, 2008), as well as the civil rights movement. As with feminism, critical race theory seeks to create a more just world by ending racial inequality and oppression. Critical race theory explains that racism is insidious and normalized. In this vein, critical race theory investigates "hierarchical racial structures of society" and posits that race is a historically and socially constructed category (Ladson-Billings & Donnor, 2005, p. 279). Richard Delgado and Jean Stefancic (2001) suggest that dominant groups racialize different minority groups at different historical moments as a result of changes in social, material, and/or symbolic context. For example, after September 11, 2001, white America has racialized Arabs as terrorists.

Research conducted from a critical race theoretical perspective might ask questions such as the following:

• How did Arab Americans experience prejudice after 9/11? What, if any, impact did this have on personal relationships?

Critical race theory can inform methodological practice in many ways. Generally speaking, this approach greatly values experiential knowledge (Ritzer, 2008). In this regard, researchers are interested in accessing the subjugated knowledges of racial minorities. Ladson-Billings and Donnor, (2005) posit that racial minorities are never able to escape "the prism (or prison) of race that has been imposed by a racially coded and constraining society" (p. 279). Over the past two decades, critical race theory has also trended toward theories of intersectionality. As noted in the last section on feminism, theories of intersectionality posit that people cannot be reduced to one shared characteristic (such as race); rather, researchers must consider the intersections of race, class, gender, sexuality, and nationality. Researchers must, therefore, be attentive to overlapping and even conflicting identities (Ritzer, 2008; see Patricia Hill-Collins, 1990, for a full discussion of intersectionality theory).

Queer Theory

Like feminism and critical race theory, queer theory is an interdisciplinary, social justice-oriented perspective that seeks equality for the sexually marginalized. Kathleen M. Ryan (2000) notes that defining queer theory is particularly challenging because queer theory posits that "naming something constitutes a form of closure" (p. 633). With this said, the main tenets of queer theory can be noted.

Queer theory rejects binary categorizations. Binary categorizations of sexuality and gender polarize difference and reinforce hierarchy. Arlene Stein and Ken Plummer (1994) note the following as a main component of queer theory:

> A conceptualization of sexuality which sees sexual power as embodied in different levels of social life, expressed discursively and enforced through boundaries and binary divides. (pp. 181–182)

Stein and Plummer are suggesting that heterosexuality is normalized in different arenas (e.g., popular culture, education, religion, health care, the law), and researchers must study sexual discourses in these diverse contexts. In this vein, Stein and Plummer assert all areas of social life are influenced by societal understandings of sexuality and must be interrogated.

Queer theorists might engage with questions such as the following:

- What is campus life like for homosexual college students? How do these experiences differ for men and women?

- How is the household division of labor organized in homes of same-sex couples?

Queer theory also problematizes traditional understandings of identity. Queer theorists assert that identity is not fixed but rather is historically and socially constructed. Moreover, queer theory rejects essentialist practices that erase differences within groups and ignore the complexity of diversity as the result of multiple shifting and intersecting characteristics (i.e., sexual orientation, gender, race, ethnicity). In this regard, queer theory challenges more conventional identity politics. Queer theorists typically avoid using minority identity status (such as homosexual or bisexual) because their use reinforces and thus legitimizes these dominant binary categories.[1]

Table 2.2   An Overview of Interpretive and Critical Approaches

	Strand	Goal	Focus
Symbolic Interactionism and the Chicago School	Interpretive	Understanding	Meaning-making through interpretive process of interaction
Dramaturgy	Interpretive	Understanding	The presentation of self in "front stage" and "back stage" contexts
Phenomenology	Interpretive	Understanding	How people experience
Ethnomethodology	Interpretive	Understanding	Meaning-making at the micro level
Postmodernism	Critical	Partial truths	Seeks partial truths and challenges dominant ideologies in postmodern contexts
Post-structuralism	Critical	Partial truths	Subversive practice of breaking down unities and decentering
Feminism	Critical	Social justice	Eradicate gender inequality and unearth women's subjugated knowledges
Critical race theory	Critical	Social justice	Eradicate racial inequality/oppression and challenge dominant constructions of race
Queer theory	Critical	Social Justice	Problematize traditional notions of sexual identity and reject essentialist practices

Conclusion

As you can see, qualitative researchers approach their research through many different methodological lenses. Some researchers tend to favor particular approaches due to their worldview and political commitments. We advocate keeping an open mind in each project and adopting a problem-centric style of research where different theoretical lenses are used for their utility in specific projects. Researchers with political or activist commitments such as feminism can combine a feminist grounding with any of the other approaches reviewed to most effectively address their research problem.

Glossary

Afrocentric feminist epistemology: Patricia Hill-Collins introduced this idea, which takes the premise of standpoint epistemology and begins with the unique standpoint of black women.

Critical approaches: Critical approaches suggest we live in a power-rich context. These approaches seek to reflexively step outside of the dominant ideology (insofar as possible) to create a space for resistive, counter-hegemonic knowledge production that destabilizes oppressive material and symbolic relations of dominance.

Critical deconstruction: Jacques Derrida developed this approach to post-structural research, which posits breaking down unities to reveal what has been rendered invisible.

Dramaturgy: Dramaturgy uses the metaphor of theater to understand social life.

Ethnomethodology: Ethnomethodology focuses on the process whereby individuals understand and give a sense of order to the world in which they live. Ethnomethodologists are particularly interested in how meaning is negotiated in a social context through the process of interaction with others.

Feminist perspectives: Feminist perspectives developed as a way to address the concerns and life experiences of women and girls, who, because of widespread androcentric (sexist) bias, had long been excluded from knowledge construction, both as researchers and as research subjects.

Feminist standpoint epistemology: This approach is based on the assumption that in a hierarchically structured social world, different standpoints are necessarily produced.

Hermeneutic tradition: See interpretive approaches.

Interpretive approaches: The interpretive approach is based on the interpretation of interactions and the social meaning that people assign to their interactions. This perspective asserts that social meaning is created during interaction and people's interpretations of interactions. The implication is that different social actors may in fact understand social reality differently, producing different meanings and analyses.

Intersectionality theory: Intersectionality theory examines the interlocking nature of race, class, gender, sexuality, and nationality.

Phenomenology: Phenomenology seeks to understand experience, arguing that there is not "one reality" to how events are experienced.

Postmodernism: Postmodern theories focus on the prominence of dominant ideology and the discourses of power that normalize this ideology to maintain a dominant world order—locally, nationally, and globally.

Post-structuralism: Post-structuralism is an engaged theoretical approach that advocates breaking down unities, decentering, and subversive practice.

Symbolic interactionism: Symbolic interactionism examines the interaction between individuals and small groups; between individuals and objects; and between individuals and small groups, on the one hand, and objects on the other. This approach suggests this interaction process is an interpretive and meaning-making endeavor where shared symbols are used to communicate meaning.

Discussion Questions and Activities

1. Briefly explain the main similarities and differences between interpretive and critical approaches.

2. What are the major strengths of each approach reviewed in this chapter? What dimensions of social reality are highlighted under each approach? To transform this question into an activity, select a current event from a newspaper. What are the issues one would need to explore to better understand the roots of this topic? What would each research approach offer this process?

Resources

Suggested Web Sites

Forum: Qualitative Social Research

http://www.qualitative-research.net/fqs/fqs-eng.htm

FQS is a peer-reviewed multilingual online journal for qualitative research. The main aim of *FQS* is to promote discussion and cooperation among qualitative researchers from different countries and social science disciplines.

Association for Qualitative Research

http://www.latrobe.edu.au/aqr/

This site is useful because although the most recent month's publication is not free on the Web site, all previous publications are. Students can access full texts.

Qualitative Research Consultants Association

http://www.qrca.org/

This Web site is for a nonprofit organization whose mission is promoting excellence in qualitative research. The site is useful for those who are interested in becoming part of an organization dealing with qualitative research.

The Association for Qualitative Research

http://www.aqrp.co.uk/

Anyone who is interested in qualitative research is welcome to join this association. Founded in the early 1980s, AQR is a recognized and respected organization in the marketing services arena.

The Qualitative Research Report

http://www.nova.edu/ssss/QR/qualres.html
http://www.nova.edu/ssss/QR/web.html

Leading online qualitative research journal with many additional sources about qualitative research.

The National Organization for Women

http://www.now.org/

This is an up-to-date Web site containing information about feminist research as well as feminist issues. It has a link to current events dealing with feminism as well as legislative updates.

The Feminist Majority Foundation (Research Center)

http://www.feminist.org/research/1_public.html

This Web site contains a plethora of information dealing with women's issues and in particular feminist research. It has links to current research, women's studies programs, feminist journals, feminist Internet search utilities, women's research centers, and feminist magazines.

The Feminist Institute for Studies on Law and Society

http://www.sfu.ca/~fisls/engines.htm

This Web site has a link focusing specifically on feminist research as well as a broader subject guide. It also contains links to feminist journals and papers, along with a list of feminist search engines.

Sociological Research Online

http://www.socresonline.org.uk/2/3/3.html

This is a link to a specific journal article about feminist research and the authors' experience with feminist research. Miller talks about such things as power in the search process, power in the research relationship, and personal experiences with feminist research. Methodologies and feminist epistemologies are also discussed.

Relevant Journals

Critical Sociology

Gender & Society

Human Studies

Journal of Phenomenological Psychology

Philosophy and Phenomenological Research

Symbolic Interaction

Note

1. The resistance to minority status identity categories has resulted in conflicts between queer theory and LGBT studies. For a discussion of these tensions, see Karen E. Lovaas, John P. Elia, and Gust A. Yep (2006), "Shifting Ground(s): Surveying the Contested Terrain of LGBT Studies and Queer Theory," in *Journal of Homosexuality,* Vol. 52, No. 1/2, pp. 1–18.

CHAPTER 3

Designing Qualitative Approaches to Research

I n this chapter, we take you through the general steps of designing a qualitative approach to a research project. We explore the types of questions qualitative approaches tackle as well as a general set of methods guidelines for answering your research questions. We offer strategies for examining your researcher standpoint by asking you to reflect on the set of philosophical assumptions you bring to your research with regard to how you see the nature of the social world and what you believe can be known about it. As noted in Chapter 2, these assumptions form the philosophical framework of a study and play a crucial role in influencing the types of research questions we ask, as well as the research methods we employ to answer these questions. But before we go on to present a qualitative approach to social inquiry, let's step back and figure out why we bother to study these approaches to inquiry in general. Why not just rely on our own common sense to figure out why something is the way it is? Why don't we call on those we consider qualified to tell us what something means, perhaps our parents or even those friends of ours whom we deem to be truly gifted and smart people? Or better yet, why not go to a tarot card reader or astrologist and let them tell us what the future holds?

How Do We Know What We Know?

Humans rely on a variety of knowledge sources to make sense of their world. The idea of taking a research methods course to gain knowledge about social reality is in fact a relatively new mode of inquiry. For many thousands of years, societies have relied on a variety of methods to understand their social world. Each culture has its own set of values and traditions that provide a window into understanding the social world that passes down from one generation to the next.

The reliance on members of authority is an important source of knowledge-building within societies; people tend to trust the authority of the chief or medicine men and women within tribal societies, of the religious elite within theocratic societies, and among the royalty in monarchies, whose authority often comes from claims of a "divine" right to rule. In their role as authority figures, these societal knowledge brokers become creators and controllers of what is seen as legitimate knowledge. Within modern-day societies, too, we defer to authority figures to tell us what is "true." We often grant authority over knowledge-building to those we believe are "experts" who can lay legitimate claim to a particular area of knowledge-building as a result of their earned expertise.

Some societies privilege a mystical mode of inquiry. This mode of knowledge-building legitimates the knowledge of those who claim access to divine or supernatural powers, such as astrologists or tarot card readers whose knowledge is legitimated through their claims that they are mediums who can tap into the mysteries of the social world and beyond.

It was only in the 17th century that a more disciplined, rule-based way of knowing evolved, what is termed the *rational mode* of knowledge-building; it encompasses objective logic of inquiry, combined with unbiased (objective) systematic empirical observation and verification. In the late 19th century, August Comte (1856/2003) coined the word *positivism* to describe a school of thought often referred to as "the scientific method." This has been "the orthodoxy in sociology" since its inception, according to Clough (2009), as it is "richly rewarded in practice" (p. 47). The scientific method is a "systematic method" that stresses the importance of unbiased inquiry, accuracy, and objectivity. The scientific method's goal is to hypothesize about cause and effect through testing out, modifying, and reformulating hypotheses in a search for causality. Positivists hold the belief that the social world, much like the natural world, consists of patterned behaviors that are knowable. There is a sense in which known truths lie within the social reality, and we can get at them if we create specific unbiased procedures. Wickham and Freemantle (2008) characterize this by saying that "positivism gives way to theory," in that positivism reveals truths that can be expostulated into knowledge and theory (p. 923).

Built into the structure of procedures is a set of rules that are meant to overcome some of the range of biases built into other modes of inquiry. One important everyday source of knowledge for many of us is the use of what we come to term our "common sense" to figure out what things mean. An example of the problems of relying on our common sense comes from a recent report on how teens view the causes of AIDS and how to prevent getting AIDS. Let's look at the six top beliefs teens hold about the cause, spread, and prevention of AIDS.

1. "You don't hear so much about it anymore, so it must not be that bad."

2. "It's really only bad in developing, third-world countries."

3. "Wearing the "Red Ribbon" is the only way to help fight the AIDS pandemic."

4. "You shouldn't kiss, hug, or share a meal or drink with someone who is HIV positive or has AIDS."

5. "Heterosexual women are not at risk."

6. "You can tell someone has AIDS just by looking at them." (From Youth Noise, www.youthnoise.com)

Using our "common sense" as a form of human inquiry has a set of biases that prevent us from getting at the range of knowledge we seek. Our common sense may serve to confirm our own biases about the nature of the social world. We may come to see what we want to see or seek out only that information that confirms our point of view. To what extent do we gather a diversity of knowledge about a given issue we seek to understand? Do we do so in a manner that ensures that all points of view on an area of knowledge are represented? Do we tend to weigh some knowledge as more important than other types of knowledge on this issue? To what extent do we rely on our intuition to tell us that something is true?

A scientific approach to knowledge-building, if carried out according to its tenets, seeks to guard against some of these foibles of human inquiry like those beliefs teenagers express about AIDS. Of course, that does not mean all scientists faithfully practice the scientific method or that science will remain free of bias. Even if all scientific procedures are carried out, bias can crop up in the types of questions scientists pose or the biases of those funding their research. If, for example, special interests such as tobacco companies decide to fund a scientific program to study the effects of nicotine on mortality rates of women, will these scientists be free to explore the range of questions and issues regarding the impact of smoking on women's health? To what extent will scientists experience a conflict of interest in terms of what questions they study? How are their data interpreted and affected by the views of the funding party?

Qualitative approaches to knowledge-building have their own set of procedures, which are also cognizant of the "foibles of human inquiry," but with a different set of goals compared with a positivistic approach: Qualitative approaches center on *understanding the subjective meanings that individuals give to their social worlds.* They seek out how individuals come to understand their world and privilege subjective forms of knowledge-building. The social reality is multiple and not unitary; there is no single truth that is sought.

What Is a Qualitative Approach to Research? Qualitative Research Inquiry: A Dynamic Dance

We develop the metaphor of qualitative research approach as a dance routine, comparing it to the more linear, steplike character of quantitative approaches to research. Typically, the quantitative research process, also known as a positivistic approach to research, employs quantitative methods and is presented as a wheel or a stepwise procedure. The various parts of the research process are part of the circumference, and one can begin one's research at different parts of the wheel. Likewise, this process can also be presented as a series of steps (Crabtree & Miller, 1999, p. 9), as depicted in Figure 3.1.

Figure 3.1 Diagram of the Quantitative (Positivistic) Research Process

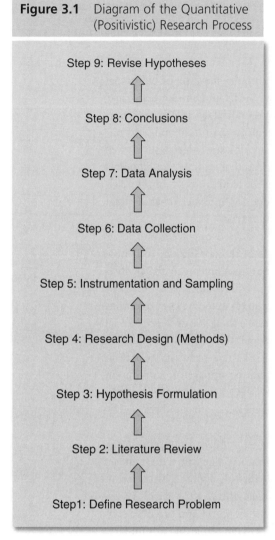

Step 9: Revise Hypotheses

⇑

Step 8: Conclusions

⇑

Step 7: Data Analysis

⇑

Step 6: Data Collection

⇑

Step 5: Instrumentation and Sampling

⇑

Step 4: Research Design (Methods)

⇑

Step 3: Hypothesis Formulation

⇑

Step 2: Literature Review

⇑

Step1: Define Research Problem

Source: Adapted from Crabtree and Miller, 1999.

Crabtree and Miller (1999, p. 8) note that this figure can best be understood metaphorically as Jacob's ladder, which connected heaven and earth in the Bible story. This form of positivist inquiry seeks the Truth. You will notice that the arrows point in only one direction, with no interaction between them. The researcher "climbs a linear ladder to an ultimate objective truth" (Crabtree & Miller, 1999, p. 8). There is a connection back to the beginning step, whereby the researcher refines the problem (Step 1) in response to research findings (Step 9). This positivistic model of knowledge-building is known as the scientific model of research. This viewpoint about the social world became popular at the turn of the 20th century and continues to operate to the present day. **Positivism** looks at the concrete social reality as something "out there" waiting to be described and explained or at least approximated (the latter is a postpositivist view). Positivistic researchers practice objectivity in conducting their research; that is, they advocate a strong separation of the researcher's values and attitudes from their research projects. They assume that to gain a true picture of reality, they must hold their ideas and biases in check—that is, by not allowing their values or attitudes or feelings to enter into the research process. Instead, the researchers hold them in abeyance by "bracketing" these attitudes and values while conducting their research project. For instance, classical ethnographers studying a community are likely to treat villagers as "foreigners" or "the other" and construct a story from the field that is thought to be an "objective" account of events.

While some qualitative approaches, as we mentioned in Chapter 2, may work from a positivist perspective, qualitative approaches in general do not subscribe to this type of stepwise model of knowledge-building. If we were to revise this positivistic framework, we might consider the following questions:

- How would this step model be revised if you were to assume that reality is not singular and "out there" waiting to be found, but instead consists of multiple realities in which there is no one overarching truth? How would this model look if the goal of research was to seek understandings of subjective experiences?

- What steps would remain, and what steps would be discarded? Would any steps need to be added?

- How would you relate these steps to one another? Does the sequence of numbering steps fit a qualitative model of research?

To answer these questions, we might begin by looking for certain omissions in this diagram when it is applied to qualitative methods practices. Perhaps the first element that is missing from this process is some acknowledgment of the influence that a particular *philosophical framework* (paradigm choice) has on the research process. Although qualitative researchers may differ in terms of their particular assumptions regarding the extent to which knowledge can be objective, as is the case of postpositivist qualitative research, as we pointed out in Chapter 2, most qualitative views on the nature of social reality can agree on the importance of the **subjective meaning** individuals bring to the research process and acknowledge the importance of the social construction of reality. In a qualitative approach to research, there is a *dynamic interaction* between the research problem and the literature review (the process of finding, summarizing, and synthesizing existing literature on a topic of interest). Research questions are tentative and most often *not* framed in terms of hypotheses (looking for "cause and effect"). The goal is one of **theory generation**.

Having said that, this does not mean qualitative researchers have no interest in testing out their ideas. In fact, some qualitative researchers, especially those employing a *grounded theory* perspective, stick close to their data and are constantly testing out their ideas as their data is being collected (Charmaz, 2000, 2006). There is an *iterative* qualitative "inductive" methods practice between data collection and data analysis and theory generation in a process known as **analytical induction** (see Figure 3.2). As one collects data, one also interprets it and formulates a range of ideas to test out on additional data collected, and so on. There is a dynamic interaction between Steps 6 (data

Figure 3.2 The Dynamic Dance: The Process of Induction in Qualitative Research

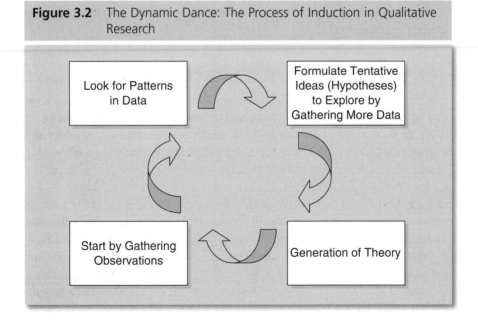

collection), 7 (data analysis), and 3 (hypothesis formulation). Data collection and data analysis can lead to the creation of ideas/hypotheses concerning the data. This, in turn, might lead the researcher to collect specific types of data via a particular sampling procedure (Step 5), that is, sampling specific cases to test out these ideas (theoretical sampling). Researchers move back and forth in the steps of research, almost as if they are doing a dynamic dance routine. The steps are often unstructured, subject to what type of music researchers happen to be listening to (the data), and researchers are open to trying new routines at a moment's notice (see also Crabtree & Miller, 1999). There is no one right dance and no set routine to follow; one must be open to discovery.

Barrie Thorne is a professor of sociology and women's studies at the University of California Berkeley and has written extensively about ethnographic research. Let's join Thorne for a backstage view of her research model.

BEHIND THE SCENES WITH BARRIE THORNE

I start with fairly broad questions, strategically choose a research site (with a case study logic in mind), and proceed to observe, and in my current work, interview, and also gather relevant statistics (about the area of Oakland I'm studying), for example, from the census and the school district. Further questions, reworked questions are "emergent," that is, there is a continual back and forth between the conceptual themes I brought in and have developed and the empirical data; it's a honing and inductive process, with a lot of discovery and reformulation along the way. (Discovery, opportunities for serendipity—those are also distinctive features of some types of qualitative research.)

The dynamic dance that often characterizes qualitative inquiry is exemplified by Thorne's approach to research.

The Importance of Knowing Your Research Position

Whether aware of it or not, all researchers start their projects with a certain set of values and ideas about social reality and the ways that it can be known, which guides their question-asking and research design process. This set of values and beliefs is called a *research paradigm,* and it constitutes the position you take on the research process. Being able to identify and articulate your research position before you start your project is critical because it serves as an important guide to making coherent, ethical, and theoretically informed choices at every stage of the research process. Any given research paradigm or position that a researcher adopts also provides a window onto social realities that may be unseen from a different position.

Sociologist Joseph Diaz (1999) started out as a classical ethnographer trained in a positivist paradigm, a worldview of social reality that assumes his positivistic perspective provides him with a ready-made window onto the social world. His paradigm assumes social reality is ordered, and an objective reality is "out there" waiting to be found. Diaz wanted to conduct a modern ethnography of a plasma-buying clinic located on the Las Vegas Strip. He began his research project by noting:

> I intended to write a colorful, but "classical" ethnography where I find causes, effects, and decipher the hidden codes of the plasma donors and workers. I think I owe this default approach to inquiry to my training as a quantitative methodologist, which teaches, within the positivist perspective, that there is a knowable reality. (Diaz, 1999, p. 1)

What Diaz soon found out, much to his dismay, is that this window onto the social world wasn't working for him:

> In the early data gathering phase of this study, I had to admit that the "plasma experience" appeared neither homogeneous nor easily modeled as a finite and discrete set of causes and effects. When I noticed that my notes, thoughts, experiences, beliefs, and observations regarding my plasma-donating experiences were often contradictory with each other, I realized that my approach needed to be changed. In short, I sought to find a "Truth" which I soon realized does not exist in human interaction and experience. . . . I tried, therefore, to employ the approach that seemed most appropriate to this confusing, and often self-contradictory practice of selling plasma: The Postmodern Ethnography. (Diaz, 1999, pp. 1–2)

The reality of events unfolding in the plasma clinic was highly subjective and filled with contradiction, and Diaz soon found himself playing a crucial role in the data gathering and interpretation of that world. As a participant observer, he uncovered a series of multiple realities or "tales" of plasma donor experiences, including his own:

> In this study I accept the postmodern notion that an author can never be truly objective . . . nor can the descriptions [of] events, people, places, and situations be entirely "true," concretely factual, or objectively representative. . . . Instead of attempting to remove myself (the author) from the study and pretend that my assumptions and interpretations of given events are correct and irrefutable, as one might in a "classical ethnography," I will instead make my presence in the study explicit and will respond to occurrences and evoke emotions and thoughts rather than try to define a given event or situation. (Diaz, 1999, p. 2)

Diaz started out his research project with a set of **philosophical assumptions** concerning the nature of the social world. These assumptions may often go unstated and unexamined, but they are crucial underpinnings to the research enterprise and help shape its process. The philosophical framework—the underlying values and ideas or theoretical paradigm of a research enterprise—guide our interpretation of reality regarding some core metaphysical issues, such as these:

- What is the *nature* of social reality?

- What is the nature of the individual (the individual's concept of social reality/humanity or *ontology*)?

- How is knowledge constructed?

- Who can be a knower?

- What can be known? (What is the individual's particular view of *epistemology*)?

What Is the Role of Methodology in the Research Process?

Our methodological perspective can be thought of as the theoretical perspective or lens we bring to bear on the social world. Our methodological viewpoint helps to shape what we study and is directly tied to the type of research problem we study and how we study it—the particular method or methods we use to address the research problem. As we discussed in Chapter 1, methodology is a bridge between our philosophical standpoint (ontology and epistemology) and methods; it is related to how we carry out our research. Methodologies are derived from our assumptions about the nature of existence (*ontology*) and are also linked to our viewpoint on the nature of knowledge-building (*epistemology*), which guides how we produce knowledge and decisions about what can be known and who can be a knower. The research problem we select is often tied to how we engage *methodologically* (theoretically) with the concrete social world, including the methods we select to answer problems.

Diaz's philosophical viewpoint took a dramatic turn as he began to conduct participant observation at a plasma clinic in the Southwest. He found that he had shifted his viewpoint toward a different view of social reality, toward that of a *qualitatively driven ethnographer* whose basic orientation embraces an interpretative approach to social reality, where the goal is to *understand and explore the nature of social life.* The basic questions of his research moved toward comprehending the lived reality of those who regularly donate blood at the plasma clinic. His research questions reflected the overarching shift in his ontological and epistemological beliefs; namely, he views the social reality as constructed and believes in a theory of knowledge-building that is open to multiple interpretations of the social world. His research question took the following shape:

- How can we understand underlying social processes—how people interact and make meaning from their participation as regular donors to this clinic?

Paradigms or worldviews are neither right nor wrong; one way of seeing is another way of not seeing. However, paradigms are powerful ways of looking at that reality, and they are windows giving us information about the social world and often frame the particular questions we seek to answer.

Reflexivity: Tips for Student Researchers

Reflexivity is the awareness that "all knowledge is affected by the social conditions under which it is produced; it is grounded in both the social location and the social biography of the observer and the observed" (Mann & Kelley, 1997, p. 392). Critical reflexivity denotes an understanding of the diversity and complexity of one's own social location and knowing the differences, and, frequently, "internal contradictions . . . complicate and enrich the analysis" conducted in a qualitative research project (Barndt, 2008, p. 355). A useful way for beginning researchers to practice reflexivity is to take about 20 minutes to complete the following exercise. This exercise is adapted from Hesse-Biber and Piatelli (2007, p. 510):

Take 20 minutes and write down the various ways your position in society impacts the way you observe and perceive others in your daily life. Answer the following questions:

- What particular biases, if any, do I bring to and/or impose onto my research?
- How do my specific values, attitudes, and theoretical perspectives influence the research style I take on? How do my values, attitudes, and beliefs enter into the research process? Do I ask questions only from my own perspective?
- How does my own agenda shape what I ask and what I find?
- How does my position on these issues impact how I gather, analyze, and interpret my data? From whose perspective do I perform these actions?

In addition, you might begin to keep a research journal where you write down your reflection on the research process as your project proceeds. Look over what you wrote on a weekly basis and reflect on your journal entries. Are there some common themes that characterize your weekly journal reflections? How do your attitudes and values enter into the research process, and do they compromise the research process in any way?

Formulating Research Questions: What Do You Want to Ask?

We often think of qualitative research questions as involving an inductive approach, which focuses on describing or generating some theories or ideas about a given social phenomenon. The researcher asks open-ended questions such as the following:

- What is happening here?
- How do individuals make sense of their lived experiences?

In qualitative research, questions are often exploratory and descriptive: to describe social phenomena and their meanings to relevant actors (the *what* questions) and to understand and explain social patterns and processes (the *how* questions). As Gubrium and Holstein (1997) note, there is a distinction between the *what* and *how* questions in qualitative research, and this can differentiate the types of *qualitative paradigms* described above:

The commanding focus of much qualitative research is on questions such as *what* is happening, *what* are people doing, and *what* does it mean to them?

The what questions address the content of meaning as articulated through social interaction and as mediated by culture. The resulting research mandate is to describe reality in terms of what it naturally is. (Gubrium & Holstein, 1997, p. 14)

The *what* questions focus on individuals and social settings, "looking for the meanings that exist in, emerge from, and are consequential for, those settings" (Gubrium & Holstein, 1997, p. 14). The *how* questions in qualitative research are different. They often set aside meaning and are interested in how meaning is constructed by those within a given setting:

How questions typically emphasize the production of meaning. Research orients to the everyday practices through which the meaningful realities of everyday life are constituted and sustained. The guiding question is *how* are the realities of everyday life accomplished? (Gubrium & Holstein, 1997, p. 14)

Qualitatively and quantitatively driven researchers can both answer the *why* questions; however, there are stark differences in the way each approach tackles a *why* question. Suppose a researcher is interested in why crime rates are increasing in the suburbs. A quantitative researcher is likely to employ a deductive approach by positing several variables that have been shown to be associated with high crime rates and then go about testing out these sets of causal factors, coming up with those factors that explain the majority of the increase in crime rates among suburbanites. A qualitative researcher, on the other hand, would answer this question using a more inductive approach, seeking to understand how certain factors play out in an individual's life that may be pivotal to his or her engagement in criminal activity, with the goal of generating a theory about suburban criminal activity that might in fact be tested later with a large-scale quantitative study. In fact, there is often a weaving in and out between macro and micro levels of understanding, with the results from quantitative study feeding into a more qualitative study.

Deriving Research Topics and Questions

The following are several questions that researchers face when beginning their research journey and formulating research questions:

- How do researchers formulate questions?

- What is a good research question?

- How does one get research ideas?

Qualitative research problems derive from many different arenas. As we have mentioned earlier, underlying any research problem are a set of set of *philosophical assumptions* within a given researcher's notion of reality. Very often, questions will arise from personal experience or from a particular issue in the research literature on a given topic. In addition, there are several factors to consider in the question-making process.

The determination of a research question intersects with the researcher's ethical values. Researchers may decide not to explore certain research questions that require the use of new technologies such as the Internet if they find it may compromise an individual user's public Web site information. While this information is in the public domain, there is the ethical issue of the extent to which the access to personal information by outside researchers compromises the privacy of Internet users. For example, problems arise when researchers collect and use personal data from Web sites such as Facebook and MySpace to conduct research to market products to users of these sites based on their personal preferences.

Sometimes, *economic* and *time* constraints can weigh on a research project. If you are a student researcher who needs to complete a research project in one semester, you may find that what type of research you do and the questions you ask are often quite limited by time and economic constraints, especially if you hold a job in addition to going to school. James A. Banks's decision to study how black Americans are portrayed in textbooks came about partly because of economic and time constraints and practical issues of access to research subjects in completing his Ph.D. thesis:

> My first idea for a Ph.D. research project was to study the effects of an experimental training program on the attitudes and beliefs of teachers in urban schools. I had to abandon this idea for several reasons. First, it was necessary that I complete my study within a one-year period, and it was unlikely that I would have been able to design and implement the kind of study I had in mind within those limitations. Second, I needed the cooperation of a large urban school district and numerous teachers to conduct the study, and the initial response I received from one large city school district convinced me that it was unwilling to cooperate with me in implementing the study. Third, the study would have been quite expensive to conduct, and I did not have the funds to finance this type of research project. Although I was disappointed because I was unable to implement my "ideal" study, I did not despair. I realized that although the classroom teacher is the most important factor in the child's learning environment, there are other variables that influence study mastery of content and acquisition of attitudes. Of these other variables, the textbook was perhaps the most important. (Banks, 1976, pp. 383–384)

A researcher may pursue a particular topic and setting because granting agencies, public (i.e., government) and private (i.e., foundations), are dispensing funds to study specific societal issues. Such was the case with Stella Jones's (1976a) dissertation study on geographic mobility. She was interested in the topic of adult socialization. Focusing on the extensive literature in this area, Jones narrowed down her topic to issues dealing with how wives and mothers cope with and adjust to new major life changes as they progress through their life cycle (p. 316). However, the type of research population she could access, as well as the funding she could receive to carry out her research interests, dictated the specific research problem and setting she selected for her research on the specific adult life change of geographic mobility:

> The sociology department in which my husband has a position . . . began planning a symposium on the effects of geographical mobility upon the wife-mother. This symposium was to be funded by a major van line. It occurred to me . . . that I might generate some input for this occasion. I assumed that being female would be helpful to my cause. The symposium format called for the presentation of original research. . . . [T]his format meant that I would need to develop a research design, get funding from the van line, and gain acceptance as part of the symposium. . . . The van line was most receptive to the research proposal. The relative ease of access to funding and a mailing list was a complete surprise to me given the understanding I had of how difficult it can be to gain access into organizations to do research. (Jones, 1976b, pp. 328–329)

One of the most common paths to obtaining a research problem involves a review of the literature on a given topic. David Karp is a sociologist at Boston College who has written several books about depression. For Karp, a literature review serves as the bridge between his interests and an area of inquiry ready for investigation. Let's join David Karp behind the scenes.

BEHIND THE SCENES WITH DAVID KARP

Well, it struck me as odd, when I looked at all this literature on depression; a literature that has really important stuff to say about which independent variables were linked to rates of depression, etc. But depression is a feeling disorder. It is an affective disorder. And so, here I was, reading all of this stuff and I wasn't hearing the feelings of the people who have had the disorder. It struck me as a kind of paradox that that was the case. And, as I said a moment ago, one goal for me, at least of qualitative work, is to let people speak, to acknowledge that the people you are interviewing are really the experts. You talk to them *because* they are the experts. So, I had work to do here, because their voices weren't being heard. There was a journal over there in the O'Neill Library [at Boston College]. . . . I was wandering in the stacks one day, and I came upon a journal called *The Journal of Affective Disorders.* It takes up about five feet of our shelf at the library, and there isn't one voice, not one word from a person who actually suffers from depression. I said, "Wow, I've got a thing to do here." That was the start.

As Karp's experience demonstrates, a literature review can directly prompt a research problem. Commonly, research problems are devised to fill in the gaps of what vital information and questions are missing within the literature.

Using the Research Literature to Formulate Questions

While this section is not intended to go over the particulars of how to conduct a literature search, we discuss the variety of ways that a review of research literature can serve to help you formulate your research question. Locke, Spirduso, and Silverman (2000) provide us with a useful metaphor for thinking about the literature review process when they note that it is like an "extended conversation" (p. 63):

> The process of locating the voices of individual conversants, for example, is called *retrieval*. That involves searching through the accumulated archive of literature to find out what has been said (when, by whom, and on the basis of what evidence). The process of listening carefully to the ongoing discourse about a topic of inquiry is called *review*. That involves studying items previously retrieved until both the history and the current state of the conversation are understood. (Locke et al., p. 64)

First, if you are interested in a general topic but uncertain about how to narrow down your interest into a specific research question, conducting a literature review on your area of interest might be a good way to begin. You might first want to familiarize yourself with the computerized literature retrieval systems that may be available to you, including the large variety of databases available online and offline. Many of these databases contain abstracts (summaries) of articles and reports, which will enable you to quickly obtain an overview of these works. You may also want to think of some important key words or phrases that you can input into these databases that will best describe the topic under consideration.

- How do the authors of these articles define their topic?
- What key terms and phrases do they employ?

Keep a list of these so that you can build up a useful set of terms to input into your databases.

- How have other researchers approached your topic? With what questions?
- What has been the history of research on this topic?
- What are the research controversies within this literature?
- What is known? Which findings seem most relevant to your interests?
- What remains to be done, that is, what burning questions still need to be addressed concerning your topic?

Returning to the metaphor of the literature review as an extended conversation, you may find that in answering many of these questions, you are given an opportunity to listen and ultimately be part of the conversation about a given topic. If you have already narrowed down your topic to some specific questions, the literature review can provide you a context within which to place these questions and will allow you to "tweak" them on the basis of what you find out in your literature review. Perhaps you will discover that several researchers have already asked a similar question. How will this affect how you pursue your topic? Will you decide to replicate their study, extend your study to a different population, or alter your question somewhat to pursue an uncharted area?

In a qualitative research design, it is important not to think of the literature review as occurring at a *fixed point* within the research process. This is often the case with conducting quantitative research, where the literature review is often conducted at the beginning of a research project and serves as a justification for why a researcher asks a particular question and its research significance. Given the iterative nature of the qualitative research process, with its emphasis on discovery, the literature review may need to be conducted at multiple points in the research process as new discoveries are made within the data and the researcher looks to the literature to provide a context within which to understand his or her findings. The function of an initial literature review in qualitative research is primarily to formulate a set of relevant and sometimes general exploratory questions about a topic or phenomenon, whereas in quantitative research the literature review serves to generate a specific set of hypotheses that can be tested. For this reason, a beginning literature review for a qualitative study may not have to be as lengthy or exhaustive as is expected for a quantitative study. This is especially true in qualitative research because the initial research questions may change early on, in response to new discoveries in the field that shift the researcher's understanding of the phenomenon and what is important to know about it.

Research Methods: How Will You Answer Your Research Questions?

Research questions, as we have shown, are grounded in a *philosophical* framework regarding the nature of reality that crystallizes in our given methodological stance. But they are also guided by a range of factors such as academic and personal interests, abilities, social values, and access of the researcher to particular resources needed to carry out the study. All of these determine the type of **research trajectory** a given research project will take. In this section, we will discuss how a qualitative researcher actually goes about planning and developing a study that can answer the questions that she or he has formulated. Particular attention will be paid to the critical issues in research design of sampling, validity, and reliability.

In choosing a research design (a plan for how the researcher will carry out the research project), perhaps one of the most important questions one needs to ask is this:

- What methodological (theoretical) traditions characterize my research problem (i.e., interpretativism, critical theory)?

If we decide to follow a feminist qualitative research perspective in studying eating disorders among college students, we might be particularly interested in studying the experience and meaning of eating disorders among college students and how eating disorders are a gendered phenomenon. We might ask the following broad questions:

- What is the "lived experience" of college men's and women's relationship to food and to their body image?

- How are men's and women's experience of these issues similar or different?

One of the first issues that a qualitative researcher must think through in designing a study that can answer such research questions is sampling: To whom will you talk? Where and when will you observe them? What information sources will you use?

Sampling

The logic of qualitative research is concerned with in-depth understanding, usually working with **small samples**. Unlike quantitative research, in which the goal is to make generalizations about the degree or extent of a problem or set of patterns, qualitative research aims to look at a "process" or the "meanings" individuals attribute to their given social situation. We investigate women's attitudes toward their bodies not to make overall generalizations about *how many* women have problems with their body image, but to understand patterns in *how* women *experience* being overweight in a thin culture. Here we would be interested in the process by which women do or do not cope with their body image and the ways in which they interact with cultural messages of thinness from the media and significant people in their lives.

Qualitative researchers are often interested in selecting a **purposive** or **judgment sample.** The type of purposive sample chosen is based on the particular research question as well as consideration of the resources available to the researcher. Patton (2002), in fact, has identified 16 different types of purposive samples, and more than one purposive **sampling procedure** can be used within any given qualitative study (p. 242). We will select a few examples of how researchers use some of these particular qualitative samples in their studies.

Katherine Hendrix (1998) wanted to study how the credibility of a professor is communicated in the college classroom and how race influences a student's perception of a professor's credibility. She notes:

> The participants in the study represented a "purposeful rather than random" sample. . . . My goal was to obtain the participation of male dyads reflecting professors who worked in the same division and possessed comparable years of teaching experience at the collegiate level. However, three of the professors would be Black and three would be White. (p. 741)

Hendrix (1998) also wanted to interview a sample of students from each of these courses who had volunteered to be interviewed. These students were selected according to their class year, race, and major, using a random procedure. However, with a limited number of students volunteering, the random procedure was revised to ensure a diverse pool, and students were selected to match specific criteria, such as race (p. 742).

Hendrix (1998) used several different *sampling procedures* in carrying out her research project. The first decision to sample came directly from her research problem; in her review of the literature on the topic of teacher communication, she noted that there were particularly difficult "restricted interactions" between black faculty and their white students. Hendrix speculated that within a predominantly white university she might find "particular challenges to building credibility and acceptance . . . for the Black teacher and professor" (p. 741). She wanted to follow up on this idea. She therefore chose a large 4-year university that had a predominantly white college student population. This was a "*homogenous* sample," which enabled her to reduce the variation in race of the student population in order to study her particular problem. However, when it came to sampling six professors and a diverse group of students from their classes, she employed a *stratified purposive sample* to ensure certain characteristics of the faculty and students were included. Sampling for these differences was crucial in carrying out her stated research goals.

Sometimes, however, sampling follows no logical plan; it just happens. Circumstance provides the researcher with an "opportunistic sampling" possibility. One anthropologist recalls his research in West Pakistan and how a sequence of events led to the unintended selection of individuals to interview:

> I recall the use of opportunistic sampling during my first ethnographic trip to West Pakistan. The abundant visitors who voluntarily came to my home served as respondents for innumerable questions; I sought to plumb their motivations and other personality characteristics, and in some cases begged them to take the Rorschach test. Occasionally I solicited my guests with my interview schedule (that had been prepared for a random sample). . . . My wife and children also utilized invitations to the homes of relatively well-to-do or high-ranking families as opportunities to observe certain aspects of domestic life and to obtain other information. (Honigmann, 1982, p. 81)

An important part of conducting fieldwork is having access to informants who can serve as guides to provide information concerning the research site. Very often, however, researchers find the selection of informants boils down to who is available, who has some specialized knowledge of the setting, and who is willing to serve in that role. This type of sample is known as a **convenience sample**. There may not be an opportunity to sample among a group of informants according to some given criteria such as age, sex, or social class. Ethnographer Michael Agar's (1996) field research among a poor migrant group known as the Lambardi, who resided in a village located in the state of Karnataka, India, notes how the researcher may have no choice in the selection of an informant. The community usually earmarks a researcher as a "stranger," and Agar named those sent to speak with him "professional stranger-handlers." He notes:

> Among the Lambardi, the professional stranger-handler was an older man named Sakrya. He was the first who came up to talk with me when I entered the *tanda* [settlement]. He pleasantly explained, for example, that the *tanda* was overcrowded. Therefore, I had to understand that it would be impossible for me to live there. It was Sakrya who suddenly appeared whenever I began doing something bizarre in the early days of fieldwork, like drawing a map or measuring the dimensions of a *tanda* hut. After a couple of months, it was partly Sakrya's decision that I was trustworthy that opened up the *tanda* to me. (Agar, 1996, p. 135)

Another important type of purposive sampling is known as **theoretical sampling.** This kind of sampling is often used as a part of a grounded theory approach to research (Bryant & Charmaz, 2007). Glaser and Strauss's classical work on grounded theory (1967) defines theoretical sampling as "the process of data collection for generating theory whereby the analyst jointly collects, codes and analyzes his data and decides what data to collect next and where to find them in order to develop . . . theory as it emerges" (p. 45). Theoretical sampling implies that the researcher decides who or what to sample next, based on prior data gathered from the *same* research project to make comparisons with previous findings. Analyses of findings in your current data and the theoretical insights you come up with provide new sampling questions such as Who will I talk with next? What additional sources of data should I explore? What data will challenge or confirm my theoretical understanding of this finding? (see Glaser & Strauss, 1967; Guba & Lincoln, 1989; Patton, 2002). Michael Agar (1996) provides the following example of theoretical sampling:

> Say you've worked with four men on agriculture. You've talked with them about their interpretation of the flow of events that constitutes agricultural work, and you've made several observations working with them in the fields. Now you seek out four more men for shorter interviews and observations who live on the other side of the village. You select them for the purpose of checking similarities in the accounts given by your original sample. (p. 172)

Agar notes that if the researcher finds that the results are the same for this group of individuals and learns nothing new by sampling again from this population, then a point of **theoretical saturation** on this group of individuals is reached. The researcher may then opt to interview another group in the village, perhaps those who do not own land, to try to ascertain if there is a different angle on the issue of agriculture. By seeking multiple perspectives, one enhances understanding (Agar, 1996, p. 172).

A common sampling technique, especially when you don't have access to a population from which to draw a sample, or if the nature of your research project makes it almost impossible, is snowball sampling. As Dattalo (2008) notes, "Snowball sampling is sampling from a known network. Snowball sampling is used to identify participants when appropriate candidates for a study are difficult to locate" (p. 6). Suppose you were interested in studying violence against women on your college campus. Women who have been victims of violence may be reluctant to talk with someone they view as a stranger. To reach this population, it might be better to ask others who are most likely to come in contact with women who have been abused if they might provide you with some information on where and how to start addressing these women on a more personal level, where you might present your credentials, and where they might hear about your study in a more protected environment. Once you are able to reach someone who meets the criteria for your study, you might ask that person to pass your name to another person who meets these same criteria; you can provide your initial contact with information about your study to give to anyone in their network who might be eligible. Snowball sampling relies on the personal networks you tap into for referrals. One research contact leads to another, and so on.

Validity

How do you know whether your findings are plausible and will be received as a credible explanation or interpretation of the phenomenon you are studying? This is the fundamental question that all qualitative researchers must grapple with in addressing the issue of validity in their research.

It is important to note that obtaining validity in qualitative analysis is not a specific entity or end goal that the researcher can easily achieve. **Validity** is a *process* whereby the researcher earns the confidence of the reader that he or she has "gotten it right." Trustworthiness takes the place of truth. Lincoln and Guba (1999) note:

> The basic issue in relation to trustworthiness is simple: how can an inquirer persuade his or her audiences (including self) that the findings of an inquiry are worth paying attention to, worth taking account of? What arguments can be mounted, what criteria invoked, what questions asked, that would be persuasive on this issue? (p. 398)

There are some guidelines to navigate important "threats to validity," such as researcher bias and measurement bias. However, there is no specific litmus test we can administer that will apply a stamp of approval on any given qualitative research project.

In qualitative research, validity takes the form of subjecting one's findings to competing claims and interpretations and providing the reader with strong arguments for your particular knowledge claim (Kvale, 1996, p. 240; Kvale & Brinkmann, 2009). As Kvale and Brinkmann (2009) note, "validity is ascertained by examining the sources of invalidity. The stronger the falsification attempts a proposition has survived, the more valid, the more trustworthy the knowledge" (p. 247).

When you are finished reading a qualitative study, ask yourself: What are the factors that make you resonate with the research findings? Does the researcher capture an understanding of the social reality of the respondents he or she has studied? Kvale and Brinkmann (2009) have come up with three criteria of validation for any given qualitative study. They define these as (1) validity as the quality of craftsmanship, (2) validity as communication, and (3) validity as "pragmatic proof through action" (p. 247).

Validity as Craftsmanship

Validity as craftsmanship has to do with how you perceive the credibility of the researcher and research. Does the researcher have moral integrity? (Kvale & Brinkmann, 2009, p. 248). This integrity and credibility is built up through the perceived actions of the researcher. How well has the research been checked? How well has the researcher investigated the findings under consideration? Have the findings been checked, questioned, and theorized? This checking process can cover a range of procedures performed on qualitative data (such as looking for negative cases in one's study, going back to respondents when you may not be clear about a point they have made, perhaps sharing your ideas with your respondents to obtain their point of view, making sure that your sampling procedures match your given research question, and so on). As we mentioned, an important aspect of checking your data is that of *negative case analysis*. Very often, this is done as an ongoing procedure throughout one's study, especially if one is using a more grounded theory approach to research (Glaser & Strauss, 1967). To validate is to look for negative cases within a study. If you think that you have come up with an idea in your data—a key relationship you found—you must go out of your way to look for negative instances where it does not hold up in your data. For example, in the study of eating disorders and body image among college-age students, we derived a concept termed "watching it." This is an abstract concept that describes the range of ways women talk about their own self-surveillance practices, as well as how others among their network of family and friends serve to "police" their eating habits and changes in body weight. Helene, a college student interviewed for a project on college women's eating issues, provides an example of what is meant by this concept from *her* standpoint:

> When I'm home I drop weight, because my mother is always on my back. When I go out to eat she tells me what I should order. When I look fine, my mother says nothing about my body, not even a compliment. But when I start gaining weight, the criticism begins. (Hesse-Biber, 1996, p. 73)

This concept appeared to be strongly related to how women talked about their relationship to food, more specifically what they ate and how much. In order for us to validate this claim, we would want to go through the interviews and look for instances in which this was not the case. If we found a "negative" case, we would want to understand why this relationship did *not* hold for this particular individual. Analyzing negative cases provides researchers with feedback concerning the extent to which their initial theoretical claims are validated by their data. As Kvale (1996) notes,

> Another important type of checking involves going out of your way to provide alternative theoretical explanations for your given findings and attempting to critically examine the relative strengths and weakness of your argument and alternatives to your argument. (p. 242)

Another important aspect of validity as craftsmanship is the ability of researchers to theorize from their qualitative data (Kvale & Brinkmann, 2009, p. 252). Is the researcher able to tell a convincing story? That is, is he or she able to fit the data to a given theoretical framework and make it credible to the reader? In the case of the study of college students' attitudes toward food and body image, has the researcher derived important theoretical insights from the data? Have you learned more about how women and men relate to their bodies, and do you have a fuller understanding of these issues? Have important aspects of a given issue been left out?

Communicative Validity

A second form of validation is **communicative validity.** One can think of this as a dialogue among those considered legitimate knowers, who may often make competing claims to knowledge-building. The idea here is that each interpretation of a given finding is open for discussion and refutation by the wider community of researchers, and sometimes this extends to the community where the research itself was conducted. There is a give-and-take of dialogue surrounding meaning, a move toward the idea of intersubjectivity or group understanding of meaning through dialogue. Not all researchers agree on who can share in this dialogue, or who has the right to interpret knowledge and how agreements should be resolved (see Kvale & Brinkmann, 2009, p. 255). One example of communicative validity might consist of asking the students interviewed in the eating attitudes study to comment on the research findings. Do they agree with the researcher's interpretation? If there is disagreement, how will alternative points of view on these findings be resolved?

Pragmatic Validity

Communicative validity attempts to reach an understanding concerning knowledge claims within the wider research community and beyond. **Pragmatic validity** goes a step further and looks to see the extent to which research findings impact those studied as well as changes that occur in the wider context within which the study was conducted (Kvale & Brinkmann, 2009, p. 257). Depending on the type of study conducted and the findings, one would expect to look for certain action outcomes. For example, we found certain factors within the college community that specifically contributed to women's binge eating. Women felt pressured not to eat in front of their friends during school cafeteria hours. They often ate only salad with little or no dressing. They had little or no time to go back to their school's cafeteria to get more food before it closed, and they relied instead on the food they could obtain in vending machines and fast food restaurants. Both these sources contained high fat content with little nutritional value. Given these findings, one might assess what impact this research had on the wider college community as a result of this report. Did the college food service change its food policies? Was there dialogue in the college newspaper around these issues, and did other students push for changes in school cafeteria policies? Are research subjects empowered to make changes within their lives because of their experience with and knowledge of this project?

One important outcome of pragmatic validity would be the launching of yet another research project, one that contains a *participatory action research* component. This model of research is often referred to as action research, emancipatory research, or collaborative inquiry. Collaboration with the research is the heart of this type of research model:

> Action research . . . aims to contribute both to the practical concerns of people in an immediate problematic situation and to further the goals of social science simultaneously. Thus, there is a dual commitment in action research to study a system and concurrently to collaborate with members of the system in changing it in what is together regarded as a desirable direction. Accomplishing this twin goal requires the active collaboration of researcher and client, and thus it stresses the importance of co-learning as a primary aspect of the research process. (Gilmore, Krantz, & Ramirez, 1986, p. 161)

Participatory action research, then, involves a collaborative model of research that seeks to include research participants in all or many of the phases of a research project—from brainstorming about the goals of the research to decisions concerning data collection, analysis, and interpretation of research findings. Not all participatory models of research involve the researched in all phases of a project; some participatory models involve the researched only in some phases or include only those who are selected to represent the researched. What we can say, however, is that despite the extent of collaboration, there is a shared goal of social activism and change. In the study we cited earlier, for example, students might begin to conduct their own research project, working with the original research team with the goal of implementing new changes in dining policies as well as improving the overall quality of life of students in the dorms during evening hours.

It is important to keep in mind the power dynamics involved in pragmatic validation. As Kvale and Brinkmann (2009) note,

> Pragmatic validation raises the issue of power and truth in social research: Where is the power to decide what the desired results of a study will be, or the direction of change; what values are to constitute the basis for action? And, more generally, where is the power to decide what kinds of truth seeking are to be pursued, what research questions are worth funding? (p. 260)

Researchers should consider these issues if they are hoping for some sort of social change to result from their research.

Triangulation as a Validity Tool

One way to check the validity of research findings is to employ the technique of methods **triangulation,** that is, using two different methods to get at the same research question and looking for convergence in research findings (Greene, 2007; Greene, Caracelli, & Graham, 1989). If two methods come up with the same finding, this serves to enhance the validity of research results. So, for example, we might use a mixed methods approach (for more information on mixed methods designs, see Chapter 11) to study the eating attitudes of college-age students by combining a qualitative design (interviewing) with a quantitative design (a survey) to see if the results concerning body image attitudes hold up using two separate methods. There are other forms of triangulation beyond using two different methods. We might use two different theoretical perspectives (a feminist approach and a critical theory approach) to study the same problem (*theoretical triangulation*). We may also have different investigators studying the same phenomenon (*investigator triangulation*) or we can use different data sources (*data triangulation*) within the same study to enhance the validity of research results. If we want to obtain data triangulation in our study of students' eating attitudes, we might include fieldnotes drawn from observations conducted in the student cafeteria and combine this data with interviews from college-age students in order to more fully understand the impact of college life on students' eating attitudes. We might also have two different investigators collect these data sources.

In this same example, we can also see how theoretical triangulation operates in a research project. A feminist perspective could be applied to understand students' attitudes toward food and body image, focusing on potential gender differences, while a critical theoretical perspective would look at the power and influence of wider cultural factors such as the mass media to understand gender differences in students' eating and body image attitudes. Using *both* these theoretical perspectives may shed *more* light on our understanding of gender differences in eating attitudes with the goal of enhancing the validity of our findings (see Denzin, 1989, pp. 236–247).

Some qualitative researchers have developed a specific set of core characteristics to ascertain the validity of any qualitative study (see Spencer, Ritchie, Lewis, & Dillon, 2003), and this raises an important question:

- Should qualitative researchers follow a set of core criteria for assessing the validity of their research?

The search for some specific criteria with which to assess qualitative findings may be harkening back to a positivistic model of the research process that assumes there is a single, objective truth waiting to be found out. Qualitative research stresses the importance of interpretation—that is, accounting for how individuals experience and make meaning from their lived reality. In fact, some qualitative researchers might find more than one function of triangulation.

Triangulation can also serve to capture alternative and multiple perspectives on social reality. Doubts are also raised concerning whether or not such core validation factors can apply across different qualitative methods. For example, is assessing the validity of a content analysis study the same as ascertaining the validity of findings from an interview project? Studies that seek to develop specific core criteria, in fact, do not always agree with each other on what these factors should be (compare Seale & Silverman, 1997, with Popay, Rogers, & Williams, 1998).

All measures of validity are not without their issues, nor is it clear that employing all of the above validity checks will result in a one-to-one convergence of research results. What these validity practices can move us toward is the more systematic practice of rigor and trustworthiness in the research process so that we can "broaden, thicken, and deepen the interpretive base of any study" (Denzin, 1989, p. 247).

Reliability

Neuman (2003) talks about the issue of reliability in terms of gathering data from observations of individuals or events within a field setting. He refers to the internal consistency of field observations: Is the data you gathered reasonable? Does it fit together? Does your data add up? Is there consistency in your observations "over time and in different social contexts?" (p. 388). External consistency refers to "verifying or cross-checking observations with other divergent sources of data" (Neuman, 2003, p. 388). Researchers who are concerned with external consistency go out of their way to look for other evidence that will confirm their findings. Neuman (2003) notes:

Reliability in field research depends on a researcher's insight, awareness, suspicions, and questions. He or she looks at members and events from different angles (legal, economic, political, personal) and mentally asks questions. (p. 388)

As you can see, validity and reliability are important and complex issues in qualitative research. Figure 3.3 shows a reliability checklist for qualitative studies that Gay and Airasian (2003, p. 536) adapted from Schensul, Schensul, and LeCompte's (1999) ethnographic volume. You might consider referencing this book in thinking about conducting a qualitative research study, especially one that involves gathering data from interviews or conducting an ethnographic participant observation study.

Figure 3.3   Gay and Airasian's Checklist for Evaluating Reliability in Qualitative Studies

- Is the researcher's relationship with the group and setting fully described?

- Is all field documentation comprehensive, fully cross-referenced and annotated, and rigorously detailed?

- Were the observations and interviews documented using multiple means (written notes and recordings, for example)?

- Is interviewers' training documented?

- Is construction, planning, and testing of all instruments documented?

- Are key informants fully described, including information on groups they represent and their community status?

- Are sampling techniques fully documented as being sufficient for the study?

Source: Gay and Airasian, 2003, p. 536.

How Do You Generalize Research Results in a Qualitative Study?

Qualitative research is often compared unfavorably with quantitative research in terms of its lack of ability to generalize its findings to larger populations. While it is true that the generally small, nonrepresentative samples typical of qualitative research do not allow for statistical generalization, qualitative research aims for another form of generalizability, called *analytic generalizability,* which is comparable in its power although different in aim from the generalizability of quantitative research. This is a crucial concept that draws on previously discussed notions of both sampling and validity in qualitative research. To gain deeper insight into this issue, let's go behind the scenes with sociologist David Karp and see how it impacts his research practice.

BEHIND THE SCENES WITH DAVID KARP

Well, I guess I would disagree with those who say that people who do qualitative research can't generalize. I make a distinction in my mind between what I think of as "empirical generalizations" and "analytical generalizations." I don't think you will find this in a textbook, but to me an empirical generalization is sort of what people do when they do statistical analysis. They are generalizing from a sample to some larger universe. Analytical generalizations, in my mind, come sort of close to what Georg Simmel talked about when he talked about "social forms"—the discovery of underlying social forms. The kind of generalization that I'm trying to make in my work is the Simmel-type generalization. And I think it is possible to do that kind of analytical generalization with smaller samples of qualitative data. But there are dangers. . . .

You're always trading off breadth for depth. I mean, the great value of survey research is breadth. You truly can, within known probabilities of error, make generalizations about a larger universe of people. It's a very, very powerful thing to be able to do. So, really, the method you use must be dictated by the problem. You don't use a hammer when you need to use a saw. . . . Every study, whether it's a statistical study, or an in-depth interview study, with 50, 60, 100, 200 people, is going to have limitations in terms of generalizability.

In the end, the test of validity, of whether you have been well-disciplined by the data, whether you really have discovered some underlying social forms, is whether the real experts, those you've studied, when they read your work say, "You've captured it!" See, to me, the ultimate test of validity is when people have read the work—this is very gratifying—and say, "You know, you really captured my experience. You found a way to convey my experience. It lets me understand my own life more deeply." Truly, I think that the power of sociological work is that when you have an experience as an individual . . . you feel so much like nobody else could possibly understand, but when I step back and listen to people, and listen well, and look for those patterns, those forms, I can see things that the individual can't see in her own life; because they have only their own life to generalize from. So, to me, if the generalization thing is off-base, people will dismiss your work. They will say, "This is off the wall . . . it's so distant from my experience that your analysis just doesn't work."

As you can see, validity, in practice, is linked to issues of representation and generalizability.

Conclusion

At this point in the book, we hope that you are getting a sense of the complexity of qualitative research on both a theoretical and practical level. In particular, every researcher operates from within a paradigm or worldview, and this perspective impacts all phases of a research project and forms the philosophical substructure of the project. These underlying issues impact the many issues pertaining to research design that we have reviewed in this chapter. In this way, qualitative research truly is a holistic activity where the varied layers of research, as well as the varied phases, interact with each other. But having said this, we have yet to properly address one ongoing component to qualitative research: ethics. In the next chapter, we turn to a discussion of the ethical substructure of research and why qualitative scholars are committed to dealing with ethics in a holistic manner.

Glossary

Analytical induction: Iterative process between data collection, data analysis, and theory generation.

Communicative validity: The idea that any interpretation of a given finding is open for discussion and refutation by the wider community of expert researchers; all research is part of an ongoing dialogue surrounding that particular research topic.

Convenience sample: Very often, researchers select a respondent who happens to be available and willing to participate in the research project and whose general characteristics fit the research study's general goals.

Philosophical assumptions: These assumptions are often unstated and unexamined, but they are crucial underpinnings to the research enterprise and help shape its process. The philosophical substructure of a research enterprise guides us and our interpretation of reality on some core metaphysical issues, such as these: What is the nature of the social world? Who can know?

Positivism: The positivists view social reality as "knowable." There is a real world "out there" waiting to be researched. One of the key tenets of positivism is the practice of objectivity. Researchers are expected not to allow their own values to intervene in their research project, thus preventing "researcher bias" from entering into the research process.

Pragmatic validity: Captures the extent to which research findings impact those studied as well as changes that occur in the wider context within which the study was conducted (Kvale & Brinkmann, 2009, p. 257).

Purposive sample: Also known as a *judgment sample*. Respondents are chosen to participate in a study based on their particular characteristics as determined by the specific goals of the research project. So, for example, a research study may call for respondents who are female and between the ages of 20 and 30. A researcher will select respondents within these specific age and gender parameters.

Research trajectory: Research questions are grounded in a philosophical standpoint regarding the nature of reality, but they are also guided by a range of factors such as academic and personal interests, abilities, social values, and access of the researcher to the particular economic and lifestyle resources. All of these determine the type of research trajectory for a given research project.

Sampling procedure: The variety of sampling methods employed to collect data in any given research project. These methods can range from non-probability to probability types of sampling designs.

Small samples: Qualitative approaches to research are often characterized by small sample sizes. The logical behind a smaller sample is that the researcher's goal is to collect in-depth information. The idea is that the researcher is trading "breath" for "depth." One of the downsides associated with small sample sizes, is the ability of the researcher to generalize their findings to a wider population. Qualitatively driven researchers might respond to this by saying that the goal of their study is to understand a given social process as opposed to generalizing their study's results to a wider population.

Subjective meaning: Although qualitative research paradigms may differ in terms of their assumptions regarding the extent to which knowledge can be objective, most qualitative paradigms agree on the importance of the subjective meanings individuals bring to the research process and acknowledge the importance of the social construction of reality.

Theoretical sampling: Another important type of purposive sample; this kind of sample is often used as a part of a "grounded theory" approach to research. Glaser and Strauss (1967, p. 45) define theoretical sampling as "the process of data collection for generating theory whereby the analyst jointly collects, codes and analyzes his data and decides what data to collect next and where to find them in order to develop . . . theory as it emerges."

Theoretical saturation: Agar (1996) notes that if the researcher finds the results are the same for a particular group of individuals and learns nothing new by sampling again from this population, then a point of theoretical saturation on this group of individuals is reached.

Theory generation: Instead of testing out a hypothesis (X is thought to cause Y), the researcher's goal is to explore a social phenomenon to come up with some type of theoretical framework or explanation that serves to place his or her research findings in a wider explanatory context.

Triangulation: Researchers often use this procedure with the goal of validating their research by employing a second method of validity that studies the same phenomenon with the goal of confirming research results.

Validity: Positivists are interested in validity especially as it is concerned with the measures that they employ in their research. Measurement validity asks, Does the measure actually reflect the specific reality it is purported to measure? Researchers working within the qualitative paradigm conceptualize validity differently than traditional positivist conceptions of the term. Generally speaking, validity is one of the issues researchers address as they make a case or argument that the knowledge they have produced is reflective of the social world and/or is compelling.

Discussion Questions

1. What is a worldview, and how does it impact the research process?

2. How is research design impacted by philosophical and practical considerations?

3. Why is it important for a researcher to be open to modifying a research project in terms of both theory and methods?

4. How do qualitative researchers think about issues of validity, reliability, and generalizability?

5. What considerations are important when selecting a sample?

6. What does it mean to say that qualitative researchers use a "dance" model of inquiry rather than a "step" model?

Resources

Suggested Web Sites

Knowledge-Building: How do we know what we know?

http://www.exploratorium.edu/evidence/

This interactive Web site challenges you to reflect and explore the process of knowing. How does science arrive at knowledge? What role does scientific evidence play in the process of knowing?

Resources for Qualitative Research

http://www.qualitativeresearch.uga.edu/QualPage/

This Web site is dedicated solely to qualitative research with useful links to resources such as publications, discussion forums, methods, papers, and organizations and interest groups.

Qualitative Research in Information Systems

http://www.qual.auckland.ac.nz/

This Web site aims to provide qualitative researchers in information systems—and those wanting to know how to do qualitative research—with useful information on the conduct, evaluation, and publication of qualitative research.

Relevant Journals

European Journal of Social Theory

Journal of Sociology

Educational Evaluation and Policy Analysis

Qualitative Health Research

Current Sociology

CHAPTER 4

The Ethics of Social Research

Why Is Ethical Practice Important?

Ethical discussions usually remain detached or marginalized from discussions of research projects. In fact, some researchers consider this aspect of research as an afterthought. Yet, the **moral integrity** of the researcher is a critically important aspect of ensuring that the research process and a researcher's findings are trustworthy and valid.

The term *ethics* derives from the Greek word *ethos,* meaning "character." To engage with the ethical dimension of your research requires asking yourself several important questions:

- What moral principles guide your research?

- How do ethical issues influence your selection of a research problem?

- How do ethical issues affect how you conduct your research—the design of your study, your sampling procedure, and so on?

- What responsibility do you have toward your research subjects? For example, do you have their informed consent to participate in your project?

- What ethical issues/dilemmas might come into play in deciding what research findings you publish?

- Will your research directly benefit those who participated in the study?

A consideration of ethics needs to be a critical part of the substructure of the research process from the inception of your problem to the interpretation and publishing of the research findings. Yet, this aspect of the research process does not often appear in the diagrams of the models of research we discussed in Chapter 3. A brief history of the ethical aspects of research will better help us understand why this still remains so.

A Short History of Ethics in Research

The history of the development of the field of ethics in research, unfortunately, has largely been built on egregious and disastrous breaches of humane ethical values. A journey through this history can provide valuable insights into the state of contemporary research ethics institutions and codes that currently guide social science and biomedical research.

The Tuskegee Syphilis Study

The Tuskegee syphilis study was conducted by the U.S. Public Health Service (USPHS) beginning in 1932. The study examined untreated cases of latent syphilis in human subjects to determine the "natural course" of the disease. Four hundred African American males from Tuskegee, Alabama, who already had syphilis, were recruited for this study, along with a matched sample of 200 noninfected males. The subjects were not asked to provide their informed consent to participate in this project. Those infected with syphilis in the early 1930s were given the standard treatment at that time, which consisted of administering "heavy metals." However, when antibiotics became available in the 1940s and it was evident that this treatment would improve a person's chances for recovery, antibiotic treatment was withheld from the infected subjects, even though the researchers knew that if left untreated, the disease would definitely progress to increased disability and eventually early death. According to some reports, "on several occasions, the USPHS actually sought to prevent treatment" (Heintzelman, 2001, p. 49). The experiment lasted more than four decades, and it was not until 1972, prompted by exposure from the national media, that government officials finally ended the experiment. By that time, "74 of the test subjects were still alive; at least 28, but perhaps more than 100 had died directly from advanced syphilis" (p. 49). There was a government investigation of the entire project launched in mid-1972, and a review panel "found the study 'ethically unjustified' and argued that penicillin should have been provided to the men" (p. 49).

At no time in the course of this project were subjects asked to give their consent to participate in the study. They were not specifically told about the particulars of what the study would entail. In fact, those who participated did not even volunteer for the project. Instead, they were deceived into thinking

> they were getting free treatment from government doctors for a serious disease. It was never explained that the survey was designed to detect syphilis. . . . Subjects were never told they had syphilis, the course of the disease, or the treatment, which consisted of spinal taps. (Heintzelman, 2001, p. 51)

In his book *Bad Blood: The Tuskegee Syphilis Experiment*, author James Jones (1993, as cited in Heintzelman, 2001) notes that the subjects in the Tuskegee experiment had a blind trust in the medical community. As one subject from the experiment notes, "We trusted them because of what we thought they could do for us, for our physical condition. . . . We were just going along with the nurse. I thought [the doctors] was doing me good" (p. 50).

There is also a question of whether or not the researchers took advantage of a vulnerable population of individuals, whom they knew did not have the resources to afford medical treatment or the education to question their medical expertise. In addition, the researchers' racist attitudes concerning black males made it easier for them to justify their decision not to provide them with treatment:

> The rationale was that the conditions existed "naturally" and that the men would not have been treated anyway, according to the premise that shaped the study—that African Americans, being promiscuous and lustful, would not seek or continue treatment. (Brandt, as quoted in Heintzelman, p. 49)

Poor decisions on the part of the researchers, influenced by bigotry, allowed this to happen. But this kind of research is simply unacceptable. As a result of this case (as well as others), the notion of **informed consent**—participants' right to be informed about the nature of a research study and its risks and benefits to them prior to consenting to participation—was born. This ethical principle in research is one of the cornerstones of modern social research ethics and will be discussed in greater detail in this chapter.

Further Developments in the History of Research Ethics

Formal consideration of the rights of research subjects grew out of the revelations of the terrible atrocities that were performed—in the guise of scientific research—on Jews and other racial/ethnic minority groups in Nazi concentration camps during World War II. One result of the revelations of these appalling medical experiments perpetrated on concentration camp prisoners *in the name of science* resulted in the creation of the **Nuremberg Code** (1949), a code of ethics that begins with the stipulation that all research participation must be voluntary. Other codes of ethics soon followed, including the Declaration of Helsinki (1964), which mandates that all biomedical research projects involving human subjects carefully assess the risks of participation against the benefits, respect the subject's privacy, and minimize the costs of participation to the subject. The Council for International Organization of Medical Sciences (CIOMS) was also created for those researching in developing nations (Beyrer & Kass, 2002). Throughout the history of scientific research, ethical issues have captured the attention of scientists and the media alike. Although extreme cases of unethical behavior are the exception and not the rule in the scientific community, an accounting of these projects can provide important lessons for understanding what can happen when the ethical dimension of research is not considered holistically within the research process.

Thus far, we have been focusing on biomedical research. To what extent do the ethical issues in the natural sciences carry over into the behavioral and social sciences? There are some classic examples of extreme violations of ethics within the annals of behavioral and social scientific research as well. Perhaps one of the most egregious comes from a 1963 research project concerning "obedience to authority," conducted by psychologist Stanley Milgram. Milgram wanted to understand the conditions under which individuals obey authority figures. His research protocol called for deceiving volunteer subjects into thinking they were involved in an experiment on the impact of punishment on memory. Volunteers first read a series of word associations to individuals (who were confederates—secretly part of Milgram's team) under a variety of experimental conditions: (1) they could not see or hear the confederate; (2) they could hear the confederate protest but not see the confederate; (3) they could hear and see the confederate; (4) same as three except the subject was required to place the confederate's hand on a shock plate. If the confederates were unable to repeat the words back, volunteers were asked to administer what they thought was an "electric shock" (it was actually fake) to them, increasing the voltage for each wrong answer to see if shocking would in fact enhance learning. Subjects had a fake voltage meter in front of them with readings "from slight to severe shock," with a sign posted next to the meter that warned about the danger of using this equipment. Some subjects protested, on hearing confederates complain about pain and other medical problems. Even though some volunteers wanted to quit the experiment, the researcher in charge insisted that they continue, saying the researcher would take the responsibility. Some subjects, however, did not protest and even went on to administer what they considered the highest and potentially lethal shock to a confederate, even when they had received no feedback that the person was even alive (Milgram, 1963).

Stanley Milgram's experiment deceived his volunteer subjects and failed to obtain their informed consent. The protocol of this experiment did not allow subjects to quit even when some protested and asked that it be stopped. In addition, some subjects experienced psychological distress knowing they actually could administer what would be considered a lethal shock to another human being.

This experiment was partially replicated more than 40 years later by Jerry Burger (2009). Burger's results differed little from Milgram's original findings in that more than 70% of Burger's respondents administered up to 150 volts to the confederate. Burger received the green light from his university's ethics board by making some specific changes to Milgram's original protocol that made sure that all his respondents were screened for psychological stress and that they would be debriefed right after the end of the experiment. He also limited the voltage reading maximum shock to 150 volts.

In spite of these protocol changes, one should ask whether or not this experiment was ethical. Respondents still needed to deal with the postexperimental reality that they were capable of administering a shock up to 150 volts to another human being. Does the end goal of this study justify the means?

Unfortunately, when the Tuskegee and Milgram experiments began, there were no review boards to oversee the goals of these projects. It was not until the mid-1960s that the U.S. federal government began the process of developing a set of official rules governing the conduct of research, partly in response to such medical abuses as the Tuskegee experiment and others (see Beecher, 1966; Jones, 1981). This ultimately led to the passage of the National Research Act by the U.S. Congress in 1974. This act set up an Office for the Protection of Research Risks (OPRR) and ultimately resulted in a set of guidelines known as the **Common Rule**, which was widely adopted by federal agencies (Alvino, 2003, p. 898). The Common Rule mandated, among other things, that any institution receiving federal funds for research must establish an institutional review committee. These committees, known as **institutional review boards (IRBs)**, have the job of watching over all research proposals that involve working with human subjects and animals. Universities and colleges that receive federal funding for research on human subjects are required by federal law to have review boards or forfeit their federal funding. IRBs are responsible for carrying out U.S. government regulations proposed for human research. They must determine whether the benefits of a study outweigh its risks, whether consent procedures have been carefully carried out, and whether any group of individuals has been unfairly treated or left out of the potential positive outcomes of a given study (Beyrer & Kass, 2002). This is, of course, important in a hierarchically structured society where we cannot simply assume racism, sexism, homophobia, and classism are not present in research.[1]

Currently, professional associations for each discipline, such as the American Educational Research Association (AERA), the American Sociological Association (ASA), and the American Psychological Association (APA), outline their own general ethical guidelines relevant to their disciplines, which elaborate and sometimes extend federal guidelines. Each of these associations has a specific Web site address that discusses a range of specific ethical concerns for each of these professions. The American Psychological Association's Web site (http://www.apa.org/ethics/code2002.html), for example, outlines specific ethical categories of conduct from "general principles" of professional conduct, which deal with issues such as integrity and justice, to more practice-specific concerns, such as privacy and confidentiality of patients and research subjects. There are also ethical guidelines on record keeping and fees, as well as on issues that may come up in a therapeutic situation, such as those especially pertaining to sexual intimacy with clients and therapy with former sexual partners. There are also guidelines for resolving ethical issues such as discrimination and handling of complaints.

How Are Research Subjects Protected Today?

Informed consent covers a range of procedures that must be implemented when your study includes human subjects. Human subjects in your study must be informed about the nature of your research project, and you must obtain their consent prior to their participation in your study. This information is usually contained in an informed consent letter that each respondent in your study needs to sign; by doing so, respondents indicate that they have read the letter and agree to participate in your research project.

The Informed Consent Letter

The informed consent letter does several things. It lets respondents know about your project and what role they will play in it. The letter should be detailed enough so that a participant is informed about the *specific nature of the project*, including any potential risks, and the letter should outline how participation will make a contribution to your project's goals. It is important for participants to weigh any potential risks with the benefits of their participating in your study. You should make sure that participants can follow up with any questions or concerns they may have about your project by providing them with information on whom to contact about the study.

You need to be sure that the study participants know that their agreement to participate is completely *voluntary* and that they are free to opt out of your study before, during, or after their initial participation. You need to be clear with them exactly how you will use the data you collect from them. You must also be sure to let them know the degree of confidentiality afforded to them once they partici-pate. For example, you need to let them know how you will ensure the confiden-tiality of study participants' contribution; this should include information on what you intend to do with the results from your study. For example, will you publish the results of this study and, if so, where? Will you present these findings at conferences? How will you ensure that the data you collect from this study will remain confidential? You might let participants know the specific ways in which you will ensure their confidentiality. For example, you might inform them that their name will never appear on any data collected and that instead you might provide a unique identification number on their data and that this information will remain secure such that only the principal investigator of this study will have access to it. You might let them know how these data will remain secure through-out the duration of the project and how data that are no longer needed will be destroyed.

Informed consent is a question of basic human rights; it is intended to safeguard participants from any mental or physical harm that might befall them as a result of their participation. Participants are made aware of any potential risks that come with participation and know that procedures are set in place to deal with any neg-ative outcomes that might ensue. In this regard, it is crucial that you build into your study the specific steps you will take to minimize any potential risks that may arise in the study (for example, by providing counseling hotline numbers if you think your study may create painful memories or even psychological trauma). Informed consent is also vital for the researcher in that it spells out the expectations on the part of researcher and participant, such as how long the study will take, whether or not the participant will receive compensation, and so on. The following is one example of a consent letter regarding a study where the participants are from a nonvulnerable population, meaning that they have reached adulthood, can fully assess the costs and benefits of participating in your study, and are freely able to give their consent to participate without feeling coerced. We have highlighted the dif-ferent parts of this letter in *italics,* to give you an idea of what sections you will need to put into your own letter of consent.

STUDENT RESEARCH PROJECT

Informed Consent Letter

Title: Drinking Patterns and Attitudes Among College Seniors

Principal Investigator and Contact Information: Here you would place the name of your supervisor and his or her contact information if this is part of a student research project.

Student Researcher's Name: You would place your name, college, and class year here.

Purpose of Your Study:

Example: I am a senior sociology major at Boston College. This semester, I am conducting a research project as part of my sociology honors thesis. I am working closely with my supervisor, Dr. Sharlene Hesse-Biber, who will be the main contact person for this project. I would like to know if you would be willing to take part in a research study on drinking patterns of college seniors. The project is part of a larger nationwide study that seeks to gather data on the frequency and extent of alcohol use among graduating seniors, as well as to understand what you consider to be the factors within the college environment that serve to promote as well as to impede the drinking behaviors of college students in general.

Procedures:

You will be asked to complete an online survey questionnaire that will ask you about your drinking patterns and attitudes toward drinking in college. We are also interested in your opinions regarding the general drinking environment at your college.

Confidentiality:

All the information you provide will be strictly confidential, and your name will not appear on the questionnaire. Instead, your questionnaire will contain an identification number that is known only by the principal investigator of this study. This identification number is used to note that you have returned your questionnaire and will not be attached to the general survey itself. Once you complete the online survey, just click on the "exit" button on the last page of your survey, and your questionnaire will be automatically sent to us via e-mail, without any identification of the sender's e-mail address.

Note About Voluntary Nature of Participation and Statement About Compensation:

Your participation is voluntary. You may refuse to participate or may discontinue your participation at any time during the online survey. While we cannot compensate you for your time, your participation will be invaluable to our project as we seek an understanding of alcohol use on college campuses and the range of factors in the college environment that exacerbate drinking patterns of college students.

(Continued)

(Continued)

Information About This Study:

You will have the opportunity to ask, and to have answered, all your questions about this research by e-mailing or calling the principal investigator, whose contact information is listed at the top of this letter. All inquiries are confidential.

Participant's Agreement Statement:

If you agree to participate in our study, we would appreciate your signing your name and date to this form and sending it back to us in the stamped and addressed envelope within one week of your receipt of this letter.

* *

I have read the information provided above. I voluntarily agree to participate in this study. After it is signed, I understand I will receive a survey form via e-mail.

_____   _____

Name   Date

As soon as we receive your informed consent letter, we will e-mail you the online survey to fill out.

Thank you.

Sincerely,

_____   _____

Your name goes here   Your supervisor's name goes here

with your affiliation   with his or her affiliation

Informed Consent: The Principle and the Reality

A major principle underlying many of the ethical policies that have historically developed around the issue of how to treat research subjects has been the use of informed consent, the right of subjects to decide—free of pressure or constraint and in a fully informed manner—whether or not they will be involved in any research endeavor (Faden & Beauchamp, 1986). Some ethicists question the extent to which informed consent has lived up to its promise (Cassileth, Zupkis, Sutton-Smith, & March, 1980). Some research has found that research subjects do not always understand the medical or social aspects of the clinical project in which they are participating, and some do not even know that they may in fact be participating in a research trial (Lynoe, Sandlund, Dahlqvist, & Jacobsson, 1991; see also Appelbaum, Roth, Lidz, Benson, & Winslade, 1987). As we have seen earlier in this chapter, in many instances, researchers fail to fully disclose to research subjects the full extent of the risks and benefits of participating in a given study. This has led to some negative and even disastrous research outcomes for some of those who have participated in both social scientific and biomedical research.

In addition, it may be particularly difficult for a researcher using a qualitative approach to approximate full **disclosure** in an informed consent letter because qualitative research, by its very nature, is open to discovery; a change in research goals may be particularly difficult to anticipate. It may be nearly impossible for the qualitative researcher to account for all of the happenings in the research setting, and it may be hard to go back and forth to a Human Subjects Committee, such as an IRB, for approval each time one's project takes an unexpected turn. Adler and Adler (2002) argue that obtaining informed consent hits those researchers practicing participant observation the hardest:

> Participant observation has a fuzziness about what is research and what is not, as ethnographers are observers of everyday life and may be generating insights and gathering data from people in all kinds of situations (a waitress at a restaurant, a fellow passenger on an airplane, a person whose child is the same age as one's own). They may not know in advance what information will drift their way and that may prove explicitly useful, either currently or in the future. (p. 40)

There is then a *principle* and a *reality* to providing informed consent. There exists a wide variation in how well researchers carry out the policy of informed consent in ongoing research projects. For example, in the following two informed consent letters to parents regarding a research project on body image, Letter A contains a much more detailed account of the research problem (including several research goals and an explanation of how the research will be carried out) than does Letter B.

LETTER A

Dear Parents:

My name is _____ and I am a sociologist and teacher at _____ College. I have previously conducted several studies on self-esteem in young girls. Currently, I am conducting a study on body image and self-esteem among African American and white preteen and adolescent girls. I firmly believe that it is essential to include a sample of African American girls. It has been my experience that the attitudes and beliefs of this important group have been all too often left out. They need a voice, and this is why I am writing to you today to ask for your help and permission to interview your daughter. I would also like to take a moment to tell you a little more about the study.

I plan on having the girls meet at the Health Center for pizza and soda after school in groups of three or four to chat about self-esteem and body image. If your daughter chooses to participate, with your permission, the interview will take no more than 45 minutes, and her participation will be completely voluntary.

(Continued)

(Continued)

This research project will study preteen and adolescent attitudes about body image and self-esteem. These are some of the questions that we will explore:

1. From whom and where do preteens learn perceptions of body image and self-esteem? For example, what role do peers and the mass media play in influencing preteens' and adolescents' attitudes concerning their weight and body image?

2. What factors (if any) appear to "protect" preteen and adolescent girls against feelings of low self-esteem, and what factors (if any) contribute to a depressed sense of body esteem?

I envision this study as a unique opportunity. As I said earlier, we need to give young black women and the black community a stronger voice. I believe that my project can accomplish that. Yet even more important, I believe that providing an opportunity for the girls to get together to chat with friends and peers about issues of black identity and self-esteem will serve as a mechanism for black female empowerment.

Attached you will find a consent form which is to be, on agreement, signed by your daughter and yourself and brought to the Health Center the day of the interview. The interview is completely voluntary and confidential.

If you have any questions or concerns, please feel free to call me at home: _____ or work: _____.

Thank you for your time, and I look forward to hearing from you soon.

Sincerely,

_____ Ph.D.

Chair, Department of Sociology

Professor

Letter B is much shorter and provides few details concerning the research goals.

LETTER B

Dear Parents:

My name is _____ and I am a sociologist and teacher at _____ College. I am conducting a study on body image and self-esteem among African American and white preteen and adolescent girls.

I plan on having the girls meet at the Health Center for pizza and soda after school in groups of three or four to chat about self-esteem and body image. If your daughter chooses to participate, with your permission, the interview will take no more than 45 minutes, and her participation will be completely voluntary and confidential.

Attached you will find a consent form which is to be, on agreement, signed by your daughter and yourself and brought to the Health Center the day of the interview.

I appreciate the opportunity to interview your daughter. If you have any questions or concerns, please feel free to call me at home: _____ or work: _____.

Thank you for your time and I look forward to hearing from you soon.

Sincerely,

_____ Ph.D.

Chair, Department of Sociology

Letter B contains the minimum information that can be given to respondents. Both letters ensure respondent **confidentiality**, that is, their names cannot be used in any written material or discussions concerning the research project, and interview materials will also be stored in a safe place free from disclosure. This means the researcher and others working on the project will not know the identity of the respondent (e.g., a respondent returns a survey questionnaire with no name on it).

These letters, however, point to some of the *political dimensions* involved in creating an informed consent letter. To the extent that they reveal the way they will conduct their research and are willing to share their research goals, researchers may be attempting to protect or not remain tied down to a particular research goal(s). For example, it may not always be in the interests of the researcher to be forthcoming regarding full disclosure. Some researchers may even go out of their way to develop a **cover story** to explain the research project, and this may be built into the original design of the research project:

> The selection or invention of details to constitute the cover story and convince intended respondents is an element in the design of a research project. That requires skills of persuasion. Investigators develop a sense of what details allay fears and what prompt suspicions. As in other types of negotiation, such as bargaining over salaries, the initiating party uses a gambit declaring a position which it may concede and which supposes an opposition of interests between the negotiating parties. The investigator will reveal further information if required but in many cases subjects will not be briefed to ask pertinent questions and the project will move on quickly from negotiation to interview. (Homan, 1992, p. 324)

If respondents initially refuse to participate in a research project, rather than accepting the right of the researched to act autonomously, this is sometimes viewed as a failure on the part of the researcher, who may then try to break down "the defenses of respondents" through a variety of means, from group pressure to exploitation of friendships. To this issue, Homan says:

> In various ways research projects trade upon a relationship with agencies in power or authority. Sutherland was able to research the secretive and exclusive Rom community, which was normally hostile to representatives of the world outside it, by exploiting her role as teacher of its children. (Homan, 1992, p. 325)

There are even times when following the ethical guidelines of informed consent may actually not be in the best interests of your research respondents in certain respects. Baez (2002) points out the ethical conundrum he experienced in maintaining the confidentiality of his respondents. Baez interviewed 16 minority faculty members regarding their personal experiences with the tenure and promotion process at one private university. He notes that maintaining confidentially can be a double-edged sword. Keeping the interviews confidential, especially for untenured faculty, allowed him to obtain candid data regarding racism and sexism within the university. On the other hand, confidentiality prevented him from reporting "serious contradictions within an institution that, through institutional documents and public comments by key administrators, purported to be supportive of racial and cultural diversity" (Baez, 2002, p. 39). For Baez personally, he stated, "I could not do so without feeling that I would be identifying my respondents to others in the institution," although he may have wanted to call attention to the contradictory, even racist transgressions and patterns he uncovered in his research (p. 39). Bear in mind that you often do not know what your research will teach you, and it can be very difficult not to try to effect social change in some situations.

Patton (2002) notes that respondents are now challenging the right to "tell their stories" while at the same time not hiding their identities, especially when they see the project as an opportunity to gain empowerment through telling their stories and perhaps becoming a catalyst for social change (p. 411). Patton suggests a number of important ethical dilemmas that flow from this new viewpoint on confidentiality:

- Should the researcher "impose confidentiality against the wishes of those involved"?

- Are human subjects committees "patronizing and disempowering" if they turn down those respondents who wish to reveal their identities?

- Do research subjects make the choice independent of others in their social context? What about the privacy of significant others in their lives, such as children, spouse, and extended family members? (p. 411)

Beyond all of these considerations, some researchers are very cognizant of ethics in practice, attempt to use informed consent, and still experience challenges in observing the principles of informed consent in a consistent and carefully considered manner. Sarah Maddison is a feminist sociologist at the University of

New South Wales in Australia, where she focuses on gender and social policy. Maddison encountered several problems when trying to use informed consent in her ethnographic work with a feminist student group. Let's join Maddison behind the scenes.

BEHIND THE SCENES WITH SARAH MADDISON

A couple of years ago, I was engaged in a project researching a group of young student feminists drawn from various university campuses in New South Wales. The Cross Campus Women's Network (CCWN) was a loose coalition of women who met on a fortnightly basis. At each meeting, there would be between five and ten women and, with the exception of the convenor, these could often be a different group of women each fortnight. It was this changing roll call at each meeting that created a major obstacle for the ethical conduct of this research: Although I had carefully explained the purpose of my research and sought permission to attend and participate the first time I went along, there were women at subsequent meetings who missed out on my spiel and became very suspicious of my presence and my intentions.

So they kicked me out! The convenor e-mailed me and asked me not to attend any more meetings until they had resolved this issue between themselves (apparently there were differing views about the merits of my research within the group). I was allowed to send an e-mail to the group explaining myself again and then I just had to sit and wait. Time to reflect on power (shared), clarity (and confusion), and consent (given—and taken away again).

I have to say I felt pretty foolish—but in actual fact it was my fear of *appearing* foolish that had put me in this situation to begin with. As a researcher wanting to begin the "participant" part of the participant observation process, I was reluctant to continually draw attention to my researcher status by outlining my project every time I saw a new face. I really wanted to blend into the group and participate in meetings as if I was "one of them," not an outsider. More than anything I wanted them to forget what I was doing there so that I could somehow observe, participate, and consume what "really" went on in their meetings. I rushed in there with the arrogant assumption that the merits and importance of my research were obvious to all and the belief that no one would *not* want to participate.

So stupid—and so wrong. They were right to kick me out because I was behaving very badly, and totally unethically. I had forgotten for a moment that the presence of a researcher always and inevitably changes the dynamics and practices of a group and that my very presence made the group a *different* group to the one that had existed before I strutted through the door. More important, I had deluded myself that, as a participant observer, I could somehow, sometimes take off my researcher hat and be "one of them." Of course I knew all these things before I began, but in my enthusiasm to get the project started, I had left my ethical practice at the door as I barged on through.

(Continued)

(Continued)

My delusions of invisibility made me forget the first and most golden rule of any sort of research—*consent*. How could my research have any integrity if even one member of the group did not realize I was a researcher? How dishonest of me! How misleading! I could really only be grateful that these young women were feisty and confident enough to boot me out while they considered their choice to participate in the project. There would be many other groups of potential research subjects who would not have the confidence to ask a researcher to leave their group. This awareness made me reflect anew on the significance of power in research relationships and the role that consent must play in clarifying these power relationships.

After a few weeks I was informed that they had decided to let me come back, and I returned gratefully and with my tail between my legs. I had learnt my lesson. Even though I had thought I had been completely open and transparent about my project, I had been careless about ensuring that *every* member of the group had a good understanding of who I was, why I was there, and what the research might achieve—an essential step for ethical research in which informed consent is crucial to the legitimacy of the entire project. This is not a lesson I will forget in a hurry, and I am thankful for these young women's patience in helping me learn it again.

There is a great deal we can learn from this example. Specifically, Maddison shows how ethical practice is an ongoing consideration. Moreover, ethical issues and informed consent provide researchers with an opportunity to learn about themselves and to develop as researchers—ethics are a doorway to reflexivity.

Beyond Informed Consent: What Are the Ethical Dilemmas in Social Research?

Although the principles of informed consent may be relatively clear, the actual practice of ethics in a given research setting can be complex and may pose a myriad of fundamental ethical questions that a researcher must navigate, often without clear guidance from a given set of ethical codes. A discussion of some of the kinds of ethical issues that may arise in qualitative social science research may serve as a guide to thinking about these issues.

The Ethical Predicament of Deception in Research

Some researchers argue that their research must be conducted in a covert manner to obtain the information they need to understand certain social phenomena. For example, some researchers have gone undercover to study underground cultures such as drug cultures (see Williams, 1996) and used **deception** to find out about the inner workings of the social life of drug dealers and drug takers, often observing individuals engaging in illegal activities and sometimes finding themselves asked to engage in these same activities. There would be no point in asking for the informed consent of the members of this closed society because they would most likely not want their organization studied. Williams (1996) conducted participant observation on a subculture of cocaine users and dealers in the after-hours clubs in an inner city and noted the following concerning his undercover activities:

> I was in a Brooklyn club where I was already conspicuous as a nonuser of cocaine. It seems that I was also overzealous. In the sense that I was staring too much and asking too many questions. One of the club's owners came over to me and said "Listen, my man, if you're undercover, I got people that'll take care of that." I was not sure whether he meant force or bribery, but in any case I stopped going to that club. . . . As a researcher, I knew what data I needed: information on cocaine users and the associated nightlife, street myths about use. . . . But as most researchers know there is a quid pro quo in every research situation. . . . I was asked to do a variety of favors, such as lending money and finding social workers. . . . On many occasions I was asked to engage in illegal acts. . . . This and similar requests put me in an awkward position. (pp. 30–31)

Any student reading this example might want to ask the following question:

- Is it ethical to go undercover to study this organization?

One can imagine those social scientists studying deviant behaviors such as life in the underground drug trafficking world and wonder how difficult it might be to obtain the informed consent of everyone involved in order to study the inner workings of an illicit drug trade. The following questions are raised:

- What does the researcher do when he or she confronts information or situations where individuals are observed engaging in major violations of the law?

- Is the researcher ethically obligated to report such activity?

- What about the risks the researcher is taking in terms of his or her own life in doing so?

Deception in research doesn't have to occur by going undercover in carrying out research projects. The Milgram experiment was a study in deception. From the start, Milgram did not truthfully explain the nature of the experiment, and he deceived subjects into thinking they were in fact applying electrical shocks to another human being. Some qualitative social science research methods, like fieldwork, can also require a more subtle type of deception between the researcher and the researched, even when fieldworkers disclose the fact that they are conducting research and its nature to those they are studying. Sociologist Herbert Gans

(1982), conducting fieldwork in Park Forest, a suburb near Chicago; in Boston's West End; and in Levittown, a New Jersey suburb, gives his personal reflections on the anxiety he experienced in what he finds is "the deception inherent in participant observation":

> Once the fieldworker has gained entry, people tend to forget he is there and let down their guard, but he does not; however much he seems to participate, he is really there to observe and even to watch what happens when people let down their guard. He is involved in personal situations in which he is, emotionally speaking, always taking and never giving, for he is there to learn and, thus, to take from the people he studies, whereas they are always giving information, and are rarely being given anything. Of course they derive some satisfaction from being studied, but when they ask the participant observer to give—for example, help or advice—he must usually refuse in order to maintain his neutrality. Moreover, even though he seems to give of himself when he participates, he is not really doing so and, thus, deceives the people he studies. He pretends to participate emotionally when he does not; he observes even when he does not appear to be doing so and like the formal interviewer, he asks questions with covert purposes of which his respondents are likely to be unaware. In short, psychologically, the participant observer is acting dishonestly; he is deceiving people about his feelings and in observing when they do not know it, he *is* spying on them. (p. 59)

Gans represents a particular point of view on the role of the researcher as participant in the fieldwork experience. The idea that researchers should remain neutral and "detached" from the research subject tells us that they aspire to the goal of objectivity in the research process. This objectivity then is enhanced by deception. Yet, as we have seen, this frame on the research process is one of many *paradigms* one can bring to the fieldwork experience. There are those who believe researchers do not need to maintain distance between themselves and the researched. Ann Oakley (1981) critiques this model of neutrality and instead argues for bridging this divide through empathy and affinity. Other ethnographers feel that this form of closeness between researcher and researched also has its problems and that one can become too close to respondents, which in turn can create a series of conflicts and deceptions as well. Ethnographer Judith Stacey (1991) comments:

> The irony I now perceive is that ethnographic method exposes subjects to far greater danger and exploitation than do more positivist, abstract, and "masculinist" research methods. And the greater the intimacy—the greater the apparent mutuality of the researcher/researched relationship—the greater is the danger. (p. 114)

Stacey (1991) notes that the more involved she became with her respondents, the further exposed she became to situations within the field that left her open to the possibility of manipulating and betraying her respondents (p. 113). Thus, personal engagement with research subjects on an interpersonal level can lead to unanticipated and unintended deception that can actually raise even more the possibility of undue power, influence, and authority in the research process. So we can see that issues of disclosure and trust are actually very complex.

Some might argue that a certain amount of strategic deception is needed when researchers are especially interested in "studying up" (see Korn, 1997). The study of elites is not a common practice within the social sciences (for an exception, see Hertz & Imber, 1995). The elite and semi-elite populations hold key positions within society, yet their activities and power remain invisible to the average citizen. Elites often protect their privacy through a myriad of self-imposed barriers, ranging from unlisted phones and e-mail accounts to the hiring of staff to screen their calls and contacts and security personnel to prevent unwanted contact with those outside their elite culture. Adler and Adler (2002) note that current IRB and professional associations, which fear lawsuits, have developed codes of ethics that now ban all aspects of covert research, using the argument that it is almost impossible to obtain informed consent. In addition, these boards cannot protect researchers from revealing the identity of their respondents if they are asked to do so by officials investigating their research findings.

Adler and Adler (2002) argue that ethics boards have overstepped their function, resulting in the unanticipated outcome of favoring the dominant classes over the weaker, saying that "powerful, elite groups can now better hide their mechanisms of control, while weak and powerless groups have lost the ability to tell their stories from their own perspective" (p. 40). These researchers lament the fact that the banning of covert research such as that done by Erving Goffman in his classic work *Asylums* (1961), providing a bird's-eye view of the treatment of the mentally ill by those who care for them, or research on the activities of control agencies such as the police as carried out by Gary Marx (1988), will no longer be possible under the new ethics guidelines.

Haggerty (2004) has identified what he terms an "ethics creep"—an expansion and intensification of ethical rules and regulations—that has taken over social science research "in the name of ethics" and in his perception has resulted in an overregulation of the field (p. 391). The issue of ethics creep has found its way into the research in which students engage. If you are a student researcher who plans to publish your research paper or present your research findings at a conference, then it is imperative that your research project be formally approved by your college or university's IRB. Very often, students who conduct research for "educational purposes only" are not required to obtain "official" IRB approval. Their supervisor's ethics oversight is usually sufficient to warrant their carrying out their research project.

If you decide to go forward with IRB approval, you may find that even when your student project is considered to be a very low risk to your research participants (in that it does not contain any deception, it does not work with a vulnerable population, and the level of invasiveness of respondents' privacy is low), your project's approval by the IRB may run into trouble. The following are some of the ethical dilemmas facing many low-risk research projects that become sidetracked at the ethics approval stage.

Divided Loyalties: An Ethical Researcher Dilemma

Bell and Nutt (2002) talk about their "divided loyalties" in terms of how their professional and occupational commitments pull them in many different directions, creating ethical dilemmas arising from the multiple roles they bring to a research setting. Bell and Nutt provide an example of how Linda Nutt's professional role as a social work practitioner, who is "bound by general social work codes of practice" (p. 79), conflicted with her role as researcher:

As she was leaving the home of a new carer following the research interview Linda Nutt noticed an unambiguously sexually explicit picture in the hallway. For most researchers this would not be an issue; art is a matter of personal taste. But Linda Nutt wasn't just a researcher; she was also a practitioner. Frequently when children are placed in foster homes little is known about their life experiences so new carers are instructed to assume that all children have been sexually abused unless specifically told otherwise. . . . There is a statutory responsibility to disregard confidentiality where children are at risk. Nonetheless, because she wanted to keep the roles clear and separate— to act as a researcher (and be in receipt of information) and not as an employee . . . (who could give them information), Linda Nutt chose not to tackle this issue with these new carers but spent several days considering this ethical dilemma. In the end the social worker practitioner identity overcame that of the researcher identity and Linda Nutt informed the local authority of her unease regarding the picture and its potential impact upon the foster children. (Bell & Nutt, 2002, pp. 79–80)

Some researchers employ research techniques that raise ethical issues regarding how human subjects are treated. Homan (1992) describes what he calls the "softening up" techniques to get at more personal information from respondents who may be unwilling to talk:

The insidiousness of softening-up techniques is demonstrated by some impertinent questions reserved for the latter and more compliant stages of the interviews and questionnaires: having scrupulously sought and obtained a general consent from respondents and their parents. (p. 328)

By its very nature, qualitative research often requires emotional engagement with those with whom we build knowledge. Jean Duncombe and Julie Jessop (2002) discuss how some researchers can lack sympathy for their respondents and "fake" their interest and concern for those they research. Duncombe describes how she wound up treating some of her respondents in a research project she was conducting on youth training schemes:

We found it more difficult to achieve rapport where we did not spontaneously feel empathy with our interviewees. For example in an early study of Youth Training Schemes (YTS), Jean felt she established a "genuine," if shallow rapport with the YTS trainees and with the more conscientious employers who took training seriously, because she was "on their side." But with the more exploitative employers and trainers (who provided neither jobs nor training), she knew she was faking rapport to "betray" them into revealing their double standards, and sometimes whilst smiling at them she almost smiled to herself, thinking: "What a revealing quote". . . . Julie felt uncomfortable and personally compromised when she found that, in order to obtain a "good" interview, it seemed necessary to smile, nod and appear to collude with views she strongly opposed. (Duncombe & Jessop, 2002, p. 115)

Researchers are human just like everyone else. Accordingly, we all bring our own likes, dislikes, emotions, values, and motivations to our research projects. It is unrealistic to expect that you will always like those you research or that you will always naturally feel 100% engaged. This being said, bear in mind that it is you, the researcher, who has initiated this process and involved others (your subjects). Consider this carefully as you contemplate your ethical obligations to your research participants, but as you think through these issues, do so with your own "humanness" in mind—be realistic and fair to all involved.

How Can I Observe Ethical Values in My Research Practice?

Ethics exist within a social context. The ethical dilemmas we discussed in this chapter serve to remind us of the importance of including an ethical perspective in the very foundation of our research project. Ethical rules cannot possibly account for all events that may arise in a given project. Rubin and Rubin (1995) note that ethical guidelines do not begin to cover all of the ethical dilemmas you may face in the practice of social research:

You cannot achieve ethical research by following a set of preestablished procedures that will always be correct. Yet, the requirement to behave ethically is just as strong in qualitative interviewing as in other types of research on humans— maybe even stronger. You must build ethical routines into your work. You should carefully study codes of ethics and cases of unethical behavior to sensitize yourself to situations in which ethical commitments become particularly salient. Throughout your research, keep thinking and judging what are your ethical obligations. (Rubin & Rubin, 1995, p. 96, as quoted in Patton, 2002, p. 411)

A useful distinction we might keep in mind here is the difference between what Homan (1992) terms *ethical codes* and *ethical values*. By agreeing to comply with **ethical codes**, as outlined in an informed consent proposal, a researcher is not absolved from adhering to the underlying ethical values contained in these codes, yet very often "they invite observance in the letter rather than in the principle" (Homan, 1992, p. 325). Homan reminds us that the danger is that many researchers think their moral obligation begins and ends with the signing of the letter of consent. In some cases, an informed consent letter is seen as protecting the researcher more than the researched. One anthropologist notes:

> I fear that informed consent, when mechanically applied using a form or some verbal formula, becomes more of a protection for the researcher than the researched. Informed consent obtained in this way is unilateral rather than bilateral and protects the researcher against charges from participants that they did not understand fully the intent or outcome of the research. (Fluehr-Lobban, 1998, p. 199)

Ethics does not exist in a vacuum. As King, Henderson, and Stein (1999) note,

> The ethics of human subjects research may be universal but is at the same time deeply particularized, so that what autonomy or informed consent or confidentiality or even benefit and harm *means* depends on the circumstances. The circumstances do not determine whether any of these "Western" moral concepts applies, but *how*. (p. 213)

Key Ethical Issues Generated by Student Research and Strategies for Overcoming Them

Novice student researchers who conduct qualitative, quantitative, or mixed methods research projects often encounter a particular set of ethical issues. This section deals with some common ethical issues student researchers often confront and how these might be addressed by both the students and their faculty research supervisors.

The following table is an adaptation of a range of ethical issues student researchers may confront as they begin their research project, as well as some strategies for overcoming these ethical dilemmas. We suggest a range of ways faculty supervisors of student research can facilitate ethical decision making for their student researchers. Table 4.1 is adapted from the work of Gough, Lawton, Madill, and Stratton (2003).

We can note from this table that an important strategy for student researchers who want to conduct a qualitative project is for them to launch a short pilot study. A student who plans, for example, to interview college seniors regarding their drinking experiences in college might begin with just one interview. This will allow both students and supervisors to assess the student's skill and comfort level in conducting an interview, and it also provides an opportunity for the researcher and supervisor to talk about any specific issues or concerns that might have come up during and after the pilot interview. To make the most use of the pilot interview, it might be good for students to write a short memo on their interview experience and to record their reflections on how the interview went from their point of view as well as that of their participant. These *reflective memos* might also be written at several points along the data collection stage of the project. Student researchers

Table 4.1 Some Potential Ethical Decision-Making Issues and Dilemmas Confronting Student Researchers

Ethical Issues Student Researchers Confront	Student Strategy for Empowering Ethical Decision Making	Ethical Issues Faculty Supervisors Confront	Faculty Strategy for Empowering Ethical Student Decision Making
Students begin a research project as a means of exploring or solving topics they are personally concerned about or involved in; use of research as a "therapeutic action" could influence the outcome of the research, as well as the involvement of the students and research participants.	Students might first attempt a small pilot study to judge how they will react to a larger research project.	Faculty advisers need to gauge the students' level of engagement or attachment to the topics and locate possible problem issues.	Faculty advisers should have an extended conversation with students prior to the beginning of the research project and check up with them throughout the project's duration. Faculty advisers should be able to advise students if the project does not appear to be working.
Students approach sample collection and interviewing without a good background of safety precautions in research.	Students must remain aware of personal safety in research (i.e., be careful about what research subjects they choose and where they are interviewed).	Faculty advisers need to provide students with an overview of safety practices.	Faculty advisers and students should discuss safety in supervisory meetings. Faculty advisers should encourage students to check in before and after they go out on an interview assignment.
Students seek to use family and friends for research purposes and run into issues of confidentiality.	Students should consider whether they will be able to honor ethical rules governing confidentiality. Students should gauge their own level of ability to conduct private research.	Faculty advisers need to inform students of confidentiality and privacy guidelines.	Faculty advisers and students need to have a meeting about ethical guidelines (both university and IRB guidelines). Faculty advisers should advise students if they think the students will be unable to follow through with these ethical guidelines.

Source: Adapted from Gough et al., 2003, p. 10.

should be encouraged to meet with their supervisors as their project proceeds and share their reflective memos with their supervisors in a nonevaluative atmosphere. The spirit of these meetings should be more of a dialogue of sharing and support for the student researcher. Having students reflect on their project and feel that they have the support of a supervisor/mentor might go a long way to head off any potential ethical issues that might arise, and it will also strengthen the research support for novice students by providing them with an access point for asking questions and expressing their concerns without an evaluative component.

How Do New Technologies in Social Research Impact the Practice of Ethical Research?

Sometimes you may want to use data that appear in the public domain for purposes other than such data were intended. For example, suppose that you seek to understand how users of an Internet community such as Facebook present themselves to their friends. You may begin by content-analyzing their online profile, looking for the type and range of information they provide about themselves, what they have listed as their interests or their taste in music, Facebook groups they have joined, the types of pictures they have posted, and so on.

After looking at this data, you as the social researcher decide to then use all the information you have collected from a range of Facebook users to create a series of profiles of those people you intend to contact later, based on the information you glean from this public Web site. In essence, you are using some type of "profiling," which may be based on one's gender and race. Suppose, in fact, you go on to categorize Facebook users and begin to make generalizations about their gender and race that appear to reproduce traditional gender and racial stereotypes.

Let's look at some of the possible ethical issues that relate to the collection of your data and the beginnings of your categorical analysis. Did users give you permission to take personal information they posted concerning their personal profile for research purposes? Does the fact that this information is public and accessible make your use of these data acceptable? Is contacting users for a future research study without their consent ethical?

We can take this example a step further. Say you are conducting research on drinking patterns among college freshmen, and you are using Facebook profiles and pictures to gather data and to identify a sample of college freshmen—those who binge-drink and those who don't drink. You may look through photos of individuals and place them in categories (consumption vs. nonconsumption) based on the presence of alcohol in five or more of their pictures. Can you use this data for a valid study? How do you ensure its accuracy (for example, what if the subject is a nonconsumer yet has alcohol present in pictures)? Is this a privacy violation (if the subjects are underage)? All this leads to our big question: How does a researcher conduct ethical research, and how does a researcher distinguish between public (i.e., usable) information and private information?

As this example illustrates, one growing ethical concern for researchers lies in the realm of Internet technology: fielding respondents and samples from sites, especially social networking sites. Doing so can raise issues of privacy and informed consent. Almost anyone can access information (in the form of user profiles, for example) from social networking Web sites such as MySpace and Facebook. This is tempting study ground for qualitative researchers in particular, argue Eysenbach and Till (2001), because

> qualitative research seeks "to acknowledge the existence of and study the interplay of multiple views and voices—including, importantly, lay voices." Internet postings are accessible for qualitative research of these voices—for example, to determine information needs and preferences of consumers. (p. 1103)

Researchers could use this information presented on the Internet and social network communities, arguing that because it is presented in a public domain, they need not seek consent to use the information as presented, nor seek consent to contact the individual in question for further questions or inclusion in a research project (Moreno, Fost, & Christakis, 2008, p. 157). This raises the following questions, among others:

- To what extent can one verify the validity or accuracy of information on these sites?

- Should the researcher inform the individuals of their inclusion in research?

- Is it acceptable to use social networking sites as a way of recruiting participants?

- How does one establish a definition of informed consent in working with this information?

In such circumstances, traditional social research practices are harder to honor. As Charles Kadushin (2005) explains, "In standard practice social science research, anonymity and confidentiality are both routinely granted to respondents, informants, and subjects in experiments and observations" (p. 140). However, researchers need to consider whether they are mining social network databases for large-scale samples or using individuals as their main source of data or for elucidation of findings. This, in part, determines how researchers approach their Internet subjects. As Eysenbach and Till (2001) note, "On the Internet the dichotomy of private and public sometimes may not be appropriate, and communities may lie in between" (p. 1104). The subject(s) may not be aware of disseminating public information, and the ideas of privacy and informed consent are often in flux.

One example of ethical implications in research based on or using social networking Web sites is that adolescents or teenagers using a site such as MySpace may misrepresent their demographic information, especially age. Although Moreno et al. (2008) acknowledge that,

> [for] researchers who are interested in studying . . . teens, social networking Web sites present a new universe both because of the sheer volume of adolescents who use them and because it is possible, at least in theory, to learn a great deal about teens by what they choose to display publicly. (p. 157)

They warn that there is a possibility that the Web profile may be fabricated (p. 159). If one is choosing to recruit a sample from this information, this misrepresentation of information may skew the sample entirely.

If the researcher chooses to use information presented publicly on MySpace, as in the example, Moreno et al. (2008) warn that "although [demographic] information is public, researchers should still use the same standards of protecting confidentiality as they do for any other research study" (p. 158). Simply because the research is done virtually, "it does not follow that it is acceptable for subjects to be recruited as research subjects without meaningful consent from the subject and/or an appropriate surrogate, such as a parent" (p. 159).

In addition to issues of confidentiality and consent, there is concern as to how the presence of a researcher affects the dynamic of the community under observation. According to Eysenbach and Till (2001), "there is increasing evidence that researchers posting or 'lurking' on [certain] communities may be perceived as intruders and may damage the communities," especially in regard to online communities (p. 1103). For example, let's imagine a community Web site that deals with individuals discussing their experiences with child abuse. On this site, the community members can find healing and solace through the shared experiences of the members. If a researcher openly announces his or her presence to the group, the group's ability to share with one another (and the researcher, if at all) may be compromised. As Eysenbach and Till (2001) show,

> There is also a considerable danger that announcing the research may influence future communication patterns or provoke many members to opt out (which may damage the community). (p. 1105)

Overcoming Ethical Dilemmas of Social Software Technologies

The following list of ethics questions comes from Dag Elgesem (2002) and is a good starting point for considering ethics in online and social network community research.

- Is there only minimal risk of harm?

- Are the integrity and the autonomy for research subjects adequately secured?

- Is the method adequate?

- Is the knowledge produced relevant enough?

Conclusion

Integrating ethics into the entire research process, from selecting the research problem to carrying out research goals and interpretation and reporting research findings, is critical to ensuring that the research process is guided by ethical principles beyond informed consent. This chapter challenges us as researchers to become aware of the range of ethical dilemmas we confront in carrying out the day-to-day tasks of any given research project. An important step beyond securing informed consent lies in the researcher engaging in self-reflexivity by asking,

- What is your ethical standpoint on the research process?

You may find the following checklist of questions useful in uncovering your own ethical perspective on the research process:

- What type of ethical principles guide your work and life, beyond the professional code of ethics you are bound by through a given discipline or professional association?
- Where do your ethical obligations to the researched start and end?

Knowing your own ethical standpoint as a researcher is an important internal guide as to how you proceed in your research. Michael Patton (2002) provides an ethics checklist to take into account as you proceed with your own research project (pp. 409–410). In Table 4.2, we have adapted Patton's list to include a range of research inquiries.

Table 4.2   Patton's Checklist of Questions for Conducting an Ethical Research Project

- How will you explain the purpose of the inquiry and methods to be used in ways that are accurate and understandable to those you are researching?

- Why should the researched participate in your project?

- In what ways, if any, will conducting this research put people at risk? (psychological, legal, political, becoming ostracized by others?)

- What are reasonable promises of confidentiality that can be fully honored?

- What kind of informed consent, if any, is necessary for mutual protection?

- Who will have access to the data? For what purposes?

- How will you and your respondent/s likely be affected by conducting this research?

- Who will be the researcher's confidant and counselor on matters of ethics during a study?

- How hard will you push for data?

- What ethical framework and philosophy informs your work and ensures respect and sensitivity for those you study, beyond whatever may be required by law?

Source: Adapted from Patton, 2002, p. 408.

A good example of ethical reflection within the research process comes from a study conducted by Huber and Clandinin (2002). They interviewed inner-city elementary school children and related the ethical "give-and-take" they engaged in to the process of understanding the lives of inner-city youth. They cite the importance of creating an "ethic of relational narrative inquiry" that goes beyond the requirements of signing a consent form:

> From a nonrelational research ethics perspective, we had met the ethical requirements, but this was not sufficient. . . . When we felt disease around who we were as researchers in relation with Azim [a respondent in the researchers' study] we realized we needed a different way of understanding what it means to live out ethical research with children as coresearchers in relational narrative inquiry. (Huber & Clandinin, 2002, p. 794)

They found that a relational model of inquiry and ethics—a view of research and ethics as embedded in the context of interpersonal relationships—requires a great deal of reflexivity on the part of the researcher (especially when studying a vulnerable population). Putting their reflexive experience into the research process enabled them to engage in a dialogue with their own ethical standpoint and ultimately to confront their own personal biases as researchers as well as teachers of elementary school children. In the end, they became more attentive to the complexities of co-creating meaning and the necessity to live within the tensions they experienced as co-researchers:

> As we entered into coresearcher relationships with children, we began to be very thoughtful about what plotlines were shaping us as teacher researchers, as researcher teachers, as researchers. Attending to the maintenance of relationships with children, now and in the future, became, for us, a first consideration. . . . We realized that our attentiveness to relationship could conflict with dominant stories of what "good" teachers and "good" researchers do. Plotlines for good researchers do not often attend to the aftermath for children's lives as their first concern. As relational narrative inquirers engaged with children as researchers, we realized that it was here that we needed to attend. (Huber & Claudinin, 2002, p. 800)

It is our hope that this chapter provides you with an awareness of the importance of the ethical dimension in the research process. We have also tried to offer some of the tools you'll need to enhance your awareness of your own ethical standpoint and its application in your ongoing research endeavors. The various components of ethical practice continue to come up throughout the following chapters, including a discussion of emergent ethical concerns linked to computer-driven research.

Glossary

Common Rule: Set up by the Office for the Protection of Research Risks, this rule was established to protect potential participants in research studies from exploitation. Most specifically, it mandated that a review board of proposals be set up for every institution that receives research funds, thereby benefiting the participants and maintaining the ethical boundaries of research studies.

Confidentiality: This means that research subjects are protected by remaining unidentifiable. That is, their names may not be used in any written material concerning the research or in discussions of the research project, and all interview materials are stored in a safe place that no one save the researchers can access.

Cover story: Researchers who choose to use deception may even go out of their way to develop a "cover story" to explain the research project (this may be built into the original design of the research project).

Deception: Researchers may be dishonest about who they are or what they are doing and thus use deception to conduct their research. Sometimes, deception may be more subtle and unintentional on the researcher's part.

Disclosure: A researcher may or may not reveal, or disclose, his or her identity and research purpose. In accordance with ethical considerations, we advocate full disclosure whenever possible.

Ethical codes: These are codes of conduct set in place to protect the research subjects and their setting—neither of which should be harmed by the research process. Professional associations have specific codes of ethics that spell out a set of rules governing research and based on moral principles.

Informed consent: Informed consent is a critical component in ethical research that uses human participants. Informed consent aims to ensure that the subject's participation is fully voluntary and informed, based on an understanding of what the study is about, what its risks and benefits are, how the results will be used, and the fact that participation is voluntary and can be stopped at any time and that identity will be protected.

Institutional review boards (IRBs): Institutional review boards (IRBs) ensure that studies using living subjects are ethical and will not cause harm.

Moral integrity: The moral integrity of the researcher is a critically important aspect of ensuring that the research process and the researcher's findings are trustworthy and valid.

Nuremberg Code: A code of ethics established after World War II that begins with the stipulation that all research participation must be voluntary.

Discussion Questions

1. What is the ethical substructure of the research process, and why must ethics be attended to holistically?

2. Although informed consent is a critical component to ensure the ethical dimension of your research project, there are instances in which there is a failure to fully disclose to research subjects the

full extent of the risks and benefits of participating in a given study. Therefore, who do you believe is responsible for any unintended consequences?

3.   The questions brought up in this chapter include the following: Where do your ethical obligations to the researched start and end? What responsibility does the researcher have to the participant after the research process has ended? Does the researcher still have a responsibility for any emotional or psychological problems that ensue in part due to the research project? What do you think about these issues?

4.   Institutional review boards were created to oversee the research process and maintain that "no one group of individuals has been unfairly treated or left out of the potential positive outcomes of a given study." However, as discussed, IRBs have proved ineffective in certain cases where members of the boards have a vested interest in the very studies they oversee. Therefore, do you believe IRBs to be an effective resource in ensuring ethical centrality in research processes? If not, what is your suggestion for improving the assurance of the ethical dimension of the research process? What would be, in your mind, the most effective means of ensuring ethical considerations and safety in research projects conducted in universities?

5.   As noted in this chapter, informed consent does not absolve researchers from all ethical lapses. Why is this? What are some ethical considerations one must keep in mind when conducting covert research or participant observation? What are some other ways of making sure that the ethical dimension is given its proper place within your research project?

6.   Do you believe it is the responsibility of the researcher to reveal information concerning the research participant if he or she feels it benefits the subject? Why or why not?

7.   If a researcher imposes confidentiality within the research process, do you see this as a way of disempowering research participants who want to reveal their identities? Do you believe it is the sole responsibility of the researcher to determine whether information should be kept confidential or not? Should the issue of confidentiality be a collaborative effort? To what extent should it be collaborative?

8.   If a sociologist is interested in studying underage teenagers' drinking and driving behaviors, what are some of the ethical considerations the researcher would have to keep in mind? Discuss some of the ethical dilemmas you would encounter. How would you structure your research project (bearing in mind the centrality of ethics in structuring your research process)?

Resources

Suggested Web Sites

National Science Foundation

http://www.nsf.gov/bfa/dias/policy/docs/45cfr690.pdf

This link is to the current law regarding informed consent/internal review boards/human subjects: "The Common Rule for the Protection of Human Subjects for Behavioral and Social Science Research."

http://www.nsf.gov/bfa/dias/policy/hsfaqs.jsp

This is a list of frequently asked questions concerning the above legislation.

The Belmont Report

http://www.hhs.gov/ohrp/humansubjects/guidance/belmont.htm

This is a link to "The Belmont Report: Ethical Principles and Guidelines for the Protection of Human Subjects of Research."

NSF on Human Subjects

http://www.nsf.gov/bfa/dias/policy/

This site has a section entitled "Human Subjects" with information concerning the basic principles of human subjects' protection as well as information about IRBs.

National Institutes of Health

http://ohsr.od.nih.gov/

This is a link to the Office of Human Subjects Research, which provides information about the existing legislation concerning the use of human subjects and research (as well as the ethical dilemmas involved). It also provides links to other governmental Web sites dealing with the issue of involving human subjects in research.

NIH on Human Subjects

http://bioethics.od.nih.gov/IRB.html

This link is entitled "Human Subjects Research and IRBs." It contains links to policies and regulations, guidance for investigators, IRB resources, short courses on bioethical issues in human studies, research resources, and human subjects research tutorials.

NIH List of References

http://www.nlm.nih.gov/archive/20061214/pubs/cbm/hum_exp.html

This is a link to a very extensive list of references, all dealing with ethical issues in research involving human participants. The table of contents (you have to scroll down the page a little to get this) breaks down the page into different categories, making it easier to find your specific topic. The bibliography contains information regarding reference materials including journals, books, and government documents.

U.S. Department of Education

http://www.ed.gov/about/offices/list/ocfo/humansub.html

This is a link to the "Protection of Human Subjects in Research" page. This page includes links to general information concerning human subjects in research and the regulations/legalities surrounding using human subjects in research. It also contains information about "Guidance and Educational Materials" (with links to "The Belmont Report" and the "Institutional Review Board Guidebook").

American Sociological Association

http://www2.asanet.org/members/ecoderev.html

This is a link to the ASA's Code of Ethics. The Code of Ethics is available on the site, and there is also a downloadable PDF version.

American Sociological Associations' Ethical Standards

http://www2.asanet.org/members/ecostand2.html

This list consists of topics such as informed consent, use of deception as a research practice, and so on.

American Psychological Association

http://www.apa.org/ethics/homepage.html

This link discusses the APA's new Ethics Code. It has two downloadable versions of the code as well as links to ethics in the news and ethics resources/reference materials.

American Association for the Advancement of Science

http://www.aaas.org/spp/sfrl/projects/intres/main.htm

This is a link to the "Ethical and Legal Aspects of Human Subjects Research in Cyberspace," which contains a link to the report prepared by the AAAS staff (which was created after a workshop was convened in collaboration with the NIH concerning Internet research involving human subjects).

Indiana University's Poynter Center for the Study of Ethics and American Institutions

http://poynter.indiana.edu/links.shtml

This site contains links to ethics centers, publications, research ethics, research policy, and general information about ethics.

Homepage for the Book Methods in Behavioral Research

http://methods.fullerton.edu/chapter3.html

This Web site contains a vast array of resources for researchers inquiring about ethics, including links to ethics tutorials, research ethics Web sites, and ethics guidelines. It is an adaptation of the book *Methods in Behavioral Research.*

Human Subject Research and Ethical Concerns

http://www.hsph.harvard.edu/bioethics/guidelines/ethical.html

This Web site contains the various guidelines involved in human subject research, specifically rights and responsibilities of the researchers, human participants, editors, publishers, and funders of the experiment.

Acoustical Society of America: Ethical Principles of the Acoustical Society of America for Research Involving Human and Non-human Animals in Research and Publishing and Presentations

http://asa.aip.org/poma/ethical.html

This Web site contains guidelines concerning recorded interviews and images of human and nonhuman subjects.

University of Virginia Institution Review Board for Health Sciences Research

http://www.virginia.edu/vpr/irb/hsr/ethical_principles.html

This Web site contains links to IRB-HSR information, including a glossary of IRB terms, ethical principles, and other Web sites that discuss IRBs in detail.

Relevant Journals

Bioethics

Journal of Global Ethics

Public Health Ethics

Nursing Ethics: An International Journal for Health Care Professionals

Science, Technology and Human Values

Note

1. Certain types of research that clearly involve no potential risks to human subjects, such as educational research dealing with "instructional strategies," may have an "exempt status" and not require a full review by an IRB (Department of Health and Human Services, 1989).

PART II

Methods of Data Collection

CHAPTER 5

In-Depth Interview

Becoming a Member of a Religious Cult

I was in the cult for 12 years and I have been out for 10 years. I'm almost 46 years old so when I got in I was about 24. . . . The way that I see it now is that I was raised by a really domineering mother and also a strong father who didn't give me very much personal space to develop so I was really used to being told what to do. I really kind of learned from a very young age to surrender myself to other people's will, desire, and wants. To really set myself far aside.

. . . I left school with a good woman friend of mine and we started traveling across the country and we were just kind of hanging out and traveling and doing what we wanted. I was very much into a hippie lifestyle. About a year and one half later she and I went to this yogi intensive that was being led by this yogi and we, it was one of those things, a week-long thing and we got up super early in the morning like 3:00 a.m. and we did this outrageous yogi all day long and it was unbelievably painful. So we were really in an altered state.

It was a big group of people who were meditating and chanting and eating a kind of light diet and here was this guy. He was leading all these exercises and talking to us about god knows what. About consciousness and he was from India and he was representing all this stuff that really didn't make much sense to me.

I really got in that state and got very attracted to the whole idea and my friend and I actually went to have an audience with him and he started talking to us. I'm trying to remember what actually happened there, but he said he would take care of us. We could forget everything that had happened to us, that had caused us pain in our lives and we would now be fine. I think for me, I was feeling kind of lost.

The experience of being out on my own was difficult because I was on my own and so I think, the way that I think of it now is that I climbed back into daddy's lap and it seemed very comforting that there was someone who had this spiritual vision about my destiny who was going to be my guide and tell me what to do. (Hesse-Biber, 2007)

This woman's experience of joining a cult and remaining a cult member for most of her young adult life is chilling reading for those of us who find it hard to understand the power of a cult and how it can become a total immersion of oneself. It would be difficult for a researcher to give this individual a survey questionnaire to fill out, asking her very closed-ended questions about her indoctrination into cult life. Surveys are good at finding out information such as the characteristics of those who join religious cults. However, getting at the "lived experiences" of why individuals join cults requires the researcher to dig deeper into the goings-on of a person's daily living. In a free-form or **open-ended interview**, this respondent is able to tell us what happened in her life at the time she became susceptible to joining a cult. In this way, we see her lived reality as if we are there with her as she is going through this life experience. We can note how deeply affected she is by her early family life and the lack of warmth she feels regarding her parents and the overly controlling atmosphere of her early family household. We empathize with her regarding her sense of vulnerability as a young woman and her lack of self-direction. It is not surprising for the reader, given her history, to find her easily caught up in a cult community, which promises to take care of her and to provide a life of certainty and nurturance. We can also note how this particular cult structure serves to "break down" and lay bare novices' emotions by building in a regime of lack of sleep and food—making her even more vulnerable to the cult's messages of kinship and promise of a better life (see Hesse-Biber, 2007).

An **in-depth interview**, also known as an intensive interview, is a commonly used method of data collection employed by qualitative researchers. The in-depth interview is important to qualitative research because it uses individuals as the point of departure for the research process and assumes that individuals have unique and important knowledge about the social world that is ascertainable and that can be shared through verbal communication.

What Is an In-Depth Interview?

In-depth interviews are a particular kind of conversation between the researcher and the interviewee that requires active asking and listening. The process is a meaning-making endeavor embarked on as a partnership between the interviewer and his or her respondent. Ideally, the degree of division and hierarchy between the two collaborators is low, as the researcher and the researched are placed on the same plane. However, as we shall see, this goal is often elusive without careful reflexivity and practice. Riach (2009) notes the danger and concern "over how we come to understand or represent another person's 'world view'" (p. 357). We therefore provide you with a set of reflexivity and interviewing tips along the way to enhance your practice of this important research method.

Qualitative interviews can be used to yield exploratory and descriptive data that may or may not generate theory. Likewise, they can be used as a stand-alone method or in conjunction with a range of other methods such as surveys, focus groups, or ethnography. Ethnographers, as we will see in Chapter 8, commonly conduct interviews when in the field. There is a synergistic link between these two forms of inquiry. In-depth interviews are generally less time-consuming than fieldwork, so when the topic under investigation is not linked to a particular setting but can be ascertained from individuals in a prearranged setting (as opposed to the individual's natural setting), in-depth interviews may be appealing and appropriate (Warren, 2002, p. 85). Typically, researchers who conduct in-depth interviews are looking for patterns that emerge from the "thick descriptions" of social life recounted by their participants. In this sense, qualitative interviews are designed to get at "deep" information or knowledge (Johnson, 2002, p. 104). In this vein, in-depth interviews yield large amounts of data in the form of interview transcripts, which are later reduced in the analytical and interpretive process. Qualitative interviews thus differ from quantitative interviews, which consist of standardized questions (often closed-ended, meaning that they have a finite range of possible answers) in search of standardized data. Qualitative interviews produce knowledge that is "contextual, linguistic, narrative, and pragmatic" (Kvale & Brinkmann, 2009, p. 18).

When Is It Appropriate to Use In-Depth Interviews?

In-depth interviews are *issue oriented.* In other words, this method is useful when the researcher has a particular topic he or she wants to focus on and gain information about from individuals. As we will see in the next chapter, this differs from the oral history method of interview, where a respondent's entire life story may be covered in the interview sessions. In-depth interviews typically occur in one session per interviewee (although more than one session can be used), centered on a specific topic in which the researcher is interested. For example, a researcher interested in how single parents balance family and work or how young girls experience body image issues may find in-depth interviews to be extremely appealing. The goal of intensive interviews is to gain rich qualitative data on a particular subject from the perspective of selected individuals.

For example, our research on body image among different populations focused on how gay, lesbian, and bisexual people experience body image. While our literature review revealed that data indicates a range of body image issues across sexual orientation, the data available is minimal and does little by way of *explaining* these differences in a nuanced way. The questions we wanted to address included the following:

- How do lesbian women feel about their physical selves?

- What are the standards by which they feel judged in the gay community and the straight community?

- How do our participants feel about these standards, and how do the standards make them feel about themselves?

- How do they view attractiveness?

- What self-esteem issues do they experience and why?

- What differences, if any, do they perceive in body ideal between the gay and straight communities?

- How has primary group support or lack of support regarding their sexual orientation impacted their body image?

These are just some of the questions that can be explored regarding this topic using an in-depth interview. This kind of study can yield both descriptive and explanatory data and is also appropriate in exploratory research, where little is known in a field. Let's take a look at a transcript excerpt from an interview conducted with a middle-aged lesbian respondent who has suffered from compulsive overeating. Let's examine the kind of information you might glean by using this method (OA stands for Overeaters Anonymous):

Interviewer:	Do you think, overall, women who are straight as opposed to women who are lesbians have more or less "issues" with their bodies?
Respondent:	I think straight women have more, but there are definitely exceptions. Like I had a girlfriend who was totally obsessed with it. I met her in OA so already she has straight up body stuff. And I know quite a few lesbians, well that might be an exaggeration, but who have a lot of body image issues, a lot are really grossed out by fat people.
Interviewer:	How does that manifest itself in a meeting, as far as . . . ?
Respondent:	It doesn't at a meeting, they wouldn't, well some people do talk about it, fat serenity, they call it. People who they consider fat but say they are abstaining from compulsive overeating, they think they are deluding themselves, they call it fat serenity, I hate it when they say that.
Interviewer:	Mmmmm.
Respondent:	So anyway, people aren't critical of other people at meetings, they would never say that. These are things people say outside of meetings. But in general, I would say in terms of the lesbian community, which is a huge generalization again.
Interviewer:	Yeah.
Respondent:	Less emphasis on having the right body shape or size.
Interviewer:	Um hmmm.
Respondent:	That has sort of been my experience. Like if you go to a lesbian function, you'll see a lot more women with different body sizes, bigger, small, all ranges in between.
Interviewer:	Right.
Respondent:	I think that you would, well that's not true, the general population is getting bigger and bigger, but more accepted as different body sizes. Yeah, I definitely think that's true, but there are definitely exceptions.
Interviewer:	Yeah.

Respondent: Well I'm sure like a lot of whatever you grew up feeling about yourself, before you even discovered your identity that would probably still affect people.

Interviewer: Yeah, in *Am I Thin Enough Yet?*, white college straight women were obsessed with being thin, really thin, thinner than they could even be basically.

Respondent: I know a few lesbians like that. But most lesbians I know aren't like that. They are pretty easy going about the whole subject. I mean what they feel in their hearts about it, I don't know, but just in terms of conversation and interactions.

Interviewer: Yeah.

Respondent: And I think part of that is that you're not buying into a lot of the cultural stuff.

Interviewer: Yeah.

Respondent: And a lot of thin women thinking they need to be thin so they get a guy.

Interviewer: Mmmm.

Respondent: I mean I think a lot of it, to feel good about themselves they need to be thin, but I think a lot of it is that message that you have to be thin to get a boyfriend.

Interviewer: Right.

Respondent: So, um, and I think in the lesbian community, that's not, ya know you don't get that message as strongly. Tons of women who are bigger have partners.

Interviewer: Mmmmm.

Respondent: So it's not such a strong issue, I think.

Interviewer: Um hmmm. Are you part of, do you have like a gay community or like is it more of like scattered friends, or is there a group of friends?

Respondent: No I don't anymore. I have some gay friends, most of my friends are in OA now, some of who are lesbians, some of them straight. I have some gay friends, I have these two friends, Ana and Jane, I have been friends with for like 25 years.

Interviewer: Um hum.

Respondent: They are a happily married couple, well not legally married, but happy couple. When I was in my 20s, I hung out with this group of lesbians, um, when I stopped drinking and I sort of moved away from that group. But I see them once in a while.

Interviewer: Yeah.

Respondent: Go to a birthday party or something. But no I don't really have a group of gay people that I hang out with for the most part.

By analyzing this transcript, several points can be made. First, an in-depth interview is a way of gaining information and understanding from individuals on a **focused topic**. In this instance, we were interested in understanding a lesbian woman's body image issues as well as her perspective on body image issues within both the gay and straight communities. Second, the in-depth interview is a very particular kind of interaction, similar to a conversation. A "normal" conversation would have much more back-and-forth interaction between the two people, with both communicating their ideas to each other. In an in-depth interview, the researcher begins by asking a question and then serves as an active listener. As you can see in the above interview excerpt, the researcher actually said very little but was engaged in the conversation through verbal support and the use of probes, responding to every point the interviewee made, either with a follow-up question or with a phrase to show her active engagement (using words such as "Mmm" and "Yeah" to encourage the interviewee to continue speaking). The respondent did most of the talking, although the researcher was present in the dialogue and resulting transcript. Last, the respondent speaks on two levels: from her experience and her perceptions. She speaks about her own experience in terms of weight struggles and body image issues, and she also speaks about her perception of social pressures on homosexual and heterosexual women based on her experience in the culture.

In-depth interviews are also very useful for accessing subjugated knowledge. Those who are often marginalized in a society, such as women, people of color, homosexuals, and the poor, may have hidden experiences and knowledge that have been excluded from mainstream use of quantitative research methods. Interviewing is a way to access some of this information. Shulamit Reinharz (1992) explains how interviewing is a way feminist researchers have attempted to access women's hidden knowledge:

> Interviewing offers researchers access to people's ideas, thoughts, and memories in their own words rather than in the words of the researcher.
>
> This asset is particularly important for the study of women because in this way learning from women is an antidote to centuries of ignoring women's ideas altogether or having men speak for women. (p. 19)

The same is the case for interviewing people of color and homosexuals, who have long been left out of the research process, along with the others mentioned above. Accessing the invisible experience of lesbian women and their relationship with their body was one of the motivators in the study we excerpted earlier.

Now that you are beginning to get a sense of what an in-depth interview is and when it is an appropriate method to address your research topic and question, let's look at research design.

How Do You Design and Conduct an In-Depth Interview Study?

Most of the research design techniques discussed in Chapter 3 apply to constructing an in-depth interview study. First, the researcher needs to select a research topic and form a research purpose (and, ultimately, now or later during initial data collection, a research question). Next, participants, sometimes called informants or interviewees, must be selected. Selecting the pool of informants, or *sample*, is a matter of figuring out what portion of the population you seek to study and then locating individuals who are members of that group. The number of individuals who will be interviewed can vary greatly, depending on the nature of the research question, your access to the sample, time, funding, and so on. Kvale and Brinkmann (2009) offer the following advice to researchers as to how many individuals need to be interviewed: "Interview as many subjects as necessary to find out what you need to know" (p. 113). However, this is easier said than done.

Researchers determine what individuals they will interview by finding a sample of the population they seek to study. *Sampling,* the process of locating respondents, can occur in any of the ways discussed in Chapter 3, such as probability sampling, theoretical sampling, or "snowball" sampling, and *convenience sampling.* The individuals selected to participate in the study should have the kind of knowledge, experience, or information that the researcher wants to know. Sometimes researchers pay the respondents a small sum of money or give them a gift (such as a gift certificate) to thank them for their participation, although this usually is not necessary. The best interviews occur with respondents who want to share their story and knowledge, and ideally, the interview experience is rewarding for them in and of itself.

Once a respondent is lined up for an interview, a time and a location need to be arranged. Often, in-depth interviews occur in the researcher's office or in the respondent's home, although any private space is suitable as long as both parties feel comfortable. These in-person intensive interviews typically last one to two hours, although some may be shorter. Interviews can also be conducted over the telephone or by e-mail. However, the quality of the interview decreases significantly when the interview is not done in person. Telephone interviews are different because they are not happening face-to-face, and thus gesturing, eye contact, and other means of showing interest and building rapport are not possible. E-mail interviews are a different kind of dialogue altogether, one in which the exchanges occur with a time delay compared with the flow of in-person or telephone interviews. Likewise, people write more slowly and differently than they speak, so responses are apt to be more thought out, less spontaneous, and shorter. We recommend using these methods only when time, money, and other pragmatic factors make in-person interviewing impossible. In this chapter, we will focus on in-person interviewing, although we want to bring these other options to your attention.

Ethical Considerations in In-Depth Interviewing

As we have mentioned, ethics need to be at the forefront of researchers' minds as they proceed throughout the research process. Before researchers can begin an interview, respondents must be made aware of their confidentiality and role in the research and eventual publication of results. To begin, informed consent should be explained in advance and executed either before or at the time of the interview. Even though the study and the participant's informed and voluntary participation will have been discussed in advance, it is important to reiterate this prior to beginning the interview. Interviewees should be given every opportunity to ask questions. This brings us to the unique aspects of in-depth interviews. There are different kinds of in-depth interviews, which vary in terms of their structure.

In addition, in-depth interviewing brings with it ethical considerations, and to this end, we provide an ethical aside on how to handle informed consent before, during, and after the interview process. This aspect of the ethics process is especially important for undergraduate researchers to review, as many may be conducting research on their fellow student population and may be part of the friendship networks of those they interview. Furthermore, it's important to note that some mistakenly believe that getting a respondent to sign a consent form is all that is needed to take care of the ethical issues involved in obtaining a respondent's consent to participate in their research project.

ETHICAL ASIDE—THE SLIPPERY NATURE OF INFORMED CONSENT: WHAT IS YOUR RESPONDENT AGREEING TO?

Researcher/Interviewer's Unidimensional View of Informed Consent	Respondent's Point of View	Possible Ethical Resolution
You believe that informed consent takes place when your respondent signs the consent form for your study. You look at consent as a "one shot" agreement that fulfills your ethical responsibility to your respondent.	*Dilemma 1.* You agree to be interviewed and have signed the formal consent letter saying that you have agreed to be interviewed. You are about to meet your interviewer, who happens to be a fellow undergraduate student at your university. You begin to have some reservations about having signed the consent form.	*Ethical Response to Dilemma 1.* The interviewer should again obtain the respondent's consent before beginning the interview.

Researcher/Interviewer's Unidimensional View of Informed Consent	Respondent's Point of View	Possible Ethical Resolution
Holistic View of Informed Consent Informed consent is not a "one time" agreement made between you and your respondent but instead is flexible and subject to change throughout the interview and after the data is collected and analyzed. Given this perspective, you might address your respondent's dilemmas as shown in column 3.	*Dilemma 2.* You agreed to be interviewed again at the beginning of the interview, but during the interview, you begin to feel uncomfortable in answering some of the questions and feel that you do not want to continue with the interview. *Dilemma 3.* After the interview, on your way home, you realize that the interviewer actually is friends with one of your friends and, in fact, you now have grave reservations about having done the interview at all.	*Ethical Response to Dilemma 2.* It is important to let respondents know that they are free to stop the interview at any time if they feel they do not want to continue and that they can withdraw their consent during the interview process. *Ethical Response to Dilemma 3.* You mention to your respondent before and during the interview that all data is confidential and will not be revealed to anyone but you. You note that all steps were taken to ensure all interview materials remain secure. You state often that informed consent is not final but that the respondent can withdraw his or her consent even after the interview is over and the data are collected and analyzed. You provide respondents with your contact information and encourage them to contact you if they have any reservations about their interview and also provide the contact information for your project director, in case they prefer to contact him or her instead of or in addition to you.

Interview Structures and Levels of Control

Depending on your research question and corresponding research goals, you may design a study with highly structured, semistructured, or low-structured interviews. A *highly* **structured interview** means that you will ask each participant the same series of questions. If the participant strays too much from the topic at hand or says some things that are interesting but are not directly relevant to the study, you guide the conversation back to the interview questions. Researchers working from post-positivist theoretical perspectives may employ such a structure for their interviews. When in-depth interviews are being used to confirm and augment data gained by other methods, such as surveys, structured interviews may also be appropriate. Highly structured interviews want concrete answers to a finite number of focused questions. Ultimately, a highly structured interview allows for a greater degree of comparison between interviews because the resulting data have a high degree of standardization. The interviewer has acted, relatively speaking, the same during all interviews and asked the same questions. Comparisons between respondents can thus be made. It is also easier to generalize (if applying standard scientific expectations of generalizability) from data that is obtained in a more uniform fashion.

Having said this, most qualitative researchers think of in-depth interviews as an opportunity to allow the words of the respondent, and his or her experiences and perspectives, to shine through. In other words, qualitative researchers are generally more inclined to impose less structure on their interviews and thus opt for semi-structured to low-structured (also known as open-ended) interviews. In addition, as seen in our behind-the-scenes visit with David Karp in Chapter 3, qualitative researchers frequently have different ways of conceptualizing generalizability, allowing them to use less structured interviews and still make larger inferences and generate social theory.

Semistructured interviews rely on a certain set of questions and try to guide the conversation to remain, more loosely, on those questions. However, semi-structured interviews also allow individual respondents some latitude and freedom to talk about what is of interest or importance to them. In other words, while the researcher does try to ask each respondent a certain set of questions, he or she also allows the conversation to flow more naturally, making room for the conversation to go in unexpected directions. Interviewees often have information or knowledge that may not have been thought of in advance by the researcher. When such knowledge emerges, a researcher using a semistructured design is likely to allow the conversation to develop, exploring new topics that are relevant to the interviewee.

In *low-structure* or completely *open-ended interviews*, this is taken even further. While the researcher has a particular topic for the study, he or she allows the conversation to go wherever the research participant takes it, and each interview becomes highly individual. The researcher is not tied to asking any particular set of questions and is more interested in letting the conversation develop and having the respondent naturally touch on or bring up the topics of importance. The data produced from these kinds of interviews are nonstandardized (Reinharz, 1992, p. 18). In a low-structure interview, the researcher asks very few but broad questions and allows the respondent to take the discussion in whatever directions he or she wants. This approach is highly congruent with the tenets of the qualitative paradigm. *Open-ended interviews* explore people's views of reality and allow the researcher to generate theory. In this way, it complements quantitatively oriented, closed-ended interview research, which tries to test hypotheses (Reinharz, 1992, p. 18). The degree of structure imposed during the interview impacts the researcher's role in the interview situation. The higher the degree of structure that is sought, the more control the researcher imposes (see Figure 5.1).

Figure 5.1   Structure of Qualitative Interviews

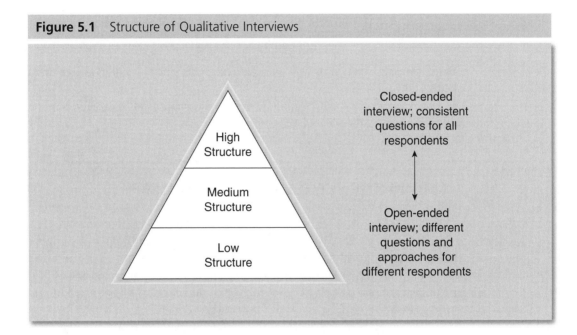

Preparing an Interview Guide

After deciding what kind of interview they want to conduct, researchers can prepare for the interview by constructing an **interview guide**. An interview guide is a set of topical areas and questions that the researcher brings to the interview. Weiss (1994) suggests beginning with a "substantive frame" or range of specific topics or issues you are interested in exploring. You may also begin to prioritize these topics and look at how they might be related or subsumed under a larger topic of interest and then use that to create a guide. When thinking about constructing an interview guide, it is helpful to think topically prior to creating specific questions. In other words, guides can be constructed by beginning with broader, more abstract areas of inquiry from which questions are developed. To begin, write down a "topics to learn about" list (Weiss, 1994, p. 46). Each topic listed is a **line of inquiry** or *domain of inquiry* that you want to pursue during the interview session. Interview questions can then be constructed to "get at" information in each of these lines. Ultimately, the interview guide is a list of topics with or without specific questions under each topic that speak to the lines of inquiry suggested during the initial drafting of the guide (Weiss, 1994, p. 48). The process of creating an interview guide, even if it remains unused, is important preparation for the interview because it helps researchers identify key issues and think about the kinds of things they may like to ask respondents (Weiss, 1994). Pilot interviews are an opportunity for researchers to test out the effectiveness of their research guide (Weiss, 1994):

- Is the guide clear and readable?

- Does the guide cover all of the topical areas in which you are interested?

- Are there any topical areas or general questions missing from the guide?

Based on early experiences with an interview guide, you can modify the guide to better suit your needs.

David Karp talks about creating interview guides as an *analytical process* in the following behind-the-scenes box.

BEHIND THE SCENES WITH DAVID KARP

Interview guides don't just come out of nowhere because I've done so much preliminary work before this. And this is really critical, because too often when people do in-depth interviews, they see putting together the interview guide as, "Well, I've got to get this out of the way." And I see this task of discovering the areas of inquiry as an incredibly important analytical step in the process of doing this work. And if we talk about the full process, when you get to the point of writing, in my case books or articles, it comes full circle because the amount of time and energy that I put into getting this interview guide together really previews what will be the central pieces that I ultimately will write about. Now, in the end, it's just a guide, and in any interview maybe 60% of the questions I ask are not on that guide. You're sitting, having a conversation with a person, and the artfulness of doing that in-depth interview is to know when to follow up on what a person is saying in the moment. By the end of the interview, I want to make sure that all the areas that I want to have covered are covered. But you would be missing the whole deal if the only questions you asked were the questions on your guide.

Karp emphasizes the importance of the interview guide not only as a tool but also as an analytical process that allows researchers to reflect on important questions and ideas they wish to address. In addition, the research guide should never limit the potential of an interview to only those questions written down.

It is important that interview guides are not too lengthy or detailed. They are meant to serve as aids to the researcher but ideally will not be heavily relied on because too strong a focus on the interview guide itself can distract a researcher from paying full attention to his or her respondent. An interview guide is meant to be glanced at when needed and ideally remains unused or as a prompt for the researcher (Weiss, 1994, p. 48). The guide can also serve as a checklist for the researcher at the end of the interview, as a way of making sure all of the topics under investigation have been addressed, even if not in the sequence suggested by the guide (Weiss, 1994, p. 48).

An interview guide is essential to a successful interview, and the preparation of an interview guide is particularly helpful for novice interviewers. Once sampling and structural decisions have been made and an interview guide constructed, data collection can begin. There are many tips for successful interviews; however, we encourage you to try to learn by practice. In-depth interviewing is a skill and craft and, as such, one gets better with experience.

How Do You Conduct an In-Depth Interview?

In-depth interviews are a *meaning-making partnership* between interviewers and their respondents. These sessions provide an opportunity for researchers to learn about social life through the perspective, experience, and language of those living it. Respondents have an opportunity to share their story, pass on their knowledge, and provide their own perspective on a range of topics. Qualitative interviews are thus a special kind of **knowledge-producing conversation** that occurs between two parties. The relationship between the interviewer and respondent is critical to the process of constructing meaning.

As discussed in Chapter 3, qualitative researchers work from theoretical and epistemological positions that are concerned with getting at respondents' lived experiences. One important way to accomplish this is to reduce the degree of status hierarchy between the researcher and the researched. During the in-depth interview situation, researchers can do this by placing themselves on the same plane as their respondents and working cooperatively to construct social scientific knowledge. In this pursuit, the relationship between interviewers and interviewees can be characterized as *reciprocal*. Furthermore, interviewees are given authority over their own stories, meaning that they are seen as "experts" on the topic. In order for reciprocity and shared authority to be possible, the two parties should feel comfortable with each other. Researchers help respondents share their stories by building **rapport**. One important goal in gaining rapport is to have your respondent feel safe, comfortable, and valued. You might, for example, engage in a casual conversation before beginning with the interview through the sharing of a short personal vignette about yourself (Lichtman, 2006, p. 121). In addition, be sure to be an active listener while the interviewee is speaking. Eye contact and appropriate gesturing (such as nodding) are important in the building of rapport. While listening, be careful not to judge your respondents' stories, but rather help them to tell their own stories.

Picking up on markers is another way to show a respondent that you are interested in what he or she is saying. Likewise, markers are a valuable source of information and often lead to the kinds of thick descriptions that characterize qualitative interview data. **Markers** are important pieces of information that respondents may offer as they are talking about something else. Weiss (1994) explains markers and how they might appear as follows:

> [A marker is] a passing reference made by a respondent to an important event or feeling state. . . . Because markers occur in the course of talking about something else, you may have to remember them and then return to them when you can, saying, "A few minutes ago you mentioned . . ." But it is a good idea to pick up a marker as soon as you conveniently can if the material it hints at could in any way be relevant for your study. Letting the marker go will demonstrate to the respondent that the area is not of importance to you. It can also demonstrate that you are interested only in answers to your questions, not in the respondent's full experience. . . . Respondents sometimes offer markers by indicating that much has happened that they aren't talking about. They might say, for example, "Well there was a lot going on at that time." It is then reasonable to respond, "Could you tell me about that?" (Weiss, 1994, p. 77)

To examine markers more closely, let's return to our example of interviewing lesbian women about the relationship between their sexual identity and body image. If a respondent is telling you about her parents' reaction to her "coming out" and in the midst of this story says, "Well it was partly due to my sister's stuff and all that craziness . . ." and then continues on with her story, you need to make a mental (or even written) note of this marker. You might, for example, make some quick notes in the margins of your study guide and think of using some standard abbreviations to save some time. You might want to briefly note a particular observation of interest that took place during the interview, in the following manner:

1. Briefly describe the respondent's mood or any significant mood change—for example, if the respondent started to cry and became upset in talking about an issue or topic. You might write the following concerning these observations with some abbreviations added:

R is L; R is S; R is having a HT describing her feelings; R is EM.

Abbreviations: R = respondent, S = sad, L = laugh/laughing, HT = hard time, EM = emotional

2. Note anything you think might have unduly impacted or disrupted the interview; for example, if the respondent had an unexpected visitor or the interview was interrupted by a phone call or other type of distraction. Include when the disruption began and how long it lasted during the interview.

3. Note where you think a question was of particular relevance or importance to your respondent or where you felt the respondent wasn't really interested in answering the question or seemed somewhat ambivalent about answering a question.

4. Include any particular happening you feel would add to your understanding of the interview. This could entail, for example, a brief note of the respondent's body language during the interview—that the respondent seemed bored, distracted, animated, and so on.

5. Briefly check in on your own feelings and attitudes during the interview. Are you distracted, bored, excited, or listening intently? Do you like or dislike the respondent? During what parts of the interview did you particularly find your own body language changing? Checking in briefly with yourself means to take a reflexive moment to make sure you are actively engaged in the listening process and thereby increasing your ability to obtain meaningful results.

Do not forget the importance of social cues in conducting in-depth interviews. Opdenakker (2006) notes that "social cues, such as voices, intonation, body language, etc., of the interviewee can give the interviewer a lot of extra information that can be added to the verbal answer of the interviewee on a question" (paragraph 7). What you do not want to do is to get off the task of listening to your respondent and take away your focus on their story. It is a fine balancing act. It is probably not appropriate to query the respondent while she is in the middle of an important and difficult story; however, you do want to go back when she is done and say something like, "Earlier you mentioned your sister was going through something at this time that bore on what was happening with you. Can you tell me a little about this?" Using the same example, your respondent could be talking about her experience in Overeaters Anonymous and say something like, "The group wasn't really helpful, but I was so depressed about other stuff anyway and so . . ." and then continue talking about the OA meetings. When she finishes you can follow up by asking, "You mentioned being depressed about other stuff during that time; can you please expand on this?" This shows your respondent that you have been carefully listening to her speak and also has clued you in to some potentially important information that you otherwise wouldn't have known to ask about.

Probes are also critical to a good interview, and it is important to be able to distinguish between when a marker has been dropped that you want to pick up on and when you should probe further into an interviewee's response. Probes are typically needed consistently during an in-depth interview, particularly if it is a low-structure interview where perhaps you ask fewer questions but delve deeper into what the respondent is choosing to talk about. A probe is the researcher's way of getting respondents to continue with what they are talking about, to go further, or to explain more, perhaps with an illustrative example. Sometimes a probe is simply a sign of understanding and interest that the researcher puts forth to the interviewee. Let's look back to a snippet of our transcript from earlier to see this kind of probe (shown in italics).

Respondent: And a lot of thin women thinking they need to be thin so they get a guy.

Interviewer: *Mmmm.*

Respondent:	I mean I think a lot of it, to feel good about themselves they need to be thin, but I think a lot of it is that message that you have to be thin to get a boyfriend.
Interviewer:	*Right.*
Respondent:	So um and I think in the lesbian community, that's not, ya know you don't get that message as strongly. Tons of women who are bigger have partners.
Interviewer:	*Mmmmm.*
Respondent:	So it's not such a strong issue, I think.

The interviewer merely has to say *right* and, at times, simply make a sound (and perhaps a simultaneous gesture such as a nod) to show the respondent that she is listening, understands, is empathetic, and *wants her to continue.* As a result, the respondent continues without the need for the interviewer to ask another question. This is critical because qualitative interviewers want as much of the interview material as possible to come from the interviewee.

At this point, let's join David Karp again to get a glimpse at how he conducts an interview and to see how he addresses some of the following issues:

- How do you get someone to start talking?

- Is it hard to be an active listener while in the role of interviewer?

- Do respondents want to share their stories?

- What do respondents get out of this process?

BEHIND THE SCENES WITH DAVID KARP

Well, I think you should be making it easy on people. You should begin by asking the easy questions. You know, "What religion did you grow up with, etc.?" And to not ask threatening questions, and to give people a sense about what you're doing. Because what they're trying to figure out, just like in any interaction, is, who is this guy? What is he after? Is he genuine? Are his intentions good? Does he listen? Does he seem to care about what I'm saying? And when you do an interview, you must make that person feel that they are the only person in the world at the time that you are talking to them. I could never do more than one interview a day, never! Because the amount of energy that is required to really listen, to really pay attention, is enormous. And to know just when to ask a lot of questions.

Part of this conducting thing is to reach a balance between . . . You should be respectful of the story that the person you're interviewing wants to tell. See, people come into your office, and they have a story that they want to tell. And when they walk in, at the beginning, maybe they want to talk about how medicine screwed them over, or something like that. That's what they really want to talk about. I have to go with that at the beginning. I'm not going to turn them off. I'm not going to say, "Well, I didn't want to talk about that until two hours into the interview." And I think it's reaching balance between allowing people to be heard, to tell the parameters of the story that they really want to tell—and every story is to some degree idiosyncratic in meaning—and at the same time, as I said, to know what you want to get covered before you're done with this person.

I find in doing interviews that if you ask the right question at the beginning of the interview, once you really get into the substance of it, you often don't have to ask much more. In the depression stuff, the first question I typically asked people was, "You may not have called it depression, but tell me about the first moment it entered your head that something was wrong. What was the first time there was any kind of a consciousness that something was wrong?" Sometimes I didn't have to say much of anything else for the next 3 hours. People had a way of telling their story, and they spontaneously covered all of those domains of inquiry that I wanted to have covered. And the other thing I would say about this is that people really do want to tell their stories. Almost invariably, people thanked me at the end of their interview for giving them a chance to tell their story. And to have a sociologist ask them questions . . . They often got a different perspective on their life than they could have gotten through years of therapy, because I was asking questions that only a sociologist would ask.

As you can see, in-depth interviewing is a process of communication that involves asking, listening, and talking. Karp shows that by beginning with good opening questions and showing enthusiastic listening, an interviewer can gain a wealth of data by doing little more than fostering a respondent's storytelling process. Intensive interview is a collaborative process of getting at knowledge that requires a unique relationship between the researcher and interviewee, based on mutual interest, respect, and compassion. When most effective, the process is rewarding for both partners, and both widen their perspective through the experience.

The following are two different listening stances one might take during the interview process. With most in-depth interviewing, the degree of structure in the interview is minimal, which means that with the exception of a few open-ended questions you might use at the beginning, your goal is to actively listen to your respondents tell their story or relate their experiences with regard to a specific event with a minimum of intervention in terms of your own agenda or set of questions. Let's examine two different modes of conducting unstructured in-depth interviews.

SOME TIPS FOR CONDUCTING UNSTRUCTURED IN-DEPTH INTERVIEWS: DEVELOPING GOOD INTERVIEWER LISTENING SKILLS

Problematic Listening	Purposive/Active Listening
Agenda Focused	*Interviewee Focused*
You focus on your own agenda. You are only half-listening to your respondent and instead become focused on the next question you want to ask. You are not directly gazing at the respondent, your body language indicates that you are preoccupied with something else.	You focus on listening to your respondent. Your body language reveals this in that your gaze is on the respondent, and your body language says you are listening—you may nod every now and then and perhaps provide the respondent with a short verbal comment such as, "Yes, I see."
Interviewer Centered: Interrupting	*Interviewee Centered: Noninterruptive*
The interview becomes about your own feelings, attitudes, and ideas. You frequently interrupt the respondent, interjecting your own point of view into the interview.	The interview is about your respondent's feelings and attitudes. You give your interviewees time to think out their responses and allow them to fully answer questions. You feel comfortable with silence without needing to fill it by asking another question. You are comfortable waiting for your interviewee to finish speaking on a given issue or topic.
Interviewer Centered: Your feelings and ideas are "right"	*Interviewee Centered: You are open and nonjudgmental*
You interject yourself into the interview and are quick to contradict or even to tell the respondent your own feelings and opinions about the situation.	You are accepting of your respondent's point of view and do not feel the need to talk over or interrupt your respondent to give your own opinion. Instead, you provide your own opinions only when asked to by your respondent. What you do instead is to encourage your respondent to tell his or her story by providing neutral probes.

Interviewer Centered: You are the judge and jury	Interviewee Centered: You are accepting of difference
You are often intolerant and judgmental, especially with respondents you do not like. Your body language may say to your respondent that you are not tolerant of his or her point of view or lifestyle. For example, you may roll your eyes, laugh inappropriately, or fidget. What is more problematic is that you may respond with a demeaning or hurtful comment.	You reserve judgment and do not make negative comments concerning the attitudes, values, and lifestyle of your respondent. Your body language shows that you are engaged in listening regardless of your personal opinion.
Interviewer Centered: You become a "mind reader"	**Interviewee Centered: You don't carry a crystal ball to every interview and do not assume you can grasp your respondent's experience**
You anticipate what your respondent is going to say and then start to finish his or her sentence. You rarely ask the respondent to repeat something, especially when you have already anticipated the answer. You rarely ask for clarification on issues with which you are already familiar.	You continue to listen and do not feel the need to finish a respondent's sentences or thoughts on a particular issue, even if intimately familiar with the issue. You are not comfortable "filling in the blanks."

How Do I Interview Across Differences Between Myself and My Respondent?

Qualitative researchers view social reality as complex and multidimensional, and this shapes how they think about the interview process. The researcher and the researched often come to the interview situation with different backgrounds in terms of their gender, ethnicity, and sexual preference, as well as class status and many other differences. Researchers working from a positivist tradition often pay scant attention to how these differences can impact the interview situation. Traditional positivistic research deals with the issue of difference through *minimizing* its effects. Positivistic researchers do this by standardizing their participation in the interview situation by being "objective," that is, "bracketing off" these differences vis-à-vis their respondent, so as not to influence the interview process itself. They seldom ask such questions as the following:

- Can a single white middle-class male researcher effectively interview a black working-class mother?

- Can a middle-class white female effectively interview a woman from the third world who is living in poverty?

- Can a straight white middle-class male effectively interview a gay working-class male?

Qualitative researchers, on the other hand, argue that it is not so easy to "bracket off" attitudes and values that emanate from any given individual's mix of positional ties. In fact, it is the acknowledgment of difference between interviewer and respondent that allows the researcher to take account of difference and its impact on the interview situation. Issues of difference impact all phases of the research process, starting with the selection of a particular research question, what hypotheses we test out on our data, and the overall process of data collection, analysis, interpretation, and the writing up of our research findings. Sandra Harding (1993) introduces the concept of "strong objectivity" and argues that by taking difference into account in all phases of a research project, the researcher in fact "*maximizes* objectivity" by ensuring that our respondent's voice is represented, listened to, and understood. Harding (2004) urges researchers to examine the questions they pose in interviews and notes that these are not "value free" but very often reflect the values, attitudes, and agendas of the researcher (p. 136). Those researchers who practice "strong objectivity" ask questions such as the following:

- How do my values and attitudes and beliefs enter into the research process? Do I only ask questions from my perspective?

- How does my own agenda shape what I ask and what I find?

- How does my research standpoint (the attitudes and values I bring to the interview situation) affect how I gather, analyze, and interpret my data? From whose perspective am I conducting my research?

A positivist scenario of the interview process is one where the researcher "asks" questions that the respondent then answers. Communication flows in just one direction, the object of the interview is to obtain information, and this is often done in the form of standardized or semi-standardized questions (see Figure 5.2). There is a specific agenda that the interviewer has in mind.

A qualitative model of interviewing, on the other hand, allows for information to flow in both directions. Qualitative researchers do not maintain a view of social reality as "out there" waiting to be captured by the objective social researcher. As mentioned earlier, the interview is often seen as a **co-creation of meaning** (see Figure 5.3). The researcher's job is to listen intently to what the researched has to say and be prepared to drop or adjust his or her agenda in response to what takes place during the interview.

Kathryn Anderson (Anderson & Jack, 1991), a speech communications expert, wanted to document the lives of rural farm women living in northwest Washington State for the Washington Women's Heritage Project. During the course of her research, however, the focus of her research project on the attitudes and feelings of

Figure 5.2   Model of the Interview Process: Quantitative Model

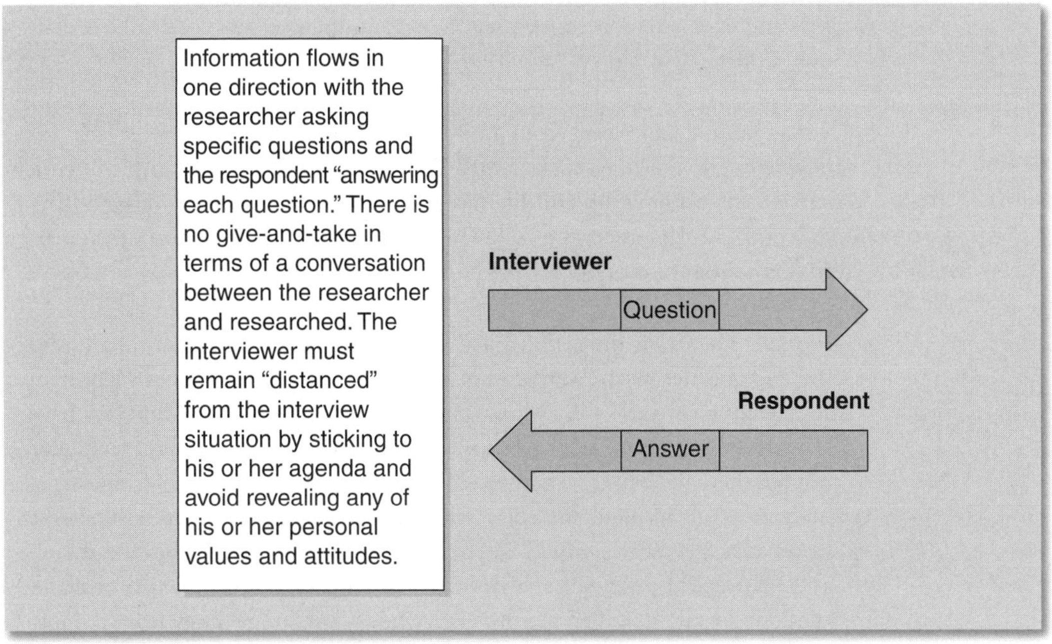

Information flows in one direction with the researcher asking specific questions and the respondent "answering each question." There is no give-and-take in terms of a conversation between the researcher and researched. The interviewer must remain "distanced" from the interview situation by sticking to his or her agenda and avoid revealing any of his or her personal values and attitudes.

Interviewer

Question →

Respondent

← Answer

Figure 5.3   Model of the Interview Process: Qualitative Model

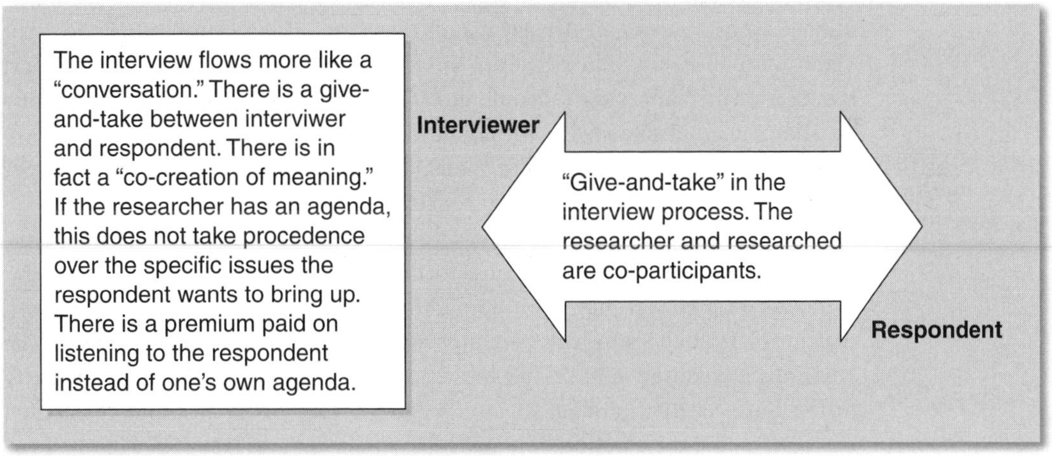

The interview flows more like a "conversation." There is a give-and-take between interviwer and respondent. There is in fact a "co-creation of meaning." If the researcher has an agenda, this does not take procedence over the specific issues the respondent wants to bring up. There is a premium paid on listening to the respondent instead of one's own agenda.

Interviewer

"Give-and-take" in the interview process. The researcher and researched are co-participants.

Respondent

rural farmwomen was often displaced by her need to produce specific descriptions of farm life that depicted women's activities on the farm in order to provide sufficient material for an exhibit. Anderson notes:

In retrospect, I can see how I listened with at least part of my focus on producing potential material for the exhibit—the concrete description of experiences that would accompany pictures of women's activities. As I rummaged through the interviews long after the exhibit [had] been placed in storage, I [was] painfully aware of lost opportunities for women to reflect on the activities and events they described and to explain their terms more fully in their own words. (Anderson & Jack, 1991, p. 13)

Let's examine an excerpt from an interview Anderson (Anderson & Jack, 1991) conducted with a farm woman named Verna. During the course of this interview, Verna reflects on how difficult life has been for her as a mother. Verna begins to open up to Anderson in the following excerpt. Notice Anderson's response to Verna's emotional remarks:

[Verna:] There was times that I just wished I could get away from it all. And there were times when I would have liked to have taken the kids and left them someplace for a week—the whole bunch at one time—so that I wouldn't have to worry about them. I don't know whether anybody else had that feeling or not but there were times when I just felt like I needed to get away from everybody, even my husband, for a little while. Those were times when I just felt like I needed to get away. I would maybe take a walk back in the woods and look at the flowers, and maybe go down there and find an old cow that was real and gentle and walk up to her and pat her a while—kind of get away from it. I just had to, it seems like sometimes . . .

[Anderson:] Were you active in clubs? (Anderson & Jack, 1991, p. 16)

From the above interview excerpt, we can observe how Anderson was single-minded in her pursuit of her agenda and does not really listen intently to what Verna was conveying to her. Instead, she has an agenda she follows, and the next question on her interview schedule deals with membership in clubs. Anderson's question fails to acknowledge Verna's outpouring of feelings concerning motherhood, and she may have missed a valuable opportunity to delve further into the subject's knowledge and experiences concerning this topic.

The qualitative interview is more of a conversation between co-participants, with information flowing back and forth during the course of the interview. Although researchers may want to pursue some specific questions of interest, their primary focus is to listen intently and take cues from the interviewee. The heart of the qualitative interview requires much **reflexivity**, which is sensitivity to the important *situational dynamics* between the researcher and researched that can impact the creation of knowledge. Anderson and Jack (1991) provide us with a guide to sharpening our "listening" skills during the interview process, especially listening across our differences. They provide the following questions and issues you might consider regarding the type of interview schedule that promotes listening:

- Have an open-ended interview style to enable your interviewees to express their attitudes and feelings.

- Probe for feelings, not just facts. For example, how does the respondent understand what is happening? What meaning does he or she give to the course of events in his or her life?

- What is not said? (Anderson & Jack, 1991, p. 24)

Anderson and Jack (1991) also suggest the following checklist you might consult *before* you conduct your interviews:

- Be mindful of your own agenda.

- Go with your own "hunches, feelings, [and] responses that arise through listening to others."

- If you are confused about something, don't be afraid to follow up on an issue or concern (p. 24).

What about your own discomfort and how this might affect the interview situation? Can your personal discomfort also provide you with a clue as to where you need to look at "what is being said" and what the respondent is feeling? For student researchers affected by feelings of discomfort in in-depth interviews, we offer the following ethical aside.

ETHICAL ASIDE—STUDENT INTERVIEWERS RESEARCHING SENSITIVE TOPICS

As a student researcher, you may be asked to conduct your own study, and you may find that your project requires that you delve into sensitive issues such as sexual assault, binge drinking, or the rise of eating disorders on your college campus. The students you might be planning to interview may be part of your wider peer group or student network. These particular interviewing circumstances may place you and your fellow student respondents under some stress, especially if you have not been trained to research sensitive topics. For example, you may find it difficult to pick up respondent cues as to whether or not they might be experiencing a high level of stress and distress with regard to your interview topic.

High levels of interviewee stress can raise some important ethical issues that you should consider. Even if you feel prepared to tackle sensitive interview topics, you might begin by conducting a pilot interview to see how things go. As you go along with this first interview, be sure to check in with your respondents in terms of how they are feeling about the interview situation. Ask yourself how you think they are reacting to your research questions. Be sure to tell them that they are free to stop

(Continued)

(Continued)

the interview at any time, especially if you feel they are showing some signs of stress. You might also want to create a short memo right after your pilot interview noting any specific issues or circumstances and first reflections on how the overall interview process went. Your project director can also help you assess the extent to which you are picking up on any stress or distress on the part of the interviewee and consider the range of strategies you might employ to address this type of issue if needed. You might be sure to discuss with your supervisors what circumstances would call for a termination of the interview.

Before conducting your interviews make sure that you have the resources and information to deal with respondents' stress during the interview. It's important to have information about local resources for counseling hotlines or services, including campus counseling services, to provide to those interviewees who experience high levels of stress and/or emotional trauma during the course of the interview.

It's also important to make sure you check in with your project director to alert him or her about any potential concerns you may have about the interviewee or your own level of stress in dealing with a sensitive research topic.

Having a good working rapport with your project director is important. You should feel comfortable contacting her or him with any overall issues or concerns you may have about your research project.

Last, it's also crucial to keep in mind that in carrying out any interview, what is most important is that proceeding with any of the above procedures is not an indication you have failed to conduct an interview properly, but instead a sign of your own professionalism and commitment to ethically responsible interviewing.

Insider or Outsider?

One strategy researchers have used to overcome the impact of difference in the interview process is to match some of their important status characteristics (race/age/gender/sexual preference) so that they can take advantage of their **insider status** in gaining access to an interview and obtain cooperation and rapport within the situation to expedite understanding their respondents. The researcher, with regard to these matched characteristics, is an insider in that he or she is familiar with the respondent's group situation. It is also important that such a balance in some of these status characteristics decreases the possibility of power and authority imbalances in the interview situation (Oakley, 1981). The standard thinking on difference in the interview situation suggests that if the interviewer has **outsider status,** this might make it more difficult to gain access and to understand the situation of "the other." Does an insider status ensure a more valid and reliable interview? How does difference impact the research process?

Doing Difference: Examples of Taking Account of Difference in the Research Process

Example—Gender Differences: What Women Are We Talking About?

Suppose we are interested in exploring the following question: What is the economic and source impact of globalization on third world women? We would need to account for the diversity of women's experiences within the global marketplace. Some important characteristic dimensions of the woman worker we might consider are (1) the geographical region in which the woman worker resides (rural/urban/suburban) and whether she is a recent immigrant to the area; (2) at what point she is in the life cycle—for example, young, not married, or with a partner and no children versus married with a partner and middle aged, and so on; (3) level of education; (4) ethnicity; (5) if married or with a significant other, is that person employed full- or part-time? These and other factors are important because they will help the researcher to understand that globalization can impact women workers differently, depending on their status along these critical socio-economic dimensions.

Helen Safa (1981), in her classic article "Runaway Shops and Female Employment: The Search for Cheap Labor," notes that the impact of women's employment in export processing zones (EPZs) on the division of labor in the home "varies with the degree of male unemployment and intensity of patriarchal tradition" (p. 427). For example, Safa states that in Mexico, the disruption of the traditional family pattern was very problematic as a result of women's involvement in the *maquiladoros* (border industrial program). She argues that women became the "primary breadwinners" of the family because the men were not employed; the men resented this and did not help out at home. On the other hand, in areas such as Jamaica, female employment did not affect the division of labor at home. Safa also notes that the age on entering EPZs is important. Older married women who had children fared better than younger unmarried women, who were more exploited by their families and the corporation (p. 427).

Embedded in this example is the realization that from the beginning of our research project, *what* and *who* we choose to study is grounded in an appreciation of difference and is impacted by how we as researchers approach and are cognizant of difference issues. An appreciation of difference allows us to ask these questions: Which women? Are all women around the world the same? How are they different, and what differences are important to my research question?

Difference is also critical in terms of the *interview situation.* Can a researcher from a first world country truly understand the plight of women working in the global marketplaces in the third world? Suppose the researcher is a white middle-class male. How will his gender, race, ethnic background, and social class affect the interview process? Can researchers overcome differences between themselves and those they research?

Example: Knowing What Differences Matter in any Given Research Project

It is easy to conclude that, if the interviewer and interviewee are of the same gender, class, and ethnic background, this might go a long way toward establishing an open dialogue between them, thereby providing a maximum opportunity for the voice of the respondent to be heard and represented. Beoku-Betts (1994) found in her field research among Gullah women (African American women who reside in the Sea Islands of South Carolina and Georgia) that fully informing her participants of her social status and background—that she, too, was raised in a rural community with similar cultural practices— enabled her to make contacts and gain data that would have otherwise not been available. Similarly, Kath Weston (2004) is reflexive about her identity as a lesbian and how it influenced her research. She writes that although she still would have studied gay families, the project would have been very different if she were not a lesbian. Weston also recognizes that her position within the homosexual community was the reason she had little trouble finding lesbian participants, while lesbians had remained virtually invisible to men conducting sexuality research. She notes:

> In my case, being a woman also influenced how I spent my time in the field: I passed more hours in lesbian clubs and women's groups than gay men's bars or male gyms. (Weston, 2004, p. 202)

Sometimes sharing some insider characteristics with their respondents is not enough to ensure that researchers can capture the lived experience of those they research. Catherine Kohler Riessman's (1987) research on divorce narratives notes that in her interviews with divorced women, just being a woman was not enough to understand the divorce experience of women whose class and ethnic background differed from hers. Her status as an Anglo, middle-class, highly educated individual prevented her from fully comprehending the particular ways these women structured their divorce narratives (episodically instead of chronologically). It became a challenge in the interview situation not to place the researcher's cultural expectations of what a narrative should look like onto individuals of different ethnic and class backgrounds.

Likewise, Beoku-Betts (1994) confronted a similar scenario in her field research among Gullah women. Beoku-Betts is a black, West African female researcher and was definitely an insider to the black community she was studying. Beoku-Betts relates how one of her respondents told her that "she preferred a black scholar like myself conducting research in her community because 'black scholars have a sense of soul for our people because they have lived through it'" (p. 416). However, Beoku-Betts found that her insider status was intertwined with other factors such as differences in class and cultural background. She found herself having to overcome some resistance within the community toward her fieldwork activities:

> My shared racial background proved instrumental in providing access to research participants and in reducing the social distance at a critical stage of the researcher process. However, my identity as an outsider was also defined by other subgroups within that identity. For example my gender,

marital status (unmarried), and profession status as a university researcher often operated separately and in combination with my race to facilitate and complicate the research process. (Beoku-Betts, 1994, p. 420)

She notes that in one of the communities she studied, her status as an unmarried female created some tensions in the research process. She relays two incidents that happened in the field because she was unmarried and educated:

In one community a local man visited the family with whom I was staying. When we were introduced, he recalled that he had heard about me and shared with me the rumor in the community that I was there to look for a husband. . . . Another incident occurred in church one Sunday with an African American minister who invoked the topic of the Anita Hill/Clarence Thomas hearing after I was asked to introduce myself to the congregation. At first the minister was very supportive and welcomed me warmly into the community as an African coming to study aspects of a common historical heritage. However, he soon switched to the Hill/Thomas hearings and began to remark on the fact that Anita Hill was also an educated woman who had used that privilege to accuse and embarrass Clarence Thomas (whose hometown was not far from this community). (Beoku-Betts, 1994, p. 428)

Beoku-Betts finds she must negotiate her differing statuses if she wants to obtain interviews with her respondents that reflect how they actually feel about her. It was not until she completed the negotiation process that she had full access to some of the research subjects and could begin to co-create meaning and understanding.

Having said all of this, being an outsider can actually be an advantage, depending on the research problem and population you are studying. By not belonging to a specific group, you may be viewed as more unbiased by your respondent. Likewise, you may be more likely to ask things that you would otherwise take for granted as "shared knowledge" and in fact learn that your participants have their own way of viewing a given issue. Sociologist Robert Weiss (1994) comments on issues of difference between the interviewer and respondent as follows:

One way to phrase this issue is to ask to what extent it is necessary for the interviewer to be an insider in the respondent's world in order to be effective as an interviewer. . . . It is difficult to anticipate what interviewer attributes will prove important to a respondent and how the respondent will react to them. . . . There are so many different interviewer attributes to which a respondent can react that the interviewer will surely be an insider in some ways and an outsider in others. . . . I have generally found it better to be an insider to the milieu in which the respondent lives, because it is easier then for me to establish a research partnership with the respondent. But some of my most instructive interviews have been good just because I was an outsider who needed instruction in the respondent's milieu. (p. 137)

What is interesting to observe is that one's status as insider/outsider is fluid and can change even in the course of a single interview. On some interview issues, you may share a given role or status with your respondent; at other times, you may find stark differences according to the particularities of your research question or topic of conversation. A good example of such a situation comes from research conducted by Rosalind Edwards.

Edwards (1990) is an educated middle-class white woman who is interested in conducting unstructured interviews with Afro-Caribbean mature mothers who are also students. She wants to understand the lived experiences of these women around issues of education, work, and family life. She describes the difficulty she had in gaining access to this population and gaining trust within the interview relationship. It was not until she openly acknowledged these differences with her respondents that they began to talk more openly with her. During the course of the interview, Edwards experienced the ebb and flow feeling of being both an insider and an outsider, depending on the issues she discussed with her respondents. She notes that when the discussion turned to being a mother, she felt more like an insider: "The black women did indicate some common understandings and position between us" (p. 488). Yet, when the discussion reverted to a more public realm like their educational experiences, even though the author also shared the positionality of having been a mature mother and student, the conversation became one where "black women were least likely to talk to me about what we had the most in common" (p. 488).

Reflexivity and Difference

Researchers can use the process of *reflexivity* as a tool to assist them with studying across difference. Reflexivity is the process through which researchers recognize, examine, and understand how their own social background and assumptions can intervene in the research process. The researcher is a product of his or her society and its structures and institutions just as much as the researched. Our beliefs, backgrounds, and feelings are part of the process of knowledge construction. It is imperative for researchers to be aware of their positionality: the set of attributes that they bring with them into the research project, including their gender, race/ethnicity, class, and any other factors that might be of importance to the research process. The research projects we recounted above required the researchers at some point during their research project to become aware of how they were similar to and different from their respondents. *Doing reflexivity* in fact empowered both the researcher and researched within the interview situation. In an interview situation, reflexivity is *discursive* due to the "active nature of data collection" as opposed to *confessional* (as traditionally found in journals and written data collection methods) (Cooper & Burnett, 2006, p. 120).

Reflecting on difference allowed Beoku-Betts (1994), Edwards (1990), Kohler Riessman (1988), Weston (2004), and Weiss (1994) to negotiate their differences and similarities with their respondents in order to gain access and obtain data that would not necessarily be available to them and to gain new insight into their data. Kath Weston's (2004) reflexivity concerning her lesbian identity and how it influences her research allows her to easily obtain access to the lesbian community. Edwards's (1990) recognition of how she is both similar to and different from the Afro-Caribbean population provides her more in-depth understanding of how that population talks about public and private issues. Weiss (1994) and Edwards (1990) also realize that the categories of insider and outsider are not fixed but fluid, depending on the given research topic and the individual ebb and flow of the interview itself.

Reflexivity also reminds us that we need to be mindful of the importance of difference to our research project as a whole. Difference enters into the projects we select, the questions we ask, and the way data are collected, analyzed, written, and interpreted. Difference needs to be explored, not disavowed. Let's listen in on a conversation Sharlene Hesse-Biber had with her research assistant Norah K. They had just finished a focus group session with several African American girls who hang out at a local community center.

DOING REFLEXIVITY: AN EXAMPLE

I am conducting participant observations and in-depth interviews with African American girls between the ages of 11 and 18 at an inner-city community center that houses an afterschool program for youth. What is it like for young teens to "come of age" in their community? I have been hanging out at the center for over a month now, meeting with the girls once or twice a week. Sometimes they ask me to join them in playing basketball, or I watch them practice their "stepping" routines. I tutor the younger children once a week.

The neighborhood surrounding the center had several drive-by shootings, and last week one of the girls mentioned that a male youth was recently shot outside the center's back door. One girl told me she rarely goes out after school except when she comes to the community center. What is it like for young girls to have their day-to-day mobility so restricted? How does violence in their community affect peer group interactions? How do girls cope with the high levels of violence within their doorstep?

Today, Nora, my research assistant, and I are the only two Caucasians in the entire community center and I have been dealing with feelings of being on the margins, concerned that my whiteness and my difference in age and social class is impacting my ability to listen to the girls. How can I bridge the differences divide? Did I expect too much of myself? Of them?

(Continued)

(Continued)

I usually stay in my car before pulling out of the community center driveway. I have a tape recorder to capture my reflections. The following are reflections on a meeting Norah and I had with the girls one Friday afternoon:

Norah: I think the girls were more open this time. I don't know if it was just because we bought them pizza, but I think that it was the fact that they have seen a lot of us and we are showing interest in the boys there as well and I felt that they were open to talking about things like discrimination and white people and I didn't feel like there was as much tension around us being white.

Sharlene: I really felt the girls opened up to me today. I think that one of the keys, it kind of fell into our laps, was that by not excluding the boys who happened to walk into our room, today, we gave legitimacy to the girls being there with us, because the boys wanted to be there as well. I think it made it a priority that day. I think in a fortuitous way, the boys legitimized the whole thing.

As I reflected on my conversation with Norah I realized that I had not thought about what our presence at the center meant for the boys who were also there. Our talking exclusively to the girls served to "de-center" the boys, and they became quite curious about what we were doing there. In fact, our openness to having the boys hang out with all of us for a brief time allowed them to know us a little and to open up an opportunity to ask them if we could talk with them as well at a later point in our visit. There were things that the girls would say about the boys especially around issues of body image and appearance, and this gave us an opportunity to see how their perceptions match up to how the boys felt about what they found attractive in a female.

One of the issues I was hoping the girls would bring up was that of what it meant to be a black female within their community. Today, one of the girls actually talked about this issue with us. It came up when one of the girls touched on what it meant to be an African American female. The girls use the term "black" and "African American" interchangeably to describe their racial identity. This moment provided me with an opportunity to directly ask the girls what being black and being female meant to them and whether they felt that one identity was first and the other second. I reflected on this interview moment.

Sharlene: I found it interesting that all said they considered themselves black first and female second. In most cases, they responded that above all they were black. They attributed this feeling to the fact that being black fundamentally shaped their sense of self and the way in which others perceived them, much more so than their gender. Related to this is the way in which the girls equated being black with a sense of strength. Many of the girls indicated that a defining factor of African American womanhood was strength, not only for one's self, but also for their family and the community.

I also reflected on what it meant for a white researcher to ask this question. What assumptions was I making concerning race and gender? Would I ask such a question if my respondents were white? How does my own positionality reflect my agenda? (Hesse-Biber & Piatelli, 2007, pp. 493–495)

Practicing reflexivity is important throughout the research process but can be especially meaningful when done directly after conducting research, when the researchers' ideas are fresh on their mind. In addition, Hesse-Biber's and Norah's reflections indicate that difference in itself is not necessarily problematic and can be an interesting aspect to deconstruct.

How Do You Analyze and Interpret Interview Data?

We go into detail about the analysis and interpretation of data in Chapter 12. However, we will provide you with some general thoughts here about generating analysis from your interview data. Sociologist David Karp, in another behind-the-scenes interview, provides us with a step-by-step approach to how you might begin the analysis of your interview data. He stresses the importance of beginning your analysis right after you begin data collection. Qualitative data analysis is an *iterative process* of data collection along with data analysis. These two processes almost proceed simultaneously. Karp stresses the importance of "memo-ing," that is, taking stock of where you are in thinking about your project by writing down your ideas about how your data do or do not fit together. If you do come up with what you consider an important breakthrough, reflect on this. Memo-ing also functions to help researchers become more reflexive about their own positionality and how it may impact what they are researching. Karp also points out the importance of going out of your way to look for "negative cases," things that do not seem to fit together or that are problematic, by asking yourself: What doesn't support my interpretation?

TIPS ON ANALYZING INTERVIEW DATA FROM DAVID KARP (PERSONAL COMMUNICATION)

1. Remember that the analytical work you do along the way is every bit as important as the task of data collection. Never subordinate the task of data collection to thinking about and analyzing your data. The great strength of methods such as in-depth interviewing is that you can engage simultaneously in the processes of data collection and analysis. The two processes should inform each other.

(Continued)

(Continued)

2. Start writing memos with the very first interview. Let your early data tell you which of your ideas seem sensible and which ones ought to be reevaluated. Especially at the beginning you will hear people say things that you just hadn't thought about. Look carefully for major directions that had just not occurred to you to take. The pace of short memo writing ought to be especially great toward the beginning of your work. We advocate "idea" or "concept" memos that introduce an emerging idea. Such memos typically run two to three pages.

3. Reevaluate your interview guide after about 10 interviews. Ten interviews ought to give you enough information to do a major assessment of what you are learning or failing to learn. This is probably a good point at which to take a close look at your research questions and emerging themes.

4. If you think that you have been able to grab onto a theme, it is time to write a "data" memo. By this, we mean a memo that integrates the theme with data and any available literature that fits. By a data memo, I mean something that begins to look like a paper. In a data memo, always use more data on a point than you would actually use in a research paper. If you make a broad point and feel that you have 10 good pieces of data that fit that point, lay them all out for inspection and later use. Also, make sure to lay out the words of people who do NOT fit the pattern.

5. Once themes begin to emerge, go out of your way to find cases that do not fit. You must try as hard as you can to disprove your ideas. Do not be afraid of complexity and ambiguity about themes. The world is complicated, and your writing must reflect that complexity. There is a tendency of social scientists to describe patterns as if they were uniform and monolithic. To do that slights the complexity of things. Don't fall in love with early, plausible theories.

6. After 15 to 20 interviews, it is probably a good idea to create coding categories. Here the task is to begin by creating as many categories as you can that seem sensible. Coding is another way of "getting close to the data" and telling you what you know. You can eventually use these codes as you go through the data for paper and memo writing.

7. Write a fairly complete memo every time your work takes on a new direction (say, a major change in sampling procedure). Provide a full explanation for changes in analytical directions. Your memos can constitute an audit trail for people who want to retrace your steps. People who do qualitative research should be as fully accountable for their procedures as those who employ more standardized procedures.

8. If you think you have a theme significant enough to write a paper on for publication, do it. Getting papers published is very affirming and brings your ideas to a point of high refinement. You don't have to wait until all your data are in to write papers. You will find that some of your papers will be on "subsamples" within the larger sample.

9. Periodically, write outlines for what a book, thesis, or report from your data might look like. Draw up preliminary prospectuses. Pretend that you were about to sit down and write a book. This is a good exercise that requires you to paint the total picture.

10. Do not get crazy about getting exactly the same data from every respondent. You will find that each respondent's story is to some degree unique. In your writing, you will want to point out here and there the unique story. It is probably a good idea to write up a summary sheet of about one page that describes the main themes in each interview.

11. Test out your hypotheses on your respondents. Incorporate your hypotheses into questions ("You know, several of the people with whom I have talked tell me that . . . Does this make sense to you?"). There is no reason to hide or conceal hypotheses, ideas, and concepts from subjects.

12. Pay attention to extreme cases, as they are often the most informative. Be on the lookout to do deviant case analysis.

In this next section, we will present an ethical aside concerning confidentiality in student research. As in the other aspects of research ethics we have discussed, respondents' confidentiality should be considered at all points of the research process.

ETHICAL ASIDE—ANALYSIS AND INTERPRETATION OF DATA FROM STUDENT RESEARCH PROJECTS: ARE YOU UNWITTINGLY REVEALING YOUR RESPONDENTS' IDENTITY?

Qualitative research projects usually work with small samples. Given the time limit on student research projects, which often span part of one semester, students who conduct in-depth interviews often collect data on a very small number of respondents. It is imperative that in analyzing their data, students do not disclose any information that might inadvertently lead to identifying a particular respondent. It is not enough for student researchers to take away any specific identifying information such as a respondent's name or dorm location; sometimes, a specific story line or event may allow others reading their project's analysis and interpretation to identify a respondent. While student researchers may believe they are abiding by the ethical code of maintaining confidentiality, the intensity of their analytical description of a given respondent's life circumstances leads to an uncovering of the respondent's identity. This is especially worrisome when the information revealed is highly sensitive and damaging to the respondent's reputation.

(Continued)

(Continued)

One might consider yet another scenario, in which student researchers find that they are talking about a given interviewee, and although they leave out what they believe are any identifying items of information, they have nevertheless provided a detailed description that reveals the respondent's identity. What can researchers do? It is not enough to make sure the documents pertaining to a given study remain confidential or that the interviewer also is abiding by a code of ethical conduct. The reporting of information from any interview must be conducted ethically whereby researchers go out of their way not to reveal any specific information from an interview that might in any way identify a respondent. That means that great care is taken to remove any specific information that might reveal a person's specific location, affiliations, telling of specific stories, age, or even gender. If any excerpts from specific interviews are taken and presented in a report, these excerpts must be free of any specific identifiers. To do this might mean that the researcher changes certain identifying information or, in fact, combines two interview stories to further ensure the confidentially of the respondents. While this will not change the researcher's specific analysis, interpretation, and conclusions, what remains intact is his or her commitment to confidentiality and the upholding of a commitment to ethical research.

It is critical that the project director be clear with student researchers concerning the extent of information that can be reported from in-depth interview data. The director should read over the specific analysis and interpretation of a student's project with an eye for possible breaches in respondent confidentiality before the report is submitted and goes public.

Conclusion

In-depth interview is a wonderful method for getting at individuals' lived experiences and perspectives. Qualitative interviews require the building of rapport and reciprocity in the interview situation. Many factors influence how a conversation will go, and as we saw, difference cannot be ignored but should be incorporated into the research design and data-gathering process from start to finish. Other issues such as sharing authority and co-creating a narrative, which were mentioned in this chapter, will be discussed at greater length in the next chapter on oral history interviews.

Glossary

Co-creation of meaning: This occurs when the researcher and research participant create meaning or knowledge collaboratively. The interview is often seen as a site for the co-creation of meaning. The researchers' job is to listen intently to what the researched has to say and be prepared to drop their agenda in response to what takes place during the interview.

Focused topic: A particular contained topic the researcher is studying.

In-depth interview: A qualitative interview where the researcher seeks knowledge from the respondent's point of view. The interview questions are usually open-ended. The degree of structure to the interview depends on the extent to which interviewers have a specific agenda, that is, a set of questions they want to be sure are answered. A less structured interview does not contain a specific interview protocol, but rather the object of the interview is to listen to what the respondent feels is important to talk about; the interviewer comes prepared with some ice-breaking or initial questions to get the process moving around the general topic of the interview.

Insider status: This is developed from an attribute, characteristic, or experience the researcher has in common with his or her research participants. One strategy researchers have used to overcome the impact of difference in the interview process is to "match" some of their important status characteristics (race/age/gender/sexual preference) so that they can take advantage of their insider status to maximize their chances of gaining permission to interview and obtaining cooperation and rapport within the interview situation.

Interview guide: A list of specific topics and/or questions constructed prior to the interview to be used at the discretion of the researcher.

Knowledge-producing conversation: The qualitative interview is a special kind of knowledge-producing conversation that occurs between two parties. The relationship between the interviewer and respondent is critical to the process of constructing meaning.

Lines of inquiry: The particular major set of themes you want to pursue in your in-depth interview. You would then construct a series of questions that explore these particular themes in your interview session.

Markers: Markers are important pieces of information that respondents may offer as they talk about something else. It is important to remember and return to markers as appropriate.

Open-ended interview: In this type of interview, the researcher has a particular topic for the study, but he or she allows the conversation to go wherever the research participant takes it, and each interview becomes highly individual. This is also referred to as a *low-structure* interview.

Outsider status: This refers to major differences between researchers and their research participants, such as a difference in race, gender, social class, sexual orientation, educational level, and so on. The standard thinking on difference in the interview situation suggests that if the interviewer is an outsider, this might make it more difficult to gain access and to understand the situation of "the other."

Probes: The researcher's way of encouraging a respondent to continue with what he or she is talking about, to go further or to explain a particular point in the interview. The researcher uses neutral language such as "Can you tell me more about that?" You might also ask a respondent to repeat something that you did not understand. Sometimes, a probe is simply a sign of understanding and support or a general show of interest that the researcher puts forward to the interviewee. This can take the form of a verbal response like "Oh, I see," or a gesture such as nodding your head.

Rapport: Researchers create a supportive interview environment where respondents feel safe and comfortable. Achieving rapport is enhanced if the researcher takes on the role of active listener and expresses a genuine interest in what the respondent is saying, without pushing his or her own agenda.

Reflexivity: Reflexivity is the process through which researchers recognize, examine, and understand how their own social background and assumptions can intervene in the research process. It is also a recognition of the importance of the role played by situational dynamics between the researcher and researched, which can impact the creation of knowledge. Researchers can use the process of reflexivity as a tool to assist them with studying across difference.

Semistructured interviews: Semistructured interviews contain specific research questions, employed by the researcher to guide the interview, but the use of these questions in any given interview is often at the discretion of the researcher, who may or may not decide to ask these questions in every interview. There is commitment to openness in following the respondents' lead in the interview situation.

Structured interview: A structured interview means the researcher asks each participant the same series of questions. If the participant strays too much from the topic at hand or says some interesting things that aren't directly relevant to the study, the interviewer guides the conversation back to the interview questions.

Discussion Questions

1. When is in-depth interviewing appropriate? What kind of questions is this method suited to answer? When should an interview be conducted instead of an ethnography?

2. What types of dialogue occur in the in-depth interview situation? How does this dialogue differ from that of a quantitative interview?

3. Explain the different degrees of structure an interviewer can impose and when it is appropriate to use a more or less structured interview approach.

4. What is an interview guide? How does one construct an interview guide, and how, ideally, should a guide be used?

5. Explain the concept of rapport in the interview situation. How does an interviewer foster rapport in the interview situation?

6. What is the difference between a marker and a probe? Why are these important to the success of an interview?

7. Discuss the importance of taking into account the differences that exist between an interviewer and a respondent. What are the benefits and drawbacks of having insider status? What are the benefits and drawbacks of outsider status? Explain how these statuses exist on a flowing continuum in actual research practice.

Resources

Suggested Web Sites

Education Online: "Collecting data by in-depth interviewing"

http://www.leeds.ac.uk/educol/documents/000001172.htm

This is a paper/presentation on the basics of in-depth interviewing. The Web site explains how to collect data by walking through the process of the presenter's own study.

Audience Dialogue

http://www.audiencedialogue.net/kya10.html

This URL leads to Chapter 10, of *Know Your Audience: A Practical Guide to Media Research,* which is about in-depth interviewing. The site breaks down the process and describes what needs to be accomplished before, during, and after this form of data collection.

Relevant Journals

Gender & Society

International Journal of Social Research Methodology

Qualitative Inquiry

Qualitative Research

Qualitative Research in Psychology

The Qualitative Report

Qualitative Social Work

Qualitative Sociology

CHAPTER 6

Oral History

To speak is to preserve the teller from oblivion.

—Alessandro Portelli

Storytelling is a natural part of the human experience. Human beings communicate meaning through talk. Oral historians have harnessed this tradition of transmitting knowledge and created an important research technique that allows the expression of voice. While storytelling has a deep history, the adaptation of this human process into a legitimated research method is relatively new.

> Oral history was established in 1948 as a modern technique for historical documentation when Columbia University historian Allan Nevins began recording the memoirs of persons significant in American Life. (North American Oral History Association, as quoted by Thomson, 1998, p. 581)

Some researchers find it helpful to distinguish between *oral tradition* and *oral history,* the former being the umbrella category in which the oral history method can be placed. Oral tradition among many Native American people refers to stories handed down for multiple generations, which can also involve nonhuman subjects (Wilson, 1996, p. 8). This differs from the more recent academic use of the term **oral history**, in which personal stories are collected from an individual.

What Is Oral History?

As we will show in this chapter, oral history is a very unique kind of interview situation because of the distinct process of storytelling on which it is based. There are moments of realization, awareness, and, ideally, education and empowerment during the process. When conducting an oral history with a college-age woman struggling in a serious battle with anorexia nervosa, there was a point, two long sessions into the oral history project, when the interviewee noted the moment in her life that culminated in a turn toward anorexia. It was a significant moment in her life narrative that could have come through only by the autobiographical telling of her story. Not only did this represent a major turning point in the participant's self-awareness, but it also helped elucidate and expand on existing substantive knowledge about eating disorder vulnerability and the onset of such disorders. The clarity with which Claire notes the moment she turned toward body obsession and the way in which it initially occurred could have happened only through the telling of her story from childhood on.

> I kind of focused more on my circumstances and the lack of opportunities that had been available to me. Like, all these things that I had, put up waiting, you know, I had waited for, for so long, and everyone was like, "one day, one day," and then that day was here and nothing was happening. You know? And so that was hard. Um, but actually it was at that time when I knew I was staying at school, that I remember thinking, OK, obviously I can handle the academics. You know, the friends, maybe I won't be developing my closest friends at college, but I still have my ones from high school. You know, what am I going to do with this time? I was sitting here looking at a three-year period going, what am I going to do with three years of my life? You know? And I think that was the other disappointing thing, is that with the exception of perspectives, my other classes were like high school. They were very structured, very like, rote memorization, as opposed to: what ideas do you have? Like, do you think this is a good idea? How do you feel about this? And so I was kinda like, what am I gonna do with three years? And I can remember that day, thinking to myself, well, at least I can come out with what I want to look like. Like, part of being successful to me, like, I had a certain image in my head, and that image was not like a woman with baby fat on her face. You know? It was very in-shape; it was funny because I never wanted to be skinny. But I wanted to be strong. I always, I mean, especially growing up with guys, I wanted to be able to take them on in basketball. And I wanted to be able to go skiing, you know? I just wanted to be in really good shape. And I was just like, OK, well at least I can, I can control my health. You know? Even though I don't really have much I can do about this decision, and now looking back I can see that I, you know, that I did have a voice. I could have said forget it, I'm just leaving, you know? But when I weighed the pros and the cons, especially because I was always someone to keep the peace in my house, to disrupt a balance, or to make unnecessary trouble, wasn't something I was willing to do. So I, you know, I remember saying to myself, well, I'll just start exercising, to watch what I eat, you know, I mean it was the first time I wasn't in organized sports, so like, I wasn't going from season to season. *And um, I was just like, ok, that's what I'll do.* [Leavy, 1998, interview two with Claire (pseudonym), emphasis added]

What a powerful moment in the research process—the revelation of when and why what would become a life-threatening body obsession began two years earlier.

As you can already begin to see, oral history is a special kind of intensive biography interview. During an oral history project, a researcher spends an extended amount of time with one participant in order to learn extensively about his or her life or a particular part of that life. The preceding excerpt is taken from a project that used oral history as a way to understand how otherwise successful female college students with eating disorders had become so focused on their bodies—to determine the life experiences that had webbed together in a way that created body image obsession vulnerabilities in Claire and others. But it is not enough to say that researchers learn about the lives of participants, as with other qualitative methods of interview and observation; oral history allows researchers to learn about participants' lives from their own perspective—where they create meaning, what they deem important, their feelings and attitudes (both explicit and implicit), the relationship between different life experiences or different times in their life—their perspective and their voice on their own life experiences. Oral histories allow for the collaborative generation of knowledge between the researcher and the research participant. This reciprocal process presents unique opportunities, continual ethical evaluation (heightened in the electronic age), and a particular set of interpretive challenges. Often used in feminist research, oral history allows us to get at the valuable knowledge and rich life experience of marginalized people and groups that would otherwise remain untapped, and, specifically, offers a way of accessing subjugated voices. Beyond contributing to social scientific knowledge substantively, the oral history process can be a rewarding and empowering experience for both the participant and researcher, as in the case of Claire, who later reported feeling empowered by gaining insight regarding pivotal moments in her life.

How Is Oral History Distinct From In-Depth Interview?

What is oral history? As we have already said, oral history is a special method of interview where the researcher and research participants spend extended time together engaged in a process of storytelling and listening. In other words, it is a collaborative process of narrative building. However, this alone does not distinguish oral history from other forms of qualitative interview. So the real question is, What makes oral history special? What is unique about this method, how do qualitative researchers use this method, and what does it add to our knowledge of the social world? To explicate the special qualities of oral history, we must differentiate it from in-depth interviewing, which is the most similar method.

As we saw in the last chapter, in-depth interviews are an excellent way to gather rich qualitative data from the perspective of the people being studied. The same is true in an oral history. However, when using in-depth interviews, an interviewer will typically have a focused topic for the interview and will follow an interview guide, which, as we saw, may be semistructured or relatively unstructured. Interviewees may or may not be asked identical questions, depending on the design and goals of the project. Oral history interviews differ in that while the researcher is studying a specific topic, the organization of the topic is likely to be far less focused. For example, if you are interested in studying the body image issues women experience while in college, in-depth interviews may be the appropriate method for focusing on that issue while still allowing participants ample room to qualitatively explain what is important in that regard, from their perspective. Now let's say that you want to study body image issues among college-age women as a part of their life process. If you are interested in the life of the participant from childhood on, such as the various life experiences that may have webbed together to create particular body image vulnerabilities once in college, oral history may be appropriate. This was the case in the study in which Claire participated. Oral history allows you to study a long period of a person's life or even their entire life. You can narrow down the topic, such as body image, work experiences, parenting experiences, and so on, but ultimately, you will get a much more in-depth story from each individual participant. This depth may sacrifice some breadth as they start to detail particular experiences at the exclusion of others, an issue we will address later.

It is not enough to say that you are studying a longer period of time with oral history; in fact, in some cases, this may not even be true. What is really underlying the strength of the method is that you can study *process*. If you are studying a woman's life from childhood through college to understand her body image issues at the present time, what you will learn about is not only what she is currently experiencing and her perspective on that but the *process* that led her there. Likewise, historical processes and circumstances will underscore her narrative in ways that help us understand individual agency within the context of social historical environments. So, while oral history focuses on the individual and her narrative, it can be used to link micro- and macro phenomena (in other words, personal life experiences to broader historical circumstances). Accordingly, oral history is a critical method for understanding life experiences in a more holistic way as compared with other methods of interview. This is in accordance with the tenets of qualitative research and can yield not only rich descriptive data but also knowledge about social processes. Some topics simply lend themselves more to one method. History-driven topics are highly congruent with oral history. For example, if you are interested in studying a historical event or a historical time period and how a certain population experienced that event or lived in that period, oral history may be the best method.

Ryan (2009) used oral history to understand the experiences of women who served in the Navy and Coast Guard during World War II. An interesting pattern emerged during the course of her oral history interviews. The participants almost always diminished the importance of their wartime contributions with statements such as "I didn't do anything important." Ryan wondered why these women would agree to participate in the oral history process and thereby place their experiences in the historical record if they really didn't think they were important. She explored this issue and came to find that the participants did not intend to downplay their military service but were rather using phrases that fit in with society's gender expectations. Therefore, their framing of their experiences occurred within the context of societal expectations. There are numerous examples of how experiences that have not yet been researched could begin to be understood from the vantage point of those who have lived them by using oral history in the way that Ryan did. In this way, previously excluded groups can share their valuable knowledge. In addition to these kinds of expansive experiences, oral history is invaluable in coming to understand how people have experienced historical events of import.

Crothers (2002) launched a fascinating project at Indiana University Southeast in which undergraduate students extensively interviewed community residents about historical events. Specifically, World War II and Korean War veterans were interviewed as were people who lived during the Great Depression. The study had an immeasurable positive effect on both the interviewers and interviewees. One dimension of this outcome could be categorized as community-building because the community learned more about its members. In terms of direct educational benefits, students learned about the relationship between individual experience and sociohistorical conditions, allowing the importance of a historical perspective to emerge during the experience of doing qualitative research.

> After interviewing World War II and Korean War veterans, students no longer view Pearl Harbor, Normandy, Iwo Jima, Hiroshima, and Inchon as distant locations on a map but as places where young Americans like themselves fought and died in miserable conditions and often without recognition. Students learn that though the veterans invariably remembered their service with pride, most had no desire to repeat the experience. Veterans left permanently disabled, both physically and psychologically, and those who were prisoners of war reinforce the lesson that war, even a "good war," should be entered only with trepidation. In short, interviews made a profound impression on students. (Crothers, 2002, p. 3)

In addition, research participants were given a voice and the opportunity to tell their story to interested listeners. This, too, is a profound and important part of the oral history experience.

> Students also interact directly with some of the community's most undervalued members, senior citizens, who share the richness of their lives and experiences. As one student noted, "I think the older people [involved in the project] were made to feel important. *They had a story to tell* and I think college students taking the time to investigate their experience made them feel like someone cared about their sacrifice. (Crothers, 2002, p. 3, emphasis added)

When used in these ways, oral history can meet ideals of education and empowerment as well as substantive knowledge-building. There are also examples of using oral history as a way of understanding current events of import from the perspective of those experiencing them while they are still fresh.

Mears (2008) is the mother of a child who was at Columbine High School the day of the 1999 shootings. She struggled to make sense of the tragedy and wanted to help others dealing with the "community-wide trauma." Using her insider status (shared experience as a Columbine parent), she was able to conduct oral history interviews, as well as other qualitative research, with other Columbine parents about the day of the shootings as well as their experiences in the following years.

Mears notes that an unintended outcome of the research was that the parents gained comfort through reflecting on their experiences. This illustrates the capability of oral history to document people's experiences as well as to "give voice" and at times empower research participants.

Merely days after the terrorist attacks, the September 11, 2001, Oral History Narrative and Memory Project was initiated at Columbia University. Bearman and Marshall Clark were cofounders of this institutionally supported long-term research project. Within 7 weeks after 9/11 the researchers had collected oral history interviews from almost 200 people, and within 6 months, they had collected an additional 200 oral history interviews, including those with volunteers, rescue workers, survivors, and others who lived or worked in the area of Ground Zero. The researchers were interested in understanding the construction of individual and social memory. Specifically, they wanted to understand the role of the mass media and government in the interpretive process of individuals coming to terms with the events that had transpired. Furthermore, as their interviewees were ethnically diverse, they wanted to understand how a heterogeneous group of people who were at the epicenter of the event had interpreted it and filtered the related information and images from the larger culture. How did feelings of patriotism and alienation impact the construction of individual memory during the immediate aftermath? In the minds of those there, does 9/11 qualify as a "turning point" in American history as it has repeatedly been portrayed by media analysts and political leaders? These were among the questions the researchers had as they listened to the stories of those who had experienced the tragedy and were now trying to make sense of it. Oral history became an important way of understanding memory construction as it was actually occurring.

The researchers found that political imagery was an important component in early memory construction. They ended up determining that there were various recurring categories of interpretation that people placed on their experiences to make sense of them. These can also be likened to frames through which people come to interpret their experience of the tragedy. Categories, or frames, included patriotism, flight and refuge, consolation, and solace (Marshall Clark, 2002, p. 7). The frame of interpretation that the researchers were most interested in was the idea of 9/11 as an "apocalypse."

> Perhaps the most important for our ultimate considerations of the significance of September 11 as an axis of national as well as international understanding, the attacks were perceived in direct and indirect ways as an apocalypse. It was registered, in that sense, as a moment that stood outside of time and an event that ended history as we had previously understood it. The interviews we conducted with survivors and eyewitnesses were frequently shot through with religious analogies and metaphors and with apocalyptic imagery from films and movies, demonstrating the ways that many wrestled with questions of good and evil, life and death outside the frame of history as they had previously understood it. (Marshall Clark, 2002, p. 7)

The ability of oral history to tap into the intersection of personal experience, historical circumstance, and cultural frame is clear in the 9/11 oral history study. Sloan

(2008) conducted an oral history project about the aftermath of 2005's Hurricane Katrina. His research raises questions about emotional trauma, historical distance, objectivity, and reflection. Oral history projects that deal with trauma, particularly recent trauma, as in the Columbine, 9/11, and Katrina examples, illustrate the importance of constantly reflecting on how you are dealing with ethical practice throughout the oral history research process. Moving away from these specific examples, we can make some comments about the relationship between biography, history, and culture as revealed by oral history practice.

In a general sense, oral history provides a way to invite people to tell their story—of their past, a past time, a past event, and so on. However, their individual story is always intimately connected to historical conditions and thus extends beyond their own experience. Oral history allows for the merging of individual biography and historical processes. An individual's story is narrated through his or her memory. This means that people's recollection of their experiences, and how they give meaning to those experiences, is about more than accuracy; it is also a process of *remembering*—as people remember, they filter and interpret. Having said this, there is a tension between history and memory—between the collective recorded history and the individual experience of that collective history—that can be revealed, exposed, and explicated though oral history. In this vein, Richard Candida Smith (2001) says, "Memory and history confront each other across the tape recorder" (p. 728). As you can see, oral history is becoming increasingly important in the growing interdisciplinary research on collective memory, which we return to in the conclusion of this chapter.

Similar to the study of historical or current events, oral history is also very useful for studying the individual experience of social change and merging social and personal problems. Slater (2000) used oral history to understand how four black South African women experienced urbanization under apartheid. The women, as perhaps would be expected, had both shared experiences and individual experiences, which are brought out during the oral history process. The data show how structural constraints shaped these women's economic realities in profound ways (p. 38). However, these women also show that their own agency ultimately impacts their lives, as does the social reality that they have in common.

> Life histories enable development researchers to understand how the impact of social or economic change differs according to the unique qualities of individual men and women. This is because they allow researchers to explore the relationship between individual people's ability to take action (their "agency"), and the economic, social, and political structures that surround them. (p. 38)

Slater makes a case that oral history can be an integral method in development research.

As globalization and our study of it increases, oral history can continue to be used to study political, social, and economic changes. In this time of world change, oral history can help us understand both the shared and the personal impact of social upheaval on the individuals living within it. For example, oral history would be a wonderful method for understanding how individuals within Iraq are experiencing the U.S. occupation, political regime shift, and rebuilding of their country.

How do individuals adapt to these major social changes? What are individual coping strategies? How do individuals filter and respond differently to these changes? How has social change impacted people's personal relationships, including courtship, marriage, and parental relationships?

Oral history is also often used to study the experience of oppression—the personal experience of being a member of an oppressed group. Sparkes (1994) conducted an oral history interview project with a lesbian physical education teacher to examine the ways that discrimination and heterosexism shaped her workplace experiences. Personalizing the shared experience of oppression is a strength of oral history.

When using oral history, researchers may interview fewer people in total but spend more time with each participant, which is likely to occur over several pre-planned interview sessions. Qualitatively inclined researchers who work with human subjects, particularly in fields such as sociology, are likely to be drawn to both in-depth interviews and oral history interviews. A choice between the two should be based on the fit between the research goals and research method. When comparing in-depth interviews with oral history interviews, the appropriateness of the method is related to the topic you are pursuing and the number of participants and depth of data that you are seeking. It is important not to privilege one method over the other but rather to focus on the strengths of each. Likewise, the two methods can be combined in multimethod designs, although this is uncommon due to their similarities and the fact that they are both very time-consuming.

Now that you are getting a better handle on how oral histories are distinct from traditional in-depth interviews, it is important to examine more closely why oral histories are special and why feminists in particular have worked so hard to revive, study, broaden, and legitimate their use.

What Techniques Facilitate Data Collection in Oral History?

Building Rapport and Dealing With Difference

During data collection, oral history relies on recording verbal communication between the researcher and research subject. We can break this down further and say that oral history is dependent on two techniques that foster the emergence of data: talking and listening. Before a story is even told, the interviewer and interviewee can begin to understand how to listen and talk in the context of producing a life narrative. It is important that the interviewer and interviewee begin to create a rapport prior to the first recorded interview session (if possible), a rapport that they must attend to throughout the interview process. While rapport is always give-and-take, the primary responsibility is with the researcher who has initiated the research process. This may mean some preliminary discussions so that both parties feel comfortable with each other and begin to become familiar with each other's "talk style."

Prior to the initial meeting, interviewers can discard their own research-oriented time frame in favor of narrators' temporal expectations. Taking time to know another means more than a preliminary interview; it entails meeting for an extended session or more. Congruent with good oral history practice, researchers take the opportunity to solicit narrators' comments and suggestions about the project, including names of potential narrators, other resource persons, and sources for photos, artifacts and written materials. However, the purpose of the initial contact is not just a preliminary interview to obtain data; the meeting is an opportunity to promote collegiality and to engage in mutual self-disclosure. (Minister, 1991, p. 36)

The process of gaining rapport and building collegiality is vital to the successful interview process. Linguistic practices are also a part of this. As we will see later in our section on storytelling, there are various structures people use to tell their stories, and each party must become comfortable with the other's style.

Although we have discussed rapport and reciprocity as critical in the use of all interactive qualitative research methods, these issues are perhaps heightened in the oral history situation—particularly for researchers who envision the process holistically. This is because, as a researcher, you are not simply asking the research participants to allow you to observe naturally occurring behavior that is independent of the research process (as in field research). Likewise, you are not asking a set of questions on a clearly defined topic (such as with in-depth and focus group interviews). When you ask someone to participate in an oral history project, you are asking that person to narrate his or her life story and, through words, to share him- or herself on a deep level. Depending on the nature of the project, you may be asking him or her to revisit difficult times in his or her life without any guarantee that once you have triggered a memory, he or she will be able to "turn it off" at will. Likewise, you may have no idea what directions the person's story will go, once the narrative takes off. Thus, you cannot define all of the topics that will be covered in advance— you simply don't know them yet. Rapport is therefore essential in the oral history process because interviewees place a high level of trust in the researcher and make themselves vulnerable to a range of emotions, feelings, and thoughts that may stretch from very positive and joyous to difficult and painful. When a foundation for trust is established, the collaborative process of oral history can proceed, and research participants will know that the researcher is truly there with them for the ride. As you will see, oral history is an intimate process of two people working together to produce a meaningful biographical narrative.

Given the collaborative nature of oral history, who can do it? Who can be an interviewer? As with all interactive research, issues of difference are an inseparable part of the research process. As such, to what extent can the researcher and narrator differ from one another? For example, some researchers suggest that because different groups within the social order have particular experiences and particular ways of expressing those experiences, "sameness" is integral to a successful oral history interview. Minister (1991) explains that women communicate differently than men, and without supportive communication in return, some women may be muted. As such, women must interview women because they share in a particular sociocommunication subculture and understand how to talk with other women. Other researchers actively incorporate difference into their research but practice reflexivity throughout the project in order to avoid claiming authority over another. For example, Sparkes (1994) conducted an oral history project with a lesbian despite the fact that he differed in terms of both gender and sexual orientation. As such, he did not share in the experience of oppression (and multiple oppressions) that framed his participant's life. As a part of reflexive practice, Sparkes wrote about the experience of interviewing someone who does not share in the unearned social privileges that he enjoys. By incorporating this difference into the entire research endeavor, including the write-up, Sparkes demonstrates that social privilege can be used to help give voice to those typically silenced within the culture. There is much debate in academia about who can be a knower, who can understand the words of another, and so forth. Ultimately, these are personal choices that the researcher must make. In thinking through some of these issues as you select your topic and design your research project, you'll have to consider your epistemological beliefs regarding the relationship between the researcher and researched. When writing up your results, you'll need to consider to what extent you are able to have authority over the life story of another, particularly if you do not share a vital social status (i.e., the experience of oppression due to race, ethnicity, social class, gender, or sexuality).

Listening

During the interview process, the researcher assumes the role of active listener. This role is not simply the role of listener we all enact with friends, family, and colleagues. As the interviewer in an oral history situation, the researcher must learn to listen with a completion and attentiveness that is far more rigorous and in tune with nuance than most of us use in daily life. As such, we must train our minds and ears to *hear* the stories of others, not just the words, but also the meaning, the emotion, the silence. We must listen to the narrator and to ourselves. This process may involve the questioning and disavowing of previously held concepts and categories that frame our understanding of social reality, making the process potentially transformational for the researcher as well. Feminist scholar and oral historian Dana Jack explains that the complexity of "listening" experienced in oral history is *the very thing* that makes this method unique. Let's join her behind the scenes.

BEHIND THE SCENES WITH DANA JACK

What I think the unique aspects are is that what it does is it allows the researcher to situate herself or himself right in the middle between the culture and the individual. And what I mean by that is as we listen to a person, what we hear is an individual's life story in its full idiosyncrasy, with all of the details and all of the sort of particulars of that person's life. But as a researcher, you're also listening for the culture, and so you also know that the very words that people use to explain their lives and their situations also come from the culture, and so they're explaining their life through culturally available stories. And yet, when we listen carefully, you can hear how the individual also participates in all those cultural stories but also brings their different experiences and so what you're listening for is how—to me I'm listening for so many things. One is how the person, the individual, the idiosyncratic story relates to the larger cultural story and how the narratives are available and how those cultural narratives can sometimes obliterate a person's meaning, a person's experience, and then they have to sort out what they think and feel in relation to the larger story, and so I guess what I love about the oral history method is that it lets you listen to the individual really carefully while also still understanding the larger cultural narrative and how the person participates in that. And of course there are many larger cultural narratives. . . .

So it lets, let's see how to say this, well, I don't know (*laughs*). It just lets us, it lets us listen to at least two large voices, one is the individual and the other is the cultural narrative that they dip in and out of. And then how, where's the tension? Where are the questions? Where's the person feeling confused by how their own experience relates to these larger narratives? How and why are they trying to distinguish their experiences, or does the larger narrative try to you know, seem to obliterate it, and what happens then? How do they feel? So I'm always listening for not just one voice, not to that subject's voice only, but how it intertwines and distinguishes itself and is in conflict with other narratives, other larger narratives.

As Jack explains, listening is complex and multifaceted in the oral history process. Listening for layers of meaning, intersecting meanings, and conflicts about meaning is what makes oral history a unique method of knowledge-building.

As qualitative researchers engaged in research involving human participants, we are searching for meaning from the perspective of those being studied. To get at this kind of meaning, we must become nonjudgmental and open listeners. The researcher needs to be right there with participants narrating their story. In this way, we need to "immerse ourselves in the interview" (Anderson & Jack, 1991, p. 18) to hear meaning from the perspective of the person speaking. But how are we to know if what we are hearing is the person's perspective? How do we know that our own life experiences and categories of understanding are not filtering the meaning we take from the experience? While, of course, as imprinted human subjects ourselves, we can't simply disavow our own understandings of social reality, there are techniques that we can apply to the oral history interview in order to better get at meaning from the participant's perspective.

Jack (Anderson & Jack, 1991) suggests three techniques aimed at helping us become more effective listeners. These are specific things we can *listen for*—places where meaning, from the narrator's viewpoint, can be heard. First, researchers can listen to a person's "moral language" (p. 19). These kinds of comments tend to be self-evaluative. How a person evaluates him- or herself can tell us a lot about where the person is placing emphasis in his or her life and how that person uses cultural constructs of success, failure, attractiveness, promiscuity, and so on as measures in his or her own life and identity formation. These comments also provide insights into a person's emotional center, the place of self-confidence and self-scrutiny.

> Although very different in tone, these moral self-evaluative statements allow us to examine the relationship between self-concept and cultural norms, between what we value and what others value, between how we are told to act and how we feel about ourselves when we do or do not act that way. (Anderson & Jack, 1991, p. 20)

For example, if you are conducting an oral history with a woman, and you are talking about some joyous event in her life, such as a special birthday party or other family celebration, and in the midst of her talking, she says, "the cake was really beautiful with ornate decorations, and it was so good, but of course I felt guilty about having so much right there," this would clue you in to several things. This is an example of using moral language—the language of guilt—to impart meaning. This may serve as a signal to the interviewer that there are some body image issues going on or that the participant has concerns about her weight and how she appears to others. Her statement is not, however, occurring in a vacuum, but rather in a cultural context that puts a premium on thinness and self-control, particularly for women. So here you can start to make some links between the participant's self-concept and the larger culture in which she lives. Both what she has said and the way she has said it are important. Such statements may also provide the interviewer with probes to be pursued later or even at a different session with the participant (as to not interrupt the flow of what the narrator wants to say).

The second thing to actively listen for is what Jack terms "meta-statements" (Anderson & Jack, 1991, p. 21). These are places in the interview where interviewees will stop and double back to critically reflect on something they have said in order to comment on the statement. This may illustrate a change in their thought process or a moment of self-realization or discomfort with how their statement may have been perceived and thus a desire to support their words.

> Meta-statements alert us to the individual's awareness of discrepancy within the self—or between what is expected and what is being said. They inform the interviewer about what categories the individual is using to monitor her thoughts, and allow observation of how the person socializes feelings or thoughts according to certain norms. (p. 22)

For example, someone who has just made a comment about race may then double back to clarify, explain, or support the original statement. This kind of cycling back may be a reflection of historically specific societal norms, such as appearing nonracist, and the interviewee's awareness that he or she may have violated those norms in the eyes of the interviewer. Such statements are then one potential space for understanding how individuals feel about and adjust to societal norms, values, and expectations. Here we can reflect back on Ryan's (2009) study of World War II military women. In that oral history project, the participants made statements that appeared to diminish their wartime contributions. However, through further exploration, Ryan found that the women did in fact value their experiences and were using language that they thought met societal expectations of how women should speak of these experiences.

Finally, we must learn to listen to the "logic of the narrative," paying particular attention to consistencies and contradictions and "recurring" themes (Anderson & Jack, 1991, p. 22). More specifically, the way that themes are brought into the person's narrative and their relation to other themes are important data. The placing of emphasis through recurring themes and both consistencies and conflicts within statements can give us insight into the logic the person is using to tell his or her story. For example, what assumptions do people hold to be true that inform how they interpret their own life experiences? What thoughts, beliefs, values, and moral judgments are underlying their interpretive and narrative processes?

Beyond using these listening techniques, Anderson and Jack (1991) also encourage researchers to learn to listen to themselves, and in our experience, this is a critical part of the listening process in oral history. As you listen to the narrator, you must listen to your own internal monitor—your feelings, confusions, questions. These are areas that may require clarification, elaboration, and exploration. You do not want to interrupt the narrator to answer these questions; remember, your primary job is that of listener. However, when pauses and transitions arise, you may want to cycle back and probe based on the various thoughts and feelings you experienced while listening. It is a fine line that through practice you will learn how to navigate. On the one hand, to be an active listener in this collaborative narrative process, you can't just "be in your own head" having an internal conversation; however, you want to be listening to your own gut reactions while you listen to the narrator.

When we choose to practice oral history, we are making a commitment to understanding meaning from the perspective of those being interviewed. We want to know what they think, how they feel, how they filter and interpret. To do so, we become highly engaged listeners. So far, we have been talking about listening to the content of what a participant is saying—the main kinds of statements that emerge as people tell their stories. Equally important to the substantive content of oral history narratives is the form through which people tell their stories; in other words, the narrative style. In this vein, the nuances in the way a person narrates his or her story are also an important data source. We recommend that you come up with a consistent way of transcribing data that allows you to note pauses, laughter, the raising or lowering of voice, tonal changes, the elongation of words, and so forth. All of this can alert you to where a person places meaning and how that person is feeling at a particular point in the interview. Putting such remarks in italics, bold print, parentheses, and so on is an easy way to retain this valuable data in your initial transcript. We will discuss this more later when we talk about transcription and analysis.

In terms of listening, what is missing from a story—silences, absences, feelings for which there are no words—is also a component to the knowledge that emerges. We will talk about narrative style more when we discuss storytelling and "talking" as a method of data building, but for now, we will elaborate on what we mean by listening for silences, bearing in mind that we are meaning seekers.

What is left out of the narrator's story can give us insight into his or her struggles and conflicts, such as differences between his or her explicit and implicit attitudes, but also the impact of the larger culture on the person's biography and retelling of that biography. Clear omissions, for example, may indicate a disjuncture between what people think and what they feel is appropriate to say. This may be the result of their perception of social norms and values or their feeling that they are in violation of normative ways of thinking, feeling, and behaving. For many researchers who practice oral history, such as feminist and multicultural researchers, the research project is imbued with an intent to access subjugated voices—the perspectives of people who are forced to the peripheries of a given social order. In this circumstance, listening for silences may also indicate that the categories and concepts we use to interpret and explain our life experiences do not in fact reflect the full range of experiences out there. The silence, therefore, indicates something about the culture at large and a gap between ways of framing experience and the experience of the individual. In other words, culture may not be providing everyone with appropriate tools with which they can fully and freely express what meaning something has for them. For many, this is the very reason why listening to the voices of individuals, particularly those long excluded from the production of culture, is imperative.

At the heart of the collaborative process of data collection is an emphasis on both listening and talking. The form talking takes is that of storytelling and narrative.

Storytelling and Narrative Styles

During the oral history interview, research participants assume the role of narrator and tell their story. This is a collaborative process of storytelling involving both the narrator and interviewer. The narrator tells his or her story, but the interviewer fosters the narration through the listening and observational techniques described earlier. In addition to the spoken word itself, the way in which a participant tells his or her story is itself recognized as an important knowledge source by oral historians.

Oral historians are interested in attending to the experience and voice of those they study in a comprehensive way, unique to the practice and historical development of the oral history method. Williams (2001) distinguishes between voice and Voice within the research process, using the capital "V" to denote a holistic conception of the term *voice*. Voice in this sense includes nonverbal gestures, intonation, expressions, bodily movements, speech patterns, and silences (p. 43). These components of the interview are a part of the interviewee's full expression of him- or herself. In other words, we must attempt to retain and learn from the *performative* aspects of the storytelling and not allow this to be lost during transcription and analysis (p. 46). Williams encourages researchers to attend to the Voice of the participant more than simply the spoken word provided by an unembellished or "clean" transcript. The researcher can then use his or her listening and observational skills (p. 45) to take fieldnotes or "memo notes" during the interview or transcription process, respectively. Returning more specifically to the role of the participant as narrator and even performer, let's examine storytelling techniques and speech patterns, central components of data building in oral history.

People have different styles for telling their stories. These varying communicative styles result in different kinds of narratives. In this vein, the researcher needs to focus on the "narratology" or narrative structure (Williams, 2001). As critical scholars have long explained, narrative form and language choice also provide important data about the narrator. In this way, the language and speech style used by the narrator do not merely frame the substantive content of the interview but are also an integral part of it. A holistic approach to oral history emphasizes all aspects of the process. Oral historians, who often work from feminist, critical race, and third world theoretical perspectives, are interested in understanding the experiences of those marginalized within society. How has their position within the culture influenced their life experiences as they interpret them, and how have these experiences in turn impacted their approach to storytelling? Etter-Lewis (1991) discusses these issues:

> Language is the invisible force that shapes oral texts and gives meaning to historical events. It is the primary vehicle through which past experiences are recalled and interpreted. Attention to language, its variations and categorical forms, enriches narrative text analysis beyond strictly linguistic concerns. On a most fundamental level, language is the organizing force that molds oral narrative according to a narrator's distinct style. Styles vary as widely as individuals, but recurring patterns indicate more than speakers' personal quirks. Speech patterns inherent in oral narrative can reveal status, interpersonal relationships, and perceptions of language, self, and the world. In the case of black women, we must ask what their narrative patterns reveal about their lives. How do their unique experiences influence the manner in which they tell their own life stories? (pp. 44–45)

To be successful at the art of oral history means, for the critical researcher, to understand, accept, and embrace different narrative styles and, moreover, to recognize their importance rather than ignoring the meanings implied by such difference. This is not without its difficulty. First, scholarly oral history developed within a patriarchal context. Second, those whom we wish to hear may themselves be accustomed to the silence. Let's examine each of these intertwined issues.

In a male-dominated world, male forms of communication are normalized, and communicative expressions that differ from this model are assumed to be less valid. Qualitative interviewing, including oral history, has not been immune to the culture in which it is practiced. The academy is deeply entrenched in male ways of thinking about knowledge construction. Even nonpositivistic research methods have been influenced by male ways of thinking about language, and this includes qualitative interviewing.

> What needs to be altered for women's oral history is the communication frame, not the woman. Oral history interviewing, influenced by its ties to academic history and by the practice of interviewing in general, has developed in the context of the male sociocommunication system. Because in an andocentric world male speaking is the norm, any other kind of speaking is subnormal. (Minister, 1991, p. 31)

Given our immersion in our culture, we are accustomed to male forms of communication (this could, of course, be broadened to include the privileging of all dominant ideals including white and middle- or upper-class styles of communication). So, to perform our role of enabling others to tell their stories, we must be attentive to diversity in communicative styles and narrative forms, which includes being reflexive about how our culture has already influenced our assumptions about "the right way to tell one's story." As such, the researcher must understand the participant's storytelling process and legitimate it.

When working within the assumptions of standpoint epistemology, this idea of communication subcultures is heightened. Standpoint acknowledges different perspectives based on differential positions within a hierarchical social order. One's experiences, visions, and voice are thus earned through being located at a particular point in the social order. Communication strategies may differ based on the intersection of race, ethnicity, class, gender, sexuality, religion, and nationality. In the context of a large oral history project involving the collection of oral history interviews from multiple participants, it is important to bear in mind that there may be differences across and within genders. Take this into account as you prepare to meet with each participant. You cannot assume that based on one characteristic alone a person will mirror the storytelling practices of a previous interviewee. Having said this, despite these differences, there are patterns by which people tend to tell their own life history. We refer to these patterns as **narrative structures.**

Etter-Lewis (1991) identifies three major narrative styles encountered in the oral history interview process: (1) unified, (2) segmented, and (3) conversational. To this, we would add a fourth category, which Kohler-Riessman calls *episodic storytelling.* As with all narrative forms, the way your participant tells her or his story may largely be influenced by factors such as race, class, and gender. Related to these characteristics are education, work, and geographic location.

Often, researchers may have the expectation that participants will hear a topic or guiding question and respond by chronologically explaining their experience regarding the topic, providing in-depth examples to illustrate their experience, and remaining focused on the topic or question. This is the unified narrative style.

> Contiguous parts of the narrative fit together as a whole, usually in the form of an answer to a particular question. Words and phrases all are related to a

central idea . . . the narrator supports her answer as completely as possible by providing several relevant examples. The result is a stretch of discourse unified by its focus on a particular topic. (Etter-Lewis, 1991, p. 45)

People who use such a style of talk may also be telling us something about how they see themselves and how they interpret their life experiences. For instance, a unified approach may indicate that a participant sees the topic clearly and has a cohesive response to it. Beyond the topic at hand, a unified approach may indicate that on a more general level, the narrator experiences life as cohesive and clearly defined. This differs in significant ways from the segmented narrative form, in which

continuous parts of a narrative [are] characterized by a diverse assortment of seemingly unrelated utterances. (Etter-Lewis, 1991, p. 46)

This form of storytelling may be counterintuitive to some researchers who are not used to this form of talk. As such, the initial meetings between the researcher and participant, where listening and talking skills are worked out and rapport is built, become critically important for the researcher to become comfortable with the narrator's speech (and vice versa).

A segmented approach to oral narrative can also reveal meaning from the perspective of the person sharing her or his story. For example, narrators may feel fragmented or believe that the various components of themselves or their experiences are disconnected. This may be true for people who have experienced multiple oppressions due to race, class, gender, and sexuality, which frame their life experiences. In this situation a discussion of female body image disturbances may result in a black narrator talking about how her female mentors taught her coping strategies for dealing with racism, which in effect helped give her the high self-esteem also needed to combat a sexist culture. Her experience of female body pressures brings her to a discussion of race because in her experience, these are interlinked. Her narrative may move around, but in ways that are inextricably linked to her experience of the topic being discussed. There are alternative reasons a narrative may be segmented. If narrators have never been given the opportunity to reflect on the many experiences that comprise their lives, the process of sharing their story may also be an intimate process of self-discovery. Thus, their narrative style may reflect "a putting together of the pieces" for themselves as well as the researcher. What may initially appear as off the subject may actually be quite connected to the primary issue. This is intimately tied to our earlier contention that many of those we ask to speak may in fact be used to being muted due to their marginalization within society. Those denied access to the social tools by which to tell their stories due to their race, ethnicity, social class, gender, or sexuality may simply not have previous experience telling their story. In this vein, Armitage suggests, "We will learn what we want to know only by listening to people who are accustomed to talking" (as quoted by Minister, 1991, p. 32). We can see this in pop culture forms as well, such as Eve Ensler's play *The Vagina Monologues,* in which some interviewed women stated that they had difficulty talking about their sexual experiences simply because no one had ever asked before. They didn't know what to say and were surprised that someone was interested. A segmented approach to narration may in these cases be the result of unearthing thoughts and feelings that had previously been untapped. A process of making the internal orally available for external use may involve a negotiation expressed through words.

Narrators may also recount past conversations as a means of providing an answer to questions. Such an approach may result in an indirect but very important and descriptive answer to a question posed by the researcher. Etter-Lewis (1991) identifies this as a conversational approach to narration which she defines as

> a contiguous part of a narrative identified by the reconstruction of conversations as they probably occurred in the past. Conversational elements are used to illustrate an idea or event. The narrator modifies voice, tone, and pitch in order to represent different speakers and different emotions (e.g., high pitch for anger or surprise). (Etter-Lewis, 1991, p. 47)

Etter-Lewis (1991) asserts that narrators may choose to recount a past conversation instead of directly answering a question as a way of mediating painful or otherwise difficult feelings that come to the surface as a past experience is recalled. In this way, it is a defense mechanism for mediating uncomfortable or particularly strong emotions. It is vitally important to enable this kind of self-protection because, as discussed earlier, neither the researcher nor the research participant can know the extent to which the oral history interview process will bring any given emotion to the surface. Participants need the freedom to deal with unexpected emotions in a way that works for them. The performative repetition of conversations may provide the details and descriptions the researcher is most interested in. Etter-Lewis explains that these recollections may actually serve as a "magnifying glass through which details can be highlighted" (p. 47).

Drawing similarities to segmented and conversational styles of storytelling, some people may use an episodic frame through which they share their story. Kohler-Riessman (1987) contrasted the episodic and linear ways women narrated their marriage life histories. Episodic narrative differs from a unified approach where a teller uses a linear (temporally ordered) model of storytelling. In episodic narration, participants speak by telling stories as episodes within their life. Their speech pattern relies on recounting experiences as episodes that are not chronologically ordered but are rather thematically driven.

Research participants may use more than one of these storytelling techniques as they share their stories with you. Shifts in narrative frames may be important indicators of a narrator's feelings or where they place importance. In keeping with the goals of understanding social meaning from the perspective of those creating it, truly developing one's craft as an oral historian involves understanding the various frames through which people communicate ideas and paying attention to nuance, such as a shift in narrative form. In this regard, the interview process results in more than the flat words on the transcript page, but rather a complex understanding of the person's story as it was told to you.

What Are the Issues of Collaboration and Authority in Oral History?

In 1990, Michael Frisch coined the term *shared authority,* which put a name to an issue of particular salience in the oral history process: the extent to which oral history is collaborative. Frisch used the term *shared authority* to denote the collaboration of the researcher and narrator during interpretation and representation (Thomson, 2003, p. 23). While Part III of this book details the broad issues of interpretation, analysis, and representation that are central to qualitative research, given the particulars of the oral history method, it warrants its own discussion of interpretation.

When using the oral history method, the data collection component of the research process is collaborative. The researcher and research participant create knowledge together through the production of a life narrative. Researchers initiate the process and facilitate the narrator's telling of his or her story. Typically, researchers then transcribe the interview(s) and may add their memo notes to the transcript to account for the performative aspects of the narration and/or add their own feelings, thoughts, questions, and so forth. So in the end, put simply, researchers and narrators work together to produce the raw data: the oral history transcript (and any additional material). But what happens once the interview data has been collected?

Does the collaborative process that shapes data collection continue during analysis and representation? Who gets to put their mark on the story that emerges out of this process? Who has authority over the narrative? What does shared authority mean in practice? Is it always possible or even desirable? What are the ethical considerations involved when determining the degree to which a project will be collaborative? What impact does collaboration have on the researcher, the narrator, and the research? Generally speaking, how do we think about interpreting oral history data? These are just some of the questions the oral historian must consider. Thinking about the qualitative research process holistically requires the researcher to consider issues of interpretation during research design and continue to revisit these questions throughout the research process because qualitative research often involves an openness to change.

At their core, questions regarding collaboration beyond the data collection stage are really questions regarding authority and what we refer to as *the oral history matrix:* the intersection of method, ethic, and politic. Who has authority over the data? Is this authority shared between the researcher and narrator(s)? The complex question of authority is where the oral history matrix of method, ethic, and politic is most clearly seen. Due to its historical development and current uses within the social sciences and humanities, oral history is a research tool merging with a particular set of ethical considerations and social justice politics. When writing about *shared authority,* Shopes (2003) says this:

> This resonant phrase neatly captures that which lies at the heart of both the method and the ethic—or perhaps one should say the politics—of the oral history enterprise: the dialogue that defines the interview process itself and the potential for this dialogue to extend outward—in public forums, radio programs, dramatic productions, publications, and other forms—toward a more broadly democratic cultural practice. (p. 103)

This raises important questions about the extent to which oral history knowledge is collaborative in terms of development as well as subsequent availability and use. The collaborative potential of oral history is not simply a choice about methodology; it also carries with it a set of politics and a host of ethical considerations. Central to these issues is the question posed by Frisch (2003): "Who is the author of an oral history?" (p. 113). In fact Frisch goes on to call our attention to the connection between the words *author* and *authority* demonstrating how representation is imbued with power (p. 113). The person who interprets, formats, and presents the narrative has a certain authority over the data—this person controls the construction of knowledge. So what does it mean for a researcher to "author" another person's story? How involved can the narrator be in this process? What options do qualitative researchers have?

As with all research projects, we recommend that the particular goals of the research project dictate the extent to which the interpretive phase is collaborative. Some projects will lend themselves more to sharing authority during all phases, while other projects will make this impossible or undesirable. Your epistemological beliefs about the relationship between the researcher and research participant will help frame these decisions, as will your ethical and political motivations, but ultimately, the research process must mesh with your goals and resources. All oral history interviews contain collaborative dimensions; however, interpretive strategies can employ a variety of perspectives. It may be helpful to think of oral history as existing on a collaboration continuum—projects can vary from being collaborative exclusively during data collection to being thoroughly collaborative from initial research design through representation. In this regard, Frisch (2003) makes an important point:

> Sharing authority is an approach to doing oral history, while a shared authority is something we need to recognize in it. (p. 113)

Let's examine some of the pros and cons of using a shared authority approach to oral history by looking at various oral history research projects and how researchers have theorized and negotiated collaboration and authority in diverse ways.

Decentering Authority and Democratic Practice

Holistic collaboration, that which engages the researcher and narrator during all phases of knowledge production, is often appealing to those working from critical theoretical perspectives. Likewise, this approach may be appropriate for research projects with the objective of creating social change or prompting social activism. Accordingly, as critical perspectives and social movement research are both on the rise, we are seeing an increase in collaborative research. This raises the question: Why are these folks particularly attracted to sharing authority?

Oral history is unique because it has the potential for decentering authority (Frisch, 1989; Shopes, 2003). As discussed in Chapter 1, historically, researchers have been privileged as the knowing party, and they have had control over the research process and resulting knowledge. The researcher's authority over the data included analysis, representation or writing, and the dissemination of the resulting knowledge. For example, will the results be published? Where? How will they be used? Oral history assumes that the research participant has life experiences, thoughts, and feelings that can help us to better understand social reality or some aspect of it. In other words, the research participant has unique and valuable knowledge. The participants alone have access to their own stories and accordingly assume the role of narrator. This method thus allows research participants to maintain authority over their knowledge during data collection. The oral history method inherently challenges positivist and postpositivist conceptualizations of the researcher-researched relationship and, moreover, necessarily shifts at least some authority to the research subject. Scholars working from critical theoretical perspectives are committed to destabilizing relations of oppression and repositioning those historically at the peripheries of the social order to the center of the knowledge-building process. Feminist and critical race scholars are interested in decentering authority as well, so that women and people of color are given a central and authoritative position within the knowledge-building process. By changing the locus of knowledge and creating engaged researchers and narrators, oral history lends itself to collaboration and the oppositional possibilities inherent in a collaborative knowledge-building process. The resistive dimension of sharing authority is also inextricably linked to ideas regarding democratic knowledge production, which may be particularly resonant for social movement and social action researchers.

The use of collaborative approaches to oral history bears traces of the earlier paradigm shift that prompted the development of qualitative research and wide-ranging changes in our conceptualizations of knowledge and the knowledge-building process. Some oral historians working in the area of social movements, public policy, and social activism advocate sharing authority during all phases of the research project in order to create democratic knowledge production, which can most effectively benefit those groups for whom we often conduct our research. This is because collaboration allows researchers to speak *with* their participants instead of *for* them. This democratic approach to knowledge construction relieves some of the questions of social power that permeate traditional research while allowing those we wish to empower to teach us how to accomplish our goals. Kerr (2003) argues that sharing authority "can play a significant role in movement building" (p. 31). Referring to Frisch's work, Kerr writes:

> He argues for "a more profound sharing of knowledges, an implicit and sometimes explicit dialogue from very different vantages about the shape, meaning and implications of history." He argues that this dialogue will "promote a more democratized and widely shared historical consciousness, consequently encouraging broader participation in debates about history, debates that will be informed by a more deeply representative range of experiences, perspectives and values." I would add that the dialogue built on this basis needs to go beyond the way we view history, but also influence the way we design public policy and more importantly, the way we reproduce the social organization of the communities we live in. (p. 31)

In this vein, a collaborative approach to oral history analysis and representation extends beyond incorporating multiple voices and perspectives into our writing of history and can help shape the organization of our communities and the formulation of public policy. In this way, oral history can promote multidirectional change. It is not surprising that social movement scholars have embraced this approach.

Kerr (2003) designed an oral history research project using collaborative analysis to study homelessness. As a part of his dissertation research, Kerr spent years working on the Cleveland Homeless Oral History Project. This research, which involved multimedia interviews, is an excellent example of applying a shared authority approach holistically because it effectively enables particular research objectives. Kerr wanted to conduct research that could create meaningful dialogue among homeless people in Cleveland, which could foster the development and *implementation* of public policy changes aimed at reducing homelessness in U.S. urban centers. Kerr argues that traditionally the research on homelessness has failed to create conversations on a street level and, thus, without substantive input from the homeless themselves, resulting data hasn't garnered the support needed to both create and execute effective social policy.

> Advocates and academics studying homelessness in the United States have primarily sought an audience of public officials, civic leaders, and middle and upper class progressives, who they believe have the power to create change. In part this focus has been structured by the public officials themselves who have encouraged this approach, seeking advice on the homeless problem almost exclusively from social service providers and academic experts. There is little incentive for academics to work collaboratively with the homeless. Those who have had the most success having their voice heard at the national policy level . . . have devised solutions without the input and oversight of the homeless and have done little to generate support for their solutions among the homeless. (p. 28)

The failure to produce knowledge that has successfully been used to alleviate homelessness is largely a result of two factors: (1) researchers cannot study misery from a neutral and detached position of authority and (2) homelessness has a structural dimension supported by powerful interests who benefit from maintaining the system (Kerr, 2003, p. 30). Accordingly, Kerr had to give up the traditional privileged position of the "researcher as knower" and work collaboratively with the homeless in order to reveal trends, generate theory, advocate sensible policy changes, and effectively implement them.

> By broadening the scientific community through the process of sharing authority with the homeless, one does not give up objectivity; rather one produces more objective and effective research. Theories and solutions that garner support are effectively implemented, and successfully address common problems [that] are objectively better than those that do not. (p. 32)

In this circumstance, sharing authority was clearly the logical approach to the oral history process and promoted the integration of the researcher's ontological, epistemological, theoretical, and methodological choices, creating a robust and layered body of applicable knowledge. This knowledge cannot be separated from its democratic process of production and, thus, in every way signifies the issues it implicitly raises about who gets to participate in the construction of our communities.

In addition, Kerr reported that the research participants were empowered through their participation. The process helped the homeless to become agents for social change in an arena that is directly relevant to their daily lives rather than remain victims of a failed system.

Empowerment, Ethics, and Conflict Within Collaboration

It is not difficult to understand how sharing authority has the effect of narrator empowerment. Certainly, people are more likely to feel empowered when they are fully included and valued and when they are operating on an even playing field. Rickard (2003) writes that the research participants in her collaborative study of British sex workers also felt empowered by the oral history process. Rickard's work is important because it raises key ethical questions about empowerment, advocacy, and sharing authority.

Is it always ethical to empower our research participants? What if they are engaged in illegal activity or an activity that we find morally or politically troublesome? As engaged researchers, where is the line between empowerment and advocacy? If we feel an obligation to benefit our research participants by empowering them (if possible), do we necessarily endorse their behavior? These are questions Rickard had to face when she shared authority with British sex workers, including using one as an interviewer. Rickard (2003) adopts a "sex positive" perspective, which has opened her scholarship up to scrutiny. Some likened her collaborative research design to promoting prostitution (p. 53).

Hence, by undertaking oral history in this area, I had to align myself with the "pro-sex work" political lobby and to become involved with the activities of national and international activist groups who support sex workers' rights. The activist involvement also came from the deep concern with sharing authority. To ensure people's stories were recorded and collected I had to be prepared to use a position of academic privilege to offer political and practical support to interviewees, to facilitate communication through international networks, and to use oral history material for political and educational purposes. For me, this has led to a number of offshoot projects, such as the organization of a U.K. conference for sex workers, and the initiation of a health education project using extracts of OHP tapes as the basic resource. It has also involved me in local and national activist meetings and the use of oral history material as an educational resource for health workers. Over time, I have slowly realized that other sex work oral history has always tended to be carried out from a similar "sex positive" perspective to my own and nearly always in a context of personal and political advocacy. (p. 54)

Rickard is reflexive about her personal political alignment with her narrators and discloses how this impacts data analysis and her resulting scholarship. While we do not think it is necessary to comment on Rickard's research choices per se, we think it provides a valuable example from which we can contemplate our own research. By engaging in a thorough discussion of both the context of discovery and the context of justification, readers of Rickard's work are given enough information about the research process and the researcher's relationship to the work that they can interpret her work as they deem fit. In this way, she has done her job and also provided a robust case study for examining how we all engage in the oral history matrix of method, ethics, and politics. This brings us to a host of additional issues surrounding collaborative interpretation.

While some research projects necessitate heightened collaboration, others may be impeded by attempts to share authority. Likewise, collaborative interpretation may alter the research in ways with which the researcher is uncomfortable. As interpretation is a fundamental component of sense making or meaning construction, collaboration deeply impacts knowledge-building and is not necessarily desirable.

Collaboration is a responsible, challenging and deeply humane ideal for some oral history work, but in certain kinds of projects, beyond a basic respect for the dignity of all persons, it seems not an appropriate goal. . . . Taking the full measures of views other than your own is one thing; failing to subject them to critical scrutiny is yet another. Is presenting differing views in point/counterpoint fashion itself a form of critical inquiry? Is it enough? We need to think more about the limits and possibilities of oral history work with those with whom we do not share a fundamental sympathy. (Shopes, 2003, p. 109)

Shopes raises several important points while reaffirming that a holistic application of shared authority is only one approach to oral history. It is perfectly reasonable and often appropriate for the researcher to retain authority over the interpretive process. As researchers we can maintain critical theoretical (and other human rights) perspectives without placing the interpretive views of our narrators at the same level on which we place our own analysis. We need not invite the narrator to participate in the research process beyond the interview sessions if our project doesn't warrant it. Our scholarship and our emotional well-being may require that we do maintain strict intellectual authority over the process of representation.

For example, the body image oral history project that opened this chapter necessitated a separation between the researcher and narrator during data analysis. "Claire" was still deeply in the throes of anorexia nervosa, and her health was rapidly declining at the time of the project. Despite her obvious ongoing battle, Claire repeatedly insisted that she was now healthy and had "clarity" over her "former" disorder. In the case of anorexia, it is clear that this kind of mind-set is common among women in the thick of an eating disorder. Her ability to judge the situation in a useful way was seriously hampered by her illness. In addition to her deep-seated denial, she was physically failing (which also had an apparent impact on her mental faculties). All of this made a collaborative analysis impossible and undesirable. In this type of situation, the researcher has to maintain intellectual authority over the data in order to generate meaning that is true to the story told by the narrator. This can be hard if you have a strong connection to your narrator; however, as the researcher you need to think of the overall process and the eventual knowledge, which may mean making a difficult decision. In our example, at the time, Claire did not have the ability to effectively help interpret the web of pressures that culminated in her body image disturbance. Even in situations where a narrator is "able" to participate in the interpretive process, it simply may not be something that interests the researcher. This is fine, too.

> At a basic level, I do think that the interview dynamic is collaborative. But I also think we need to think carefully where we wish to share intellectual control over our work and where we don't. We do need to be clear where and how we want to differ with narrators, perhaps in the interview itself, more likely in what we write based on interviews. We need to be clear when we wish to be critical of narrators, when there is no room for a shared perspective. (Shopes, 2002, cited in Shopes, 2003, p. 109)

For example, what if your narrator is racist, sexist, or homophobic? If we are committed to the spirit of social justice, then there are times when shared authority simply isn't an option. Regardless of whether or not we share a "fundamental sympathy" (Shopes, 2003, p. 109) with those we interview, we need to seriously consider the place of our own intellectual voice within our work. This requires us to construct, question, negotiate, and renegotiate the boundaries of collaboration within any particular project—always reflecting on the fit between our choices and our research objectives. Likewise, we think it is important for qualitative researchers to write openly about this process to assist others in thinking through the complexity of collaborative research and make informed decisions about where on the continuum any given project will fall. Let's look at an example that illustrates the importance of staying true to one's voice and the potential pitfalls of ill-defined collaboration.

Sitzia (2003) wrote a case study about the relationship she had with her oral history narrator as they tried to share authority while producing his autobiography over a 6-year period. Her experience illuminates the rewards and dangers inherent in collaboration.

Sitzia (2003) shared important insider traits with her narrator, Arthur, particularly a working-class background, and common interests, which together facilitated a wonderful data-building rapport between the two.

> This constant dialogue between me and Arthur enriched the process of working on another's life story. I quickly moved from being an interviewer to a facilitator in helping Arthur uncover his past. The development of the dialogue within the process was only possible through our relationship. (p. 94)

The kind of mutual engagement with, and shared ownership of, the project produces data that may otherwise remain hidden. However, the engagement required for collaboration has an emotional price and can at times be overwhelming. Likewise, while some scholars feel their work is enriched through shared interpretation, others may experience an unwanted loss of intellectual authority over their research, as Sitzia (2003) explains.

> When our work began . . . I felt very pleased with the way the project was progressing . . . [but] as . . . we drew closer to the publication of a book, Arthur began behaving aggressively; putting substantial pressure on me to work more quickly, threatening to complete the work with another editor, and most importantly, raising issues of ownership: "our" book became only "Arthur's" book. This situation was made worse by the fact that Arthur was going through a severe emotional and mental health crisis, which also meant that he became very dependent on me, calling in varying states of distress at all times of the day and night. I felt—and still do feel—a huge responsibility for Arthur and felt I should help him resolve his crisis, but did not feel equipped to do this. On reflection, these complications partly arose because of the experimental nature of the project: neither I nor Arthur had worked in such a collaborative way before. My approach to the project was an informal learning experience. . . . I now believe that it is crucial to define clear boundaries and guidelines when embarking on a project of this nature. At the beginning of this collaboration I directed the work to a large extent and certainly had a "voice;" one consequence of this lack of clarity is that as the project progressed I felt that I gradually lost authority, that Arthur became more and more dominant—and in fact bullying—and my own voice seemed to be lost. (p. 97)

This illustrates the tensions a researcher may face when trying to determine where to place a project on the continuum of shared authority. In the end, Sitzia (2003) came to understand that, in the case of her project, both she and Arthur could "own" it by being open to multiple outcomes from the one study. She and her narrator are thus free to draw on the work in various ways and, through those unexpected avenues, they can each make their own mark on the knowledge they have created. Sitzia uses aspects of the project in her writing while Arthur is able to use it in his performance pieces. This required them to let go of the idea that "one book" would be the outcome of this process and consider multiple outcomes. We think it is important to remain open to the data being used in multiple ways, as was the resolution here; however, we caution that this is not always appropriate and must be carefully contemplated by the researcher. Make choices and find resolutions that make sense in a particular circumstance.

Despite the difficulties that can arise, collaboration can be a worthwhile or necessary practice. It is therefore helpful to be proactive, design your study well, and remain open to modifications as practice dictates. If you decide to share authority with your narrators, we suggest the following strategies for dealing with the specific challenges you may encounter.

- Create clear boundaries regarding the relationship between the researcher and narrator. In other words, devote some substantial time to defining your relationship. Talk this through together so there is mutual clarity. Continue to have these conversations throughout the various phases of the process so you are constantly reinforcing your definitions and expectations (while modifying them as appropriate to growth in the relationship). This relationship must be tended to holistically.

- Set up precise expectations regarding each person's role(s) in the collaborative process. Issues to discuss and come to an agreement on include the following:
    - The transcription process
    - Fieldnotes and theoretical memo writing
    - Analysis procedures
    - Interpretation and theory-building
    - Writing and/or representation
    - The use of the results (including how many possible outcomes are expected)

- Construct practical ideas for how to deal with potential interpretive conflicts.
    - What degree of difference does each party expect to have included in the final write-up?

By thinking these things through, you can avoid many potential pitfalls—this is time well spent. You can thus be open to less traditional approaches to oral history that may allow the asking and answering of new social scientific questions. Don't be afraid to create new methodologies as long as you remember that experimentation necessitates both openness and rigor.

Archiving Oral Histories

As you have already seen, qualitative research in general, and oral history in particular, demand a high degree of ethics in practice. The archiving of oral history transcripts or projects is an important part of the oral history process. The American Historical Association has determined that arranging to deposit oral history interviews in an archival repository is a part of ethical research. The archiving of oral history materials, which makes them available for a host of future uses, may influence the research process in many ways. If a participant is well informed about the research and its outcomes, as they should be through informed consent, then the knowledge the interview will be archived may influence their storytelling. This is particularly salient when unedited interviews will be archived as narrators understand their initial telling of their story will be documented and made available forever.

The deliberate consideration of what can and should be said, and how it should be said, is pronounced when interview transcripts are specifically prepared for archival purposes because narrators will seek to prepare their narratives for an undetermined public audience. This has a double-edged effect.

On the one hand, it can produce more accurate recollections and fuller accounts if narrators take the time to refresh their memories by consulting old documents, and/or other people who experienced the same events. On the other hand, however, it may produce more of a "canned speech," or a more carefully crafted statement that is sensitive to wider implications of what is said. (Wilmsen, 2001, p. 72)

Edited interviews, intended for archival deposit, present their own set of challenges.

Analyzing, interpreting, and writing up your data is always a part of meaning making. Producing a version of the work can be equated with producing meaning itself—creating knowledge. Editing is therefore tied up with the construction of meaning (Wilmsen, 2001). As the researcher, how are you going to edit the transcript? Will you "clean it up" in terms of pauses, "ums," "likes," and the other informal ways people speak? Will you fix grammar? Will you change the particulars of the narrator's way of speaking, and, if so, what implications does this have in terms of meaning construction? Will you delete or add emphasis to convey meaning? And, if so, meaning from whose perspective: yours, the narrator's, or your interpretation of the narrator's meaning? How is all of this influenced by social class, race, gender, and other characteristics? In other words, what are the implications in changing the grammar of a narrator from a lower socioeconomic background? What are the implications of changing, or adding your own explanations for slang words, which may be the product of ethnic background and other social characteristics? These are all considerations when determining how to edit the transcript. Wilmsen (2001) cautions that these choices are interlinked with social power—the power to construct and disseminate what is deemed "knowledge."

A significant feature of the social relations of oral history interviews is the power relations between the interviewer and the narrator. Gender, class, race, and other social considerations enter into every interview situation to a greater or lesser extent. They affect editing through narrator and interviewer/editor perceptions of the social status similarities or differences between them, which in turn shape their understandings of their respective roles. The importance this has for editing is the way in which power relations are interwoven with differing experience with the written word. The fact that narrators have varying experience with the written word, the world of publishing, research archives, libraries, et cetera, affects what editing decisions are made, who makes them, and why. (p. 75)

As with all of the choices a researcher makes when thinking about interpretation and representation, editing is an important arena in which meaning production occurs. Reflexive researchers must consider issues of difference and research power relations as a part of ethical practice.

The extent to which the research process is collaborative will also impact the editing process. If narrators are involved in the interpretive process, they will likely have input on reflection. In other words, when reviewing the raw transcript, it is very likely that narrators will recall things that were forgotten at the time of the interview, which they may want to add. Likewise, they may want to elaborate or edit parts of the transcript. As a part of ethical practice, we encourage you to share your transcripts with your narrators for their approval and input; however, we caution that this, of course, raises many possible responses. Ultimately, the degree of influence the narrator will have on the editing process is linked to the issues of authority previously discussed.

Technological advancements have also impacted the practice of oral history with respect to editing and archiving. In addition to audiotaping, some researchers now videotape their interviews. Audio or video interviews can be turned into digital data. Frisch (2008) has been at the forefront of discussing the role of these emerging technologies on the practice of oral history. He suggests there are two major impacts of digitization. First, in digital form, there is no difference between text, photos, music, visuals, and so on. Data in all of these forms "can be expressed as digital information that can be organized, searched, extracted, and integrated with equal facility" (p. 226). Second, in digital form, any point in the data can be accessed immediately. A researcher or reader can move to any point in the data in a nonlinear manner to code, search, and so forth. For example, one can move to any scene on a DVD or any point on a CD. These technological changes impact data analysis considerably. Software programs make it possible for researchers to tag, annotate, or link pieces of data in a variety of ways. Whereas in the past software could assist only with textual data, now software can perform these functions for "nonlexical content or qualities" such as tone, voice, body language, and so forth (Frisch, 2008, p. 226). Digitization also means that oral history interviews that are archived in digital form can be accessed and used with ease in comparison with the "old" ways of searching through transcripts for the data in which one is interested. As researchers and archivists continue to take advantage of these technological possibilities, the ethical implications of digitization will need sustained reevaluation.

Conclusion

As you have seen, oral history is an intense, rewarding, and flexible research method. It is particularly useful for gathering rich data from the perspective of those who have traditionally been marginalized within the culture and excluded from their own documented representation. In this way, oral history allows narrators to use their voice and reclaim authority in an empowering context where their valuable life experiences are recognized as an important knowledge source. Oral history is also an excellent tool for situating life experience within a cultural context. In other words, personal stories can be interlinked with collective memory, political culture, social power, and so forth, showing the interplay between the individual and the society in which he or she lives.

Oral history is a collaborative process that must be conceptualized holistically. Special attention must be paid to the relationship between the researcher and narrator, and clear guidelines should be employed through a rapport-building dialogue that is revisited throughout the project. As we have outlined, a researcher needs to consider the oral history matrix: the interplay between the method, ethical considerations, and politics.

Glossary

Narrative structures: There are three major narrative styles encountered in the oral history storytelling process: (1) unified, (2) segmented, and (3) conversational. To this, we would add a fourth category, which Kohler-Riessman calls *episodic storytelling*. As with all narrative forms, the way participants tell their stories may largely be influenced by factors such as race, class, gender, education, work, and geographic location.

Oral history: A method of open-ended interview, usually occurring in multiple sessions, where a researcher aims at interviewing a person about her or his life or a significant aspect of it. This is a highly collaborative interview method resulting in a co-created narrative.

Discussion Questions

1. Discuss some of the differences between oral history and in-depth interviews.

2. In what ways does oral history benefit the researcher and participant?

3. What is the significance or importance of building rapport with your research participant? How does the establishment of a good relationship between the researcher and research participant contribute to a successful oral history?

4. What is shared authority, and how is it distinct in oral history? We note a few instances in which a shared authority would not be beneficial to the research process. Can you think of any other instances? What are some of the problems that can arise?

5. What are some things a researcher should consider when deciding whether to use a collaborative strategy? What are some of the ethical considerations a researcher must keep in mind when determining the degree to which an oral history project will be collaborative? What kind of guidelines can help collaborative research work effectively?

6. How does oral history help us to bring about social change and aid in social activist efforts?

7. Do you believe the collaborative process that shapes data collection should continue on during the analysis and representations phases of the research project?

8. In what ways can society impact the ways in which a person tells his or her story, and why is it critical for the researcher to cue into this?

9. Oral history can be an empowering experience for both the researcher and the research subject. In what ways can this be true?

10. If, for example, you were interested in how teenage females internalize images of female beauty in American society, how would the use of oral history be beneficial as opposed to an in-depth interview method?

Resources

Suggested Web Sites

The General Commission on Archives and History

http://www.gcah.org/oral.html

This Web site is a clear-cut, easy-to-understand guide to oral history interviewing. It gives the steps of interviewing as well as useful tips and a reference list of books and articles.

How to Collect Oral Histories

http://www.usu.edu/oralhist/oh_howto.html

This Web site explains what recording oral histories entails. It also has a link to other useful Web sites dealing with collecting oral histories.

Oral History Interviewing

http://www.cps.unt.edu/natla/web/oral_history_interviewing.htm

This Web site gives a step-by-step easy guide to understanding and conducting oral histories. It also has a link to a sample release form and sample interview questions.

Center for the Study of History and Memory

http://www.indiana.edu/~cshm/oral_history.html

This site has links to techniques for oral history interviewing, resources, newsletters, and forms. The most useful link at this site is the techniques link, which provides a lengthy description of techniques for oral history.

Center for Oral History

http://www.lib.lsu.edu/special/williams/index.html

This Web site offers a list of publications including some online publications. It also has links to projects, forms, other sites, and its newsletter. The mission of the Williams Center is to collect and preserve, through the use of tape-recorded interviews, unique and valuable information about Louisiana history that exists only in people's memories and would otherwise be lost.

American Sociological Association

http://www.asanet.org/public/IRBs_history.html

This link contains information about oral history interviews and protection provisions.

Relevant Journals

History & Memory

Memory Studies

Oral History Review

The Journal of American History

CHAPTER 7

Focus Group Interviews

Comparisons to other methods have thus led to the conclusion that the real strength of focus groups is not simply in exploring what people have to say, but in providing insights into the sources of complex behaviors and motivations. (Morgan & Krueger, 1993, as cited in Morgan, 1996, p. 139)

Sometimes as researchers, we are interested in topics we don't know that much about. The area we are interested in may be a new or underresearched topic. As noted in Chapter 1, this is an appropriate situation in which to conduct *exploratory research* (also called *discovery*). Let's say that we are interested in Internet dating among 30-somethings. Why do people turn to Internet dating? How do they make this decision? What is their protocol for evaluating possible dates? In what ways are Internet first dates qualitatively different than non-Internet first dates? These may be some of the questions guiding our research process. As with any new project, we would begin by conducting a literature review to see what research we already have available in this area. Let's say our initial literature review indicates that very little has been done on this newly widespread phenomenon. As such, focus groups may be a useful method to gain **exploratory data** that can stand on its own or then be used to shape future research, such as qualitative in-depth interviews or quantitative surveys.

What Are Focus Group Interviews?

In a focus group, multiple participants are interviewed together, making the focus group distinct from the one-on-one methods of interview discussed in the last two chapters. Focus groups have a distinct advantage over other available research methods when the researcher doesn't know what all of the issues surrounding a topic are. Focus groups can help the researcher inductively figure out what the key issues, ideas, and concerns are from multiple participants at once. The data will be qualitative in nature and thus descriptive and process oriented, giving the researcher depth and breadth to a subject about which very little is known. In other words, focus groups can be used to gain needed exploratory data. This is one example of why a qualitative researcher may use focus groups. However, focus groups are used for more than just exploratory research. Focus group interviewing is not simply about interviewing several people at once but constitutes an entirely specific approach to research.

Some Background on Focus Groups

Focus groups developed in the 1940s (Betts, Baranowski, & Hoerr, 1996) and are used for a variety of purposes in many different fields. Although famed sociologist Robert K. Merton used focus groups in the 1950s (Merton & Kendall, 1946), market researchers have historically made most frequent use of focus groups. This is because focus groups are an economical way to gather a relatively large amount of qualitative data from multiple human subjects. To increase the vendibility of their products, companies often employ market researchers to conduct focus group interviews with consumer target groups. This strategy is used to evaluate a product's likability, to help market new products, and to aid in the advertising of new, old, and "improved" products. Researchers conducting these kinds of focus groups may face unique pressures "to perform," as clients often watch the group from behind one-way mirrors. As we will see later, these pressures may significantly influence the structure of the group and level of researcher participation. In market research, focus groups are also frequently video recorded (Puchta & Potter, 1999). Focus groups are effective in market research because they are good for exploring people's feelings, thoughts, and behaviors (Costigan Lederman, 1990). More specifically, Bristol and Fern (1996) outline three different purposes for which focus groups are used in market research: (1) clinical, (2) exploratory, and (3) phenomenological. They are used for "clinical purposes" to "uncover consumers' underlying feelings, attitudes, beliefs, opinions, and the subconscious causes of behavior" (Bristol & Fern, 1996, p. 186). When used for "exploratory purposes," which Fern and Bristol explain they are particularly well suited for, they help "generate, develop, and screen ideas or concepts" (p. 186). Researchers have "phenomenological purposes" when they are interested in "discover[ing] consumers' shared everyday life experiences, such as their thoughts, feelings, and behavior" (p. 186).

Focus groups are also a common method of data collection in evaluation research. They are used when a program of some kind needs to be evaluated to help measure its success, strengths, and weaknesses and also to help qualitatively *explain* the nature of what is and is not working. For example, new educational programs are frequently evaluated through focus group research to understand their strengths and weaknesses. Focus groups are also useful in developing the content of new programs. Likewise, focus groups are an effective method of evaluating a range of early intervention programs in a multitude of social welfare organizations and agencies (Brotherson, 1994). The qualitative data yielded is important because it can help us to develop an understanding of the issues with which families, individuals, and agencies deal (Brotherson, 1994). Focus groups are also employed to evaluate issues and programs within the criminal justice system (Matoesian & Coldren, 2002). For instance, Matoesian and Coldren (2002) review how focus groups were used to gain insight into a community policing program. In that case, a small focus group was used consisting of three members of the community and a moderator who was a member of the community policing program.

For the past four decades, focus groups have been increasingly used across academic disciplines including criminal justice, education, health care, media studies, psychology, and sociology. Kitzinger (1994) explains that focus groups are particularly useful in gaining data from populations traditionally referred to as "difficult" (p. 112). These people may feel unsafe, disenfranchised, or otherwise reluctant to participate in research. Examples of such groups include AIDS patients, welfare recipients, and drug users. Focus groups may become more popular in medical sociology as a means of accessing stigmatized populations about a range of topics, such as fertility, grief, depression, and cancer (p. 112). Likewise, focus groups are an important tool for accessing the experiences and attitudes of marginalized and minority groups, including racial/ethnic minorities, sexual minorities, women, children, the mentally and physically challenged, and so on. Dodson, Piatelli, and Schmalzbauer (2007) advocate using focus groups composed of people from marginalized or disenfranchised groups as a part of a feminist participatory methodology. They suggest that, in this context, focus groups can serve as "safer spaces" for people to share experiences and perspectives. The ability to access "subjugated voices" may be a part of the recent surge in focus group exploration by academics, which corresponds to increased attention to critical race, feminist, postmodern, and queer theory perspectives. In addition to working with marginalized groups, Goltz (2009) suggests that focus groups can be used for education, exploration, and collaborative generation. Overall, the wide use of focus group interviews indicates that they can be a part of research design for a breadth of research questions and agendas.

Focus groups may be a profound experience for both the researcher and participants. They also generate a unique form of data. They tell the qualitative researcher things about social life that would otherwise remain unknown. In this chapter, we will explain qualitative focus groups as a method and source of data. We will discuss the varied ways they are used across disciplines in contained and multimethod designs, why we feel they are a distinctive experience, and what they contribute to our overall knowledge. As you will see, focus group interviews result in data that is not comparable to the sum total of individual interviews or oral histories. We will now move into a discussion of the data collection process, followed by research design and mixed and multimethod approaches,[1] and finally data analysis and representation.

The Differences Between Focus Group Interviews and In-Depth Interviews During Data Collection

When thinking about why a researcher would use focus group interviews as a part of research design versus in-depth interviews, we must look at the differences between these two interview methods. While an obvious distinction is that focus groups are the only method of qualitative interview where multiple participants are interviewed simultaneously, what does that actually mean in terms of the kinds of research questions focus groups can help us answer and the particular form of data generated by focus groups?

Focus group interviews are fundamentally different from in-depth interviews because data are generated in a group composed of the researcher and participants. It is a dynamic process based on interaction between multiple people. This dynamic can be thought of as producing a "happening" that cannot be replicated. In other words, the interaction and conversation within any given group will not be reproduced in another group (even if conducted by the same researcher). This is because participants, even if they hold similar views, attitudes, and life experiences, are not merely responding to questions posed by a researcher but they are also *responding to each other* and the group dynamic as a whole. The same researcher could conduct two focus groups on the same topic, with participants who share common characteristics, yet the data will differ because it is produced within a different conversation. Sometimes, researchers use "repeat focus groups" (Morgan, 2008), which are repeated focus groups with the same participants, and still a different conversation occurs. Likewise, a conversation fosters kinds of communication that are unlikely to occur in an in-depth interview (and remain almost exclusively untapped by quantitative survey research). Kitzinger (1994) notes, "Everyday forms of communication such as anecdotes, jokes, or loose word association may tell us *as much,* if not *more,* about what people 'know.' In this sense focus groups 'reach that part that other methods cannot reach'—revealing dimensions of understanding that often remain untapped by the more conventional one-to-one interview or questionnaire" (p. 109).

These forms of communication are an important source of data and can be a significant part of the knowledge-building process—particularly in qualitative research.

A focus group can be thought of as a happening in which a rich conversation occurs, but while dynamic and unpredictable, it is not a naturally occurring conversation. It is important not to confuse the conversational structure of focus groups with naturally occurring talk, as focus groups are always arranged by a researcher for the purpose of research. The fundamental characteristic of focus groups during data collection is that the group dynamic starts to create a story. The narrative produced by the group begins to take hold and guide the production of data. Accordingly, group interviews are extremely useful for identifying the language, definitions, and concepts that the research participants find meaningful as they navigate through their daily life experiences.

> Group work ensures that priority is given to the respondents' hierarchy of importance, *their* language and concepts, *their* frameworks for understanding the world. (Kitzinger, 1994, p. 108)

As we will discuss later, the production of this kind of data makes focus groups an increasingly common tool in survey question development. This aspect of group work, however, may also be very attractive to researchers working from "power-sensitive" critical theoretical perspectives. In this vein, Frey and Fontana (1991) explain that group interviews can alleviate some of the concerns postmodern researchers have regarding the hierarchy between researcher and researched even in an in-depth interview. Typically, the researcher is ultimately privileged as the "authoritative voice." However, focus groups create data from multiple voices, which together create a narrative (p. 178).

While we refer to the *context* of a focus group as a happening, the dynamic produced *within* the group is termed **the group effect** (Carey, 1994; Morgan, 1996; Morgan & Krueger, 1993). The group effect serves as an important and unique source of data and is why focus group data are not equivalent to the sum total of individual interviews.

> What makes the discussion in focus groups more than the sum of individual interviews is the fact that the participants both query each other and explain themselves to each other. . . . [S]uch interaction offers valuable data on the extent of consensus and diversity among participants. (Morgan, 1996, p. 139)

When a participant makes a comment that appears to indicate disagreement with another participant's comment, the researcher may make a note of this, using it as a marker to return to later (Myers, 1998) for clarification, elaboration, or additional questioning. While agreement and disagreement are interesting aspects of focus group data, as well as serving as potential stimuli within the group for the production of data, these are not the only kinds of data enabled by the group effect. Participants may also change their minds, challenge previously held attitudes or beliefs, or reconsider their own behaviors when they are reflected back at them by the mirror of the larger group.

Unique data develops as participants disagree, explain themselves, and query each other, often negotiating their original ideas with new thoughts resulting from the conversation. This form of data often helps to both elucidate *and* challenge taken-for-granted assumptions that, like water to a fish, are difficult to discern. One fairly common goal for sociologists in particular is **denaturalization** of common-sense assumptions about the social world. Yet, because culture becomes a second skin, this process of understanding normative ideas and customs is quite complicated for the researcher and research participants. This general challenge for the social sciences is another reason that focus groups are a useful method of data collection, particularly when the researcher is explicitly studying issues that are largely taken for granted by the participants.

Frances Montell (1999) found focus groups to be highly effective in revealing assumptions about sex and sexuality in her study of gender, sexuality, and the mass media. Montell credits the group dynamic created in focus groups for fostering an informative discussion that exposed and challenged the closely held beliefs of different women.

> In a group, if even one person expresses an idea it can prompt a response from the others, and the information that is produced is more likely to be framed by the categories and understandings of the interviewees rather than those of the interviewer. Participants can help each other figure out what the questions mean to them, and the researcher can examine how different participants hear possibly vague or ambiguous questions. This is important in studying sex and gender because these issues are "naturalized" to such an extent that it is very difficult to recognize one's own preconceived notions, much less challenge others' taken-for-granted assumptions. The expansion of the roles available to women in a group interview, beyond the strict separation between "interviewer" and "interviewee" allows for interactions that are more likely to reveal and even challenge these taken-for-granted assumptions. (p. 49)

In addition to encouraging participants to explain their recognizable assumptions, given the generally private nature of the subject matter (sexuality), Montell (1999) used focus groups as a means of making the participants more open to discussing this highly personal and taboo aspect of social life. While at first glance it may seem that the group atmosphere would deter people from discussing intimate issues, once a relaxed environment is created, participants may feel more comfortable than in a one-on-one interview because the "spotlight" is not constantly on them. Once a comfort level is established, participants may actually feel less pressure within the group. Likewise, Montell used the group dynamic to get at ideas and assumptions that underlie the attitudes the participants were aware that they held.

> I just wanted them to state ideas explicitly that usually "go without saying," to articulate the beliefs and categories that underlie their conscious attitudes. It is very difficult for people to talk about these kinds of attitudes and assumptions in an individual interview. In a group interview, however, the ways participants respond to and interact with each other can provide richer and more complex data. (p. 47)

Another example comes from Goltz (2009), who used focus groups to investigate the meanings gay youth attach to their future. In this research, Goltz was working with minority participants in a project that focused on attitudes regarding a very personal topic. The results were surprising and indicated strong gender differences with respect to attitudes held about the future. The gay male participants largely attached negative meanings to the future whereas the lesbian women largely associated positive meanings with the future. The results suggest that the male participants were heavily influenced by cultural myths of the "bitter old man" whereas the female participants viewed their futures within the socially normative model of family and children, albeit lesbian.

In addition to exploring *attitudes,* the group dynamic can be equally fruitful for encouraging group members to provide detailed explanations of normative *behaviors* that are mundane to them. In our study of black females' body image, we find an excellent illustration of focus group interview as a method for gaining "thick descriptions" of routine behaviors. The group interaction allowed the girls to weave together a robust description of normative behaviors as banal (to them), but analytically important to us, as hair care.

Interviewer:	Is that good for some girls and bad for others?
Sasha:	Well some people don't look good in either cut, though.
Deb:	Caesar cuts are like a man's hairstyle.
Interviewer:	I understand.
Deb:	If your head looks like a football it's not going to look right.
Interviewer:	Do you spend a lot of time on your hair?
Michelle B:	Yes.
Sasha:	I know I do.
Jen:	Only when it's straight enough to do something . . .
Deb:	. . . Right . . .
Jen:	This morning I threw some curls in it, got in the shower, got out and called it a day.
Interviewer:	What happens when you go in the shower . . .
Sasha:	Shower cap.
Interviewer:	Why do you have to wear a shower cap?
Jen:	Because we don't have hair like y'all. No offense but we just can't get ours . . . if we go in the shower, it depends . . .
Interviewer:	Tell me what happens when you go in the shower.
Jen:	When you first get a perm and you in the shower your hair still comes out straight, but if you wash your hair continually, like get your hair wet every day . . .
Sasha:	. . . You'll get bald headed . . .
Jen:	. . . And you got a perm on Monday, it will be nappy, it will be an Afro, we just can't get in the shower.
Interviewer:	Why don't you want an Afro here? Why wouldn't you want hair to be nappy?

Jen:	It's not about wanting to have an Afro, if I was born to have one, or made to have one, if the Lord wanted me to have one, I'd have one . . .
Deb:	. . . He would have gave you one, and kept letting my hair fall out . . .
Jen:	The Lord wants my hair to be short because I've had my hair short for a while. Therefore this is just how it's going to be.
Deb:	Afros don't look pretty on girls.
Sasha:	Rashina has an Afro, but that's an exception.
Deb:	Rashina?
Sasha:	Yes.
Interviewer:	So you can't wash your hair every day is what you are saying to me.
Jen:	There's no reason to.
Sasha:	It breaks.
Jen:	There just isn't a reason to. There's just no reason why I have to wash my hair every day. I go to the hairdresser's every two weeks.
Interviewer:	You go to the hairdresser?
Jen:	I get a perm every six weeks.
Sasha:	I go home and shower, every two weeks I wash my hair. I get my perm every eight weeks, but at the present time I'm letting my hair grow until August because I'm getting my hair cut. I'm getting my hair cut.
Interviewer:	You say you went to get a perm; what does that mean?
Sasha:	A relaxer . . .
Deb:	. . . You get a relaxer to get your hair straight . . .
Jen:	. . . A relaxer straightens your hair.
Interviewer:	It does straighten your hair.
Sasha:	Chemical-bound relaxer.
Interviewer:	When we're talking permanent we usually say it curls your hair, but your permanent relaxes your hair is what you're saying.
Jen:	Exactly. If you got a perm, your hair would be curly. . . .
Sasha:	. . . or wavy . . .
Jen:	. . . If we got a perm our hair would be straight.
Interviewer:	I understand. Why is it important to have straight hair?

| Deb: | Because it's nappy. You can't do anything with it. |
| Jen: | It's not necessarily important, it's just your image. You don't have to have straight hair. I wouldn't want to walk around. . . . |

The preceding transcript is actually a brief snippet of the data elicited on this subject alone. As you can see, the group atmosphere fosters detailed descriptions of mundane experiences, which might provide very important data.

The dynamic produced within a group is very different from the experience of a one-on-one interview. Interaction influences all members of the group (the researcher as well as participants, which we will talk about more when we discuss the role of the moderator in focus groups). Focus group participants often change their mind based on the influence of the attitudes and values in the group—this is a key part of the dynamic, and it is an important part of the data collection process. As we saw in the chapter on in-depth interviews, what a person says in the context of a one-on-one interview is influenced only by the researcher and the rapport created between the researcher and that particular participant.

In the case of focus group interviews, what any given participant says is mediated by the group and subsequently reflected through the eyes of the others in the group as they continue the conversation. For example, in an exploratory study about gay men and body image, Jesse might explain why he feels the pressure to work out in order to be valued in the gay community, but his comment is then thrown back into the conversation by the other members of the group who respond to the statement and/or are influenced by the statement when they comment on their own experience. It is for *all* of these reasons that the data produced within a focus group differs from in-depth interview data.[2]

The group dynamic is impacted by many research design choices and impacts data collection and analysis. The researcher's role in creating the group dynamic through the level of moderation he or she provides as well as the level of structure he or she imposes is important and will be discussed in detail. Likewise, the dynamic is brought to bear during analysis when the researcher decides at what level analysis occurs and when she or he interprets the data and uncovers emergent patterns. These aspects of the group will be fleshed out later in this chapter. First, we will discuss research design, where choices about moderation and structure as well as many other considerations are made. Through an examination of how to design a focus group study, some more of the unique aspects of this method will become clear.

How Do You Design a Focus Group Study?

As we saw in Chapter 3, the research design process, including methodological decisions, should always be guided by the research question(s). The research design process is about formulating research procedures (Krueger, 1994) linked to your research purpose. The importance of the fit between the research question and methodological design becomes even more salient in a project using focus groups because of the sheer multiplicity of design options for data collection alone.

Morgan (1996) finds it helpful to distinguish between "project-level" design issues and "group-level" design issues. We caution you that while conceptualizing qualitative research as a holistic process in the ways we have explained, some of the distinctions between project level and group level become artificial in actual practice. This artificiality in practice may also be linked to the theoretical framework of the study. For example, a study using a **grounded theory approach** may merge some of these design choices in practice. Having said that these categorizations are not always so clear-cut in practice, Morgan's model is very helpful when considering the design of your focus group project.

Considerations to be made at the *project level* include (1) mixed method and multimethod frameworks, (2) group selection (sampling), and (3) standardization of data collection procedures. Sampling and standardization are related decisions, so we will discuss them together. At the group level, the most important design consideration has to do with the role of the researcher. Specifically, what degree of moderation will the researcher provide in regard to managing the group dynamic and structuring the flow of topics? Issues of moderation, as we will see, are ultimately about structuring the proper balance between control and flow to produce the best results from the group for the specific research purposes. All of these research design issues, at both the project and group levels, should be worked through in relation to the research questions and research goals. In this vein, Morgan (2007, 2008) advocates a "pragmatic approach" to research design, where the goals determine the methodology.

Mixed Method Designs: Combining Qualitative and Quantitative Data

Focus groups can be used as a self-contained research method or as a part of a mixed method or multimethod design (for a complete discussion of mixed-method designs see Chapter 11). Most frequently, focus groups have been used in mixed method studies (Morgan, 1996). Whether your study uses focus groups on their own or in conjunction with another method, either quantitative or qualitative, will depend on your research question. For example, there are many questions that we could ask about male body image. The way we frame our research question will help determine an appropriate method, including whether focus groups will be used to help yield exploratory, descriptive, or explanatory data. Let's review some of the most common mixed method focus group designs, using our research examples of gay male body image and black female body image as a means of illustrating the appropriateness of each option for different kinds of questions and purposes.

Creating research projects that use both focus groups and survey research is one of the most common methods of combining qualitative and quantitative techniques in mixed method designs (Morgan, 1996). It is important to bear in mind that a holistic approach to knowledge construction necessitates that the methods are not simply used to generate a greater volume of data but that the methods inform one another and are used in a way that creates a more complex understanding of social reality. Focus groups and surveys can be used with another research method in studies that practice **triangulation**, which is the use of three research methods; however, we are going to focus on two-method designs. It should be noted that group interviews can also serve in a "pretest" capacity to make sure that the language of a survey is appropriate to the population (Frey & Fontana, 1991, p. 177). Morgan (1996) outlines the four major ways that focus groups can be used in conjunction with survey research. We will highlight how the methods can be combined in ways that encourage interaction between the qualitative and quantitative components.

Survey research can be used to generate data that will guide the focus groups, from sample selection to topics and questions. Surveys are an effective method for generating large amounts of "flat" data from many respondents. The respondents can be stratified based on any number of characteristics, including race, sex, social class, age, and sexuality, through demographic questions typically placed at the beginning of a survey. This kind of information can be useful to a researcher who has not yet decided whether to use homogeneous or heterogeneous focus groups (as we will discuss later, these are groups with members who are similar or dissimilar, respectively). When surveys are used in this kind of preliminary capacity, they are essentially being employed to explore a topic that will then be fleshed out through qualitative focus groups. This kind of exploratory data is critical when a researcher is not sure what the key issues are.

For example, if we are to study gay men's body image, and we decide to use focus groups as our primary method because of their usefulness in gaining exploratory and descriptive data and also in making participants feel comfortable discussing taboo subjects, we may want to use surveys as a preliminary way of discovering some key themes and patterns that we can use to shape our interview guide. Although this is a perfectly legitimate way of combining these methods, one major weakness should be noted. If, in fact, we know very little about gay men's body image, which is why we are going to use focus groups, then how are we going to create useful survey questions? Based on our literature review, we would create a range of closed-ended questions that give respondents a limited choice of how to respond. While these data could certainly be used to guide the structuring of focus groups, it is important to realize that the survey data reflect our own categorizations— what *we* think some of the key issues may be. Because the entire study in our example is *exploratory* in nature, the data we derive from our surveys, which then guide our group interviews, may have framed issues in ways that are different from how our respondents *themselves* would have discussed them, may have distorted the importance of some issues over others, and may leave out many important issues altogether. The value of a survey rests solely on the ultimate usefulness of the questions asked, which is especially difficult to gauge in exploratory research.

A different and more common twist on this combination is to use focus groups as the preliminary method and surveys as the primary method. In this instance, a researcher uses focus group data to help shape quantitative survey questions. Market researchers who ultimately want breadth to their data often use this economical structure. This framework is also useful in exploratory research when the researcher does not know all of the key issues and terminology because the participants can create categorizations, choose what to emphasize, and explain their perceptions and experiences. Focus group data are very helpful when formulating survey questions whose value rests on their applicability to respondents' lives. Nassar-McMillan and Borders (2002) discuss the "highly effective" use of structured qualitative focus groups to generate and modify questions for the Volunteer Work Behavior Questionnaire. In this instance, survey respondents were educationally diverse but shared the experience of being "direct service volunteers." Focus groups were used to help find language and terms appropriate to the population. The focus group interviews resulted in substantial alterations in the survey instrument, which the researchers labeled an additional "quality control measure."

In our own exploratory focus group interviews with gay men about their body image, the research participants had the opportunity to help guide the conversation, introduce their ideas, explain their meanings, clear up misconceptions, and educate the researcher. In this instance, the participants helped the researcher to understand that gay subculture not only is a source of body image pressure, but also acts as an important source of acceptance and positive self-esteem. The data we gathered would be very helpful for the generation of pertinent survey questions in the future.

Cliff: Thanks to the gay subculture, I now am very self-conscious about things that I wasn't really self-conscious about, one of them being weight. Another being this whole question of genitals, which is so overemphasized. One of the most important things about my body to me is my heart and how that works; because emotions are physical, I experience this feeling and I don't know, these one-night stands are not, they don't tend to that. It's hard. So that's important—the physical relationship. (silence)

Tony: I have changed quite a bit in the way I have dressed and the way that I think of myself. Before . . . I used to wear clothes that did not look good on me at all, they looked terrible, black and dark colors, or bright colors. But since coming out and being more comfortable with myself, I have seen change in the clothing I buy now that aren't screaming out and saying look I'm very fashionable. I'm still well dressed (group laughter), but I have definitely noticed a change, and I do feel much more comfortable with myself. (silence)

Jesse: I think a lot of it has to do with confidence, which is a result of having come out. (pause) I used to hate my legs, because they seemed disproportionate to the rest of my body, which is very slim, and I have big tree trunks down here. I used to do a lot of cycling—whichever came first! (group laughter) I'm hyperconscious of putting weight on. It's less of an issue now. I don't know why. The only thing that has changed is that I have come out, and I'm more confident and what not.

The importance of gathering qualitative focus group data before constructing survey questions is also evident in our focus group study of black girls and body image. Many of the issues the principal investigator may have assumed to be of importance were in fact secondary issues to the girls. Given that the study centered on body image and body disturbance, which the investigator had explored in-depth with white populations, there was a seemingly reasonable assumption that the girls might exhibit fears of being fat and desire to embody the media ideal of thinness, as white samples routinely did. However, weight was not a primary source of body concern for the girls.

Interviewer:	How do you feel, Nicole? You're 10 pounds [heavier] now; how do you feel?
Nicole:	I feel fine. I feel on top of the world.
Interviewer:	Come on now.
Nicole:	No really, it won't make any difference, I may have to buy some new clothes and stuff, but otherwise it's nothing.
Interviewer:	If you were to gain 10 pounds tomorrow, how would you feel?
Joy:	I'd be happy.
Tasha:	I'd just go on feeling, but I mean, I'd probably change my way of thinking, but if I feel comfortable with it I'll just adjust to it, there is nothing else I can do.

The interviewer's assumptions were directly questioned, and as the transcript shows, she asked for clarification and confirmation with the phrase "come on now" to make sure that she understood the feelings of the participants, which clearly challenged her own ideas.

The major concern qualitative researchers have with this way of combining qualitative focus groups with quantitative survey research is that by using surveys as the primary method of data collection, the quantitative data is privileged. The resulting quantitative data has been intimately shaped by the qualitative data if questions were formulated that would otherwise have been excluded or worded differently. However, it is likely that when research results are reported or represented, the quantitative survey data, generally presented statistically, will be emphasized. This fails to take into account the interaction between the methods and the holistic nature of the research design. It is possible that the use of focus groups will be mentioned (in an introduction or appendix) and never elaborated on, masking the importance of the qualitative data. Alternatively, the preliminary focus group data may not be discussed at all.

Morgan (2002) explains that focus groups became popular in the social sciences when used with quantitative methods in evaluation research. This trend gave qualitative researchers more legitimacy as well as access to funding formerly restricted to quantitative projects; however, these combinations were based on the privileging of the quantitative data, allowing researchers to ultimately remain within the conventions of quantitative approaches (Morgan, 2002).

The most common combination also uses surveys as the primary research method but employs focus groups during the later phase of data collection as a "follow-up" (Morgan, 1996, p. 135). This design is chosen so that researchers can use the qualitative focus group data to aid in interpreting and analyzing their survey results. When applied in a manner that is appropriate to the research question, this can be a highly effective way of combining quantitative and qualitative data holistically—in a manner that expresses the different dimensions of the research. For example, a researcher may conduct survey research with white and black populations of college-age women to examine differences in body image perceptions and disturbances. Such data would likely indicate that black women have more positive body images and are less likely to exhibit body disturbances; however, the survey would not help us to understand *why* that is. By following up with respondents with qualitative focus groups, patterns or anomalies in their initial closed responses could be explained and clarified, adding descriptive and explanatory data to the statistical data. The two forms of data would "speak to each other" when represented, which is critical in holistic practice.

The final way of combining focus groups and survey research is when focus groups are used as the primary research method and surveys are employed in the follow-up manner we just described. What is appealing to us about this less common design is that qualitative data are conceptualized as the primary data form—this is rare and, when it occurs, exemplifies an important shift in thinking about the relationship between qualitative and quantitative data. Researchers may opt for this kind of design when they want to see the pervasiveness of particular attitudes, behaviors, experiences, or themes. This may be a preplanned part of the research project, or researchers may decide to go back and try to gain survey data from participants after the focus groups have occurred because they seek clarification or some issues unexpectedly emerge from the transcript. When researchers present their findings from this kind of project, the quantitative data may in fact be used as a heuristic device. This means that the quantitative data are being presented as a means of highlighting themes within the qualitative data. With the advent of computer-driven qualitative data analysis programs (which we discuss in the chapter on analysis), there are several methods of accomplishing a similar end. Thus, the rarity of this mixed methods design may not only reflect epistemological issues but also be linked to the availability of other ways of presenting qualitative data with similar quantitative components.

Qualitative Multimethod Designs

Focus group interviews can be used in multimethod designs with other qualitative research methods. The possible combinations run the gamut of available qualitative methods. We will discuss the mixing of focus groups with in-depth interviews because this is the most typical and straightforward pairing (nonetheless, we encourage you to consider other creative combinations as your project dictates, and we conclude this section with a brief mention of focus group and diary research).

For researchers asking qualitatively oriented questions that can be addressed via methods of interview, the benefits of combining focus groups and individual interviews are abundant. There are two major design strategies: (1) focus groups are used as a follow-up to in-depth interviews, and (2) individual interviews are used as a follow-up to group interviews. In both instances, it is important to look at each method as a phase in the overall project. When the process is conceptualized in this comprehensive way, the qualitative data yielded by the two methods can inform further data collection, analysis, and interpretation.

A qualitative researcher may design a study using these two methods because the research question requires both breadth and depth (Morgan, 1996). In-depth interviews provide greater depth from individual participants, whereas focus groups can give researchers a greater range of responses in a shorter time period. However, we caution you to take these as generalizations because, as we have seen from the examples in this chapter, focus group data can also be quite rich. It is appropriate to follow up in-depth interviews with focus group interviews to verify individual interview data, examine how individual responses differ in a group setting, expose individual interviewees to the group dynamic as a means of education or empowerment, and include larger populations that may not have been available for in-depth interviews.

A more common design strategy uses focus groups as the primary research method and follow-up in-depth interviews with some or all of the focus group participants. This research design allows researchers to gain initial group data, which produces an overall group narrative, and then seek more data on specific components of the narrative. This design allows participants to share their experiences in the group setting and then have individual time to elaborate on their personal experiences, attitudes, and beliefs, including any impact of the focus group. In addition, although a focus group interview is "focused" on a particular topic, it is likely that many other issues come into the conversation. By following up with in-depth interviews, the researcher is able to go back and gain more data where needed to best answer the research question. This was the strategy we employed in our study of black girls and body image. The principal investigator conducted the focus group interviews, which provided a range and depth of data. She then conducted in-depth interviews with the focus group participants who wanted to continue their participation in the project. This allowed her to explore particular perspectives and themes at a greater depth. These interviews, however, were intimately shaped by the data gathered during the primary focus groups, and thus the two methods interacted to produce richer data.

A more recent combination is the use of focus group interviews with diary research (see Hyers, Swim, & Mallett, 2006, for a discussion of diary research). Markham and Couldry (2007) conducted a multimethod qualitative project in the United Kingdom, asking a sample of citizens to reflect on their relationship to the public world over the period of a year. Markham and Couldry were particularly interested in the role people's media consumption plays in their relationship to the public world. As such, they designed a study that combined focus groups and diary research (a method where participants routinely record their experiences and feelings). As you can see, focus groups can be combined with a variety of other methods as appropriate to particular projects.

Whether your project uses focus groups as a part of a multimethod design or in a self-contained format depends entirely on your research objectives and material constraints. We have provided you with some standard examples of how you may conceive of a multiple method design; however, these are simply models. Beyond deciding the application of methods, there are many other choices that must be made when using focus groups.

Sampling and Standardization

Morgan (1996) identifies sampling and standardization as two of the key components in focus group design. Sampling addresses this question:

- Who makes up your focus group?

This question is intimately connected to your research purpose—the population or populations about whom you are interested in learning. However, other realities, not within your control, may also impact the selection of research participants. For example, the populations to which you can gain access, your geographic location, and your timeline all impact recruitment and sample selection. The recruitment process is important in ensuring your design requisites are met. Morgan (1995) wisely notes that recruitment is about getting participants, and sampling is about getting the "right" participants (p. 519). He cites inattention to recruitment as the single greatest source of focus group failure (p. 517). While our holistic approach to the research process stresses the interconnection between all phases of the research project, it is also clear that recruitment procedures and group composition are key to success. Morgan (1995) suggests several strategies to proactively avoid the potential pitfalls of recruitment: overrecruit, send reminders, provide incentives (such as money). Moving beyond these structural realities and recruitment techniques, you should try to construct samples composed of people who can best shed light on your topic through their personal thoughts and life experiences. When participants are invested in the topic, they will have more to say.

Focus groups vary in size but typically consist of four to eight participants. A major decision researchers confront is whether the focus groups will be **heterogeneous** or **homogeneous**. A heterogeneous group consists of dissimilar participants. While these kinds of groups are relatively uncommon in academic research, heterogeneous groups are appropriate when the researcher wants a range of responses and is willing to sacrifice a more in-depth understanding of how a particular segment of the population experiences the topic under investigation. For example, let's say we are interested in what different kinds of people think about the mass media's portrayal of President Obama. Heterogeneous focus groups would speak to this kind of research topic. Groups would be mixed in terms of gender, race, sexual orientation, social class, political affiliations, and perhaps age. The resulting data would not give us a deep understanding of why different people in the population have different attitudes about the portrayal of President Obama; however, these data would provide us with some insight into the different kinds of perceptions and attitudes prevalent in society at large. Such data, perhaps a preliminary phase of data collection, would be highly valuable in the thinking-through of future research and could inform the development of subsequent focus group questions or other forms of data collection, such as in-depth interviews or quantitative surveys.

Generally, qualitative researchers opt for homogeneous focus groups. These are groups with members who are similar to each other. Depending on the research question, it may be important that group members all share the same sex, race, sexual orientation, social class, age, occupation, educational level, religion, medical condition, particular life experience, or some combination of the above. Homogeneous groups are appropriate when the researcher wants to gain in-depth understanding about how members of a particular group experience or think about a given issue. For example, when we were interested in studying the unique ways gay men experience body image, it was important that we used homogeneous groups consisting of gay males—this is of course pretty clear-cut. In this instance, in terms of the initial research, we did not feel that the race of the participants was central, and thus, our participants were racially dissimilar to each other. Homogeneous groups have an important built-in advantage, which is that they are typically helpful in creating a comfort level within the group that fosters conversation. People tend to feel more comfortable speaking in a group when they have things in common with the other group members right from the start. This becomes more pronounced in the case of sensitive matters such as sexuality, body disturbance, violence, depression, addiction, racism, and so forth. As the group dynamic is integral to the development of the narrative, the advantage of homogeneity is significant.

In addition, the composition of the group is likely to affect *who* will be more or less likely to fully express themselves. This happens in fairly predictable ways. Minority voices tend to be "muted" in majority populations (Kitzinger, 1994, p. 110). This process produces knowledge that is privileged from the position of dominance. In other words, unequal societal power relations along lines of race, class, gender, and sexuality are likely to be replicated in mixed-status focus groups. This is another reason why some researchers may opt for homogeneity, particularly critical scholars and other researchers committed to accessing the voices of marginalized groups.

A widely used design feature that maximizes the benefits of homogeneity while allowing for comparison among populations is called **segmentation**. This occurs when each group consists of similar members, but the different groups within the study as a whole are different from each other. Put differently, segmentation is a way of stratifying groups based on the particular traits in which you want to examine difference. Let's say we wanted to be able to compare how men and women think about the mass-mediated female beauty ideal. We could construct two solely female groups and two solely male groups. The study could be complicated further if we were interested in gender and racial differences—our literature review would indicate, for example, that race impacts the internalization of the media ideal in female populations. We might then construct two groups of each of the following: white males, black males, white females, black females. Depending on whether we think social class and age are relevant, we could control for these factors by making group members similar to each other in those ways. A major appeal of segmentation is that it creates a **comparative dimension** in the research (Morgan, 1996, p. 143). Our study of gay male body image would produce another level of knowledge if we also conducted focus groups with otherwise similar heterosexual males. This dimension of the research would give us a greater understanding of the link between body image and sexual identity in males and allow us to make powerful comparative claims. As exciting a design feature as segmentation can be, it also creates additional work (typically, more groups and more complex data analysis), and thus time and other practical constraints also come to bear on the feasibility of this decision. Sampling decisions always impact both the overall number of groups and the size of those groups. Ideally, sampling decisions should always be considered in relation to the research purpose, although practical constraints like time and funding come into play.

The degree to which a **standardized approach** will be employed is also a critical issue when developing focus group-based research. **Standardization** refers to "the extent to which the identical questions and procedures are used in every group" (Morgan, 1996, p. 142). The degree of standardization used should be based on a logical fit to the research question. Market researchers typically maximize standardization because of the kind of information they are looking for—they want each group to stay on track and answer preconstructed questions. The main advantage of standardization is that it allows researchers to make valid comparisons between all of the groups in the study. This is particularly salient when dealing with segmented samples, where presumed comparability is a part of the research purpose.

Thinking back to the example of our gay male body image study, we saw how applying segmentation to our sampling procedures would add additional dimensions to our data. Specifically, such a design would help illuminate the relationship between sexual identity and body image within male populations. The emergence of any patterned differences between the homosexual groups and heterosexual groups would constitute very important contributions to our knowledge about sexual identity and male body image; however, clarity about differences between our groups based on sexual orientation alone requires a high level of comparability between the straight and gay groups. In other words, to link differences between the groups to the sexuality of group members—critical to how we have framed our research purpose—the groups must be similar on all other counts *and* have experienced a highly comparable interview situation. A quantitatively inclined researcher might refer to this as controlling for confounding variables, which can also be thought of as reducing mitigating circumstances. Despite the potential rewards of applying stringent standardization, particularly when comparison among groups is part of the research purpose, there are also considerable advantages to applying the **open-ended approach** (or grounded theory approach) to group interviewing and thus opting for less standardization.

While standardization fosters comparability, open-ended designs allow the participants more freedom to speak to their own experiences and use language in ways that are meaningful to them. Likewise, open-ended formats allow the group dynamic to flow, creating a unique narrative whose power does not lie in conventional conceptions of generalizability. Less standardized approaches allow data to emerge from interaction. Furthermore, a more "learn-as-you-go" approach allows the researcher to apply what was learned in one group to the next. Thus, any errors or omissions in the interview guide don't impact every group in the study. The widespread appeal of open approaches is in many ways congruent to the appeal of qualitative research more generally.

Qualitative researchers are interested in understanding social life from the perspective of those experiencing it. Focus group interviews conducted in an open format allow participants to help shape the topic in ways that are meaningful to them. Research participants transform into coauthors of the emerging narrative. Researchers have the opportunity to allow important concepts and themes to emerge directly out of the interview situation. What is learned in one group can be used in later groups. Any theories about what is significant to the population develop *inductively* through data collection and are not merely constructed by the researcher and reflected by a firm research guide used to yield data that likely support previously held theories.

This way of conceptualizing the research process is often particularly appealing to critical scholars committed to accessing subjugated voices, as was the case in our study of black girls' body image. Those focus groups were conducted in an open format so that the research participants could help shape the discussion in ways that were meaningful to them. Furthermore, applying a grounded theory approach to both data collection and analysis allowed themes to emerge directly from the girls, drawing directly on their ideas, language, and ways of understanding their own behaviors and attitudes.

There are also ways to design your project that draw from the benefits of more and less standardized approaches. Morgan (1993, 1996) explains two mixed designs. One option is to apply a *funnel pattern* (1996, p. 143). In this instance, each focus group begins with a high level of standardization (all groups begin with a fixed set of questions), and then the group becomes less controlled as subsequent topics are allowed to emerge (1996). The other approach is to use the initial groups within a study in an exploratory way, thus applying a low level of standardization (1996). The data collected are then used to develop a highly standardized research guide for subsequent groups. This kind of design is very similar to the use of focus groups as a means of developing survey research that is language- and concept-appropriate to the target population.

The Role of the Researcher in Focus Groups: Moderator

The researcher has a very particular and important role in focus group interviews that is different from the interviewer/listener role in the in-depth interview situation. In the context of a focus group, the researcher assumes the role of **moderator**. The moderator greatly influences the flow of the conversation and therefore the group dynamic and manner of the group narrative. Moderation styles can vary greatly, which is one of the general appeals of focus groups—they can be designed in many ways to meet the needs of a particular research objective. Also, contrary to popular conceptions, some of the important work of moderation is actually done before the focus groups meet (Morgan, 2002).

Recruiting participants is linked not only to sampling but also to moderation. This is because an open approach to the interview, in which participants are allowed to speak freely, is a possible design option only if in fact the participants will speak extensively. In other words, low levels of moderation and researcher control are viable only in talkative groups. So, if you are anticipating employing a less structured approach to moderation (which we discuss in detail shortly), then it is vital to recruit participants who are deeply interested in the subject matter (Morgan, 2002). Typically—we all have to face it—as researchers, we are generally more interested in our particular research project than anyone else is likely to be. Having said this, we can go a long way to creating a range of possible design options by recruiting people who are also personally invested in the topic we are studying.

The interview guide is another critical component in the success of a focus group. Depending on the overall goals and research design, an interview guide can be a very detailed listing of major topics and subsets of specific questions, or an interview guide can be less rigid, with a set of general topics and/or some open-ended questions. Good questions, that is, questions that are designed to elicit the kind of data the researcher is seeking, are essential to focus group success. Accordingly, Morgan (1995, p. 520) suggests pretesting questions. You can pretest questions with individual or group interviews depending largely on the time and resources you are able to allocate to validating the interview guide.

The opening question is perhaps the most important part of the research guide because it helps set the tone for the entire interview. A good opening question will prompt participants to speak and ideally lead them in additional directions that you already had in mind. In other words, a well-written question (especially the first question, but this is also true for all questions in an open-ended format) will not only ignite discussion but also suggest directions for the group conversation to pursue. When this occurs, the moderator may have many interview questions answered without even having to ask them. We will talk more about this when we discuss level of moderator involvement, but for now, it is important to note the significance of the opening question. However, a focus group interview, and thus the guide, may in fact begin with something other than a question. This is also a possibility the researcher must consider prior to meeting with the group.

Morgan, Fellows, and Guevara (2008) suggest two alternative ways of beginning focus groups. First, they suggest using "stimulus materials" such as pictures, stories, photos, media, or videos as a way of stimulating conversation. Second, they suggest *projective techniques,* which are more interactive, such as a game or role-playing approach. Kitzinger (1994) suggests beginning groups with an exercise such as a card game or vignette. Such an activity serves as both a "common external reference point" and a "party game" that "warms up" the participants and helps make them feel comfortable in the group (p. 107). Kitzinger has used various kinds of card games that typically involve participants putting cards into piles. The cards may have pictures, advertisements, opinions, or accounts of events or people on them, for example, and participants place cards into groups based on the level to which the participants agree or disagree with something the researcher says (p. 107). For example, participants may be given advertisements and asked to place them in a pile based on things such as how "effective" or "offensive" they find the ad to be (p. 107). This kind of game can be particularly helpful when the focus group is about a difficult topic. Kitzinger found the card game method very useful in her research on the effect of media images of AIDS.

We also found an alternative way of opening a focus group very effective in our work on gay male body image. In that instance, the principal investigator (Hesse-Biber) thought that using someone else to moderate the focus group would be beneficial. As the group was exploratory in nature, it was important for the group to feel as free and comfortable as possible. This is always particularly true when dealing with marginalized groups, which are often victimized because of their status, in this case, a sexual minority group. As an alternative moderator was available, who himself is a gay male living in the same geographic region and in the same age-group as our participants, he was employed to moderate the group and was given a research guide consisting of 12 open-ended questions. The opening of the guide, however, was actually a quote about gay male body image taken from a book published in 1980. The moderator started the group by reading the paragraph-long quote. He then introduced himself and went around the room allowing everyone to introduce themselves. He then asked for people's reactions to the quote. This opening was so effective in beginning an in-depth dialogue that the moderator barely had to ask any of the remaining questions—the conversation naturally supplied the answers. It is here that we start to move away from moderation preparation to issues of moderation during the actual focus group interviews.

The way in which a researcher chooses to moderate during data collection is intimately linked with decisions about standardization. In a research project with high standardization, it is more likely that the researcher will maintain a high level of *control* as a moderator, whereas in more evolving designs the researcher may opt for less control and a more open style of moderation. Morgan (1996) identifies two main areas in which the researcher exercises a level of moderation, which can range from very high to very low. The moderator decides how much he or she will control the issues that are discussed. Will the moderator allow the group to veer off in its own direction as the conversation progresses, or will the moderator carefully control the topic flow, making sure that participants stay on track answering a predetermined set of questions or focusing on predetermined topics? The moderator also acts as the manager of the group dynamic. Accordingly, the moderator can create a more structured conversation in which all participants have relatively equal speaking time, or the moderator can allow the participants and their group dynamic to lead the conversation. In the latter instance, this means some people may dominate the conversation while others speak far less. As you can see, when we talk about the role of the moderator, we are really talking about *structure* and *control*. Issues of moderation also exemplify the push-pull relationship that qualitative researchers using focus groups must come to grips with between *standardization* and *flow*.

In marketing research, moderators typically exercise a high level of moderation in terms of asking questions, controlling topics, and managing the group dynamic. Often in this kind of research, the moderator will make sure that every research participant answers the same set of questions and the conversation does not stray off topic. The high level of moderator involvement reflects the goals of market research (Morgan, 1996). Performing for paying clients, as we discussed earlier, may also prompt high moderator interaction and thus high control. According to Puchta and Potter (1999), because market researchers are typically after highly standardized data, focus group moderators have the task of "managing spontaneity." To address this particular undertaking, a phenomenon has emerged in market research: Focus groups often rely on "elaborate questions" (p. 319). By complicating questions through the use of additional question components, moderators help direct the responses they receive. Participants are more likely to stay on topic and answer questions in the ways anticipated by the researcher if the questions are complex and specific, and if possible answers or answer suggestions are located within the questions themselves. Having said this, we are more concerned with how scholarly researchers deal with issues of moderation.

Social science approaches to focus group moderation can vary greatly but tend toward less control (Morgan, 1996, p. 145). Highly flexible approaches to moderation are sometimes viewed as more congruent with the main tenets of qualitative inquiry because they give participants more of a voice in shaping the topic and conversation. Low levels of moderation allow the research participants to do most of the talking, providing rich descriptions of social life and in-depth explanations of social processes. When the researcher does not stick to a rigid interview guide but rather allows the group to take hold of the narrative, the interview may move in directions that the researcher couldn't have anticipated. When this occurs, the researcher is likely to learn about things that are of importance to the group being studied that he or she may not have known to ask. The group ends up placing emphasis on the areas that are significant to its members, and the researcher is given the opportunity to follow the group discussion in new directions. The resulting data are directly grounded in the experiences of the research participants as they perceive them. In addition, if the group dynamic itself is a part of what's being studied, then it must be allowed to take its course freely. This would be true, for example, in a study about how members of dominant social groups and members of minority social groups interact in a group setting—who speaks freely, who dominates, who is silenced.

Another benefit of employing low levels of moderation is that the research participants are more likely to develop and shape the categories and concepts being used to understand their experience. In other words, if the researcher does little by way of providing the participants with language (which guides responses), the research participants will tell the researcher and other group members what language and concepts are appropriate to their group. For example, in our study of black girls and body image, the moderator employed an open format with low levels of control. This allowed the girls to focus on the issues that were of importance to them as opposed to preconceived issues thought up by the researcher. This approach allowed the girls not only to shape the flow of topics but also to use language that was meaningful to them. In other words, it isn't just what is said, but the way that it is said—these are both influenced by the amount of control the moderator exerts. For example, there were times when the moderator did not understand a term the girls were using. All the moderator would have to say is, "I don't know what that term means," and the girls would provide a richly detailed explanation of the term and its significance. In their words, they would "break it down." Open formats are often used in exploratory research; however, for many qualitative researchers, less structured formats that encourage participants to share their ideas, feelings, experiences, and language are simply most congruent with their qualitative projects.

> The ideal group would start with an opening question that was designed to capture the participants' interest, so that they themselves would explore nearly all of the issues that a moderator might have probed. . . . [O]ne of the partici- pants in the ideal group would spontaneously direct the others' attention to the topic for [a] second question. . . . Anyone who has done much moderating has experienced this magic moment, as the group goes right where you want it to, without any help from you. . . . [T]he moderator could move toward closure with a typical wrap-up request, such as, "This has really been wonderful, and I'd like to finish by having each one of you summarize . . ." In this ideal version of a less structured group, the moderator would have to ask only the first and the last questions. Beyond that, the group itself would cover every topic on the guide. (Morgan, 2002, p. 148)

When the researcher has participants who are themselves deeply interested in the research topic and has created a conducive group composition, this kind of approach is possible. Again, this is why recruitment and the opening question (or opening exercise) are so important. Furthermore, the instructions given to the group are vital in open approaches (Morgan, 2002). Most research participants have never been subjects of social research. Because the researcher, whom they may view as the expert, recruited them, the onus is on the researcher to clearly explain that he or she has brought the group together because they are the experts on this topic, and the researcher is there to learn from them. The best way to accomplish this is for the participants to speak freely and be as in-depth as possible. The researcher's role is that of active listener. This kind of direction is key if an open for- mat is being employed. With any luck, beyond asking the first and last questions, the researcher will have to say only things like "can you explain that" or "what do you mean by that" from time to time.

The dynamic of a group is one of the most unique features of the focus group method. Given the significance of the group dynamic, the researcher's role as moderator deeply impacts the research process. Accordingly, great care must be used when considering how to moderate, which includes issues such as what level of structure will be imposed, how much control will be used, and how much the participants will be called on to shape their own story. Moderation itself is a skill that requires time and patience on the part of the researcher. The best way to learn how to moderate effectively is to practice; you will get better and better over time.

Julia Johnson Rothenberg and Peter McDermott, education professors at the Sage Colleges, used focus groups to research education and parental involvement in urban schools (McDermott & Rothenberg, 2000). Here's what Julia Johnson Rothenberg recently said about research design and moderation, in practice:

BEHIND THE SCENES WITH JULIA JOHNSON ROTHENBERG

Peter McDermott and I read several journal articles and reviews concerning focus groups after we had been questioning our work with subjects in our research on good teachers in economically distressed school districts. We knew we had strong feelings about our subjects and their work. It seemed that using the focus group approach in research would allow us to describe more fully our own biases and positions in the narrative of our research.

Another aspect to this became evident in our work with parents. These subjects were much more open with us when they were not described so much as "subjects" or "objects" of our research armed with questionnaires and questions already written. Seen as their allies and friends, they shared their experiences more openly.

Clearly the disadvantages are inherent in this plan: we do not have those objectively designed questionnaires, Likert-type scales, prearranged questions asked of all subjects. . . .

It was extremely gratifying to be an advocate for the parents of urban school children. We have strongly held beliefs in equity and justice for children in school, and we were pleased to share these with parents. Likewise, they appeared to be gratified by our discussions. We thought the parents were honest in their discussions, too, as they freely disagreed with each other and also verified each other's data. One example of this was their talking about how teachers never visited their part of town, never came to community events. When we asked if there were any exceptions, all the group members named one kindergarten teacher who came to their community fairs and visited families in their homes.

There was one concern we had about the discussions and their veridicality, however. We were aware that people kind of urged each other on—especially in complaining. When we would intervene and ask more pointed questions, they persisted in their complaints about schools and teachers. Perhaps all this was true, but the effects of the group appeared to operate as well. I think we needed more time with them, over time, to establish communication patterns and group dynamics that reoccurred over time. I think this is the primary role of the researcher with focus groups, to assess the dynamics and determine where verification is needed.

As you can see, Rothenberg notes that the group atmosphere allows focus group participants to view themselves as collaborators in the research project while also allowing researchers opportunities for reflexive practice regarding their own previously held assumptions.

How Is Focus Group Data Analyzed and Represented?

Once focus group data has been collected and transcribed, it is time for data analysis and then representation. The most unusual aspect of this process, particular to focus group interviews, is determining the unit of analysis. At what *level* does analysis occur, the individual or the group? The short answer is, both. Just like the group "happening" and the role of the researcher as moderator role of the moderator, focus group analysis is unique.

Focus group transcripts can be analyzed, in part, as a conglomeration of individual responses, in other words, on the **individual level of analysis.** This refers to what each individual group member has said and is similar to how one would analyze any interview transcript. What makes focus group analysis unique is that the transcript can also be analyzed at the **group level of analysis.** While individual accounts compose the transcript, there is also a group narrative that emerges, which is larger than the sum of its parts. In other words, the group dynamic and group interaction influence the data and become a part of the data. So researchers can analyze components of the data such as the interaction between research participants, interruptions, agreements, and so forth.

When thinking about how to represent focus group data, one must consider the following:

- What is the research question? What information am I trying to get at?

- At what level has analysis occurred (individual, group, or ideally both), and how can this best be represented accurately?

Depending on the research question and the kind of analysis employed (i.e., by hand, by computer), different kinds of representation will be appropriate. For an in-depth discussion on analysis and interpretation please consult Chapter 12, bearing in mind that focus group analysis differs as a result of the data at the group level.

Concept Mapping

Concept mapping is a new strategy for conducting focus group research (Morgan et al., 2008). Concept mapping impacts data collection as well as analysis; however, we place our discussion in the section on analysis because, as you will see, even when used as a part of data collection, it is an iterative process that involves a back-and-forth between data collection and analysis. Morgan et al. (2008) explain this strategy as follows:

Concept mapping uses stimulus materials in the form of concepts and ideas that are either prepared beforehand or generated by the participants themselves. It also uses projective techniques by getting the group to work together in the process of arranging those concepts into a physical map. This combination of more open-ended, creative thinking and more active group-based teamwork not only gives the participants a change of pace from analytical questioning but also has the potential to produce insightful data in its own right. The goal in concept mapping is for the participants to produce a diagram or "map" that summarizes their thinking on a key topic or issue. The process involves making map-like patterns by arranging and connecting a set of ideas that are relevant to the discussion topic. (p. 199)

There are two main strategies for using concept mapping. In one scenario, the researcher chooses a list of concepts related to the topic, and the list is used as "stimulus material" in the making of a concept map (Morgan et al., 2008). In the other scenario, the researcher provides a clear and brief description of the central topic and the participants generate the concepts (Morgan et al., 2008). This process usually requires the participants to refine their initial list (Morgan et al., 2008).

An excellent example of concept mapping comes from Morgan, Fellows, and Guevara's work with Peter Collier (2007) on how first-generation college students cope with problems regarding their coursework. For this project, the research team combined in-depth and focus group interviews with a sample of graduate teaching assistants in the yearlong Freshman Inquiry program. The participants had brainstorming sessions to generate a typical freshman problem, which became the "primary issue" in their map (for example, one identified problem was when students have two papers due on the same day) (Collier, 2007; Morgan et al., 2008). The next step was to create a list of issues linked to the problem and organize them into a hierarchical map (for example, talking to professors, requesting extensions, etc.) (Collier, 2007; Morgan et al., 2008). The result was a list of the different categories of academic problems first-generation college students face "and a clear sense of how various coping strategies fit into each of those problem areas" (Morgan et al., 2008, p. 202). In this example, the expert research participants generated the concepts and organized them, which is an analytic activity.

Conclusion

As focus group research has grown greatly in practice even since the publication of the first edition of this book, we conclude this chapter by suggesting two emergent trends in focus group research that we expect will continue.

First, there is an increase in the use of focus groups in international and cross-cultural research (Hennink, 2008). Given the rapid changes brought about by globalization as well as the marked increase in academic attention to issues of globalization, this research is likely to continue to emerge. International or cross-cultural focus groups can cover a range of pertinent topics such as the diverse impacts of development, health issues (living with HIV, caring for those with HIV), international adoption, environmental issues, and so forth. These kinds of projects raise a host of practical and ethical issues. For example, informed consent can be challenging because of language barriers, the nature of how participants are recruited, and different (or nonexistent) institutional review board standards in different geographic contexts. Hennink (2008) advocates using bilingual moderators to conduct the focus groups (raising many issues with respect to training, translation, and transcription) (for a full discussion of these issues see Hennink, 2008).

The second major trend in focus group practice is the emergence of electronic or online focus groups (for a full discussion, see Morgan et al., 2008). Researchers can now use chat rooms, discussion boards, and video conferencing as means of creating "spaces" for focus groups (Morgan et al., 2008). Researchers have also begun using instant messaging technology to conduct "synchronous online interviewing" (see Hinchcliffe & Gavin, 2009). These practices all come with various considerations and constraints. For example, video conferencing is expensive, and there are practical issues with setting up the technologies. However, these technologies are also enabling research that would otherwise be totally cost prohibitive or geographically impossible. As these practices continue to be honed, it is important to pay attention to the ethical issues that develop. For example, is it ethical to recruit people for focus groups while they are in chat rooms? How can message board data be ethically used, if at all, in the construction of an interview guide?

Focus groups are a valuable and time-efficient method for gathering qualitative interview data from multiple participants at one time. Particularly useful in exploratory research when little is known about the topic under investigation, or as a part of a mixed method or multimethod design, focus group interviewing allows the qualitative researcher to unearth individual narratives and a group narrative that is larger than the sum of its parts. In the context of focus group interviews, the researcher serves as moderator and determines the degree of control and structure the interview will have. Although this is a strength of the method, it also presents many challenges as researchers try to manage a group dynamic and later make sense of it, including the extent to which group members may have influenced each other and the resulting data. As always, this method should be used when it serves the guiding questions posed by a researcher and his or her research objectives.

Glossary

Comparative dimension: A major appeal of segmentation is that it produces another level of knowledge by comparing groups that are similar in every way except the areas of difference that are relevant.

Concept mapping: A strategy that combines stimulus materials and projective techniques. Through an analytic process, participants arrange concepts into a physical map.

Denaturalization: The process of understanding normative ideas and customs by challenging taken-for-granted assumptions that, like water to a fish, are difficult to discern.

Exploratory data: This is preliminary data that is used during the research design phase.

Grounded theory approach: Allows themes to emerge directly from the data, in this case the subjects, drawing directly on their ideas, language, and ways of understanding their own behaviors and attitudes.

The group effect: The dynamic produced within the group, which impacts individuals and their responses.

Group level of analysis: The analysis is focused on the "group narrative" that emerges, which is larger than the sum of its parts.

Heterogeneous: A group consisting of dissimilar participants.

Homogeneous: A group consisting of similar participants.

Individual level of analysis: The analytical focus is on what each individual group member has said.

Moderator: The researcher must take on the role of the moderator in the focus group; she or he greatly influences the flow of the conversation and thus the group dynamic and manner of the group narrative. The main concerns of the moderator are *structure* and *control*.

Open-ended approach: Under this frame, the moderator imposes less structure on the interview situation.

Segmentation: A design feature that maximizes the benefits of homogeneity while allowing for comparison among populations; this occurs when each group consists of similar members, but the different groups within the study as a whole are different from each other. Segmentation is a way of stratifying groups based on the particular traits where you want to examine difference (such as race or gender).

Standardization: Every research participant answers the same set of questions so the conversation will not stray off topic.

Standardized approach: Standardization refers to "the extent to which the identical questions and procedures are used in every group" and allows researchers to make valid comparisons between all of the groups in the study.

Triangulation: The use of three research methods.

Discussion Questions and Activities

1. How does data produced within focus groups differ from that which is produced in in-depth interviews?

2. In what ways do focus groups conducted for market research purposes differ from those conducted for sociological purposes?

3. How do group members influence each other in focus groups? How does this have an impact on data produced by focus groups? What is the group dynamic?

4. In what ways can focus groups be disempowering for some members? How can focus groups be used to empower participants? What is the link between participant empowerment and the theoretical tradition that guides the research?

5. What is the role of the researcher in focus groups? What issues of control come up for the researcher, and how are these issues informed by epistemological beliefs and research goals?

6. In what ways can survey research serve as a guide for structuring focus groups? How can focus groups and surveys be combined?

7. Discuss the strengths and weaknesses of conducting a less-structured focus group.

8. How does one sample for a focus group? Discuss the benefits of homogeneous versus heterogeneous focus groups. Discuss segmentation.

9. For this activity, get into groups of four to six participants. Use the topic "challenges balancing school demands and personal life" and create a concept map. First, come up with a list of possible major challenges. Then select the problem you want to focus on and branch out to related issues. Organize the issues hierarchically and create your concept map. How does this technique help you understand this issue and how various components are interrelated? What was the experience of group work like? What are the limitations of this procedure?

Resources

Suggested Web Sites

Basics of Conducting Focus Groups

http://www.mapnp.org/library/evaluatn/focusgrp.htm

This Web site contains a comprehensive outline of how to set up a focus group, what questions to ask, and how to run the session, as well as what to do after the session is over. This Web site also provides a link to other useful focus group Web sites on the Internet.

The University of Surrey Social Research Update

http://www.soc.surrey.ac.uk/sru/SRU19.html

This Web site contains an article on focus groups written by Anita Gibbs, which appears in *Social Research Update,* Issue 19. The article comments on the definition of focus groups, as well as how to run such a session, the benefits and limitations of focus groups, and the ethical issues that come to light when using this method.

Qualitative Research: Telephone Focus Groups, Face-to-Face Focus Groups

http://www.mnav.com/qualitative_research.htm

This Web site contains many links that deal with how to conduct various types of focus groups, as well as tips and strategies to use when dealing with focus groups, either in person or on the telephone. This Web site also introduces online focus groups. The articles mainly deal with marketing strategies but can be related to other areas as well.

Focus Groups

http://imwww.hhi.de/USINACTS/tutorial/focus.html

This Web site offers a tutorial on what focus groups are, how and why they are used, and their applications, as well as advantages and disadvantages.

Using Focus Groups for Evaluation

http://ag.arizona.edu/fcr/fs/cyfar/focus.htm

This Web site, based at the University of Arizona, contains an article written by Mary Marczak and Meg Sewell. The article answers questions concerning what a focus group really is, what focus groups can demonstrate and cannot demonstrate, and how to set up a focus group. The article also addresses the advantages and disadvantages of this method.

Relevant Journals

Qualitative Health Research

Qualitative Inquiry

The Qualitative Report

Notes

1. In this chapter we use the term *mixed method* to denote research designs that combine qualitative and quantitative approaches and we use the term *multimethod* to denote research designs that combine two or more qualitative approaches.

2. This is not to imply that arranging a focus group interview is easier than arranging in-depth interviews. In fact, the contrary may be true, as it may be very difficult to arrange a time when all of the interviewees are available. In addition, sampling and recruiting may be particularly challenging in focus group research.

CHAPTER 8

Ethnography

Robert Park, an urban sociologist, gave his students the following advice:

> You have been told to go grubbing in the library, thereby accumulating a mass of notes and a liberal coating of grime. You have been told to choose problems wherever you can find musty stacks of routine records based on trivial schedules prepared by tired bureaucrats and filled out by reluctant applicants for aid or fussy do-gooders or indifferent clerks. This is called "getting your hands dirty in real research." Those who counsel you are wise and honorable; the reasons they offer are of great value. But one more thing is needful: firsthand observation. Go and sit in the lounges of the luxury hotels and on the doorsteps of the flophouses; sit on the Gold Coast streets and on the slum shakedowns; sit in the Orchestra Hall and in the Star and Garter Burlesque. In short, gentlemen, go get the seat of your pants dirty in real research. (quoted in McKinney, 1966, p. 71)

What Is Ethnography?

Ethnographic research aims to get a holistic understanding of how individuals in different cultures and subcultures make sense of their lived reality. The literal meaning of the word *ethnography* is "writing culture." Ethnographers are researchers who "go inside" the social worlds of the inhabitants of their research setting, "hanging out," observing, and recording the ongoing social life of its members by providing "thick descriptions" of the social context and the everyday activities of the people who live in these worlds, spending a good amount of time engaging with the events, people, and activities in the setting (Geertz, 1973). Ethnographers provide detailed accounts of the *everyday practices and customs* of a culture, subculture, or group, often collecting artifacts and other cultural materials and paying attention to religious, familial, political, and economic life. This method is "up front and personal" and usually takes place in **natural settings**—those places where individuals go about their daily lives—rather than a place "set up" by the researcher at a specific site.

The ethnographic method has often been associated with the field of *anthropology,* in which research is conducted on foreign cultures to capture understanding of the "native" population—the customs, values, and artifacts associated with a given group and its wider culture. Bronislaw Malinowski was a Polish-born British social anthropologist who conducted several fieldwork visits among the Trobriand Islanders in the Western Pacific from 1915 to 1916 and again from 1917 to 1918. Malinowski (1922) wanted to live among the peoples he studied. He felt that fieldwork must begin by "cutting oneself off from the company of other white men, and remaining in as close contact with the natives as possible which really can only be achieved by camping right in their villages" (p. 6). The following is an excerpt from his fieldnotes, which illustrate the experience of cultural immersion that an ethnographer may experience in studying another culture or subculture:

> Soon after I had established myself in Omarkana Trobriand Islands, I began to take part, in a way, in the village life, to look forward to the important or festive events, to take personal interest in the gossip and developments of the village occurrences; to wake up every morning to a new day, presenting itself to me more or less as it does to the natives. . . . As I went on my morning walk through the village, I could see intimate details of family life, of toilet, cooking, taking of meals; I could see the arrangements for the day's work, people starting on their errands, or groups of men and women busy at some manufacturing tasks. Quarrels, jokes, family scenes, events usually trivial, sometimes dramatic but always significant, form the atmosphere of my daily life, as well as theirs. It must be remembered that the natives saw me constantly every day, they ceased to be interested or alarmed, or made self-conscious by my presence, and I ceased to be a disturbing element in the tribal life which I was to study, altering it by my very approach. . . . In fact, as they knew that I would thrust my nose into everything . . . they finished by regarding me as part and parcel of their life, a necessary evil or nuisance, mitigated by donations of tobacco. (Malinowski, 1922, pp. 7–8)

The sociological practice of ethnography dates back to the late 19th century and is rooted in the social reform movements that sought to understand and provide assistance to the underclass urban poor (Emerson, 2001). Early ethnographies by sociologists contained a variety of mixed methods, from survey research to **field** observations and intensive interviewing. Early ethnographic research was influenced by a social survey movement. An example of this type of ethnography comes from Charles Booth's (1902) study of London's underclass in his classic work *Life and Labour of the People in London.* Ethnographer Robert Emerson (2001) notes the following concerning Booth's work:

> In his studies, Booth combined statistical data, widespread interviewing, and direct observation to amass an extremely detailed and systematic description of the lives of the London poor. In their use of direct observation, Booth and his colleagues at times entered directly into the world of the poor. (p. 9)

Writing over a half century later, sociologist Elijah Anderson (1976) relates his experiences in conducting fieldwork in a poor black establishment on the South Side of Chicago he calls "Jelly's place." Jelly's was a bar and liquor store frequented by working and unemployed black males. Anderson also employs the technique of **participant observation** in his research. However, he does not go to an isolated island in the Western Pacific, but like Charles Booth is drawn to an urban setting— an American city, home to a part of American subculture whose life and activities remain "hidden" from the wider culture's purview—a subcultural island within the dominant culture of the city of Chicago. Anderson's purpose was to uncover the social life of Jelly's place—to understand the interactions among those who came to Jelly's.

Anderson's work in the inner city of Chicago has its roots in the fieldwork tradition known as the *Chicago School* of sociology, founded by Robert E. Park and Ernest W. Burgess. Both of these sociologists were influenced by the work of late 19th-century social reformers, such as Jane Addams, who founded Hull House, a social settlement institution, and they trained and supervised students in the use of ethnography from around 1917 to the early 1940s (see Addams, 1910; Deegan, 2001). They urged their doctoral students to obtain first-person accounts of the everyday lives of those individuals living in "natural areas" of the city. "Natural areas" are thought of as concentric zones that emanate out from the city's center, with each zone containing individuals with different racial, ethnic, and social class backgrounds. Park's and Burgess's students went on to produce a wide range of important ethnographies dealing, very often, with the city's "underside," invisible populations and issues such as homelessness (Anderson, 1923), gangs (Thrasher, 1927), taxi-dance halls (Cressey, 1932), and race relations (Frazier, 1932), to name a few.

Malinowski, Booth, and Anderson are part of the ethnographic tradition. They are not there as interviewers primarily but are engaged in observation and conversation with those in the setting. They record their observations and interactions as **fieldnotes,** which are written accounts of their everyday experiences in the field, sometimes jotting down notes on the fly, but usually writing up their fieldnotes shortly after leaving the setting. Ethnographers may also employ other methods such as in-depth interviews and focus groups with members in the setting and are interested in any documents that may give them insight into the lives of those in the setting. Ethnographers may also *content analyze* a variety of historical and present-day documents and cultural artifacts to better understand the wider historical context of a given setting.

The concept of a *field* in ethnography differs depending on the type of research project you pursue. For an anthropologist studying a foreign culture such as Malinowski's study of the Trobriand Islanders in the Western Pacific in the early 1900s, the field is a *cultural* setting. For Anderson, studying a local bar or local neighborhood, the bar or neighborhood becomes the *field*. This type of research is often known as **urban ethnography.** Another classic example of an urban ethnography is sociologist William Foote Whyte's (1943) study of Cornerville, an Italian American neighborhood located in the inner city of Boston. Whyte wanted to understand the social interactions taking place within this community.

The popular image of places like Cornerville was one of disorganization and suspicion on the part of the dominant culture. Especially during World War II, there was a feeling that the "Italian slum dweller might be more devoted to fascism and Italy than to democracy and the United States" (Gubrium & Holstein, 1997, p. 20). Through "hanging out" with local residents, Whyte was able to gain insight into the life of this neighborhood from the perspective of its inhabitants. Let's go "behind the scenes" with Whyte as he reflects on his publication of *Street Corner Society* (1943), 12 years after the publication of the first edition. Whyte talks about how he first got involved in studying Cornerville and some of the specific challenges this type of research project entailed.

BEHIND THE SCENES WITH WILLIAM FOOTE WHYTE, REFLECTING ON *STREET CORNER SOCIETY*

I began with a vague idea that I wanted to study a slum district. Eastern City provided several possible choices. In the early weeks of my Harvard fellowship I spent some of my time walking up and down the streets of the various slum districts of Eastern City and talking with people in social agencies about these districts. . . .

I made my choice on very unscientific grounds: Cornerville best fitted my picture of what a slum district should look like. Somehow I had developed a picture of run-down three- to five-story buildings crowded in together. The dilapidated wooden-frame buildings of some other parts of the city did not look quite genuine to me. . . .

At the time I was completely baffled at the problem of finding my way into the district. Cornerville was right before me and yet so far away. I could walk freely up and down its streets, and I had even made my way into some of the flats, and yet I was still a stranger in a world completely unknown to me. . . . I sought out the local settlement houses. They were open to the public. . . . As I look back on it now, the settlement house also seems a very unpromising place from which to begin such a study. . . . However that may be, the settlement houses proved the right place for me at this time, for it was here that I met Doc. I had talked to a number of the social workers about my plans and hopes to get acquainted with the people and study the district. They listened with varying degrees of interest. . . . In a sense, my study began on the evening of February 4, 1937, when the social worker called me in to meet Doc. She showed us into her office and then left so that we could talk. Doc waited quietly for me to begin, as he sank down into a chair. I found him a man of medium height and spare build. His hair was light brown, quite a contrast to the more typical black Italian hair. It was thinning around the temples. His cheeks were sunken. His eyes were a light blue and seemed to have a penetrating gaze. . . . I began by asking him if the social worker had told him about what I was trying to do. "No, she just told me that you wanted to meet me and that I should like to meet you." Then I went into a long explanation. . . . Doc heard me out without any change of expression, so that I had no way of predicting his reaction. When I was finished, he asked: "Do you want to see the high life or the low life?" "I want to see all that I can. I want to get as complete a picture of the community as possible."

"Well, any nights you want to see anything, I'll take you around. I can take you to the joints—gambling joints—I can take you around to the street corners. Just remember that you're my friend. That's all they need to know. I know these places, and, if I tell them that you're my friend, nobody will bother you. You just tell me what you want to see, and we'll arrange it."

Source: W. F. Whyte, "On the Evolution of Street Corner Society," in A. Laureau and F. Schultz (Eds.), *Journeys Through Ethnography: Realistic Accounts of Fieldwork* (pp. 9–74), Boulder, CO: Westview Press, 1996. Originally published as an appendix in W. F. Whyte's second edition of *Street Corner Society,* University of Chicago Press, 1955. Used with permission of University of Chicago Press.

Ethnography is a useful tool for creating an in-depth picture of a cultural setting, particularly an exclusive urban environment that requires a researcher's physical presence in order to get at lives hidden from the outside world.

Using an Ethnographic Approach: When Is It Appropriate?

As we have discussed in earlier chapters, the *research question* dictates the type of methods one pursues. If your research question requires an in-depth understanding of the social *context*, in particular the culture within which individuals engage in a particular set of behaviors, then ethnography is an important method for getting at this understanding through direct observation of behaviors and through interactions with others in your research setting. Ethnographic methods allow you to understand social reality from the participants' perspective, which is why it remains a staple practice in qualitative inquiry. You have the opportunity to explore the range of activities that may even remain unconscious to your participants. Ethnographers ask questions such as these:

- How do individuals view their world?

- What is their story?

- How do members of a given culture understand a custom or behavior?

As we observed in Chapter 3, the selection of a particular research problem is related to a number of different factors. Your own biography may be the decisive reason for wanting to find out more about a given group or community. Perhaps growing up in a small town, inner city, or suburban lifestyle provides you with a set of specific ideas and interests or particular curiosities concerning aspects of the social world. It may be that a given research question becomes sparked by a personal, professional, or academic experience, or even a memorable event, whether it be tragic or uplifting. Peggy Sullivan and Kirk Elifson happened to attend a church service run by a religious group known as Free Holiness. This group was a part of the Pentecostal Christian Church in a rural Georgia community; it used serpent handling as part of its religious ceremony. Sullivan and Elifson (1996) stumbled onto their research question almost by accident:

> What began as a curiosity visit grew into a two-year research project. Kirk orig-inally went to the church with an undergraduate class he was teaching and later returned with graduate students from a sociology of religion seminar. Peggy was among those students. We arrived and sat on the last pew near the back door. Our curiosity was mixed with trepidation as we waited for the service to begin. . . . At first it was a half-joke-half-dare between us that we should con-duct a participant observation research project focused on the church. Several days after the seminar group had visited the church we decided to learn if studying the church would be possible. We knew practically nothing about rural Pentecostal religion and even less about serpent handlers. We had no idea whether we would be welcomed to the church enough to study it. (p. 34)

There may also be a set of economic and practical constraints that determine whether you decide to conduct an ethnographic study. Ethnographic work is labor-intensive and requires a good deal of time, energy, and resources.

An ethnographic perspective relies on a set of philosophical or epistemological assumptions concerning the nature of the social world. Ethnographic work relies, for the most part, on an *interpretative* rather than a *positivist* perspective on the nature of social reality. The goal of this type of research is exploring and describ-ing social phenomena. However, this does not mean that some ethnographers are not also positivists who employ quantitative methods to get at an understanding of their setting. Some ethnographers may "test out" their preconceived hypothesis in the field as well. The ethnographic research question, however, is usually a *guid-ing* one that is not phrased in terms of hypotheses or a set of propositions. Participants in ethnographic research projects may hold a variety of different per-spectives on reality within the same setting, and there is a dynamic interplay between the researcher and the researched in identifying and making sense out of these different realities.

There are also ethnographers whose perspective goes beyond that of description and understanding. Some ethnographic fieldwork is also *activist* and sets a goal of social change and empowerment of those within a given setting as well. This more activist ethnographic stance provides an interpretive as well as a *critical perspective.* The goal of a *critical ethnography* is to understand social life in order to change the way that those in power marginalize those with less power (Bailey, 1996, p. 25). Christine Sleeter (1992) studies multicultural education with the goal of wanting to change school systems, saying, "I have sought to understand why schools so consis-tently serve children from the dominant society better than children from poor families, families of color, and girls" (p. 55). She conducts a critical ethnography of an inner-city school system to understand the inner workings of multicultural edu-cation with the goal of developing social policy concerning multicultural education:

The book . . . suggests why the mix of people who work in schools should reflect a much wider diversity of life experiences in order for teachers to generate for themselves richer concepts of what cultural diversity means. Diversifying the teaching force is a policy issue; this book addresses that issue. (p. 56)

There are a range of feminist approaches to ethnography, depending on the particular disciplinary perspective, theoretical stance, and political goals of any given feminist ethnographer. What unites these varying approaches is a deep commitment to understanding the issues and concerns of women from their perspective and the quality of being especially attentive to the activities and "goings on" of women in the research setting. The work of Patti Lather and Chris Smithies (1997) is an important example of feminist ethnography "giving voice" to women's concerns and issues. Lather and Smithies interviewed and participated in the ongoing lives of women they met through HIV/AIDS support groups in three cities in the United States. They studied this epidemic by concentrating on the female HIV/AIDS population, whose voice has remained muted. Their research provided in-depth accounts of women's experiences living with HIV/AIDS and took an openly critical, feminist look at the perception and role of HIV/AIDS in women's lives.

How Do You Get Started?
Negotiating the Research Setting

As we saw with Peggy Sullivan and Kirk Elifson's participant observation study of a Pentecostal Church, familiarity with a setting may in fact propel an individual to be curious enough about the setting to want to research it. At other times, the choice of a specific research question may determine what research sites are acceptable or not acceptable, when it is imperative that you select a research site that will give you the information you need to specifically address your research question(s). Sometimes you may need to select more than one setting. Several factors are important to consider in selecting a specific research setting:

- Can you conduct research in this setting?

- How accessible is the site to you as a researcher?

Some sites that may at first appear inaccessible might in fact open up to the individual as a result of specific network ties the researcher has to that setting; other settings that one might think would be easy to enter can be impervious to outsiders. Who is considered an "outsider" also depends on the type of setting. For example, some settings may restrict specific types of individuals based on their age, sex, race/ethnicity, and social class background. Terry Williams is a black American sociologist who is interested in cocaine culture. Most researchers would find studying this culture quite inaccessible. His status as a black man and as a former well-received prison teacher are key factors that assisted Williams in gaining access to after-hours clubs as a setting for his study of cocaine culture. Williams (1996) notes:

> In 1974, after completing several years of graduate study in sociology at the City University of New York, I accepted a teaching position at John Jay College of Criminal Justice. My first assignment entailed commuting from the main campus to Rikers Island to teach in the satellite program established by the college. After a year in this special program, I became friendly with several of the inmates, many of whom were serving relatively light sentences. Upon their release, three of them called me and offered to take me out on the town. They showed me the nightlife of New York City as I had never seen it before. In the small, intimate clubs known as after-hours spots, I was introduced to a bewildering variety of people—musicians, drug dealers, punk rockers, transvestites, secretaries, doctors, dancers, gamblers, actors, policemen, prostitutes—all of whom were there to share in a lifestyle based on the enjoyment of cocaine and the pleasure and excitement brought on by the intensity of their interaction. (p. 28)

Williams's status as a male of color as well as his credentials as a teacher within a prison setting might have been two crucial elements of his status that provided a positive link to the inmate population, perhaps providing him with credibility as well as some base on which to build trust with the inmates.

Sometimes the selection of a research setting depends on a consideration of practical issues such as economics (How expensive will it be to conduct research in this setting?), time constraints (How much time do you have to spend in the setting? Does your research conflict with other obligations?), and potential risks to you as the researcher (Are you risking bodily harm by entering a setting where illegal activity takes place?). Ruth Queen Smith (1998) provides an example of how one of these practical issues adversely affected her ability to select a setting in which she was interested. Smith (1998) was a doctoral candidate in education, and while she wanted to conduct research at a particular setting, her class schedule conflicted with her ability to make crucial observations in that setting:

> At first, I considered three different cultural settings for this ethnographic study. Two of the three choices involved researching people of poverty in racially integrated environments. These two research possibilities required that I conduct observations and interactions within the culture between the hours of 9:00 pm and 3:00 am because that was when the majority of sociocultural interactions were evident in the sites. Reality quickly awakened me. Both of these potential sites presented strong potential for engaging an ethnographic researcher. However, with a demanding doctoral student schedule, I knew that it was not in my best interest to take either study at this time. I surrendered to practicality. This recognition created a reflective space in which I could discover my own process concerning the identification, selection, and ranking of research choices. (p. 81)

Once a research question and site are chosen, the next step is to negotiate access into the setting as well as establish what role you as an ethnographer will take in this setting.

Gaining Entry Into the Setting

How you gain *access* to a community or group setting is critical in determining the type of data, if any, you will be able to collect and how difficult or easy the process will be. First, you will need to think about how you will gain permission from a human subjects committee, if there is one in the setting you propose to study, as well as how you will gain the permission of the institutional review board (IRB), if you are working within an organizational setting such as a university. There are a myriad of ways to gain access to your setting, but a general way to begin is by making a *personal connection* to someone who knows a member of the setting you wish to study or who can serve as a liaison to some key members of your setting. You might begin by thinking about how best to set up this contact. Would you write a permissions letter or make a call? What type of letter? How much do you reveal about your study?

Settings often contain **gatekeepers** whose approval is crucial to gain access and acceptance. **Formal gatekeepers** grant you formal permission to enter a setting for the purpose of conducting research, and may be, for example, a principal of a school or a director of a social service agency. While formal permission is important, some in the setting may see your connection to a higher level official as threatening to them. This may be especially true in settings where participants do not necessarily see themselves in alliance with the formal officials or gatekeepers in the site of interest (i.e., inmates in a prison or students in a school setting). What may matter more in gaining access to this kind of setting is the approval or support of **informal gatekeepers** who hold key positions in the informal culture or subculture you are studying and whose influence on others in this group shapes your level of access (i.e., the leader of a social clique you are studying in a high school). Informal gatekeepers have the power to give their approval with regard to your presence in the field. Several factors affect your ability to gain entry into a setting. The first is the degree to which the setting is *public or private.*

Public settings like cafés, bars, or laundromats are not typically difficult to access. Access to *private settings* may be more difficult because members may be motivated to protect the boundaries of their setting and, in some cases, keep their affairs hidden from public view. If illegal activities are a routine part of a setting of interest, gaining access may be next to impossible for the researcher, and entry into such a setting may place the researcher in harm's way. It may be in fact that the setting is quite public, like a restroom, but that there is a strong motivation by those in the setting to keep their activities under cover.

Several options are available for gaining access to more private settings. One role, of course, is to go "undercover" into the setting as a way of gaining entry. Laud Humphries studied the activities of male homosexuals who engaged in "illicit" sexual activities in public restrooms. Humphries was able to gain access to the setting covertly by assuming the role of a gay male and taking on the job of a "watch queen" or "lookout" who alerted the *insiders* (those engaging in illicit sexual activity) to the impending presence of *outsiders,* such as the police, and others who only saw the setting as a public restroom. Humphries (1976) notes:

> By serving as a voyeur-lookout, I was able to move around the room at will, from window to window, and to observe all that went on without alarming my respondents or otherwise disturbing the action. Being a watch queen enabled me to gather data on the behavior of participants in homosexual acts. (p. 104)

Another important strategy to gaining access to a setting involves establishing relationships with central figures who become **key informants.** Some key informants may in fact be the gatekeepers of the setting. Recall the figure of "Doc" in William Foote Whyte's (1955/1996) study, *Street Corner Society,* who played a central role in helping Whyte both to gain entry into his setting and to understand the subculture of Cornerville (p. 20). Through his initial contact and friendship with Doc, Whyte was able to find his way into the goings-on of this close-knit community. In effect, Doc took on the role of key informant:

> Doc introduced me as "my friend Bill" to Chichi, who ran the place and to Chichi's friends and customers. I stayed there with Doc part of the time in the kitchen, where several men would sit around and talk, and part of the time in the other room watching the crap game. . . . [W]hen I went to the toilet, there was an excited burst of conversation in Italian and he had to assure them that I was not a G-man. He said he told them flatly that I was a friend of his, and they agreed to let it go at that. (p. 26)

Throughout the study, Doc provides Whyte (1955/1996) with insightful interpretations of the social life of Cornerville:

> Without any training he [Doc] was such a perceptive observer that it only needed a little stimulus to help him to make explicit much of the dynamics of the social organization of Cornerville. Some of the interpretations I have made have been more his than mine, although it is now impossible to disentangle them. (p. 28)

While Whyte (1955/1996) relied on Doc for gaining a perspective on Cornerville life, depending too much on any *one* informant or becoming too aligned with a specific informant in the setting can have its drawbacks. Seeing the setting only through the eyes of a specific informant may serve to bias one's observations. Doc has a specific point of view on the setting, and while his observations and interpretations shed much light onto Whyte's understanding Cornerville, *one way of seeing is also another way of not seeing.* For example, if Doc had made enemies in the setting, Whyte's close alignment with Doc might have served to alienate some important segments of the community from Whyte's research or might have prevented him from seeking additional informants whose perspective or engagement with the community were different from Doc's.

Sometimes gaining access to a setting depends on the very attributes of the field researcher—his or her age, gender, social class, and racial/ethnic background. Some of these social attributes in and of themselves may make the researcher a perceived insider or outsider to the setting. Interestingly enough, in any given setting, the researcher's role may become quite fluid, with the researcher taking on both insider and outsider roles. What specific social attributes matter depends on how these attributes mesh with those of the setting. Elijah Anderson's ability to gain access to Jelly's bar and liquor store was probably enhanced because of his status as a black American male. He shared some *key attributes* with those who hung out at Jelly's (his race and gender). Although Anderson can be considered an "outsider" especially in terms of his education (a PhD student at the University of Chicago), he was able to move across some important social hurdles to gain entrance into the inner world of the regulars at Jelly's because Herman, an important group regular at Jelly's, befriended him and asked Anderson to become his "cousin." Anderson took on a "fictive kin" role with Herman, allowing him to access an insider status with Herman's friends and coworkers.

Some researchers find that their gender can be an impediment to their gaining access to the setting, especially when that setting is male dominated. Arlene Kaplan Daniels (1967) wanted to study military officers but encountered obstacles when she found that they wanted her to maintain a traditionally feminine role, expecting her to exhibit a range of deferential behaviors. Some balked at being interviewed unless they placed her in a subservient position such as that of a mascot (pp. 285–286). She notes:

> I developed mediating and soothing strategies. . . . I learned the necessity of changing my tone. And, once I was in the field, I abandoned my picture of myself as the director of a research project and returned to the role of student and humble observer. . . . What I began to learn was that certain kinds of deference to the idea of superior male status had to be paid. Certain behavior was considered inappropriate or even insulting from women: a firm hand clasp, a direct eye-to-eye confrontation, a brisk, business like air, and assured manner of joking or kidding with equals were all antagonizing. (p. 273)

Female researchers in settings that hold traditional expectations for women find that to offset these roles and gain access, they need to be perceived as nonthreatening. Exhibiting more "feminine attributes" like those described by Arlene Kaplan Daniels, or taking on specific roles in the setting like that of daughter, may, in fact, increase a female researcher's probability of gaining access and information in more traditional male-dominated settings (Myerhoff, 1978).

Negotiating Your Research Role in the Setting

An ethnographer participates in the research setting to varying degrees. There is often a tension between wanting to get close to those in the setting and at the same time maintaining the role of researcher, which involves a degree of detachment. Some research may require more attachment while other research may require less attachment or no attachment at all. Finding a balance between the two is crucial in most fieldwork settings, and as a result, participation ranges along a continuum from complete observer, observer-as-participant, participant-as-observer, to complete participant (Gold, 1958). We can consider our participation diagrammatically as shown in Figure 8.1.

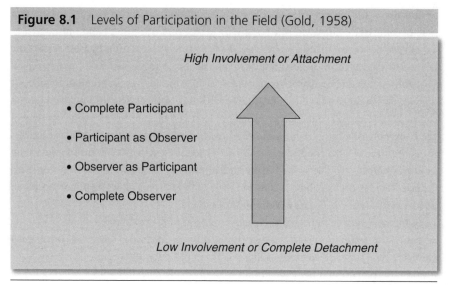

Figure 8.1 Levels of Participation in the Field (Gold, 1958)

High Involvement or Attachment

- Complete Participant

- Participant as Observer

- Observer as Participant

- Complete Observer

Low Involvement or Complete Detachment

Source: Used by permission.

None of the roles is set in stone for the life of a project; in fact, a researcher may progress through each of these roles as fieldwork progresses by moving back and forth on the continuum between observation and participation, depending on the circumstances encountered in the setting. There are limits in the amount one can go back and forth between these roles. Once one begins to participate in the field to some degree, there is a chance that certain expectations for participation will evolve. It is easier to begin as a complete observer and gradually get involved in the setting than to start at the other end of the continuum as a complete participant. It may be harder to go in the other direction and diminish your level of participation, especially when those in the setting may have come to expect your presence and active participation. This may tarnish the rapport the researcher has developed with those in the setting. If in doubt about your role in a specific setting, start out slowly in terms of the extent to which you participate. It is easier to pull back from a position on the observational end of the continuum than to move from complete participant to observer.

Complete Observer

A **complete observer** role requires that the researcher's identity remain hidden; the researcher does not interact with those in the setting but instead makes observations of the setting by using such devices as a hidden video camera or by remaining invisible behind a one-way mirror or a screen to avoid detection. The complete observer role allows the researcher to study a setting without interfering with its day-to-day operations, thereby minimizing the bias (or *reactivity*) that might result from the presence of the researcher interacting and possibly changing the very nature of social relationships in the setting. It is possible that those in the setting will change their behavior if they know a researcher is present.

Taking on the role of complete observer has its drawbacks. It does not allow the researcher to clarify meanings and ask questions concerning things that are not readily understood. How do we know that our understanding or observation is shared with those we research? Most fieldwork requires more than observation. It may not be easy for the researcher who is in the field to maintain the stance of complete observer. Sometimes people in the field unwittingly draw the researcher into a more heightened participation level than the researcher may feel comfortable with, as Emerson and Pollner (2001) note:

> Unlike laboratory researchers whose one-way mirrors provide distance and allow completely unengaged observation . . . fieldworkers cannot necessarily stand back and watch social interaction with absolutely no involvement with those engaged in that interaction. Nor can the fieldworker simply declare a detached position by fiat: host members may resist the researcher's definition of his level of (non-) involvement and even ignore his self-definition as a researcher, analyst or observer. (p. 241)

What is important to note about the complete observer role is that the researcher's role remains hidden in the setting. The lack of cognizance on the part of the respondent in the field is what defines the role of the researcher as strictly an observer. An important question that stems from this point is the following:

- How can the researcher maintain distance in the setting so that the observer role is not compromised?

Yet, given the social dynamics in the field, whether encouraged by others to take more of a participant role or embracing opportunities for fuller participation, researchers often try to strike a balance between intimacy and distance.

Observer-as-Participant

Along the continuum and moving toward more intimacy in the setting is the role of **observer-as-participant.** This role requires researchers to reveal their researcher identity in the setting, but the extent to which they actively engage with the members of the setting is *limited.* Pamela Fishman's research on social interaction between married couples provides an example of this type of role identity. Fishman (1990) was interested in analyzing the power relations in conversations between couples in the privacy of their homes:

- How do couples interact with each other in their everyday lives?

- How are power and authority produced and maintained in an intimate relationship?

Fishman (1990) intensively studied the conversations of three couples who agreed to have her record their conversations in their homes. She notes the following concerning her role:

> The tape recorders were present in the apartments from four to fourteen days. I am satisfied that the material represents natural conversation and that there was no undue awareness of the recorder. The tapes sounded natural to me, like

conversations between my husband and myself. Others who have read the transcripts agreed. All six people also reported that they soon began to ignore the tape recorder. Further, they were apologetic about the material, calling it trivial and uninteresting, just the ordinary affairs of everyday life. Finally, one couple said they forgot the recorder sufficiently to begin making love in the living room while the recorder was on. That segment and two others were the only ones the participants deleted before handing the tapes over to me. (p. 227)

While Fishman does have contact with the couples in her study, her presence in the research setting is invisible. While couples are aware of her research presence by the intrusion of a tape recorder into their everyday lives, for the most part, Fishman's role remains very peripheral in the research setting.

Participant-as-Observer

The **participant-as-observer** participates fully in the ongoing activities of the research setting and members of the setting know the identity of the researcher. There are *degrees of participation* in the research setting and degrees to which members of the setting view the researcher as an insider to that setting.

William Foote Whyte (1955/1996) does some negotiating of his role in Cornerville. At times, Whyte himself is unclear about his degree of participation in the setting. While residents know that he is a researcher who wants to know more about the life of Cornerville, it takes Whyte and the residents of Cornerville a bit of time to find a balance between these two roles:

> At first I concentrated upon fitting into Cornerville, but a little later I had to face the questions of how far I was to immerse myself in the life of the district. I bumped into that problem one evening as I was walking down the street with the Nortons. Trying to enter into the spirit of the small talk, I cut loose with a string of obscenities and profanity. The walk came to a momentary halt as they all stopped to look at me in surprise. Doc shook his head and said: "Bill, you're not supposed to talk like that. That doesn't sound like you." I tried to explain that I was only using terms that were common on the street corner. Doc insisted, however, that I was different and that they wanted me to be that way. . . . I learned that people did not expect me to be just like them; in fact, they were interested and pleased to find me different, just so long as I took a friendly interest in them. (p. 30)

While Whyte's (1955/1996) role allows him to maintain some distance so that he does not directly influence those he wants to study, he finds that he is not involved enough with the group to obtain more specific information and insights, which might be obtained through complete participation. What is he missing by not fully participating in the group? Complete participation would allow those in the group to develop a better sense of who Whyte is. If he were able to garner their trust, they might open up to him about their lives, especially those aspects that still remain hidden to him. However, there is a downside to complete participation. The more involved Whyte becomes, the higher the chance that he might lose his objectivity as the outsider. There is also the issue of ethical dilemmas he may confront once he gets more involved with this group. How much can he reveal in his published study about the group? What happens if he uncovers any illegal activity? By remaining at a distance, there is in fact less of a chance that he will confront an ethical dilemma with which he must then grapple.

Complete Participant

The **complete participant** actively engages with members of the setting; however, the participants in the setting do not know the researcher's identity. The researcher participates in a *covert* manner by not revealing his or her researcher identity in order to "pass" as an authentic member of that setting. Judith Rollins (1987) chose to go under cover to study the plight of domestic workers. She notes:

> I began the field research process by working for a month as a domestic. . . . I chose to submerge myself in the situation before even designing the research in order to sensitize myself to the experience of domestic work and of relation to a female employer. . . . I obtained my jobs by placing advertisements in city-wide and suburban newspapers. (p. 9)

When engaging in undercover research, the researcher must address a variety of ethical concerns, which we will discuss in the following section.

The Ethics of Deception in Ethnographic Research

As Calvey (2008) states in his article on **covert research**, undercover research "is a situated business and not open to rationalistic planning" at all points throughout the research process (p. 908). Due to the nature of the field and often what the study entails, researchers must contend with ethical issues when they make a decision on the type of role they will take up in an ethnographic setting, especially when this role involves deception. Those who favor deception argue that it is necessary because certain types of field research would be impossible to conduct if the researchers' identity were revealed. Douglas (1979) goes so far as to suggest that covert researchers are *entitled* to do this type of work "in order to achieve the higher object of scientific truth" (p. 17). Others point out that going under cover provides the researcher with an opportunity to study individual or group behavior that might otherwise remain invisible; such is frequently the case with "studying up," as in the case of research done on elite groups such as surgeons (see Jan Famradt, 1998) or groups whose activities are often secretive, such as cult organizations (Galanter, 1989). For Judith Rollins (1987), in her study on domestic workers, the defining criterion for her decision to use deception hinged on whether or not the "gains" outweighed the "losses":

> The immediate question became: is what can be gained worth the loss? I decided it was. I decided that because this occupation had been such a significant one for low-income women and because so little research had been done on it despite

its presence throughout the world, the understanding that might be gained by my putting myself in the position of a domestic, even in this limited way was worth the price. (p. 15)

We can see that researchers make a range of ethical decisions with regard to the issues of deception in research that range from ethically relativist arguments that argue for basing decisions about deception on the particular situation at hand, to those researchers who advocate an ethically absolutist stance, claiming any deception in research is an invasion of respondents' privacy and morally wrong. Between these two ends of an ethics of deception continuum are those researchers who advocate a position that weighs the benefits of doing a research project against the perceived harm to both the respondent and the researcher.

Beyond the important ethical issues concerning deception in research, taking on a complete participant role can interfere with the very in-depth understanding a researcher hopes to gain (Bailey, 1996, p. 15; Wax, 1971, p. 52). Researchers who go under cover may start to believe that they are in fact "one of the natives," and this may cloud their ability to understand the very setting in which they are working. During her research, Rollins pretends to be a domestic only for a rather short period of time: "In all, I worked for ten employers: for seven of them I worked four weeks, one day . . . a week; by one, I was fired after the first day . . . and for two, I worked six months, one day a week" (1987, p. 10). This length of time may *not* be sufficient for Rollins to gain an in-depth understanding of the everyday working conditions of domestic workers. Consider the following questions:

- To what degree is Rollins's experience as a domestic worker equivalent to the everyday realities of domestic working life?

- To what extent does taking on the "insider" role prevent or interfere with an understanding of the setting?

Assuming the role of insider prevents Rollins from asking questions that might "blow her cover." Bailey notes that "most people allow researchers to ask certain questions, such as those that are stupid or blunt, that are not allowed of insiders. . . . The role of researcher also allows one to go places that otherwise might be taboo" (1996, p. 15). Added to this is the increased inability of the researcher to readily jot down observations "on the fly" to accurately capture ideas and observations of what is happening in the setting. Waiting for an appropriate time to do so may result in loss of information and inaccurate accounting of important events (p. 15). In addition, by completely immersing herself in the setting and taking on the specific role of a domestic, Rollins's vision of her employer is limited. To what extent can Rollins get "outside" the role of domestic within the setting and reflect on the social interaction between domestics and their employers, from the point of view of the employer? The context of understanding the social interaction is missing the vantage point of the employer.

Most ethnographic fieldwork lies in the middle of the observer-participant continuum. We can think of each of these as parts of a seesaw. At one end of the rise, we have the observer part of ourselves, at the other end the participant part. When the seesaw is not balanced, we might move too much to one side or the other, and the researcher's selves may get out of balance—one self is in the air (participant role) while the other is on the ground (observer role). Each of these sides can become unstable, and the balance point is when both of these roles are equal. The fun and understanding, however, sometimes lie in the constant interplay between these roles. These roles are *not fixed* in a research setting; the researcher can traverse this continuum depending on the social situation and the demands of the research problem.

The more you participate in a setting, however, the harder it may be to pull back and become more of an observer. You may find yourself already well-connected in the setting, with certain members of the community expecting you to maintain your networks of activity. You may also feel that you have created a personal bond and persona in the setting that intimately ties you to it, such that it may be difficult for you to return to more of a researcher role in the setting. This over-identification with your participant role, in fact, may place your project in jeopardy if you do not maintain some type of boundary between your researcher role and your participant role. Bourgois (2007) offers the following question of caution: "Is rapport building a covert way of saying 'encourage people to forget that you are constantly observing them and registering everything they are saying and doing'?" (p. 296). Remember that you are both participant and observer and that reflecting constantly on the fact that you are, primarily, a researcher working in a given field is one key to balancing your ethnographic roles.

Exiting the Field

The particular role you take on in the setting—how enmeshed you are in the day-to-day life of the setting—can determine how easy or difficult it is to depart. The ending of a project can happen for a variety of reasons. You might have to abruptly exit the field because of time constraints or economic or personal reasons; these are unforeseen disruptions. Other factors may stem from unfortunate events in the setting that make it difficult for you to continue your work. What often occurs, however, is that you reach a **saturation point** where you are no longer finding new information in the setting; you may even feel that if you stay any longer, you may start to lose your research perspective. Dorinne Kondo (2001) is a bilingual Japanese American researcher who conducted fieldwork in a confectionery factory in the city of Tokyo. She is particularly interested in the idea of treating workers as part of one's "family." Is the Japanese factory really like a family? Do the workers consider themselves part of a family? She spent almost three years in the field, and she describes how difficult it was to finally leave:

At a tea ceremony class, I performed a basic "thin tea" ceremony flawlessly, without need for prompting or correction of my movements. My teacher said in tones of approval, "You know, when you first started, I was so worried. The way you moved, the way you walked, was so clumsy! But now, you're just like

> an ojosan, a 'nice young lady.'" Part of me was inordinately pleased that my awkward exaggerated Western movement had finally been replaced by the disciplined grace that makes the tea ceremony so seemingly natural and beautiful to watch. But another voice cried out in considerable alarm, "Let me escape before I'm completely transformed!" And not too many weeks later, leave I did. (pp. 199–200)

There are degrees of exiting the field as well. Some researchers may depart abruptly, severing all ties to the setting. This may happen because the researcher or the researched are feeling uncomfortable with their interactions in the setting or perhaps because personal or economic circumstances require that the research project end early. Ruth Horowitz (1986) wanted to conduct research on a Chicano gang; however, unwanted sexual overtures from gang members made it impossible for her to remain in the field. She notes: "As the pressures increased to take a locally defined membership role, I was unable to negotiate a gender identity that would allow me to continue as a researcher" (p. 423). Others may maintain close ties to their setting, visiting and keeping in contact with the researched; some may even form friendships that last a lifetime.

There are some important **exiting strategies** you might employ in leaving the field, such as preemptively informing members of the setting that your stay is only temporary and giving others a sense of your own research timetable. Inherent in the field research process is the forging of reciprocity (rapport) between the researcher and the researched. Those in the setting can come to rely on the researcher for emotional support and advice, and when this is withdrawn, it may create a sense of loss and abandonment for both the researched and the researcher.

Whatever the situation of your exit, it is important to come up with some strategies for your departure. It might be prudent to check in with others to get a sense of how they are feeling about your departure. Perhaps you may arrange with those in the setting to mark your departure in a more public way, as with a party, and also plan for a follow-up, whether that follow-up is a letter or a return visit.

The particular role or set of roles you take on in a setting directly influences the types of data you are able to access. You will find that the amount of ethnographic data you collect will quickly multiply, and you may soon find yourself in need of a way to manage this data so as not to become overwhelmed. We now turn to a different type of ethnographic experience, known as autoethnography.

What Is Autoethnography?

Sometimes researchers use themselves as the subject of their research. If you are interested in your own personal experiences and how they are situated in a cultural context, **autoethnography** may help you meet your goals.

Qualitative researchers often use autobiographical data in both explicit and implicit ways. As we have mentioned, field researchers often keep a journal, ethics diary, or reflective diary where they document their thoughts, feelings, emotions, and so forth during field research (Tenni, Smith, & Boucher, 2003, p. 2). In this way, autobiographical data is a part of the research process because the researcher records his or her thoughts, opinions, and interpretations of what is happening in the field. In addition, particular theoretical and epistemological positions may influence a researcher to explicitly include autobiographical data. When using standpoint epistemology, as conceptualized by Sandra Harding (1993), and thus using "strong objectivity," researchers necessarily disclose information about their own biography and how it informs the knowledge-building process.

The term *autoethnography* can mean different things depending on how it is applied and what theory is applied to it. However, in this section, we are focusing on autoethnography as a very general form of autobiographical oral history. Autoethnography refers to writing about the personal and its relationship to culture that displays multiple layers of consciousness (Ellis, 2004, p. 37, quoting Dumont, 1978). Ellis (2004; see also Ellis, 2009) expands on this definition to illustrate the richness of this method and variability in representational forms it can use, which include books, essays, poems, plays, novels, and performance pieces:

"What is autoethnography?" you might ask. My brief answer: research, writing, story, and method that connect the autobiographical and personal to the cultural, social, and political. Autoethnographic forms feature concrete action, emotion, embodiment, self-consciousness, and introspection portrayed in dialogue, scenes, characterization, and plot. Thus, autoethnography claims the conventions of literary writing. (Ellis, 2004, p. xix)

This method allows us to use our own experiences, thoughts, feelings, and emotions as data to help us understand the social world. This kind of research can be empowering for the researcher-subject and raise our self-consciousness and reflexivity. Having said this, these potential rewards carry their own burden. The ethnographic research process is intellectually and emotionally draining. When conducting a field study, we are never fully prepared for what we might find. Nor can we fully prepare our field subjects for the range of possible emotions that could flow from telling their story or leading the researcher through their field. The same is true for when we use ourselves as the subjects of our research. Heightened emotions during the research process can be markers of important data that we need to flesh out and try to make sense of. These moments also represent times where we may need additional support because the strains of the research process may be more than we can comfortably handle alone. Keeping track of one's emotions during the process can thus serve as both data and signals to the researcher about how he or she is coping with the autobiographical process.

The data analysis process may also require external assistance, in the form of a supervisor or adviser with whom the researcher interacts during the autoethnographic study. Instead of maintaining a neutral or detached role, the supervisor role means becoming engaged in assisting with the researcher's autoethnography (Tenni et al., 2003, p. 3). The adviser's role can take the form of dialoguing with researchers to help them stay grounded, and this can also serve to alleviate some of the concerns about validity that are often raised when researchers use personal data (Tenni et al., 2003, p. 3). In addition, an external party, but one who is committed to the project, can add complexity and nuance to the data analysis process—he or she may help the researcher "see" more broadly, enhancing both the data and what the researcher takes away from the project in terms of self-consciousness.

Autoethnography can also be challenging, as researchers open up their own experiences for public consumption, which requires a degree of vulnerability on their part. In this next behind-the-scenes box, we examine an autoethnography conducted by Sharlene Hesse-Biber, coauthor of this book.

BEHIND THE SCENES WITH SHARLENE HESSE-BIBER

I never intended to write an autoethnography about the death of my younger sibling, Janet, from breast cancer a few years ago. However, I happened to be attending a qualitative conference on Long Island and was invited to join an autoethnographic workshop conducted by sociologist and renowned autoethnographer Dr. Carolyn Ellis. It was then only a few months since my sister died, and Ellis encouraged members of my workshop to write about a significant event in their lives. As a sociologist, I was used to listening to the experiences of others, not taking myself or my personal experiences as the subject of inquiry. I did so with much trepidation and felt vulnerable writing about my experience, especially when Ellis asked us to share our writing with other members of the workshop.

I began my autoethnographic journey by writing a series of letters addressed to my deceased sister. The autoethnographic process allowed me to uncover my feelings toward my younger sister, some of which stemmed from growing up with three siblings in a poor female-headed household. I reflected on how difficult it was to relate to my younger sister. It was during her one-and-a-half-year illness, ironically, that we grew extremely close to one another. I realized during the writing process how much guilt I carried with me regarding my lack of closeness to my younger sister. I remember feeling that I was not a "good enough" sister, especially upon her death. I was experiencing "survivors guilt" by always thinking, "Why her and not me?

The following autoethnographic entry is the first of a series of letters I wrote to my sister after her death, which were written over the course of several years. I feel that this first letter best captures some of my early feelings of guilt as well as remembrance of our childhood and adolescent years. The title reflects my need to not forget my sister, Janet, a concern that often plagues those who are left behind, who often pledge to themselves not to forget their lost sibling. Also contained within the text are the analytical seeds of understanding the wider social factors that intersect with the grieving process.

A Letter to Janet

Do you remember sister?

I want to remember your warm caring smile. You lit up a room with your presence. You were my kid sister, but I didn't spend enough time with you. I mourn not knowing you enough, not being the sister who was good enough.

Remember the time I picked you up from the daycare center? You were waiting anxiously by the large metal fence with its diamond shaped pattern, pressing your face deep against the steel mesh that separated us. I can see your blond curly hair tangled in all directions, your high pitch squeal telling me how much you missed me.

Do you remember sister?

You had the boyfriends who drove us anywhere you wanted, you with the cigarette in your hand brazenly smoking, violating all of mom's rules. Your infectious laugh filled the car as we careened down the road to the next party.

You were the sister who didn't like school and the trouble you got into always fooling around—talking back to Sister Jones. You were expelled from St. Peter's High School, having only arrived there the week before.

You made the cheerleading squad on your first try at your new high school, the public high school I also attended. While I diligently practiced each cheering routine, I was rejected for a third time at the cheerleading trials. Instead, I became the second-class booster, cheering our basketball team from the sidelines. What I didn't realize and you did was that I wasn't part of that clique of girls. I was the scholar of the family. You took all the risks, I was the cautious big sister, who aimed to please my teachers while you forged ahead, breaking traditional female gender boundaries.

Janet, you did things your way. Your many friends quickly became your new family, the close-knit family you never had when we were growing up. Education was my ticket out of the projects that I used to negate my feelings of disappointment at not being able to afford many of the basic necessities other kids seemed to take for granted.

I vividly recall the last days of your terrible disease. I was going to make you some chicken soup. Even though it was hard for you to swallow, I remember how your face lit up, and there you were, my kid sister of many years ago, waiting in anticipation for the soup. Gone were your curly locks, your hair now ravaged by chemo, yet a few curly locks still jut out, hoping to grow more roots. But, your smile and excitement, they are there, lighting up a sorrow-filled room. I eagerly scoop up the hot steamy contents in the bowl and serve you a teaspoonful of "my" chicken soup as you quickly shout out: "This is awful! It has no taste!" Upon tasting the chicken myself, I agreed—it lacked your spices!

Janet, even now you remind me that I must go after the spices of life—I must not be afraid to take risks; going for those things I believe in. You have the

(Continued)

(Continued)

courage of your convictions even in the last months of your battle with breast cancer, your courage, humility and humor remain strong. You get outside your own illness, caring and asking about everyone else: "How are the kids doing? How do you feel? How is Michael doing?"

You don't give up on your passions too easily my sister. Even in your last few days of life, you play your ultimate passion game, *Scrabble*.

I remember your delight in counting up word scores and nine times out of ten you would beat me at this game. Even when cancer spread to your brain, you refused to give in to your illness, how you fought for each Scrabble word.

Janet, let's beat another game, together let's try to hang onto each moment, each minute, each hour.

Janet succeeded in bringing our family closer together; something she could not accomplish while she was still healthy. Upon her death, it was as if our now very close family lost a major limb and part of its soul. Janet's death also changed the sibling dynamic, as I now became the "youngest *surviving* sibling," leading me to wonder how I might accomplish taking on the identity of a surviving sibling.

While this autoethnography is evocative in that it provides a way to get at the emotions regarding her sister's death, the letter and writing extends our understanding of this experience by using a series *of analytical lenses* that consider the wider societal factors involved in the grieving process. C. Wright Mills once noted that "personal troubles" are often symptomatic of "public issues." To quote from Mills (1959):

> Know that the human meaning of public issues must be revealed by relating them to personal troubles—and to the problems of the individual life. Know that the problems of social science, when adequately formulated, must include both troubles and issues, both biography and history, and the range of their intricate relations. Within that range the life of the individual and the making of societies occur; and within that range the sociological imagination has its chance to make a difference in the quality of human life in our time. (p. 226)

Turning this "private problem" into a public issue was a key consideration for the author in applying her sociological imagination to her own experience. How do we as a society deal with death? How do we deal with the grieving process? What are the structures of support available to those who experience loss? While the experience at times felt unbearable, the author notes that, at the core, she would remain resilient, and as a researcher, she asked herself why that was the case. What were the factors in her life that allowed her to be resilient? What are the factors that promote or inhibit resilience in others?

Now that we have discussed the various ways of designing and working through the process of ethnographic research, let's turn to gathering and management of data encountered in these types of research projects.

How Do You Gather and Manage Your Ethnographic Data?

It is crucial for you to determine what type of data you want to collect in the setting and the best way to go about doing that. Your role in the setting will determine what types of data you will or will not be able to collect. Will you obtain data only through observing and/or participating? Will you collect data using other methods such as interviewing those in the setting, both informally and formally? Will you rely on previous information about the setting collected by others (i.e., research studies, documents)? Most of these decisions should be guided by your research question. Here are some important pointers to keep in mind in planning your data collection:

- If you are gathering data through observation and participation in the setting, it becomes critical that you collect data on an *ongoing* basis. Data collection and data analysis should proceed simultaneously. For the ethnographer in the field, this means writing down your observations and ideas (data collection) and trying to figure out what is going on (data analysis). This is done each day as soon as you leave the field, and if possible, while you are in the setting; otherwise, it is easy to forget important details and events. Analysis of your fieldnotes may lead to asking new questions and making new observations and interactions in your setting.

- It is important to remember that you cannot observe all interaction that is going on. Ask yourself what particular part(s) of the setting you want to observe.

- Remember that there are multiple levels of observation contained within a setting, and not all can be observed at any one time.

- These are some levels of observation you might want to consider: What are people doing in the setting? What are their activities? What sensory observations do you take from the setting (i.e., specific sounds and smells in the setting)? What is being said (pay attention to language—write down specific quotes or phrases you feel capture the story of what is going on in the setting)? What is not said? Are certain things taken for granted? Sometimes what is not present is just as important as what is present.

The following are some common mistakes that student researchers make in the field. The key to combating these mistakes is to engage in reflexivity through the research process, and to keep these mistakes in mind as you progress through recording and analyzing fieldnotes.

- Only observing what you feel is important from your own cultural and academic standpoint.

- Assuming that what is true or common in your own culture must be so for those in the host culture.

- Closing inquiry prematurely and rushing to judgment about what is happening in a setting.

Keeping Fieldnotes

Not all ethnographers agree on what is the best way to record their observations in the field. This section concentrates on how you might do this by writing them up in the form of fieldnotes; however, other valid methods include using a tape recorder or even a video or digital recorder. Fieldnotes are the data that you gather to make sense of your research setting, and they serve as an aid in writing your research results. Researchers have suggested several types of fieldnotes you might create for yourself (see Bailey, 1996, pp. 80–85).

On-the-fly notes can consist of some key words or phrases to help you remember important events or ideas that occur while making your observations. They can be written on a small memo pad. Some researchers use whatever paper they can find, including the back of a matchbook cover or paper napkin so that this does not disrupt their ongoing observations in the field. Remember to record the date, time, and location.

Thick descriptions of the setting are all the things that you can remember about exactly what took place in the setting. Be sure to record, whenever possible, the exact *in vivo* words or phrases of respondents, or as close to their words as you can get. Be sure not to forget the sensory observations in the setting: What do you smell? What about specific visuals? While you might think some of these details about activities and events are very mundane, it is important that you not censor your descriptions but stay open to the range of events and details in the setting. These notes and their relevance can be sorted out after you leave the field. Something you thought was unimportant may in fact be crucial once you fit some of these descriptive pieces together.

Data analysis and interpretation notes are linking notes you gathered *on the fly* and your "thick descriptions" from the setting. These are the "what does it mean?" notes to yourself. What things go together? What new questions do these observations bring up for you? What have you learned thus far and what does it mean now? These notes can also contain your innermost ideas. Allow your "analysis" self to have free rein here through the process of brainstorming (see also Bailey, 1996; Lofland & Lofland, 1984).

Personal matters and reflexivity: This is a space for you to explore your own positionality as the researcher in the research process. What are you feeling about this setting? What are your concerns? How might you analyze your role in the setting? Were you open to new ideas, or were you shut down that day because the people you met were critical? Write down your emotions vis-à-vis those you are researching. For example, are you limiting your observations of X because you really don't like him or her—he or she reminds you of your college roommate who went out with your ex-lover? What are your fears? What are the "to do" things you need to remind yourself of? Do you need certain research supplies such as computer paper or index cards? These "to do's," while seemingly trivial, are important to keep your project moving along (see Bailey, 1996, and Lofland & Lofland, 1984).

Accounting/summary memo: You also might want to conduct a mini-accounting or summary of what data you gather on a *daily* basis by providing (a) a brief summary of what you found and (b) a short memo on what you think it means so far. Ask: What are the implications of (a) and (b) for how I will proceed the next day with my observations? What should I examine next? This mini-accounting or summary doesn't have to be a long memo; a few paragraphs will do. About midway through your data collection, you might provide a more substantive accounting by going over all the data you collected from the beginning up to the midpoint and writing a substantive memo on what you think it means, asking the same questions.

There is no perfect formula for writing fieldnotes; everyone's fieldnotes take on a life of their own. Some of us may like to draw visual diagrams, while others like to doodle as a way to get at some of their ideas. Some of us may cut and paste various clippings that we acquired that day into our fieldnotes; maybe someone gave you a newspaper article, a brochure, or even a letter or card that he or she wanted you to have. Remember, field research can also consist of documents you gather in the field, and these also need to be analyzed.

Let's go inside the research process and look at how one researcher writes up her fieldnotes. Notice how *thick description* and *analysis* are running together in these notes. These fieldnotes are written by a white, middle-class college student named Nora who is doing participant observation in a predominantly black inner-city school, which also serves as the local community center after school hours. The following is an excerpt from fieldnotes written shortly after she observed this setting. She takes on the role of *observer-as-participant* in the setting. Nora's professor accompanies her to the research site, called Cityville, to begin to recruit black adolescent girls for a research project on adolescent black identity and body image. She and her professor were invited by the center's director to meet parents and their children. Let's look at how the student researcher approaches the writing up of her field observations after spending her first time in the field for several hours.

Field Note: Number 1

Date: July

Place: Community Center, Cityville

Event: Mother-Daughter Day

Total Observation Time: 2.5 hours

Personal Reflections: It was so different to drive into Cityville, a neighborhood and part of the city that I have never seen before. The difference between where I live and go to school and Cityville is amazing. It is almost two separate worlds.

(Continued)

(Continued)

Description of Setting: The Cityville public school was hidden back off a side road; you would never even know that it was there. The school itself was so much different than the schools that I have seen in my area. It was a huge school but very old and not very well taken care of. I was a little nervous about what we would find when we walked in.

Personal Reflections: The first thing that struck me was how white I felt. My professor and I were the only two white people in sight and I felt like everyone was looking at me and thinking "Who is this stupid white girl and what the hell does she want?" I read an article in my professor's class called the "Invisible Knapsack" and it talked about white privilege and the fact that no matter where we go, as white people, we can bet that the majority of the people around us will be white as well. So I have always been aware of what it must feel like to be black and to walk into an all white room but not as aware as I was when I walked into an all black room. The tables were turned and I have to admit, I didn't like it. I felt so uncomfortable and unwanted. I felt like I needed to show or prove to all the people there that I was the same as them, even though deep down I knew it wasn't true.

Description of Setting—Focusing Observations on Parents' and Children's Interactions: Well the second thing that struck me was what a huge commotion the place was. Kids were running everywhere; adults were shouting orders here and there. Then we walked into a room where tables were set up and a group of kids were practicing a stepping routine with their coach. A lot of people were all dressed up and as I sat there, I knew that this couldn't have been a normal day at the center. A few minutes later, my Professor and I found out that there was going to be some type of show. Well this was a surprise. And the even bigger surprise was that my professor would be speaking at the show to all the kids and parents. So much for advanced notice.

As my professor got ready I watched the steppers continue to practice. They were really cute kids, ranging in age from about 7 to 14, and there were about 12 girls and 1 boy. Their coach was really into it. He was very stern with the kids and demanded their attention and precision, but stern in a very caring way. The kids were also very serious about the stepping and practiced very hard.

Well after a while the parents started pouring in and the steppers left. My professor and I got a pamphlet from one of the ushers and discovered that we were at the Mothers' and Daughters' Night. My professor's name was on the pamphlet as a speaker and in a few minutes she was going to be on.

Personal Reflections—On Being an Outsider: Finally some other white people showed up, now I didn't feel like I stuck out as much. There was a mother and a sister of one of the singers, the only white girl in the group of kids that I saw. Very interesting! The two other white people who came were speakers as well.

Description of Setting—Focus on Mother-Daughter Program Activities: Well, the show began. My Professor spoke first; she was pretty brave because you couldn't have paid me to get up in front of that group. But she gave a great talk and most of the mothers seemed pretty interested. Then the new director of the center spoke about how happy he was to be the new director and about how excited he was to get some new programs going. Next came a group of singers. There was a lead singer about 10 or 12 and a group of back up singers of about 8 girls and 1 or 2 guys. They sang "You Have to Be Strong."

All of the parents looked very proud. The next speaker, who was Caucasian, got up to speak about her Family Van. She is a doctor who drives around a van with a team of professionals and provides free health services to those who need it. She said that she wanted to introduce her van and make sure that the community really wanted it in Cityville and to ask if they had any questions. A few questions were asked and then she seconded what my professor said. Next came the steppers. They had matching outfits and they performed their routine to perfection. Their coach looked very proud and so did all of the parents. The mother at my table said "there's my baby" as her daughter marched out. The kids seemed really proud and pleased as well. At the end I saw their coach give them a big hug. Their message was about knowledge and success and trying your hardest, it was a powerful message.

A couple of women told my Professor that they wanted to talk to her so she first spoke with the grandmother. I was a little nervous for her because I thought that the grandmother might be upset but she wasn't. In fact, she wanted to be interviewed and with her 2 daughters and her grandchild. She was very interested in our project, and she told my Professor that black men and the black community are more accepting of big women.

Personal Reflections—Being an Outsider and Observing Mother-Daughter Interactions through a Prism of Difference: I, myself, noticed such a difference between all the women in the room compared to a room full of white women. There were a few very large women but they were all well dressed, they all carried themselves with confidence, they all looked happy and they all looked at ease. I've never really seen that among the white females. Usually when people are bigger in the white community they carry themselves differently, they don't look confident and at ease. I know that this is a generalization but it is what I have noticed. Black women, big or little, all carried themselves the same.

There was so much pride and love and culture and strength in the room. It was overwhelming and amazing to be a part of this event, even as an outsider. I would like all the people who make comments and generalizations about blacks to go to a center like Cityville's for a day and see how wrong they are.

Another woman got up and spoke, she was a black woman and she brought her mother. It was interesting to listen to her speak as she called for "Amens" and to see how much more responding the audience was to her than to my Professor and the other white speaker.

After this we left and as we were asking for directions a woman who was leaving offered to give us a ride to the trolley. She was very generous and also very friendly. She has lived in Cityville for 25+ years and runs a drug hotline/clinic.

On the trolley ride home the tables were turned back and I was the white majority again. Amazing how much more comfortable I felt.

These fieldnotes are broken down and the sections labeled to illustrate what goes on when taking fieldnotes. When you enter a setting, it's important to begin with *a brief description of the setting*. This description is usually general in the beginning, and as one spends more time in a setting, these descriptions become more and more detailed. Realize that you cannot focus on everything in the setting; instead, begin with a single *focus*. This focus can be a particular set of interactions. In these fieldnotes, we observe Nora homing in on interactions between mothers and daughters. She then changes her focus to the specific set of activities presented at the mother-daughter event. Starting with a focus prevents you from becoming overwhelmed by all the interactions within the setting. Nora also reflects on her positionality as a white student from the suburbs in her interactions with this predominantly black community. She reflects on her outsider status as one window into understanding the interactions and events in the setting in order to ascertain their meanings. By reflecting on her outsider status, she sees what appears novel or similar.

Tips for the Beginner Taking Fieldnotes

- Identify and describe the setting. Remember to describe the setting in as much detail as possible. You might start to focus in detail on a few aspects of the setting and then move to other elements in subsequent visits.

- Start with focusing on a particular set of interactions in the setting. Why did you home in on this particular interaction? What is going on within these interactions? Be sure to record as many quotes of interest as you can obtain.

- Begin to reflect on how your presence in the setting is affecting you. What do you find unusual or problematic for you? What surprised you and why? Did you feel you fit in? Why or why not?

- What influence do you think you have on the setting and its activities? How do others relate to you or treat you? Be sure to write down any particular quotes of interest to you. These quotes help to retain the ambience of the setting. They give you an idea of the emotive aspects of the setting as well as detail the cultural aspects of a particular interaction, especially when studying and observing across cultural differences.

Analyzing Your Fieldnotes: The Ethnographic Puzzle

We can think of ethnographic analysis as an *inductive process,* that is, a process of discovering what the data you gathered means. Description is the bedrock of ethnographic analysis, and fieldnotes are the record of the in-depth observations you garnered from the field that provide a window into the research setting—its people, the physical attributes of the setting, and so on. We can think of fieldnotes as pieces of a puzzle. The object is to put these pieces together to create a puzzle picture (analysis) and then to tell the reader what you see (interpretation). You might begin to organize this descriptive story simply by reading over what you have gathered and ask some sensitizing questions such as the following:

- What is going on in the setting?

- Have I fully captured the social setting, the physical layout of the setting, the sounds, and conversations? How have I sampled observations for this setting? How do I determine that I have a good representation of what goes on in this setting?

- How well do I take note of my own impact on the setting? What do I perceive as my effect on the setting? How do those in the setting react to my presence?

Part of your analysis is to arrange these descriptive pieces into a story. Your analysis (how you organize these pieces into a whole puzzle picture) leads to interpretation (what the puzzle depicts). As you know, there are false starts to creating a puzzle. We move the pieces back and forth, sometimes forcing pieces of a puzzle together. Certain problems may arise in the analysis process. Along the way, ask yourself:

- Am I moving too fast from description to analysis? If so, the picture may be blurred and your explanation too weak.

- Am I spending too much time at the level of description? If so, you may describe all of the pieces of the puzzle in accurate detail but not have a clue as to what the puzzle depicts or what it means.

Analysis helps us to fit the puzzle pieces together. When certain pieces of the puzzle fit together, we have grabbed onto a **theme**, something that provides us with an idea of what the puzzle is and allows us to move toward our goal of completing the picture. You might consider memo-ing about how your analysis is going. **Analysis memos** are ideas that you write down to help you think through how you are going about your work or what something means. Just as with fieldnotes, there are a variety of memos you might write to assist with your analysis, and we will cover some of these techniques in the analysis and interpretation chapter.

You might employ a variety of analysis methods for putting the pieces together. For example, you could code each piece by its size (assign the code categories large, medium, or small to each of the pieces) and place (sort) all the pieces into these three categories. We can think of this technique as employing the ethnographic analysis method called the *constant comparative method,* which is part of grounded theory (see Glaser & Strauss, 1967). We will talk about this method in more detail in Chapter 12. In effect, this technique consists of looking at how puzzle pieces are the same or different from one another in the context of your research question. This method asks,

- What is this piece?

- What does it mean?

- Are there other pieces like this?

- What makes Piece A different from or the same as Piece B?

Comparing analysis to putting a puzzle together is meant to remove much of the jargon that has cropped up when researchers try to explain how to analyze and interpret data. To take this analogy and apply it to your project, you might begin by just reading over all your fieldnotes and other written documents and interviews. You should try to reach a comfort zone about your data—the point at which you feel very familiar with the data you have before you. You might also begin by "marking" up the text as you go along; perhaps you would like to make notes or memos about what is happening and what you think are the important points to which you might want to return. You might also think about inputting your data into a computer software program such as HyperRESEARCH (www.researchware.com) to assist you with this task (we will take up the issues of computer software and data analysis in Chapter 12).

In the first run-through of your data, you might begin to see and identify some major categories or **codes** that illuminate your research topic. You might want to look at things that "go together" and things that don't seem to fit anywhere (*analytic comparison*). Think about this process and write about how codes are similar or different and why, in light of your research question. Once you have grabbed onto what you feel is a potent theme or code, look for several independent sources that might support this idea—documents or interviews, in addition to your observations. This is called *triangulating* your data among different sources. You might even have your respondents read over your ideas to see if they can corroborate your theories or perspectives. Be sure to memo about your important theme idea. How is it related to other ideas you have also isolated? Doing this will help you see the links between various code categories. Little by little, your story will emerge (see Hammersley & Atkinson, 1995, pp. 157–174; see also Hammersley & Atkinson, 2007).

Conclusion

The ethnographic method provides the researcher with an important window into understanding the social world from the vantage point of those residing in it. Ethnographies provide the reader with an in-depth understanding of the goings-on of those who inhabit a range of naturally occurring settings. Participant observation is a primary means of data collection, although other forms of data such as interviews, documents, and photography may also be used. Writing and analyzing fieldnotes are important features of this method. Data analysis requires the researcher to be open to discovery, with data analysis and collection proceeding almost simultaneously. Interpretation of the data requires sensitivity on the part of researchers to the variety of multiple meanings in the setting and an awareness of their own positionality.

While ethnographic methods cannot be used to make broad generalizations about a given social phenomenon, they provide an important context for understanding the results from large-scale research such as surveys. Ethnographers take a range of approaches to observing the social reality depending on their specific discipline and theoretical bias. Some ethnographers may be more interested in social change than others (*critical ethnography*); others are more focused on studying populations that have been overlooked by traditional ethnography, such as women (*feminist ethnography*). What characterizes and underscores all of these approaches, however, is the emphasis on interpretation—getting at meaning from the perspective of those who are researched.

Glossary

Analysis memos: Ideas that you write down to help you think through how you are going about your work or early reflections on specific interviews and so on.

Autoethnography: This type of ethnography refers to reflecting and writing about one's own personal experience and its relationship to culture.

Codes: Ways to break down and reorganize your data into categories or themes as a way to get at meaning.

Complete observer: The researcher's identity remains hidden; the researcher does not directly interact with those in the setting but instead makes observations of the setting from a distance and sometimes using such devices as hidden video cameras or by remaining invisible behind a one-way mirror or a screen to avoid detection.

Complete participant: The researcher actively engages with members of the setting; however, the researcher's identity is not known to the participants in the setting.

Covert research: The researcher does not reveal his or her identity in order to "pass" as an authentic member of that setting.

Data analysis and interpretation notes: These are field notes that ask questions of the data you are gathering in the field. This type of field note asks: What is going on? What does it mean? What things go together? What new questions are sparked by these data?

Ethnographic research: Seeks an in-depth understanding of how individuals in different cultures and subcultures make sense of their lived reality. Ethnographers "go inside" the social worlds of the inhabitants of their research setting, "hanging out" and observing and recording the ongoing social life of its members by providing "thick descriptions" (Geertz, 1973) of the social context and the everyday goings-on of the people who live in these worlds, spending a good amount of time engaging with the events, people, and activities within the setting.

Exiting strategies: Plans which allow the researcher to leave the setting easily and without causing harm to the people in the setting.

Field: In ethnography, this concept differs depending on the type of research project you pursue. For an anthropologist studying a foreign culture, the field is a *cultural* setting. A chapter example is Anderson's (1976) research where the field consists of studying a local bar or local neighborhood; the "bar" or "neighborhood" becomes the field. In short, the field is the setting a researcher studies.

Fieldnotes: Written accounts of the researcher's everyday experiences in the field, which are written while in the field, on the fly, or shortly after leaving the field.

Formal gatekeepers: Those individuals in the field who have the formal or legitimate authority to grant the researcher permission to enter the "official" research site if formal permission is needed.

Gatekeepers: Gatekeepers are people in a setting whose approval is crucial in order to gain access and acceptance. Their authority to grant access to the field may be formal or informal.

Informal gatekeepers: These are people who hold key positions in the informal setting, and their influence on others in the site determines your level of access. Informal gatekeepers have the power to legitimate your presence in the setting by virtue of their role as a leader or person of influence among the group being studied.

Key informants: These are people in the setting who provide the researcher with critical information and tips.

Natural settings: Places where individuals go about their daily lives, rather than a place set up by the researcher at a specific site.

Observer-as-participant: The researcher is required to reveal his or her identity in the setting, but the extent to which the researcher actively engages with the members of the setting is limited.

On-the-fly notes: Notes that can consist of some key words or phrases to help you remember important events or ideas that occur while making your observations. These can be thought of as "jottings" that you elaborate on further when you leave the field.

Participant-as-observer: The researcher participates fully in the ongoing activities of the research setting, and the identity of the researcher is known to the members of the setting.

Participant observation: A primary research tool of ethnography and its practice; researchers live in or make extensive visits to the setting they are studying, observing as well as participating in the activities of those they are researching.

Saturation point: The time in the research where nothing new is found in the setting and in which researchers may even lose their perspective if they stay in the setting any longer.

Theme: An aspect of the coding process whereby code categories start to come together and show a larger pattern in the data. Put differently, when certain pieces of the puzzle fit together, a theme provides us with an idea of what the puzzle is and allows us to move forward toward our goal of completing the picture (meaning).

Thick descriptions: This term was coined by Clifford Geertz (1973) and refers to all the things that you can remember about exactly what took place in the setting. These are very detailed descriptions and rely on a researcher's acumen in the setting to capture the full essence.

Urban ethnography: Study of a neighborhood or city.

Discussion Questions

1. Discuss the meaning of *ethnography* and when it is appropriate to use it as a method of social research.

2. What is the importance of adopting an interpretative (as opposed to positivist) model when conducting ethnographic fieldwork?

3. In ethnographic fieldwork, the researcher's understanding comes from the members of the social setting being researched. How can that, therefore, serve as an empowering experience for the researched (i.e., aid in social activism efforts)?

4. What is the importance of fieldnotes in ethnographic fieldwork?

5. How does gaining entry into a specific social setting have an impact on data collection?

6. How does your role in the social setting shape what types of data you will or will not be able to collect?

7. When studying members of a certain social setting, researchers may be introduced to unfamiliar rituals and customs (perhaps rituals or customs with which they do not agree). Discuss how these factors would impact your research project.

8. Although it is important for the researcher to gain access to a social setting through a gatekeeper (of some sort), the authors warn that it is important that a researcher not be *too reliant* on one member of the setting. Why is that?

9. How do constraints on gaining access to private settings affect the extent to which you, as the researcher, can understand the members of the social setting you wish to study?

10. This chapter discussed the role that you, as a researcher, should have when carrying out your research process. Discuss the factors that influence what role or identity you should adopt when conducting your research. What role will you take on in the setting?

11. Discuss some of the options available to researchers as they attempt to gain access to more private settings.

Resources

Suggested Web Sites

Center for Ethnography

http://www.socsci.uci.edu/ethnog/

Established in 2006, the Center for Ethnography is housed at the University of California, Irvine. According to its Web site mission statement, the center seeks to promote "a series of sustained theoretical and methodological conversations about ethnographic research practices across the disciplines that will have a broadly transformative effect on ethnographic research methodologies and theoretical developments. The center will support innovative collaborative ethnographic research as well as research on the theoretical and methodological refunctioning of ethnography for contemporary cultural, social, and technological transformations."

Participant Observation

http://www2.chass.ncsu.edu/garson/pa765/particip.htm

This Web site is an overview of a course offered at North Carolina State University. There is an extended bibliography and a link to a journal that has information on participant observation and other field studies.

Relevant Journals

Ethnography

International Journal of Fieldwork Studies

Journal of Contemporary Ethnography

Journal of Ethnographic & Qualitative Research

CHAPTER 9

Content Analysis and Unobtrusive Methods

Social science research has to confront a dimension of human activ-ity that cannot be contained in the consciousness of the isolated subject. In short, it has to look at something that lies beyond the world of atomistic individuals.

—Lindsay Prior (2004, p. 318)

ontent analysis is one of very few research methods that can be employed qualitatively or quantitatively, opening up a wide array of methodological possibilities. Up until this point, we have been reviewing qualitative methods that rely on obtaining data directly from people, using interviewing and observational skills. How can qualitative researchers use nonliving materials to study the social world? How can texts, in their varied forms, be used as the starting point for understanding social processes and generating theories about social life?

What Is Content Analysis?

Unobtrusive methods were developed out of the assumption that we can learn about our society by investigating the material items produced within it. In other words, we can learn about social life, whether it be norms or values or socialization or social stratification, by looking at the things we produce that reflect macro social processes and our worldview. Embedded in the texts and objects that groups of

AUTHORS' NOTE: Parts of this chapter are adapted from S. Hesse-Biber and P. Leavy, "Unobtrusive Methods, Visual Research, and Cultural Studies," in *Approaches to Qualitative Research: A Reader on Theory and Practice*, edited by S. Hesse-Biber and P. Leavy, New York: Oxford University Press, 2004.

humans produce are larger ideas those groups have, whether shared or contested. The other major qualitative research methods rely on collecting data from individuals and groups through interactional and observational ways of knowing. Unobtrusive methods use texts or artifacts as the starting point of the research process. There are two primary benefits to working with nonliving data forms: (1) the data are noninteractive, and (2) the data exist independent of the research (Reinharz, 1992, pp. 147–148). Because the data are not influenced through researcher interaction, as with interviews, and they already exist in the world regardless of the research currently being done, the data are "naturalistic." This quality gives the data a unique level of authenticity. Researchers do not intrude into social life by observing or interviewing but rather examine existing noninteractive texts, and, thus, the research process is classified as unobtrusive. Many different kinds of texts and artifacts can be studied, including, but not limited to, historical documents, newspapers, magazines, photographs, books, diaries, literature, music, cinema, television, Web sites, and so forth. While unobtrusive methods encompass a wide range of methodological possibilities, historically, **content analysis** has been the major method under this rubric. Content analysis is now used across the disciplines including but not limited to communications (e.g., see Yoon, 2005); criminal justice/criminology (e.g., see Gerkin, 2009; Phillips & Strobl, 2006; Rothe & Ross, 2008); education (e.g., see O'Connor, Netting, & Thomas, 2008); and sociology (e.g., see Leavy & Maloney, 2009).

The Uses of Content Analysis

Content analysis can be used to study mass-mediated representations of historical or current events. The 2008 presidential campaign was a particularly long campaign process. First, there was the historic competition between Barack Obama and Hillary Clinton for the Democratic Party's nomination. Then, historic tickets of John McCain/Sarah Palin and Barack Obama/Joseph Biden competed. With all of the media coverage, from journalism to entertainment shows like *The View* to stories in popular magazines such as *People* to imitations on *Saturday Night Live,* the campaign was represented in numerous media forms, creating a vast repository of representations. Content analysis could be used to systematically analyze the content of those representations. For example, there was speculation during the campaign that Clinton and Palin were treated in sexist ways by journalists. Conversely, some people expressed concern that Obama got a "free ride" from the media. These kinds of issues can be addressed via content analysis.

Content analysis can also be used to compare media coverage of similar events. For example, Leavy and Maloney (2009) compared newspaper coverage of the 1999 Columbine High School shootings with coverage of the 2005 Red Lake Indian Reservation school shootings, which at that point was the largest school shooting spree since Columbine. The project consisted of a qualitative content analysis of three newspapers over a 2-week period following each event (the *New York Times* as the national paper of record, the *Denver Post* as the major newspaper local to Columbine, and the *Star Tribune* as the major newspaper local to Red Lake). Leavy and Maloney found, as they hypothesized, that Columbine became a major event in the American collective, whereas Red Lake did not, for four primary reasons: (1) Columbine received far greater national coverage; (2) newspaper reporting was racially biased, assuming white youth represented "all-American" kids; (3) newspaper reporting was biased with respect to social class (privileging middle- and upper-class narratives); and (4) Columbine reporting was more infused with political rhetoric and was thus elevated from an event into a political platform.

Content analysis can also be used to study topical areas, as noted in other chapters. Let's take the example of body image and ask this question: What is the relationship between media images and female beauty ideals? This kind of research question could be explored through a variety of interview methods: We would define the sample of girls in whom we are interested and ask them about their media consumption, their body image ideals and issues, and what they perceive as the relationship between popular culture and their own body image. One question might be, How do you feel when you see images of models and actresses? This kind of research design privileges the way individuals subjectively think about and feel toward their bodies in relation to their media consumption. The knowledge gained reflects the experiences of individuals. While important, this is merely one way a qualitative researcher can go about studying this topic. A researcher interested in how cultural forms are created and projected in a given society may use content analysis. For example, a qualitative researcher interested in how media images *themselves* reflect and construct a particular ideal of female beauty, instead of how women subjectively relate to such images, will find content analysis very useful.

A qualitative researcher might wish to study women's magazines to critically investigate the portrayal of women. Guiding questions might include the following: What are the body sizes of women represented? What positions are women shown in? What text accompanies visual images? Unlike researchers conducting in-depth interviews, researchers in this project study how body ideals are created and reflected by the mass media. The focus of inquiry here is on the *cultural forms* in which beauty ideals are distributed and the *cultural processes* that construct these ideals. When using this approach, the point of departure for the research is no longer individuals, who themselves live in a social context and have been "imprinted" by the media images that constitute part of the socialization process in their society. Critical scholars explain that individuals are imprinted by their culture's power-knowledge relations, and researchers must use "texts" as their starting point to more accurately investigate social power (Taylor, 1987).

Let's take an example. If a researcher were to approach you, present you with a variety of parenting magazines, and ask you to interpret the images of boys versus girls, how would you go about performing the task? How would you respond to questions about activeness versus passiveness and pastels versus primary colors? Given that you live in the context where these images circulate and have thus been exposed to comparable images over an extended period of time, it is fair to assume that the very images to which you are now being asked to respond are also mediating your perception of boys and girls, or masculinity and femininity. A qualitative researcher interested in going beyond the mediated vision of individuals whose vision is already filtered by societal norms may use the magazines themselves as the starting point for research. By deconstructing preexisting images of boys and girls in popular magazines, the researcher is interrogating the process by which the images came to be (and to be normalized) and how they represent (or in some cases challenge) the prevailing worldview. As you can see, depending on the research question and the researcher's goals, content analysis may be more appropriate than interactional methods such as interviewing.

As the preceding parenting magazine example illustrates, content analysis can be used to study difference. Let's return to our body image women's magazine example, which focused solely on representations of females. Instead, a researcher could also study racial *differences* in portrayals. For example, what are the different roles women are shown in depending on their race? How do these images impact stereotyped attitudes?

Covert and Dixon (2008) designed a mixed methods research project investigating portrayals of race in mainstream women's magazines and their effect on readers. They conducted a content analysis of a sample of women's magazines produced in a 5-year period. They found that white women were overrepresented whereas Latina and black women were underrepresented in articles, although this trend decreased over the 5-year period. Covert and Dixon also conducted an experiment to study the effects of counterstereotypical portrayals on racially diverse readers. They found that when white readers were exposed to these depictions, their occupational expectations for women of color increased (a positive outcome). People of color did not have elevated expectations based on exposure to counterstereotypical representations. Ultimately, Covert and Dixon were able to generate theory about these differences. As we can see, in this instance, content analysis was very useful for contributing to our knowledge about racial differences within mass-mediated forms. In addition to exposing and describing a cultural phenomenon over time, Covert and Dixon also generated theory from their data about the implications of these racial differences.

Another example comes from Diana Rose, a researcher in the United Kingdom, who used audiovisual content analysis to study representations of "madness" on British television. In the following behind-the-scenes box, Rose talks about how she came to study this topic and where it has taken her.

BEHIND THE SCENES WITH DIANA ROSE

I have been working in the field of mental health research for 12 years. Before this, I conducted research on language and education and gender studies. There was a gap between the two types of research. This is because I have a diagnosis of bipolar affective disorder and for some time was too unwell to work. I lived on state welfare benefits and a small pension.

The first piece of research on mental health which I undertook was for my PhD, for which I studied quite late in life (40 years old). The topic I chose was "Representations of Madness on British Television." I considered this a "safe" topic, one that would not require me to disclose my mental health problems. I was very aware of stigma. After a while, I became unwell at the university, and it all came out. Everybody knew where I was drawing my inspiration. I did not really mind—I had a political commitment. In the British media at the time, there was much criticism of the policy of care in the community, and I wished to expose how biased this was. I was not a disinterested scholar!

In the last year of my doctoral studies, I was offered a job at a mental health charity to do research. This was *because* of my experience of mental health problems—having a diagnosis was a qualification for the job (Rose, 2000). I decided to embrace this whole-heartedly, be upfront about my diagnosis and treatment, and use my experience of treatments and services to inform my research practice.

This has led me to develop an "empowerment" epistemology. In terms of enlightenment thought, mental health service users (we don't like the term *patient*) are in a similar position to that described for women by feminist epistemologists—only worse. Irrationality defines us according to psychiatrists and the public; we have no intellectual capacities—only out-of-control emotions and chaotic lives. There are still psychiatrists who believe that mental health service users are damaged in the "cultural" parts of their brains and so are closer to nature. An empowerment epistemology seeks to overturn these beliefs.

Just as the women's movement contributes to feminist scholarship, the user/survivor movement has contributed to my own thinking. I first became aware of this movement in the mid 1980s when I was not working. It was a consciousness-raising experience, just like feminism. I came to realize that the way I was being treated by the mental health system was unjust. Later, I theorized this in terms of the mental health system being a dominant discourse and practice, drawing on the work of Foucault.

What does this mean in terms of research practice? It leads to a participatory form of research. There are two ways this can happen. First, when other service users are participants in our research, we are able to understand their perspectives as we have been there, too—we share their experiences. From a methodological point of view, we are also very careful that we capture exactly what individuals and groups think—often going back several times to check on the contents of an interview or focus group. This is good qualitative research practice, but it is also informed by a deep respect for our participants. This does not happen in mainstream mental health research.

The other form of participatory research is to involve service users as *researchers*. People with little or no research experience are trained to do research, alongside experienced researchers. They design interview schedules drawing on their own

(Continued)

(Continued)

experience. Using these schedules, they conduct interviews with other service users. The general view is that when users interview other users, the situation is more open and relaxed and the information is different to what a professional would obtain.

My preferred method of analyzing data from qualitative projects is qualitative content analysis. This is more a methodological choice than a choice informed by my experience as a mental health service user. I do not believe it is possible to come to a set of data with no preconceptions. I do not believe this is ever possible. Having a coding frame, albeit informed by initial examination of the data, makes one's preconceptions explicit. In the research I do and the research I supervise, many of our coding categories are developed from our personal knowledge of distress, treatments, and services.

Some would say that this constitutes bias. But I have yet to meet a professional researcher in the mental health field, which is mostly quantitative, who is not researching a topic that is close to his or her heart, where there is some personal investment.

User involvement in research is quite fashionable in the United Kingdom at the moment. I am now responsible for a unit of five researchers, all of whom are or have been mental health service users. I am committed now to developing the ideas outlined here.

As you can see from Rose's work, content analysis can be employed in social justice-oriented ways, just like the other qualitative methods reviewed in this book. Now that we are getting a sense of how content analysis can be used, and used differently than other methods, let's look more closely at the quantitative origins of content analysis.

Qualitative and Quantitative Traditions: What Are the Main Approaches to Content Analysis?

Traditionally, content analysis referred to the systematic examination of written texts. Originally, this practice was quantitative in nature, and researchers would count the occurrence of a particular thing in which they were interested, such as gendered or racialized terms in a newspaper. These early researchers were considered "bean counters." Many researchers now don't think in terms of qualitative or quantitative when they think about content analysis—content analysis merges these categories and can be considered a hybrid. Content analysis can be conceptualized as an inherently mixed method of analysis, or a method that always contains the possibility of both qualitative and quantitative applications. Bauer (2000) refers to content analysis as a "hybrid technique," which has always, even when performed quantitatively, been an implicitly hybridized approach to inquiry. He explains as follows:

> While most classical content analyses culminate in numerical descriptions of some features of the text corpus, considerable thought is given to the "kinds," "qualities" and "distinctions" in the text before any quantification takes place. In this way, content analysis bridges statistical formalism and the qualitative analysis of the materials. In the quantity/quality divide in social research, content analysis is a hybrid technique that can mediate in this unproductive dispute over virtues and methods. (p. 132)

Regardless of the extent to which we think about content analysis as implicitly hybridized or a method with deductive and inductive capabilities, there is no doubt that with this method of inquiry, social scientists have contributed to our overall body of knowledge in significant ways with statistical and descriptive power.

Historically, quantitative researchers have demonstrated the importance of content analysis as a method of gaining "hard data" about macro phenomena in both single method and multimethod studies. This kind of research has contributed significantly to social scientific knowledge and directly influenced social policy. In briefly reviewing the history of content analysis, we will see how it can be an effective tool for promoting social change on a policy level.

Quantitative content analysis has been integral to creating our repository of social scientific knowledge, including that aimed at social justice. The strength of this method is that it enables researchers to examine patterns and themes within the objects produced in a given culture. Researchers can analyze preexisting data to expose and unravel macro processes. The quantitative practice of content analysis is important because researchers are able to present their findings on easily readable charts and tables, often in numerical form. The force of this form of data cannot be underestimated when trying to call attention to systemic practices of inequality and when attempting to change public policy. In terms of adding to our knowledge about social inequality, quantitative content analysis has been a standard method for analyzing the role of mass-produced texts in the socialization process.

For example, Gooden and Gooden (2001) studied gender representation in 83 notable children's books that were published from 1995 to 1999. Their research showed that sex stereotyping is lower than it was in the 1970s; however, sex stereotyping remains prevalent in children's literature. As children's books are a significant source of socialization, this research indicates more work must be done in terms of making children's books more gender neutral. In their present form, these stereotyped representations can negatively impact girls' self-esteem and self-identity. Moreover, these texts reinforce traditional gender roles and thereby may limit the behavioral choices boys and girls believe are available to them.

Likewise, traditional content analysis has been used to help shape social policy by calling attention to systemic inequalities in need of change. For example, Thomas and Treiber (2000) conducted a quantitative content analysis of 1,709 advertisements taken from four magazines, two marketed to white consumers and two marketed to black consumers, in order to examine race, gender, and status stereotyping. Their research indicated that there are a few patterns of gender and racial stereotyping within image-based media. For example, the white subjects often appear to be of higher status than the black subjects. Thomas and Treiber conclude:

> Racial and gender stereotypes endure as exaggerated, over-simplified images used to sell products. We have demonstrated that magazine advertisements differentially use these superficial images when targeting products to women, men, Blacks, and Whites. The use of stereotypical images in magazine advertising confirms to the readership that subordinate groups should remain in lower status. In this study, both gender and race were found to be strong underlying principles of organizing everyday experience. One of the tragic characteristics of media-generated stereotypes is their ability to generate self-fulfilling prophecies, although stereotypes in ads often provide an incorrect image of race and gender. (p. 370)

This research was enabled through quantitative content analysis. The use of clear statistical charts facilitated the researchers' generation of convincing theory regarding the social implications of socializing people via harmful stereotypes.

Altheide (2009) used content analysis to examine the extent and nature of news reports that use the sociological concept of "moral panic." This method allowed him to note several patterns about the use of this term: (1) It is most commonly used in news reports in the United States, the United Kingdom, and Australia; (2) it is most frequently used in print news; (3) it is most frequently used as a form of resistance in articles about "deviant behavior"; (4) it is associated more with topics like sex and drugs and less with topics likes terrorism; and (5) usage has increased over the past decade. Based on these findings, Altheide suggests areas for future research, which may lead to calls to reevaluate Western journalistic practices. Even beyond exposing patterns and themes, unobtrusive methods can help researchers to *describe* and *explain* macro social processes.

Content analysis has historically been conducted quantitatively; however, now there is a rich tradition of qualitative content analysis as well as mixed approaches. The primary difference in these two broad applications is in research design. Quantitative approaches to content analysis are largely deductive and follow a **linear model** of research design. Qualitative approaches are mainly inductive and follow what we term a **spiral model** of research design.

Let's take the former first. When using a *linear design* the researcher has a preconceived set of steps to follow in a linear (vertical) path through each phase of the research process. A *spiral design,* employed by qualitative researchers, allows them metaphorically to dive in and out of the data as they proceed. In this model, a researcher generates new understandings, with varied levels of specificity, during each phase of the project and uses this information to double back and gain more information. This forms a "spiraled" approach to knowledge-building, if one were to visualize the process. The flowchart in Figure 9.1 depicts the phases of the research

Figure 9.1 Phases of the Research Process

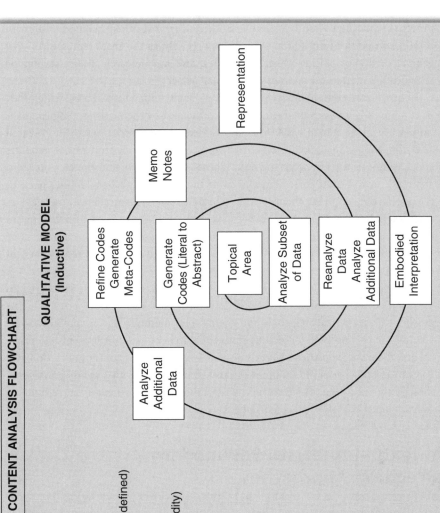

CONTENT ANALYSIS FLOWCHART

QUALITATIVE MODEL
(Inductive)

Representation

Memo
Notes

Refine Codes
Generate
Meta-Codes

Generate
Codes (Literal to
Abstract)

Topical
Area

Analyze Subset
of Data

Reanalyze
Data
Analyze
Additional Data

Embodied
Interpretation

Analyze
Additional
Data

QUANTITATIVE MODEL
(Deductive)

1. Research Question and Hypothesis

2. Conceptualization
   (What variables are used and how they will be defined)

3. Operational Measures
   (Aimed at gaining internal validity and face validity)
   3a. Unit of analysis
   3b. Measurement
      – categories can be exhaustive and
      mutually exclusive or a priori

4. Coding

5. Sampling
   (Randomly sampling a subset of content)

6. Reliability
   Can use: Two codes for intercoder reliability
   or computer program for validation

7. If reliability was determined by hand (Step 6)
   then apply a statistical check

8. Tabulation and Representation

Source: Quantitative Model adapted from Neuendorf, K. A. (2001). *The content analysis guidebook.* Thousand Oaks, CA: Sage.

process in quantitative and qualitative studies—linear versus spiral models. Bear in mind that one need not follow these steps precisely, as the chart represents a very general depiction of these two approaches, and any research design should be specifically suited to the goals of a particular project.

In qualitative content analysis, researchers begin with a topical area, which they start to investigate from their standpoint, influenced by their epistemological position. Early in the process, the topic is also examined in relation to the research question. Researchers do not begin with preconceived codes but rather generate code categories directly from the data. These codes can range from very literal to abstract. As code categories emerge from the data, researchers double back to reexamine data applying the new code categories. Many researchers also engage in **memo writing** throughout this process as a way of interpreting and reflecting on the data as they go. This is why we refer to inductive approaches as a process of "diving in and out of the data." The resulting knowledge can be represented in numerous ways.

The wide-ranging ways in which unobtrusive methods can be employed to yield varied kinds of data with both descriptive and explanatory power distinguishes this set of research tools and their broad methodological configurations. During the past 30 years or so, qualitative researchers from diverse epistemological and theoretical positions have dramatically enlarged the conceptualization and use of unobtrusive methodologies. Increased attention to this set of practices is directly linked to the growth of cultural studies and the postmodern critique of social scientific knowledge construction.

Qualitative Textual Analysis: Postmodern and Post-structural Approaches

Traditionally, text analysis has been the most commonly used form of content analysis. Text analysis is when a researcher uses written texts as the primary form of data (although a researcher might combine textual and visual data or combine text analysis with another method). At the present time, the term *text* is used more broadly to encompass the range of media in which cultural texts appear. Over the past few decades, new scholarly conceptions about the nature of social reality and the nature of social inquiry have led to increased use of and elaboration of unobtrusive methods. In particular, the postmodern and post-structural critiques of research have influenced the practice of unobtrusive research by changing the theoretical perspective from which many researchers practice these techniques. Although we briefly reviewed these theoretical frameworks in Chapter 2, we will now review them again in relation to unobtrusive methods.

In essence, postmodernism posits a shift from the modern era into the postmodern era. In this new era, there has been an implosion of media forms, constituting what Jean Baudrillard refers to as a *hyperreality* in which "the real" and "the imaginary" have become blurred to an unprecedented level. In such a context, it becomes important to investigate the material aspects of culture such as texts (broadly defined), which, during production and dissemination, are embedded with historically specific power relations. But what do postmodern and other critical scholars mean by studying the power imbued in texts?

Michel Foucault was at the forefront of influencing conceptions of power. Foucault (1978) theorized that power and knowledge are inextricably linked, creating a complex web of power-knowledge relations. In short, Foucault's work shows that all knowledge is contextually bound because it is produced within a field of shifting power relations. Scholars must interrogate cultural texts to reveal traces of the dominant worldview embedded within them as well as the "silences" (what has been marginalized or left out of the text, which in Avery Gordon's terms "haunts" that which is there). Specifically, researchers in this tradition examine the discursive practice embedded in the text, which means the specific ways that language is used within texts. Foucault proposed an archaeological method of investigation to unravel how a text assumed its present form (Prior, 1997). This specific technique relies on tracing the text's process of production and distribution. Stuart Hall (1981) explains that within cultural texts, dominance is enacted. Hall goes on to explain that popular texts also have an "oppositional" possibility, and within texts, hegemony is also contested, resisted, and challenged. Texts do not simply mirror social reality but are also an integral component in shaping that reality (Hall, 1981) or hyperreality. Prior (1997) asserts that we can "know the world through the representational orders contained within the text" (p. 67).

We now turn to post-structural thought. As noted in Chapter 2, Jacques Derrida (1966) coined the term *deconstruction,* which is a method of conducting an internal critique of texts. In essence, a deconstructive approach to textual analysis aims at exposing what is concealed within or has been left out of a text (but, in Gordon's terms, "haunts" the text). Deconstruction is based on the notion that the meaning of words happens in relation to sameness and difference. In every text, some things are affirmed, such as truth, meaning, and authorship/authority; however, there is always an "other" that contrasts with that which is affirmed. This other, that which has been left out or concealed, appears absent from the text but is actually contained within the text as a different or deferred meaning. Through the process of deconstruction, these different and deferred meanings are revealed. The aim of deconstruction is, therefore, not to find "the truth" of the text but rather to displace assumptions within the text (such as the meaning, the truth, and authorship/authority). Ultimately, this process shows that the meaning of a text is never single or fixed. For example, applying a deconstructive approach to the analysis of outdated U.S. history textbooks might reveal a predominance of nationalistic viewpoints about the founding of the country and the exclusion of Native American perspectives.

Since the advent of postmodernism and post-structuralism, many qualitative researchers who use textual analysis now do so to provide a critical (power-reflexive) analysis of the text in question. We have already discussed deconstruction, and while there are many other approaches researchers can take, we will review discourse analysis and semiological readings of texts.

Influenced by post-structuralism, ethnomethodology, and linguistics, discourse analysis is a strategy employed when one is concerned with the social meanings within language and discursive practices. In other words, discourse analysis is concerned with the process of communication. For Foucault, discourses are practices that are composed of ideas, ideologies, and referents that systematically construct both the subjects and objects of which they speak. Thus, discourses are integral to the construction of social reality. Many qualitative researchers perform discourse analysis when studying texts to reveal the hidden ideas embedded within written language. Researchers can investigate how the dominant discourse is produced, how it is disseminated, what it excludes, how some knowledge becomes subjugated, and so forth. This kind of research is rooted in the postmodern and post-structural conceptualization that language reflects power. Moreover, the structure of society is embedded within language (and representational forms). A qualitative researcher conducting discourse analysis of texts can follow the "spiral model" of knowledge construction and dive in and out of the text to gain deeper insights into the ideology within the text and how language is being used to create social meanings. For example, over the past two decades, gay marriage has become a major social and political issue. A researcher could study the texts (political advertisements and so forth from the two major sides of the debate) using discourse analysis to investigate how ideas of "the family" are created and arguably how these ideas in turn create the kinds of people we become (the kinds of attitudes we come to hold).

Semiological readings of texts are another approach. Roland Barthes (1998) suggests that semiological analyses of representations are a necessary part of social research. Semiological analyses examine the way meaning is constructed through a process of signification or connotation. Barthes created a three-part system detailing how people, places, times, and events (the signified) are distilled into signifiers (concepts), which are then planted in a host of signs (representations) (Hesse-Biber & Leavy, 2004). From the point of view of a semiologist, this three-part process is the way in which cultural interpretive practices become naturalized—take on the appearance of fact when they are actually socially constructed. Researchers can analyze the signs or representations produced within a society to break down the process of meaning construction that created them. This process generally occurs in a contextualized way. By this, we mean that in addition to analyzing isolated texts, researchers can analyze how meaning is constructed within a given text by the placement of words next to other words, or images next to other images, or images and words together. Meaning is not constructed out of one aspect of the text alone, but also in how the various components of the text sit in relation to each other (thereby creating different connotations or meanings). In short, semiological textual analyses center on revealing social processes of making meaning. Given that postmodernists conceptualize a "crisis in representation" brought about by the high-speed flow of images and texts within popular culture, this kind of research is becoming increasingly popular, particularly in media studies. Let's look at an example of semiological textual analysis.

If we are to create a semiological reading of this *Time* magazine cover, what would it look like? Let's begin with the image: a pumpkin pie with an American flag stuck in it. This image is composed of two images (the pie and the flag) and creates a connotation between the two images through their placement. These images are the signs (representations), but what is signified with the fusing of these two images to create one image? What signifiers (concepts) have been implanted into this sign (the image)? The American flag contains the concept of patriotism, and thus, patriotism is being signified within the pumpkin pie. But this is only part of the story. To get a full read, we have to consider the image in conjunction with the words. The caption next to this image was "Thanksgiving 2001: Next week American families will set their tables, count their blessings and discover how their lives have changed—and how they haven't." Clearly, this image, with the words, is meant to evoke patriotic feelings on the first Thanksgiving after the September 11th attacks. The words and image work together to create a particular connotation—the signified (9/11) is distilled into the signifier (the concept of patriotism), which is presented in the representation (the image of the flag in the pumpkin pie). A semi-ological approach to content analysis rejects the idea of naturalistic meaning in favor of examining how meaning is socially constructed. Let's take the same image of the American flag in the pumpkin pie. Now let's pretend the image was created in 1991, 10 years earlier. What if *the same image* had the following words next to it? "Leading Native American Activist Questions the True Meaning of Thanksgiving."

The same image now takes on a very different meaning—it was constructed and presented to do so. Instead of overarching patriotism in the wake of 9/11, the image now evokes thoughtful contemplation about how the United States was founded, about genocide, about a more textured questioning of patriotism. The same image connotes a very different meaning.

Lindsay Prior is a reader of sociology at the University of Wales, Cardiff, and author of several books, including *Documents in Social Research: Production, Consumption, and Exchange*. Prior has written extensively about what it means to use content analysis and to study nonliving forms of data, as well as the theoretical underpinnings of such investigation. He addresses these issues in the following behind-the-scenes box.

BEHIND THE SCENES WITH LINDSAY PRIOR

I have always been fascinated by the ways in which the spaces within buildings are arranged, which is why I always include plans of hospitals or mortuaries or whatever in my studies (Prior, 1989, 1993). Elements of front stage and back stage, entrances and exits, areas where only women can enter or men can leave, rooms for children that restrict where they can and cannot learn or play or sleep—all these are of utmost significance. So, studying the arrangement of the material space in which people live and work is for me an essential precursor to any ethnographic study, and I always find it worthwhile to find an architect's plan of the key sites in which such ethnographic work is to be based. This is so even though a building will be used in ways undreamed of by its creators. Indeed, the similarities and differences that can be noted between the ways in which a site is used and the intentions of its designer can often highlight fundamental changes in the ways in which people see things over time. Hospital plans, for example, certainly illustrate major shifts in the ways in which "disease" and sickness have been conceptualised over the decades, and this can be noted in the smallest detail—such as the positioning of windows in a hospital ward.

Although people think with things as well as words, it is also important to note that humans arrange things in words as well as in space and time—which leads us to a second great source of social scientific data: documents. I always find it something of a puzzle as to why, when people consider social scientific research, they almost always rule out a study of documentation in favour of interpersonal interviews. Perhaps it is something to do with those aforementioned anthropologists who worked in societies where written documentation was negligible or non-existent. I don't know. Nevertheless, almost every study of the contemporary social world will involve documentation of some kind. In my own work the documentation that has most concerned me are the notes and descriptions made by health professionals of the people they care for. In other words the kinds of things that doctors and nurses write about when they encounter "patients"—including dead patients. How, for example, do doctors explain death in official terms? We know that they have to write on a death certificate, but how do they know what to put on that certificate? And what kind of things can they *not* put on that certificate? Questions such as these normally lead one into an investigation of other types of documentation—generative documents such as are represented in nosologies or classifications of disease. Nosologies and other "big" classificatory schemes are invaluable for a number of reasons. First of all they change at regular intervals, so one can actually track thinking in progress. The *Diagnostic and Statistical Manual of Mental Disorders* (DSM)—a publication of the American Psychiatric Association—for example, documents the ways in which psychiatric disorders have been theorized between 1952 and the present day. Second, these big documents constitute the frame in which people at street or health centre level have to operate. If a disorder is not in the DSM then it can't be diagnosed, it can't be billed for, it can't be treated—and disorders come and go in the DSM with interesting consequences. In the same way there exists an international list (classification) of diseases and conditions that people can die from—if a condition isn't on the list then people can't die of it. You will be glad to hear, perhaps, that old age and poverty are not on the list.

The issue for me, then, is how people represent and arrange worlds in documents, and how such documentation is subsequently used in social interaction. I am especially keen to note how people use and make sense of the *rules* that are contained in documents (Prior, 1989). As I have explained elsewhere (Prior, 2003), the notion of use and circulation of documents can form an entire theme for research in itself—and all this without recourse to a single interview. However, even when one is right there in the midst of human interaction, there is no necessary call on behalf of the researcher for intrusive acts of questioning. Instead, one can often get what one wants from judiciously recording the "naturally occurring" data that arises from routine activities—as for example in studies of medical decision-making (Wood, Prior, & Gray, 2003).

In Belfast, the city where I undertook a large part of my work on death and psychiatric illness there was a phrase that was in common use during the 1970s and 80s. Viz. "Whatever you say, say nothing" (in Belfast, of course, the "nothing" is pronounced more like "nathn"). The advice to say nothing was advice to be wary of declaring details about oneself. Advice not to declare too much about one's identity, or of one's views on matters political or religious, or an opinion on anything at all that might be sucked into the whirlpool of sectarian strife that formed the backdrop to everyday life in the city. In the context of this book, such a keenness to say "nothing" can also stand as a reminder to the social researcher that asking people questions does not always get answers—or at least, true and reliable answers. More importantly, it serves as a reminder that even should people remain determined to say nothing, there is a whole world of data just laying around and about, waiting for the keen eyed and systematic observer to collect.

(Continued)

(Continued)

References:

Prior, L. (1989). *The social organization of death: Medical discourse and social practices in Belfast.* London and New York: Macmillan and St. Martin's Press.

Prior, L. (1993). *The social organization of mental illness.* London: Sage.

Prior, L. (2003). *Using documents in social research.* London: Sage.

Wood, F., Prior., L., & Gray, J. (2003). Making decisions in a cancer genetics clinic. *Health Risk and Society,* 5(2), 185–198.

Prior raises important issues concerning the kinds of research questions that can be addressed via the study of documents. These kinds of research projects can have social justice foundations and also illustrate how the built-in authenticity of pre-existing documents can be useful as researchers try to deal with these issues.

Visual Research: Photographs, Images, and Interactive Visual Research

Qualitative researchers can use visual representations as the starting point of inquiry. We have already discussed the use of media images, such as magazine covers or advertisements, but the media are merely one source of visual imagery. In addition to media-produced images, researchers can study photographs. Broken down further, the researcher can use preexisting photographs or photographs taken for the purpose of research (taken by the researcher or someone hired by the researcher). In this section, we will discuss these different forms of visual research and how researchers must conceptualize images in relation to their philosophical framework in order to holistically construct a cohesive research project (see Chapter 1 for our discussion of the philosophical framework).

When working with photographs and other visual images, you must consider how you conceptualize the images, broadly speaking, with which you are working. Prosser and Schwartz (1998) explain that photographs can be conceptualized in two different ways: (1) as visual records and (2) as visual diaries. This distinction is important and is intimately linked to your epistemological position. If you choose to conceive of photographs as visual records, then you imbue them with a sense of authority. It is like the saying "a picture is worth a thousand words." In other words, a record is a representation of some aspect of social reality—it is an aspect of social reality that has been captured. If you decide to conceptualize photographs as visual diaries, then you are implying that photography is a medium used by embodied actors who *take* the pictures and *view* them *from particular perspectives*. Under this conceptualization, the researcher uses photographs much like memo notes that are *marked by the researcher's position within the project.* This is a way of infusing reflexivity into the research process.

Neither of these approaches is necessarily right or even better, but again, the choice will be influenced by epistemological and theoretical commitments. For example, researchers working from a post-positivist frame who are studying images of the terrorist attacks of September 11th might conceive of photographs as visual records for the sake of that particular research project. In doing so, they are able to conceptualize the photographs as material records of one of the darkest days in American history. The photographs can be used as "memory enhancers" under this frame (Hesse-Biber & Leavy, 2004, p. 312). Typically, researchers working from critical perspectives are more likely to view photographs as visual diaries influenced by their point of production as well as the context of viewing. For example, a postmodern researcher interested in studying how meanings about September 11th were constructed in American newspapers might conceive of newspaper images as visual diaries. In this situation, researchers would examine the social power embedded in the photos, the connotations created through the placement of photos, both on each page and in the newspaper as a whole, and the standpoint of the researchers themselves viewing the photos. By situating the images in these ways, the researcher can begin to disentangle how ideas about September 11th were constructed, disseminated, and consumed in ways that created a dominant collective memory of the event.

Instead of using preexisting photographs, researchers can also adopt the role of photographer and take photographs that will then serve as data. Researchers interested in studying social change might act as photographers to document and then interpret different forms of social change. This could be done, for example, to study changes surrounding the urbanization of a particular area or to study how social and economic change impacts a residential environment, community center, or work site.

> If you are interested in exploring or revealing the precise nature of change, then photographs taken at regular intervals from exactly the same place can be revelatory. Changes in urban neighbourhoods, landscapes or the contents of a room; the condition of a tree, a wall or human body "before" and "after" a significant change; all these, when properly attested and witnessed, and logged for time, place and circumstance, can have powerful evidential or persuasive value. (Loizos, 2000, p. 96)

Likewise, historical research can be conducted by combining preexisting photographs with those taken by the researcher to document and analyze change.

Reflexivity becomes critical when using a traditionally unobtrusive method in this way. First, this is one of the rare instances in which the research is unobtrusive but nevertheless **interactive research.** The researcher impacts social reality by being present and taking photographs. In addition to changing that aspect of visual research from noninteractive to interactive, the data is produced directly from the vantage point of the researcher. Consider Paul Byers's (1964) assertion that "cameras don't take pictures [people do]." This is always true; however, when the researcher is the one taking the photos, the practice of reflexivity, examining and disclosing one's position within the process, becomes critical. Let's return to the example of studying 9/11 photo images. Let's say that you wanted to study the 9/11 recovery process immediately following the event or the search for survivors. One way to do this would be to go to Ground Zero and the Pentagon site and take photographs, which then serve as your data. You may even conceive of your photographs as visual fieldnotes.

Researchers often use preexisting visual images as data to study media bias. For example, Nikolaev (2009) conducted a content analysis of the coverage of the war in Kosovo in three American magazines (*Time, Newsweek,* and *US News & World Report*) and found the photographic coverage was imbalanced, with bias against the Serbs.

In another example, this time about the bias produced from sensationalistic news reporting, Jones and Wardle (2008) conducted a content analysis of the British press's visual coverage of a major murder trial: the Soham murder trial, which occurred in 2003. Two girls had been abducted and murdered, and their school caretaker, Ian Huntley, was charged. His girlfriend, Maxine Carr, provided a false alibi for Huntley and was charged with "perverting the course of justice," although she was not charged as an accomplice. Carr was released in May 2004 and granted "indefinite anonymity"; however, public contempt toward Carr (and her "light" sentence) was intense. Jones and Wardle conducted a textual and visual content analysis of trial coverage in three British papers to understand how Carr was visually constructed as compared with Huntley. They examined three papers: one national newspaper, one middle-market newspaper, and one tabloid. They considered many dimensions of the data, including but not limited to frequency of images, color, page layout, montages, and juxtaposition of images to each other and to headline text. They found images of Carr were more frequent, larger, and more frequently in color. They also found newspaper formatting would lead readers to misleading conclusions not supported by the evidence that formed the basis for her sentence, thus explaining the public contempt of Carr relative to the court's ruling.

These are clear examples of how mass media images can be used as the starting point for research. But once you decide what you want to study and what data you will use, research design becomes critical to the practice of visual studies. The primary issue regarding research design centers on analysis. Let's say you have decided to study mass-mediated images of female beauty, and you have selected a sample of fashion magazines. What will be the unit of analysis? Typically, individual images or ads would serve as your unit of analysis. But how do you code this data? There are many strategies qualitative researchers can employ for coding visual data. For example, codes such as "still shot" and "action shot" can be employed. Likewise, researchers can code for gender, race, and other social attributes. This process can occur from a grounded theory approach, where code categories emerge from analysis, or alternatively, preconceived code categories can be employed.

The following is an exercise aimed at familiarizing you with the process of conducting visual content analysis, although it can also be modified for audiovisual analysis. This exercise can be adapted to suit particular skill sets or can be adapted as a part of exploratory or preliminary research protocol.

Exercise on Coding Advertisements

We suggest that you work in pairs to add a dimension of reliability to the research process. In pairs, select a sample of 10 advertisements (any number of sampling strategies can be employed). Then, code them. Both scholars should agree on the primary figure(s) in the advertisement and then independently code the following characteristics: sex of the primary figure, basis for credibility, setting, category of product, and the arguments given on behalf of the product. Below are details of the coding categories, which are adapted from McArthur and Resko (1975). This exercise can be adapted and conducted in groups or by individuals.

Primary Figure: Primary figures are the individuals who play a major role in the advertisement, as denoted by prominent visual exposure. If more than two adults are present, choose those that appear central (where the looker's eye is drawn). If it is unclear which two figures are most central, you can pick primary figures of each sex or racial group represented. If there are only two adult figures present, both should be coded.

Basis for Credibility: When determining who the primary figure is you must consider how to justify your decision. The basis for credibility of the primary figure usually falls under three main categories: (1) product user, (2) authority, and (3) other. The primary figure is a product user when he or she is depicted as the primary user of the product or service being advertised. The primary figure is an authority when he or she is depicted as having the information about the product being advertised. The primary figure is "other" if he or she is being persuaded by another central figure to use the product, that is, if the primary figure is represented as a potential consumer.

Role: Primary figures should be coded according to the major roles in which they are shown, such as teacher, worker, parent, spouse, child, and so forth.

Setting: Primary figures should be coded according to their location, such as home, work, store, outdoors, vacation setting, school, concert, and so on.

Type of Product: The category the product best fits should be coded (such as beauty products, food products, home products, automotive products, technology-based products, etc.).

Persuasion Arguments (some may be more relevant to audiovisual advertisements, so adapt accordingly): The argument made on behalf of the product should be coded. The argument made may be based on factual or scientific evidence aimed at encouraging consumers to use the product for its "proven" benefits or superiority. The argument may also be based on opinions consisting of personal testimonies that encourage consumers to use the product. In some cases, there aren't any arguments on behalf of the product, and the advertisement doesn't make any truth claims about the quality of the product. In this case, the primary figure is simply displaying the product or creating an atmosphere around the product.

In lieu of the above more in-depth exercise, try analyzing the following magazine ads taken from an array of magazines aimed at different demographics. Try analyzing them using the exercise above. Then try analyzing them from different theoretical perspectives. Try a deconstructionist approach. Then read the texts from a semiological perspective—what connotations are created in the representation by implanting distilled concepts (such as beauty) in the signs? How would a feminist interpret these ads? By applying different "lenses" to these ads, do you *read* them differently?

Audiovisual Analysis: Working With Multiple Fields

Many scholars across the disciplines use audiovisual material as their data. If researchers are interested in studying cinema or television, they can content-analyze audiovisual footage. Although it can be researched as another narrative form, audiovisual data is unique and requires a particular set of considerations. What makes audiovisual data distinct from the kinds of texts we have been discussing is that it has *multiple components*, including visual, sound, and dialogue. Rose (2000) refers to audiovisual material as a *multiple field* because of its distinct but interrelated components. Furthermore, the data is *moving*.

During research design with audiovisual data certain considerations arise. Sampling issues are relatively consistent when performing content analysis with any kind of material. What to sample, how much to sample, and the extent to which sampling is randomized are all things to consider. For example, let's say we are interested in studying television news coverage of the terrorist attacks of September 11th. We have to choose networks from which we will sample. Then we must decide what to sample. We could use all coverage in a certain time frame, such as 2 weeks. Or we could use coverage between certain hours of the day for a selected number of days. We could also select certain news programs, and they would be our data. Beyond sampling issues, we would have to decide what the unit of analysis is and what the coding procedure will be. The coding process is one of the most important decisions when working with moving data.

As discussed in Chapter 3, as a part of research design, researchers create a research question, which is linked to their research purpose. In the case of audiovisual content analysis, researchers also construct a definition of the kind of representation they are seeking. After creating an operational definition, researchers must determine the unit of analysis and coding scheme, all of which is complicated by the multidimensional nature of audiovisual data. Let's look at an example.

Ramasubramanian and Oliver (2003) wanted to study the portrayal of sexual violence in Hindi films. They chose this topic because rates of male sexual violence against women are higher in male-dominated countries, including India. The public sexual harassment of women, referred to as "eve-teasing," is prevalent in urban India. A literature review also revealed two important factors: (1) there is a relationship between media sexual violence and real-world aggression and "rape myths," which culturally legitimate the sexual violation of women, and (2) prior research on Hindi films showed that violence and sexuality were often intertwined, and sexual violence was normalized and even portrayed as "expected" in romantic relationships. So Ramasubramanian and Oliver decided to analyze the content of Hindi films regarding violence and sexuality and thus analyzed the films' portrayals of sexuality. They first developed a definition of the kind of representation they were seeking. Films were watched in their entirety for the presence of sexual scenes. They defined a sexual scene as "one in which two or more characters were involved in activities such as having sex, kissing, petting, initiating or suggesting sexual contact, displaying nudity, engaging in sexual talk, bathing in an erotic way, wearing provocative or revealing clothing, or shown as a sexual object of gaze" (p. 330).

After constructing an operational definition of the kind of scene they were looking for, the next step was to determine the unit of analysis. Their units of analysis were characters and scenes. Characters who spoke and were present in sexual scenes were coded. The coding method here was to code for gender and type of character role. Then characteristics of the characters were coded only after the film was viewed in its entirety. A scene was defined as a "continuous action in one place such as a single situation or a unit of dialogue in the film" (Ramasubramanian & Oliver, 2003, p. 330). Sexual scenes were further broken down into (1) mutually consenting scenes and (2) sexually violent scenes. The coding method of scenes consisted of a list of variables considered relevant to the topic. These codes included gender, character role, presence of sexual violence, severity of sexual violence (moderate to severe encompassing harassment to rape), primary perpetrators/victims, and fun/seriousness of scene. Their findings show that a significant number of sexual scenes in Hindi films consist of sexual violence regardless of the audience the film is aimed at (including those rated for children younger than 12 years old). In addition, females are almost exclusively the victims of male violence. Most disturbing, the way in which the sexual violence is portrayed normalizes it. It is not just "bad guys" who commit sexual violence but also those who are portrayed as hero figures. Sexual violence is shown as a marker of masculinity.

While we have reviewed how this particular project created a definition of the kinds of representations under investigation and then determined the unit of analysis and constructed a coding scheme, there are other ways to determine the unit of analysis and coding strategy.

The method of using scene change is common among film and television program analyzers, and the change of camera shot is another option. In addition, one could demarcate units based on a time-fragmented system. This might be appropriate in our example of studying 9/11 news coverage. The unit of analysis could be every 5 minutes of coverage, for example. The specific kind of audiovisual data being used (i.e., films, news, etc.) in conjunction with the research goals help determine an appropriate unit of analysis.

In terms of coding, several strategies can be employed depending on the degree to which the study will be deductive or inductive. It is helpful to think of deductive and inductive approaches as existing on a continuum rather than as an either/or decision. Coding categories, such as those used in the study of Hindi films, can be constructed prior to data analysis. In this deductive approach, researchers already have a set of coded representations that they are seeking. When this kind of strategy is used, it is helpful to have other scholars participate in the construction of the code list. In addition, validity and reliability can be enhanced by having multiple coders examine the same data, which is what occurred in the study of Hindi films, where two coders coded the data set and verbally discussed discrepancies until reaching a consensus. If you employ a preset code list, we suggest adding a category such as "other" or "miscellaneous" in the event that there is additional pertinent information in the data that you hadn't considered before data analysis. The usefulness of this extra code is dependent on the research goals. This includes the extent to which you want to be able to replicate the study and achieve generalizability. Researchers can also blend deductive and inductive strategies. For example, a researcher can determine some codes in advance of analysis and then, as analysis is under way, the codes can be modified. This might include the removal of codes no longer deemed appropriate, the renaming of codes based on the language of the data under investigation, and the adding of codes to categorize information not previously known to be there, or any combination of the aforementioned.

On the inductive side of the continuum, researchers can create code categories as they analyze and interpret the data. This can be done using a grounded theory approach or the similar spiral model of diving in and out of the data that we have explained. In this instance, the code categories develop directly out of the data. The researcher analyzes a portion of the data and constructs code categories based on what was in the data, often using the language of the text itself as code categories. With some categories in place, the researcher goes back through the data, and another portion of the data, to see if the code categories "hold up," and adds more as the data warrant. The researcher may begin with very specific literal codes and through the process develop large code categories, or "meta-codes," under which the subcodes will be placed. Conversely, but perhaps less frequently, you could begin with broad-based meta-code categories, and as you cycle back through the data, code categories could be refined and new, more specific categories added.

The strategy of coding, particularly with the complexity of working with a multiple field, will be dependent on the research goals and theoretical framing of the topic. The methodological and epistemological components of the project should fit as tightly together as possible.

There is one final issue that must be considered during the coding, analysis, interpretation, and representation phases: **translation**. All qualitative research produces an abundance of data, such as the thick descriptions common in ethnography and the hundreds or thousands of pages of transcripts produced in the various methods of interview. These data then go through a process of reduction whereby large amounts of data are reduced so that the data can tell a story or explain some aspect of social life. Audiovisual content analysis also requires a process of reduction. For example, the researcher doesn't actually reproduce all of the television shows or films studied in their entirety—one wouldn't need research to simply present this material as it already is. The key difference between reducing audiovisual data and other forms of qualitative data is that an additional process of *translation* occurs as we move from one medium to another (Rose, 2000). In the other examples discussed, the original data are in textual form; so is the resulting representation. In the case of audiovisual data, we are moving from moving pictures, sound, and words to words alone. In addition to reducing or simplifying the large amounts of data studied, we are also translating it, as if into another language. Researchers should be cognizant of this as they consider how to best interpret and represent their data. This is another reason why thoroughly disclosing coding strategies is so important.

Computer-Driven Content Analysis

A recent development in content analysis has been the use of computer-driven data or "virtual documents." Similar to audiovisual data, this kind of data may appear in the form of a multiple field (although this is not always the case). Computer-driven data is very unique and raises its own set of issues as it simultaneously pushes the practice of qualitative research in new directions while raising questions about ethics.

First, computer-driven content analysis can be unobtrusive, but it isn't necessarily unobtrusive. And even when the practice is not obtrusive, particular ethical concerns not present with other forms of text analysis may arise. Frequently, computer-directed data is data obtained from Internet Web sites, message boards, and chat rooms. Let's look at Web sites and message boards first.

Web sites, message boards, and social networking sites are three sources of computer-driven data. Web sites may consist of multiple fields containing graphics and words and should be coded accordingly. Message boards are typically text-based. If we are interested in going to a message board to study people's responses to the Susan Boyle talent show loss, we can simply go to a site and print its content. This textual data can then be analyzed using the variety of perspectives discussed in this book. This kind of research is unobtrusive, and the information placed on Web site message boards is placed there freely by people who know that it can be seen and used by anyone who wishes to do so. However, it likely doesn't occur to people that their posts will be used in research. Let's look at an example of using this kind of data.

Harmon and Boeringer (1997) were interested in exploring sexual content on the Internet. Web-based forms of pornography were relatively new at the time, and so they decided to conduct content analysis as a means of conducting exploratory research. After a preliminary review of Internet Web sites, they decided to collect 200 "postings" from a Web site with explicit sexual content. Postings refer to information (comments and so forth) placed on the site. They decided four postings were "unusable," and so they ended up with a sample of 196 postings collected over a 2-week period. Using a line-by-line method of analysis with codes developed directly out of the text, they assigned each line of text a code such as "pedophilia" and other "fetishes." When they completed the coding process, they were stunned by the presence of "nonconsensual" expressions, which dominated the postings. The research process and findings were so troubling that one of the researchers sought a professional "debriefing" from a university counselor—showing that researchers using content analysis are susceptible to some of the emotional challenges field researchers and other qualitative researchers face. For example, a content analyst studying representations of tragic events such as September 11th may experience emotional and psychological difficulties traditionally attributed to the practice of interactive methods such as ethnography. Researchers should bear this in mind as they select research topics.

The Harmon and Boeringer study is an excellent example of using qualitative content analysis as a method of developing data in an emerging field. The computerized form of the data is actually a part of what is being studied. This is a method of using computer-driven data in a way that is congruent with the principles of unobtrusive research. However, other forms of computer-driven data blur these lines, raising a host of new ethical considerations.

Emergent Ethical Concerns
With Computer-Driven Content Analysis

Qualitative researchers can study ongoing interaction using chat rooms as the location of social data. What is interesting about chat room data is that even though it is dialogue to the extent that multiple people are typing in their responses in a fluid manner, it is not the same as face-to-face talk. People write differently than they normally speak (including more slowly). Likewise, the people in the chat room cannot see each other and have a technologically created anonymity. Typically, you really don't know who you are speaking to in a chat room (from their gender to their age, etc.). Researchers who use chat room discussion as data can do so in two ways: as an observer or as a participant (much like in ethnography). Let's look at the former first.

A researcher can observe chat room discussions and perform discourse analysis (Mann & Stewart, 2000). The chat room data appear as line-by-line text, although the data occur in the form of mediated conversation. In this kind of research, the researcher assumes the role of voyeur to interaction (Mann & Stewart, 2000). The researcher can conceal his or her presence, and the dialogue would be occurring regardless of the research, thus maintaining the principles of unobtrusive research. However, this kind of voyeuristic research does raise ethical issues. What are the implications of sitting in on a conversation for the purpose of research? Is it fair to the people participating in the chat room discussion for a researcher to use that information without obtaining informed consent? Is it possible to obtain informed consent in a chat room situation when people enter and exit the chat room routinely? Likewise, because chat room participants can assume false identities, how does a researcher know whether or not there are minors present? How can one code for demographics that may be falsified? These are some of the issues one must consider when thinking about this kind of research.

Researchers can also choose to disclose their identities and, thus, to some extent participate in the chat room discussion. On the flip side, researchers can participate in the chat room discussion, and this becomes a part of the text they use as data, without disclosing their identity. In these instances, the research is no longer unobtrusive, as the researcher directly impacts the development of the data. This raises considerations regarding ethics, confidentiality, disclosure, and researcher effect, all of which must be carefully considered.

Using pages from social networking sites such as MySpace or Facebook raises additional ethical concerns, as noted in Chapter 4. People who use these sites do not do so with the understanding that their "virtual documents" could be used as data in research. When these sites are open to the public (or open for a fee), who "owns" the information posted? Should informed consent be obtained? Similar questions are raised by Internet dating sites and the profile pages users generate.

As Web-based technology increases, computer-driven data in even more forms will likely emerge. The extent to which newer data can be studied unobtrusively and ethically is something that remains to be seen. With that said, following the basic principles of ethical research, as discussed in Chapter 4, will help qualitative researchers explore these new terrains, asking and answering a host of social scientific questions.

Conclusion

We hope this chapter has introduced you to some of the many ways that qualitative researchers can investigate texts as the starting point of research or as a part of a mixed method or multimethod design. The primary advantage of working with nonliving data is that it allows us to go beyond the subjective perceptions of individuals, which, while very important, are not the only point of departure for knowledge-building. By interrogating texts from a variety of epistemological and theoretical positions, we can continue to ask new research questions and offer new insights about social reality.

Glossary

Content analysis: Systematically analyzing texts.

Interactive research: When the researcher impacts social reality by being present (e.g., by taking pictures), and thus the data are produced directly from the vantage point of the researcher.

Linear model: A method of research design in which the researcher has a preconceived set of steps, which follow a vertical path through each phase of the research process.

Memo writing: Used by a researcher engaged in the spiral model of research design as a way of interpreting and reflecting on the data as they go.

Spiral model: A method of research design that allows the investigator to, metaphorically, dive in and out of the data as she or he proceeds. In this model, a researcher generates new understandings, with varied levels of specificity, during each phase of the project and uses this information to double back and gain more information.

Translation: This is the process through which large amounts of textual data are reduced into codes. In the case of visual or audiovisual analysis, translation refers to the process of putting data in one medium (visual or moving images) into words, as if translating the data from one language into another.

Discussion Questions

1. How has the growth in cultural studies and postmodernism impacted the use of content analysis? What are the congruencies between these theoretical traditions and this particular method, particularly in terms of the nature of knowledge and its construction?

2. What is unique about working with nonliving data? How does this impact the research questions and resulting knowledge?

3. What does it mean to say that content analysis is a "hybrid technique"? How can qualitative and quantitative approaches to content analysis be combined? What benefits does this have?

4. Explain the difference between linear (quantitative) and spiral (qualitative) approaches to content analysis.

5. What are the specific issues that arise when using visual and audiovisual data? Explain the process of translation that occurs. What are different strategies for dealing with this kind of data?

6. Discuss emergent practices in unobtrusive methods. What ethical issues are raised by these new approaches?

Resources

Suggested Web Sites

Cultural Studies Central

http://www.culturalstudies.net/

This Web site allows for interactive learning. You can participate in online discussions. This site offers links to cultural Web projects as well as other related links. We think this Web site provides a lot of options to the viewer.

Cultural Studies Study Group

http://members.tripod.com/~warlight/

This Web site appears to be privately owned but offers discussions, articles, and links to various types of culture studies, including youth, media, and popular culture.

The Critical and Cultural Studies Division of NCA

http://www.vcsun.org/CCS/

This Web site appears to be appropriate and useful for people looking for information on cultural studies. This organization publishes newsletters and holds conventions and conferences related to the field. The site includes related links.

Cognitive Cultural Studies

http://cogweb.ucla.edu/

This Web site is from UCLA and offers the viewer conference dates, forums, and papers related to the field. It also has an extended bibliography, including links to more information.

Relevant Journals

Communication Research

Crime, Media, Culture

Critical Sociology

Discourse Studies

Sex Roles: A Journal of Research

CHAPTER 10

Case Study

What Is a Case Study?

A case study differs from the research methods reviewed in this book because it is *not* a research method. Although often referred to in the literature as a method, methodology, research design, and even paradigm, these are inappropriate conceptualizations (Van Wynsberghe & Khan, 2007; Simons, 2009). **Case study** is a decision about what is to be studied, not a methodological decision, although it also guides how inquiry proceeds (Stake, 2005b). Case study has no disciplinary or paradigmatic orientation and can be conducted from any of the theoretical approaches reviewed in Chapter 2 (Van Wynsberghe & Khan, 2007). It is employed across the disciplines, most commonly in education, health care, management studies, organizational studies, public relations social work, and sociology. All disciplines need exemplars, so case study research, which results in the ongoing production of exemplars (Flyvbjerg, 2006), is vital toward making a discipline effective.

One of the problems in defining *case study* is that the term is not used in a consistent way across the literature as there are no agreed-on definitions (Gomm, Hammersley, & Foster, 2000). Moreover, researchers who do case study research often refer to their work by the methods they employed within the case study, such as ethnography or oral history (Gomm et al., 2000), and thus, a great deal of case study research is not defined as such. Even a history of the emergence of case study research spurs debate. "Cases" are used in many fields including medicine, law, and social work, and "case study" has been influenced by all of these fields (Gomm et al., 2000). Becker (1967) links the development of case study to the medical model, Stenhouse (1975) to education, and Platt (1992) to social work (Gomm et al., 2000). Van Wynsberghe and Khan (2007) argue that case study is a *heuristic device* because "at its most general, [it is] an approach that focuses one's attention during learning, construction, discovery, or problem solving" (p. 81). Graebner and Eisenhardt (2004) refer to case study as a research strategy. We concur and further suggest that case study is not a method or methodology but rather for our purposes *an expansive field within the qualitative paradigm.* Case study is both the way we proceed in research and the result of the research (Stake, 2005b). In this vein, we also concur with Stake, who writes, "a case study is both a process of inquiry about the case and the product of that inquiry" (2005b, p. 444). Simons's definition builds on that of Stake by noting the reasons for a case study as well as the research focus of a case study project. Simons (2009) states,

> "Case study is an in-depth exploration from multiple perspectives of the complexity and uniqueness of a particular project, policy, institution, programme or system in a "real life" context. It is research-based, inclusive of different methods and is evidence-led. The primary purpose is to generate in-depth understanding of a specific topic . . . , programme, policy, institution or system to generate knowledge and/or to inform policy development, professional practice and civil or community action. (p. 21)

The unique contribution of a case study approach is that it provides the researcher with a holistic understanding of a problem, issue, or phenomenon within its social context. Cases can be individuals, events, programs, institutions, or a society. Case study research usually relies on one or a few cases to investigate (typically, one case for which ample multidimensional data is collected and analyzed). Case study also allows us to study systems, which is particularly useful in both the social sciences and health studies (Anderson, Crabtree, Steele, & McDaniel, 2005). Because case study enables holistic understanding, it is often performed with social justice purposes in mind. In other words, because the case is investigated from many different angles and pays attention to many different dimensions of the issue, case study is typically able to avoid the kind of essentialist and context-free analyses that have historically been harmful to disempowered groups. Case study allows for a highly complex and nuanced understanding of the subject of inquiry. Case study aims to build understanding by addressing research questions and triangulating "thick descriptions" with interpretations of those descriptions in an ongoing iterative process (Stake, 2005b). Stake notes the following:

> For a qualitative research community, case study concentrates on experiential knowledge of the case and close attention to the influence of its social, political, and other contexts. For almost any audience, optimizing understanding of the case requires meticulous attention to its activities. These [are the] five requirements—issue choice, triangulation, experiential knowledge, contexts, and activities. (p. 444)

Researchers conducting case studies use more than one method to collect extensive data about the case. The methods can vary depending on the case and related research questions but often include interviews, oral history, ethnography, and document analysis. Both qualitative and quantitative methods can be employed in a case study and data can be original or preexisting. Statistical data, such as a census, are often used in case study research. Yin (2008) provides a table of data collection strategies you might use in thinking about the types of data to gather for your case study, along with the strengths and weaknesses of each type of data form (p. 101). It is important to take into account the important link between your research question(s) and the type of data that will serve to answer your question(s). While case studies incorporate many different types of data—qualitative and quantitative—as depicted in Table 10.1, not all these data may be appropriate for your particular study. More data is not necessarily better.

Your case study research question(s) guides the type of research design you will select. For example, will your study use a qualitative method or set of methods, quantitative methods, or mixed methods? One method is not necessarily better than another, but your guide to the selection of a particular case study design should flow from the research problem(s).

Table 10.1 Types of Case Study Evidence

Source of Evidence	Strengths	Weaknesses
Documentation	Stable: can be viewed repeatedly Unobtrusive: not created as a result of the case study Broad coverage: long span of time, many events and settings	Retrievability: Can be difficult to find Biased selectivity if collection is incomplete Reporting bias: reflects (unknown) bias of author Access: may be deliberately withheld
Archival Records	Same as those for documentation	Same as those for documentation Accessibility due to privacy reasons
Interviews	Targeted: focuses directly on case study topics Insightful: provides perceived causal inferences and explanations	Bias due to poorly articulated questions Response bias Inaccuracies due to poor recall Reflexivity: interviewee gives what interviewer wants to hear
Direct Observation	Reality: covers events in real time Contextual: covers context of case	Time-consuming Selectivity: Broad coverage difficult without a team of observers Reflexivity: events may proceed differently because they are being observed Cost: hours needed by human observers

(Continued)

Table 10.1 (Continued)

Source of Evidence	Strengths	Weaknesses
Participant Observation	Same as for direct observation Insightful into interpersonal behavior and motives	Same as for direct observation Bias due to participant observer's manipulation of events
Physical Artifacts	Insightful into cultural features Insightful into technical operations	Selectivity Availability

Source: Yin, 2008, p. 101.

Let's look at the types of data we have listed in Table 10.1. Suppose you have just entered your first research methods course, and your instructor asks the class to conduct a case study. As you have learned thus far from this chapter, you first need to decide what you will use as the unit of analysis for your case study.

What Specific Type of Case Study Do You Want to Conduct?

The unit of analysis in a case can consist of an individual, a group (such as students in your college dorm), an institution (such as your college), or more broadly a whole community and even a larger social entity (such as a state or nation, etc.). You might also consider a case to consist of a nonliving entity, such as a program or a specific social policy. You need to establish clear boundaries to your case, that is, what it includes and excludes. This boundary line may change as your study proceeds, and you may need to adjust what you consider to be a case, but this does not change the need for you to be clear on what it is you are studying and making statements about. To understand this, we will now look at the various parts of conducting a case study in more depth.

Stake (2005b) identifies three general types of case studies: (1) **intrinsic case study** (to understand the particular case holistically); (2) **instrumental case study** (a case is studied to generalize or provide insight into a larger topic); and (3) **multiple case study** (multiple cases are studied together to investigate a larger phenomenon or population from which the cases are drawn).

Case study research can serve many different purposes and can be conducted with different goals with respect to generalizability and related issues. In other words, the extent to which one learns about a case to enable generalizations to other cases, or to learn about a case purely in its own right, is variable. For now, it is important to note that case study research can be (1) theory based, (2) problem based, (3) descriptive, or (4) exploratory (Gomm et al., 2000). More specifically, case study can be used to test, illustrate, or generate theory; identify the sources of problems or solutions to problems; describe something; and explore something (Gomm et al., 2000).

Table 10.2, reprinted from Gomm et al. (2000), offers a schematic comparison of case study research with experimental and survey approaches to research. The table helps clarify the parameters of case study research.

Table 10.2   A Schematic Comparison of Case Study, Experimental, and Survey Approaches

Experiment	Case Study	Survey
Investigation of a relatively small number of cases	Investigation of a relatively small number of cases (maybe just one)	Investigation of a relatively large number of cases
Information gathered and analyzed about a small number of features of each case	Information gathered and analyzed about a large number of features of each case	Information gathered and analyzed about a small number of features of each case
Study of cases created in such a way as to control the important variables	Study of naturally occurring cases, or in action research, study of cases created by the action of the researcher, but where the primary concern is not controlling variables to study their effects	Study of a sample of naturally occurring cases, selected in such a way as to maximize the sample's representativeness in relation to some larger population
Quantification of data is a priority	Quantification of data is not a priority; indeed qualitative data may be treated as superior	Quantification of data is a priority
The aim is either theoretical inference—the development and testing of theory—or the practical evaluation of an intervention	The main concern may be with understanding the case studied in itself, with no interest in theoretical inference or empirical generalization. However, there may also be attempts at one or the other or both of these. Alternatively, the wider relevance of the findings may be conceptualized in terms of the provision of vicarious experience, as a basis for naturalistic generalization or transferability.	The aim is empirical generalization, from a sample to a finite population, although this is sometimes seen as a platform for theoretical inference

Source: Reprinted with permission from Gomm et al., 2000.

Variations in case study research are based on the following criteria:

[in] the number of cases studies, and the role of comparison; in how detailed the cases are; in the size of the case(s) dealt with; in the extent to which researchers document the context of the case, in terms of the wider society and/or historically; in the extent to which they restrict themselves to description and explanation, or engage in evaluation and prescription. (Gomm et al., 2000, pp. 3–4)

These design features, as with all qualitative practice, always relate to the research purpose, the research questions, and the grounding from which the research is conducted. When trying to make sense of the practice of case study, bear in mind that above all case studies are comprehensive research studies. However, not all research, even holistic ethnographies, produces case studies, nor are case studies necessarily produced with qualitative methods (Yin, 2008).

Continuum of Perspectives on Case Study Research

There are different perspectives on how a case study should be conducted with respect to the goals and purpose of the particular project. We suggest there is a continuum on which these perspectives can be placed, and we note three main points on the continuum depicted in Table 10.3, which we classify as (1) high generalizability, (2) **transferability** (characterized by the Lincoln & Guba approach), and (3) a focus on the particular (characterized by the Stake approach). We briefly review each perspective.

Generalizability

Some researchers conduct case study research with the goal of generalizing to the larger population of cases from which the particular case was selected (Gomm

Table 10.3 Comparison Points of the Continuum of Perspectives on Case Study Research

Perspective	Main Tenets	Advantages
High Generalizability	Maximize generalizability through comparative analysis	Facilitates theoretical conclusions
		May strengthen applied research
Transferability	"Thick descriptions" can produce "working hypotheses" which can sometimes be transferred from one case to another based on "fit"	Allows nonpositivist generalization as well as in-depth qualitative description

Perspective	Main Tenets	Advantages
The Particular	Cases as "bounded systems" in which the particular (or uniqueness) of each case is examined via developing "thick descriptions"	Avoids essentialism and the erasure of difference
		Results in "naturalistic generalization" and vicarious experiences for readers

et al., 2000). Schofield (2000) favors high generalizability and suggests that generalizability does not have to produce general laws, as suggested in positivist and quantitative understandings of the term. Schofield offers strategies whereby qualitative researchers can maximize generalizability in three possible ways: (1) to what is, (2) to what may be, and (3) to what could be. He advocates using published studies to increase generaliziblity via the "aggregation or comparison of independent studies" (p. 69). This kind of generalizability, which is developed through **comparative analysis**, can assist researchers interested in making theoretical conclusions (Hammersley & Gomm, 2000, p. 13).

Generalizability can be important in a variety of research scenarios. It may be particularly important when there are public policy implications or other "real world" applications of research findings. For example, sometimes, case study is conducted in education research to evaluate particular educational environments or programs. Research findings can be used to advocate for changes in educational policy, curriculum or programming changes, and funding. In these kinds of contexts, generalizability is necessary. Similarly, case study is used in health care research to understand a wide range of issues including the effectiveness of particular health care systems and their organizational strategies, as well as issues pertaining to patient rehabilitation and emotional well-being. In these instances, the ability to generalize allows for the application of relevant research findings to other populations, who may be served better as a result.

Transferability

Some researchers critique the use of generalization as a goal of social scientific inquiry, arguing that it is necessarily grounded in a positivist conception of valid research and thus legitimizes positivism. Lincoln and Guba (2000a) have been at the forefront of this critique, famously noting, "The trouble with generalizations is that they don't apply to **particulars**" (p. 27). They go on to write,

Generalizations are not found in nature; they are active creations of the mind. Empirically, they rest upon the generalizer's experience with a limited number of particulars not with "each and all" of the members of a "class, kind, or order." . . . . [T]hat is to say, while generalizations are constrained by facts (especially if the facts are the particulars from which the generalization is induced), there is no single necessary generalization that *must* emerge to account for them. There are always (logically) multiple possible generalizations to account for any set of particulars, however extensive and inclusive they may be. (Lincoln & Guba, 2000a, pp. 30–31)

Lincoln and Guba (2000a) suggest there are numerous possibilities in between studying general laws and total uniqueness or particularity (the final end of the continuum). They write that there is "the broad range of the related" where conclusions derived in one context might be relevant to another context (p. 38). Using Cronbach's (1975) term **working hypotheses**, Lincoln and Guba (2000a) suggest that working hypotheses produced out of one case study can be used to understand other cases. They urge researchers to produce "thick descriptions" of cases to (possibly) be able to *transfer* conclusions from one case to another based on **fittingness**. Lincoln and Guba explain as follows:

The degree of *transferability* is a direct function of the *similarity* between the two contexts, what we shall call "*fittingness*." Fittingness is defined as the degree of congruence between sending and receiving contexts. If Context *A* and Context *B* are "sufficiently" congruent, then working hypotheses from the sending originating context may be applicable in the receiving context. (p. 40)

Lincoln and Guba (2000a) offer a metaphor to help explain their perspective. Using an analogy to holographic film, in which any fragment can produce the whole picture, they coin the term **holographic generalization** (p. 40). Again, this can be accomplished only if highly detailed descriptions of cases are produced.

For example, case studies in sociology often aim for transferability, allowing both a deep understanding of the case at hand and the use of the findings in other contexts. Let's take the example of binge drinking and related behaviors on college campuses to look more closely at transferability and fittingness. A sociologist may use the case study approach to study this topic in relation to one specific college community; the case would center on campus culture at a particular college. Data collection might include ethnography or participant observation at parties; interviews with students, campus police, and resident advisers; document analysis of campus policies and campus police records of involvement with drinking-related issues; and a geographic analysis of the community in which the campus is situated (bars, entertainment venues). The result would be a highly detailed rendering of the case within its social context. Sociological researchers, however, may be interested in transferring their hypotheses to other contexts to extend the usefulness of their findings (and perhaps build theoretical assessments). When selecting appropriate secondary contexts, a range of dimensions of fittingness or "sameness" must be considered, including but not limited to campus size, residential/commuter ratios, gender and race ratios, geographic location, drinking age, and campus policies regarding drinking.

The Particular

Some researchers argue against generalization and suggest cases must be investigated as unique and closed systems. Stake (1995, 2000, 2005b) suggests that generalizations may render cases more simplistic than they actually are. This view assumes the case is a **bounded system** that exists independent of the research, a system with features, patterns, and boundaries (Stake, 2005b). Stake advocates a thorough investigation of "the particular" instead of striving for generalizations. This belief is based on the grounds that if researchers collect extensive data and come to a deep understanding of the particular, case study research can facilitate **naturalistic generalization**, which is not grounded in positivism. This form of generalization is based on a natural process where readers can see themselves and/or their experiences in the case study.

Ultimately, according to Stake (1995, 2000, 2005b), the aim of case study is to understand, in a meaningful and nuanced way, the view of those within the case. Although case study can be conducted from any theoretical grounding, we suggest that Stake's perspective is closely aligned with an interpretive approach that emphasizes creating thick descriptions of social life from the viewpoints of participants to understand meaning from their perspectives. As an example of what is meant by truly thick descriptions, Stake (2000) further explains that even descriptions of physical environments become critical as the researcher aims to create vicarious experiences for the case study reader. He notes the following:

> To develop vicarious experiences for the reader, to give them a sense of "being there," the physical situation should be well described. The entryways, the rooms, the landscape, the hallways, its place on the map, its décor. There should be some balance between the uniqueness and the ordinariness of the place. The physical space is fundamental to meanings for most researchers and most readers. (Stake, 2000, p. 63)

BEHIND THE SCENES WITH ROBERT STAKE

The case to be studied is a complex entity located in a milieu or situation embedded in a number of contexts or backgrounds. Historical context is almost always of interest, but so are cultural and physical contexts. Other contexts often of interest are the social, economic, political, ethical, and aesthetic.

The case is singular, but it has subsections (e.g., production, marketing, sales departments), groups (e.g., patients, nurses, administrators), occasions (e.g., work days, holidays, days near holidays), dimensions, and domains—many so well-populated that they need to be sampled. Each of these may have its own contexts, and the contexts may go a long way toward making relationships understandable. Qualitative case study calls for the examination of these complexities.

Source: Stake, 2005b, p. 449.

This approach to case study requires extensive data collection, which is built into in-depth descriptions of all aspects of the case necessary to convey the particularity of the case to readers.

Robert Stake elaborates on the issue of describing context(s) in the following behind-the-scenes box.

As you can see, in case study research, identifying and describing contexts is vital in generating meaning and creating understanding. The issue of contexts, which may be complex, overlapping, and multidimensional, is perhaps more pronounced in case study research than in other approaches to qualitative research.

How Do You Design Case Study Research?

Case study design is particularly complex because it involves the collection, organization, and interpretation of large amounts of data. Case studies use multiple methods, often more than in typical multimethod research, where only two methods may be used. In short, there are a lot of data to keep track of and make sense of.

Research Purpose

As with any research endeavor, the process begins with the determination of a research question and selection of a research purpose. A case (or cases) must also be selected out of a population of possible cases, chosen for the ability to address research questions and purposes. This may mean selecting a particularly anomalous case or a case that, on a surface level, appears congruent with other cases in the pool. When developing your research purpose, consider the three main perspectives on case study research and contemplate your goals with respect to where your project goals stand on the continuum from generalizability, transferability, to particularity. Also, consider whether your project is primarily theory based, problem based, descriptive (as suggested by Hammersley and Gomm), or exploratory. In formulating your research question and choosing your case study, consider the following questions (alluded to earlier):

- Do I aim to test, illustrate, or generate theory?

- Do I aim to identify the sources of problems or solutions to problems?

- What dimensions of my topic must be described and understood to meet my goals?

- Am I exploring a new or underresearched topic?

- What am I seeking?

- What type of case study will be most beneficial to my research?

Research Methods and Researcher Role(s)

Next, researchers must consider the research methods—data collection tools—that will be used, as well as their role in the case study. We note these two features together as there is always interplay between a researcher's position in the research process and the tools he or she deems appropriate to use (as evidenced throughout this book). With this said, case study always necessitates the use of multiple methods and data sources. Triangulated approaches are generally used as they build validity into the case study: by adopting a triangulated approach, researchers are using multiple techniques to clarify meaning (Stake, 2005b). When mixed methods are used synergistically, findings can be substantiated (Cutler, 2004). Therefore, the researcher ultimately bears some responsibility for the validity of the reader's interpretation of the final representation (Stake, 2005b). In this vein, consider validity with respect to "descriptions, interpretation, theories, generalizations, and evaluative judgments" (Stake, 2005b, p. 453, drawing on Maxwell, 1992). We suggest that case study is a quintessential example of a *problem-centric approach to research:* Methods are selected based on their effectiveness in gathering data about key dimensions of the case. The case must be investigated from many angles by gathering data on many dimensions.

With respect to the researcher's role(s), just the act of choosing the particular case or set of cases that will be studied, and possibly represent a larger population of cases, intimately shapes the research. The case or cases selected should contain elements typical of the wider population of cases, knowing that the case or cases you select will form the basis for making generalizations and building theory. The researcher must also constantly negotiate the relationship of the parts to the whole and the whole to the larger population.

In addition to the aforementioned issues, Stake (2000) suggests case study researchers become teachers (to inform readers), advocates, evaluators, biographers, and interpreters (the latter of which is their central role). Researchers wear many hats in the case study process and must constantly negotiate their roles. Some of these roles may be in conflict with each other. For example, the act of evaluation and interpretation is very different than the role of advocate. As a researcher, you might be asked to evaluate a health program or an educational program. Alternately, you may also be asked by your research participants (or your own social justice grounding) to advocate for funding for these programs or for their expansion. This can potentially raise conflicts. For example, if you find that the program is somehow ineffective, how do you negotiate reporting these deficiencies while at the same time advocating for increased funding? The roles of biographer and interpreter may also produce tensions. For example, there is often a push-pull between trying to tell the stories participants have shared with us while also retaining the roles of interpreter and evaluator.

Data Organization, Analysis, and Representation

As noted earlier, case study involves collecting massive amounts of qualitative data. Therefore, the organizational aspects of the process are vital to the successful execution of case study. Issues of data collection, data organization, conceptualization, and analysis must be built into the research design. A data storage system is, therefore, vital in case study (Stake, 2000). New computer-assisted technologies can enhance data organization, conceptualization, and analysis.

Computer-Assisted Software for Case Study Analysis and Interpretation

To manage the increasing amount of qualitative data you will gather in your case study project, you might want to consider using a computer-assisted software product. Some commercial software packages, such as ATLAS.ti, HyperRESEARCH, and QDA miner, are available for downloading, and you might consider perusing the CAQDAS Web site for more information on a variety of these types of programs. It is critical to remember that software programs do not do your analysis for you; they help you organize and retrieve large amounts of textual data. Certain programs, such as HyperRESEARCH and ATLAS.ti, can analyze audio and video data as well as still images. These programs allow you to use a variety of analytical strategies such as grounded theory (Corbin & Strauss, 2007). Some of these programs can also assist with the grouping of your qualitative data into meaningful categories, creating frequency counts and matrices (see Miles & Huberman, 1994). We cover a variety of analytical strategies for analyzing your data in Part III of this book. It is important to remember, in all of this analysis, that you, the researcher, are making decisions on what types of analytical procedures to use on your data. It is critical to go back to your research question and connect this to your analytical decisions.

Let's look at a hypothetical case study to see how the research question plays a primary role in the selection of data and your overall research design.

A Case Study of a Sorority

It is the first day of class, and already your instructor wants you to begin planning a term paper based on a case study approach. It seems like putting the method before the problem, but now you need to ask yourself: What type of problem or set of problems might lend themselves to a case study approach?

You go to your professor and ask for more clarification regarding exactly what you should be thinking at this stage of your case study project. He or she replies by saying that students in the research methods class are asked to select an on-campus organization as the unit of analysis for their case study. Several weeks go by, and school has already been in session for over a month. You happen to pass by your university's most popular sorority house on a walk to campus and remember that this particular house was in fact deemed "sorority of the year" by the student newspaper this month. Your past experience with sororities left you a bit dismayed because a once-close friend stopped talking with you once she joined this particular sorority house. Your general feeling is that perhaps sorority life tends to exclude students who are not part of their newfound sorority clique.

However, this seems like an interesting case study that would fit the parameters of your research project. You decide to put your prejudices about sororities aside to find out if your impressions about sorority life are confirmed.

Reflexivity

You might begin your project by practicing reflexivity (see Chapter 3 on research design for more details) around this particular project. That is, you may begin by reflecting on how your own feelings about this topic might influence the data you collect as well as how you analyze and interpret these data. Our values are present in the research process, whatever topic we decide to focus on. Even if your feelings about a particular research project are unconscious, they can influence the process.

Focusing on Your Case Study Research Question

Once you have decided to study sororities, try to read some of the research literature on sorority life. As you begin to take notes and read more of the literature on this topic, several research questions may be derived from these studies (see the research literature section of Chapter 3). Your research questions can derive from your own personal experience, as is the case with this hypothetical project. After carefully considering a range of research literature and your own observations concerning sorority life, you decide on the following set of research questions: (1) What is the overall climate of sorority life? and (2) How do sororities sustain themselves over time?

Methods of Data Collection

Yin's (2008) table of data collection methods (Table 10.1) provides a good starting point for deciding on the type of data you will collect for your case study project. These two research problems are complex and will require that you put in extensive time collecting those data that pertain to each of these research goals. The first thing you might want to do is to prioritize your research questions and start out with one question to see how long it takes you to gather the information you need, as well as to conduct your analysis, interpretation, and the writing up of your results. In doing so, you may find that these questions overlap and that you might be able to use some data to answer both, or you may decide to drop a question because you are running out of time.

You could employ a range of data collection methods to help answer these research questions. Documentary data might consist of the back copies of your college's student newspaper. You can visit the sorority's Web site to collect any documents and to ascertain the overall climate of the sorority by examining the layout of the Web site itself. For example, what is most prominently displayed? Does the Web site contain any testimonials from sorority members through the years? These types of data can range from informal personal accounts to more formal reports. Increasingly, a significant amount of documentary data is gathered via the Internet, using popular search engines. However, you do need to remain aware of the validity or reliability of the data you use. One way to check out the Web site's authenticity is to talk with a university librarian, or you might consider also using databases whose veracity has been established, such as those academic databases suggested by your college's reference librarian. This is also the case for any archival data you may come across on the Internet. You might, for example, use your library's archive and see what information they have concerning sorority life on your campus.

Say you decide to go out and collect your own data in the form of face-to-face in-depth interviews. The interviewing chapter in this book can provide you with some tips on how to conduct and analyze your interview data. What is most important in gathering your own data is to let your research question guide the type of data collection procedures you use. Interviews with sorority members will provide with you with an understanding of sorority life. You will need to decide on whom you want to interview and the types of questions you will ask. How many individuals will you interview? What type of sample will you collect? Will you interview only those women who are members of the sorority this year? Do you want to collect information from former sorority members? To what extent is it important for you to interview the officers of a sorority? Do you want to interview members (if any) who dropped out of this sorority during their college career?

You might also decide that you want to gather data by using a focus group method, whereby you gather a group of sorority sisters and ask them to talk about sorority life. In this instance, you take on the role of moderator. You will need to decide on the makeup of the focus group: How many respondents? What types of sorority members—new recruits only? To what extent do you focus on the diversity of representation of sorority members by class year, race/ethnicity, and so on? Remember, the methods you decide on should follow from your set of research questions. You might consult the focus groups chapter in this book for more tips on this method of inquiry.

As you can observe in our example, the research question lends itself to a variety of data-gathering procedures. You might in fact decide that you need to gather data by directly observing sorority life. Here you might attend open events sponsored by this particular sorority. You may need to decide whether or not you will tell others about what you are doing, or whether you will be conducting this project "under cover." If so, what are the ethical implications of doing a covert study? On the other hand, you can conduct this project in the open, with direct observation. Direct observation in a case study occurs when the investigator makes a site visit to gather data. The observations could be formal or casual activities, but the reliability of the observation is the main concern. Using multiple observers is one way to guard against this problem. What are the costs and benefits of your collecting this type of data, and when should you do so?

You might also consider looking at any physical artifacts that will give you clues to life within a sorority and what a sorority values. For example, what is the physical layout of the sorority's Web page? What is prominent on the Web site? Going by size and placement is a good measure perhaps of what the sorority deems important. For example, is a quarter of their Web page devoted to displaying the faces of sorority members? What objects are displayed on the Web site? You might also want to ask for a tour of the sorority or go to an open-house event with the goal of observing the physical surroundings and the objects contained therein. For tips on how to do this, you might go to the chapter that discusses unobtrusive research, including the section on content analysis.

The overall goal of your particular case study is to come to a *comprehensive understanding* of sorority life and those factors that help to sustain the sorority's existence on campus. The sorority is your unit of analysis for your case study. You are, in effect, conducting an *intrinsic case study.*

An important thing to remember in selecting methods to apply to your case study is whether or not these methods will add to your understanding of your research question or set of questions. A case study approach relies a great deal on the person or set of persons who are carrying out the project. Your role is vital in determining what is considered valid and reliable data for your project. Being reflexive about your own standpoint in the research process is a critical first step. We noted earlier that in conducting case study research on a sorority, you had some upfront misgivings about sororities in general. It's important not to push these ideas under the rug and pretend they don't exist, but rather, to deal with these biases up front and develop strategies to counteract any tendency to go for more negative than positive data about sororities, especially if you, the researcher, serve as the data collector. Chapter 3 has a range of reflexive strategies you might want to review before undertaking your research project. At stake as well are a range of ethical decisions that you as a student researcher will bump up against, especially if you decide to go undercover for this type of project. If you are a male or a female, your gender may play an important role in the types of data to which you may have access. There may be female-dominated spaces within a sorority that no males will have access to, and this may make it harder as a male to collect certain types of data, and so on. You might want again to look at the interviewing chapter in this book, especially the section that deals with interviewing across differences.

Analysis, Interpretation, and Writing Up of a Case Study

Analysis and interpretation of case study research takes place in an iterative way. The researcher collects some data, performs an analysis to get at what the data are saying (analysis), and seeks to understand what it means (interpretation). There is also along the way some validation, perhaps of different data sources. Are these data telling the same story? If they are not, then are these data valid or just telling a different aspect of the story?

Going back to our sorority example, we might ask: What type of analysis will assist in answering the research problem(s)? Does performing a grounded theory analysis on the data you gathered from interviews with sorority members allow you to get at the lived experience of sorority members? A grounded theory approach is iterative, in that you gather a bit of data, begin to analyze it by writing memos, coding your data—attaching what you perceive to be a word or phrase that best captures the excerpt you are reading—and then begin to look at the range of codes you accumulate over time. In what sense are these codes related? In what way are they different? Can some code categories be combined to a larger, more analytical code? The following excerpt is a hypothetical interview you might gather from a member of your college's sorority.

Hypothetical Excerpt From Sorority Member	Partial Coding of Excerpt
The minute I joined this sorority I felt like I was transported to a large family. If you can imagine it, I have over 80 sorority sisters. Here I feel secure and cared about. I have made so many close friends as well.	**Sorority as a form of belonging** Sorority as a family Feel secure Close friendships
Since I have joined this sorority I have had a number of networking possibilities. I have met former alumnae who have approached me about job opportunities. I am also able to access a range of academic resources.	**Opportunities for networking** Meeting alumnae
I have been given a number of leadership skills in the sorority as well.	**Opportunities for leadership** Leadership skills

Even from this short hypothetical excerpt about the environment of sorority life, we can see that this respondent feels a wealth of positive affect from joining a sorority. We note that some of the codes we used are more literal: "feels secure" reflects the exact words of the respondent. We term this an "in vivo" code. The codes that are bolded, such as "opportunities for networking," are larger thematic categories that have other codes subsumed under them, such as "meeting alumnae." Coding consists of creating a label or title for a chunk of text that captures its meaning (reflected in the title of your particular code name). The idea of coding is to begin to decontextualize these texts into meaningful chunks of coded materials. Further analysis would require that you begin to think of ways you might combine some of these codes into larger thematic categories, such as those code titles that appear bolded. As you collect your data, you need to begin the coding process or your analysis—that is, what the data are telling you. You might begin to create some memos (ideas you write up) about what these categories mean and so on.

It is best not to collect your data all at once but to take a more iterative approach by interrogating each interview along the way and by asking yourself questions about these data through writing up a short memo on what these excerpts might mean for your general case study questions. How do these interviews begin to give you a sense of the climate of a sorority and the factors that perpetuate these organizations on a college campus? We depict a diagram of this iterative process in Figure 10.1.

Figure 10.1 The Iterative Process of Data Analysis

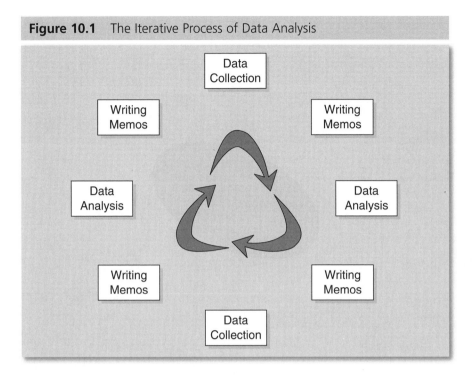

This is a process of synthesizing, clarifying, chronicling, and producing "history, meanings, and understandings" (Zucker, 2001, p. 3). Stake (2000) also advocates beginning the organizational and writing processes early. This allows researchers to build the conceptual structure of the case in a way that is grounded in the data, and it also allows the researcher to keep track of the data, learn what new dimensions must be accessed, and see when saturation has occurred. We offer the following template for how a case study project might be organized (see Table 10.4).

Table 10.4 Template for a Case Study Project

Title of Your Project

What is the basic essence of your paper? A title should describe in a nutshell what your paper is about. Your title should also be written to draw the attention of your audience. If you are writing an article, you might want to mention some **key words** that you feel best capture the basic ideas or concepts in your case study project. These words usually go right after the title of your research article. Key words help to enhance the retrieval of your project from a larger database.

Abstract

This is a short summary of your research project in no more than 200 words. Be sure to state the research problem, method, and major research findings.

(Continued)

Table 10.4 (Continued)

Introduction

What is the purpose of your project?

Background of your problem

Significance of your project

State your problem or set of research problems

Define any specific terms utilized in your study

Discussion of theoretical framework you may employ

Literature Review

A summary of the research literature most relevant to your research problem

Research Design

Data Collection

What is your unit of analysis?

What are your data collection method(s)?

Provide the rationale for the use of your methods (remember that your research question should determine your choice of method(s).

Sampling Procedure(s)

What type of sampling procedure did you use for gathering your data for each method you employed?

Discussion of issues of validity and reliability, especially the measures you may be using in your study

Data Analysis and Interpretation

State the rationale for each analysis that you employ. How will this type of analysis help you answer your research problem(s)? Be sure to keep in mind the unit of analysis of your study since this is what you will be making statements about. Summarize what you found (analysis). Think about using visuals (table, diagram, etc.) and what the data mean (interpretation). Go back to the research question to make sure you have answered it.

Summary and Conclusion

Provide an overall summary of what you found out and talk about any limitations of your study.

Bibliography

Appendix

Any documentation you want to include about your case study: for example, photos, charts, or documents that you may refer to in your case study

As you can see, case study is a multifaceted endeavor requiring the collection of different kinds of data, the wearing of different researcher hats, the organization of large quantities of data, and an ongoing process of conceptualization and analysis.

A final issue to consider is representation. What format will be used for writing up the case study? One approach is a *storytelling* model (Gerring, 2006). When adopting this approach, Gerring (2006) suggests considering the following questions:

- How does the researcher put the story together?

- What will be included and excluded?

- How much does the story become the researcher's story of the case? (pp. 456–457)

Another representational choice is a *comparative* model. Gerring (2006) suggests considering the following question:

- Cases are compared to each other by readers, so, how much does the researcher note comparative cases? (p. 457)

Gerring (2006) notes that highly detailed descriptions can facilitate comparison; however, Stake (2005b) argues that comparison can obscure noncomparative dimensions of data as well as the uniqueness of the case as a bounded system. For example, Stake suggests that those aspects of the case which are not comparable to another case may be inadvertently glossed over or trivialized. Decisions about comparison are inextricably linked to the research purpose and the extent to which they facilitate comparison. Perhaps most important, you must consider your goals:

- Is this an instrumental or intrinsic case study?

- Do I aim to explore, describe, or explain?

- What usefulness might my research findings have? How can I maximize this?

It is also important to reflect on the data collection and analysis procedures you are using and the extent to which they do or do not facilitate comparison. All this should be considered during research design so that the most effective research design can be employed.

Let's join Robert Stake again behind the scenes for a fuller discussion of the writing process.

BEHIND THE SCENES WITH ROBERT STAKE

Even when empathic and respectful of each person's realities, the researcher decides what the case's "own story" is, or at least what will be included in the report. More will be pursued than was volunteered, and less will be reported than was learned. Even though the competent researcher will be guided by what the case indicates is

(Continued)

(Continued)

most important, and even though patrons and other researchers will advise, that which is necessary for an understanding of the case will be decided by the researcher. It may be the case's own story, but the report will be the researcher's dressing of the case's own story. This is not to dismiss the aim of finding the story that best represents the case, but instead to remind the reader that, usually, criteria of representation ultimately are decided by the researcher.

Many a researcher would like to tell the whole story but of course cannot; the whole story exceeds anyone's knowing and anyone's telling. Even those inclined to tell all find strong the obligation to winnow and consolidate. The qualitative researcher, like the single-issue researcher, must choose between telling lots and telling little.

Source: Stake, 2005b, p. 456.

Again, as a result of the large amount of data produced by case study, the researcher has many considerations when it comes to the final write-up. As Stake notes, the whole case cannot be told, but when done properly, the report can be a window into the case as a whole.

Multiple Case Study

Multiple case study research, or multicase study research, involves studying multiple cases that share a commonality. The cases may be an exhaustive list of all possible cases or may be selected out of a larger population of possible cases. For example, when studying some sort of fairly unique educational program, there may be only a handful of cases, all of which may be examined in one study (Stake, 2005a). However, when the cases are phenomena of some kind, there may be many more cases than those selected (Stake, 2005a). When investigating phenomena, as social scientists often do, researchers are looking for both common characteristics and "situational uniqueness" (Stake, 2005a, pp. ix–x). Often, a team approach is used in multiple case study projects, although this is not a requirement. Stake explains that a project begins with "recognizing what concept or idea binds the cases together" (p. 23). Then, cases are selected. Stake (2005a) recommends 4 to 10 cases; however, as he notes, there may be reasons to use fewer or more cases in any particular study. According to Stake (2005a), the main selection criteria for cases are these:

- Is the case relevant to the **quintain** (the larger group of cases)?

- Do the cases provide diversity across contexts?

- Do the cases provide good opportunities to learn about complexity and contexts? (p. 23)

In multiple case study projects, the aim is to describe the *quintain* (Stake, 2005a). This does not mean that researchers should solely focus on similarities between and across cases. In fact, the particulars that vary across cases can be just as and even more important, depending on the research goals. Stake (2005a) advocates seeking out differences between cases and emphasizing each case's uniqueness in relation to the quintain or the larger group of cases under study.

Conclusion

Case study research is both the process by which research proceeds and the outcome of research. Case study relies on triangulated methods employed for their fit to the problem or issue at hand. In this respect, case study is the quintessential example of the problem-centric approach to research that we are advocating in this book. Case studies are also necessarily examples of mixed method or multimethod designs (discussed in the following chapter). Because case study requires the collection and ongoing analysis of large quantities of detailed data, having an organizational structure is vital to the successful completion of a case study project.

Glossary

Bounded system: This refers to the conception that case studies are closed systems that exist independent of the research and contain unique features and patterns specific to the system.

Case study: An expansive field within the qualitative paradigm. Case study is a research strategy or a process of inquiry, as well as the result of inquiry.

Comparative analysis: Aggregating or comparing independent studies to create generalizations.

Fittingness: Lincoln and Guba (2000b) define fittingness as the degree of congruence between two contexts (strong "fit" between contexts allows for the transfer of working hypotheses from one case to another).

Holographic generalization: Term coined by Lincoln and Guba (2000b). They suggest that researchers must create "thick descriptions" of case studies to develop generalizations, and they pose an analogy to holographic film, in which any fragment can produce the whole picture.

Instrumental case study: A case is studied to generalize or provide insight into a larger topic.

Intrinsic case study: The goal of the case study is to understand the particular case holistically.

Multiple case study: When multiple cases are investigated in one case study project.

Naturalistic generalization: A term coined by Stake that denotes non-positivist generalizations that are formed through the analysis of "thick descriptions." This requires two simultaneous forms of analysis: analyzing particulars and aggregating the particulars or instances so that something can be said about them as a group.

Particulars: The unique features and details of the case, as well as the instances in which these features emerge or take on meaning.

Quintain: In multiple case study or multi-case study, this refers to the larger group of cases to which the selected cases belong.

Transferability: The extent to which you can transfer working hypotheses from one case study to another.

Working hypotheses: Hypotheses developed out of one case study that can be used to understand other case studies.

Discussion Questions

1. What is case study research? How does case study differ from the research methods reviewed in earlier chapters?

2. Briefly explain the three main perspectives on case study research. Try to identify research questions best suited to each perspective.

3. How is case study an excellent example of a problem-centric approach to research?

4. What research design features become particularly salient in case study research? Why?

Resources

Suggested Web Sites

http://ublib.buffalo.edu/libraries/projects/cases/webcase.htm

State University of New York at Buffalo's Web site on Case Studies in Science.

http://www.guisd.org

Georgetown University's Case Studies in International Affairs.
    The Institute for the Study of Diplomacy provides case study examples for undergraduate and graduate students interested in international affairs.

Relevant Journals

Clinical Case Studies

The Management Case Study Journal

Qualitative Sociology Review

CHAPTER 11

Mixed Methods Research

Thus far, we've concentrated primarily on qualitative methods for research. However, some research projects cannot be adequately completed using only qualitative methods and require a quantitative component as well. To this end, the practice of mixed methods research has become increasingly broad and popular, especially over the past decade (Bergman, 2008; Bryman, 1988; Creswell, 1999, 2003, 2008; Creswell & Plano Clark, 2008; Greene, 2007; Greene & Caracelli, 1997a; Hesse-Biber, 2010; Morgan, 1998; Sandelowski, 2000; Sieber, 1973; Tashakkori & Teddlie, 1998, 2003; Teddlie & Tashakkori, 2008). We present you with the following case concerning the study of the tsunami that devastated Southeast Asia in 2004 as an example of mixed methods research.

The following excerpt is an account from a BBC news reporter on the efforts of one Thai village to rebuild its community in the aftermath of one of the worst natural disasters to strike South Asia:

At first glance, the small island community of Khlang Prasang might count itself lucky.

Like much of Thailand's west coast it was hit by the devastating Asian tsunami, yet no one in the 400-strong community died.

But the tsunami changed the lives of far more people than those now mourning loved ones. Away from the famous resorts and tourist beaches, hundreds of small communities like Khlang Prasang now face a long, difficult challenge to rebuild.

Before the disaster, the people of Khlang Prasang had two sources of income—fishing and tourism.

Now they are struggling to make money from either.

"We're afraid we're going to get forgotten, and all the aid is going to go to Phi Phi island and other areas where the destruction is greater," said Donjit Hafah. . . .

Two weeks on from the tsunami, the people of Khlang Prasang are still suffering from the trauma of their experience.

"I still can't sleep. I keep thinking another tsunami is going to come. The waves and the tides are still not normal and I'm very scared," said Samari Koonlong.

"Last night I was just sitting watching the waves," Maad Oonbutr said. "I thought about the children who ran towards the sea when the tsunami came, and how near they were to drowning." (McGowan, 2005)

A massive tsunami struck South Asia on December 26, 2004. It was one of the largest natural disasters in recorded history. In its wake, private and public relief efforts were launched from all parts of the globe to aid the survivors and help rebuild much-needed infrastructures. Newspaper reports warned of the severe psychological trauma among the survivors. One CNN report told of posttraumatic effects from the tsunami, especially on its young survivors.

"The psychological effects are immense," explains Dr. Michael Wasserman, a pediatrician with the Ochsner Clinic Foundation in New Orleans, Louisiana. "Children understand sameness. And for reasons out of everybody's control, you've yanked that away. You've devastated their world." (Cox & Brown, 2005)

It is unclear how survivors are coping with the aftermath of this devastating event. While media reports give anecdotal information, much more is needed to assist with relief efforts. Social scientists can provide funding and relief agencies with a fuller understanding of the economic and personal scope of this tragedy at the village and national level, as well as ascertaining the lived experiences of those whose lives have been dramatically impacted by this disaster. To do this, they can design and implement research experiments concerning events such as this. The following research questions can provide some important data toward that effort:

- How many people died as a direct result of this disaster? What villages were affected? What is the extent of property damage? Who are the survivors (in terms of their demographics such as age, sex, class, etc.)?

- How are survivors managing their lives on a day-to-day basis? What are their lived experiences? What are their specific needs and concerns?

What Is Mixed Methods Research?

A mixed methods research approach might be a good starting point for beginning our inquiry. Mixed methods is a research design for data collection and analysis. The term usually refers to the use of *both* qualitative and quantitative methods in *one* study or *sequentially* in two or more studies. An important logic behind the application of this design is that "the whole is greater than the sum of its parts" (Greene & Caracelli, 1997b, p. 13). Greene and Caracelli (1997b) note that having a "conversation" between different methods and the paradigms that they represent promotes "more comprehensive, insightful, and logical results than either paradigm [interpretivist or post-positivist] could obtain alone" (p. 10; see also Greene, Benjamin, & Goodyear, 2001). Tashakkori and Teddlie's (2003) *Handbook of Mixed Methods* refers to mixed methods research designs as the "third methodological movement" (p. x). Mixed methods research requires that researchers, who are usually trained in only one method or who have more experience in one method over the other, reach out of their comfort zone and think beyond their usually implemented methods. In this sense, the practice of mixing methods may even upend the researcher's ongoing philosophical and methodological practices.

The combination of two different methods can create a **synergistic** research project in which one method enables the other to be more effective. Together, both methods can provide a fuller understanding of the research problem (Greene & Caracelli, 1997b; see Sieber, 1973, for an early example of the synergy in mixing the methods of fieldwork and survey research). Mixed methods designs can also help to get at "subjugated knowledge" and give voice to those whose viewpoints are often left out of traditional research (Greene & Caracelli, 1997b, p. 14). Combining methods can assist the researcher in tackling highly complex problems involving several layers of understanding that may require different analytical techniques.

The selection of a particular research method *should be tightly linked to the research problem.* Some methods are more effective than others for answering certain types of questions and specific dimensions of a research question. *Qualitative methods* are useful for getting at the "lived experiences" of the individual by asking such questions as the extent to which long-term psychological trauma is experienced by tsunami survivors. Qualitative collection methods require an analytical design that often deals with the analysis of textual data for meaning; they are not particularly useful for getting at the "overall picture." *Quantitative methods,* such as surveys, answer questions such as How many? How often? Quantitative methods allow researchers to test hypotheses and draw out generalizations from their data. As we will discuss later, the use of mixed methods is also subject to some practical constraints, including the cost of conducting research, the training of researchers, and so forth, as well as the type of funding available for the particular research design (Brannen, 1992, p. 17).

In deciding on a research design for our tsunami study, we would begin with our specific research questions:

- How many people died as a direct result of this disaster?

- What villages were affected?

- What is the extent of the damage?

- Who are the survivors (in terms of their demographics—age, sex, class, etc.)?

This set of questions is asking for some numerical data: How many? and How widespread? A quantitative method such as a *demographic survey* of the social and economic conditions of the population, as well as a comparison of these demographic figures with the latest national and regional census and population data, will provide a context within which to assess the extent of the devastation at the village and national levels. This method provides the researcher with an overall picture within which to place survivors' lived experiences. Understanding this framework helps researchers place their qualitative findings in the larger context.

The next set of questions is qualitative and concerns experience and how people make meaning of their social world. These are questions such as the following:

- How are people within affected areas managing their lives on a day-to-day basis?

- What is their lived experience?

These questions address issues of *interpretation*. As qualitative researchers, we will want to listen to the narratives of those who have experienced the disaster firsthand: their attitudes, feelings, and concerns. We might consider a range of interpretative methods such as intensive interviews, focus groups, or participant observations gathered from a cross-section of individuals from villages destroyed by the tsunami. These data collection techniques allow for a fuller understanding of the disaster's effect on individuals' lives, including the extent to which people are able to cope with the loss of relatives and friends, as well as the economic loss and destruction of their property and livelihood. This type of method allows researchers to listen to the specific needs and concerns of survivors while capturing nuances in their stories of survival. In essence, we are employing a mixed methods design by gathering both qualitative and quantitative data to answer our research questions.

To address the set of questions we have posed, you might begin with an *exploratory study* of a sample of villages affected by the disaster. This exploratory study begins with a survey to locate a sample of villages (quantitative data collection and analysis) and is followed by a qualitative study, such as a series of interviews or focus group sessions with survivors. We present this as a qualitatively driven mixed methods project because the qualitative aspect of the project is given priority. Let's take a more in-depth look at why and how we should proceed with this type of design.

Reasons for Using a Mixed Methods Design

Greene, Caracelli, and Graham (1989) discuss five specific reasons why researchers might want to use a mixed methods approach. The first and perhaps most common reason is **triangulation.** This strategy involves using more than one method to study the same research question. The researcher is looking for a convergence of research findings to enhance credibility. As an aside, it is important to note that while we are using the term *triangulation* in this context to mean using *different methods* (**methods triangulation**), it has also come to mean using different theoretical perspectives (**theoretical triangulation**), as well as different data sources using the same or different methods (**data triangulation**; see Denzin, 1978). In the case of the tsunami project, we might opt to administer "paper-and-pencil" quantitative psychological tests to ascertain the well-being of those we interview, together with conducting a more extensive in-depth interview. The quantitative scales would serve as a *validity check* on the in-depth psychological findings gathered from our intensive interviews.

A second reason for employing a mixed methods design is that of **complementarity**, whereby the researcher seeks to gain a fuller understanding of the research problem and/or to clarify a given research result. Mixed methods are employed in the service of assisting the researcher's total understanding of the research problem. For example, a researcher may use a qualitative study of the tsunami disaster to ascertain the lived experiences and in-depth feelings of disaster survivors, while also using a quantitative component, such as a survey, to assess how those impacted perceive the effectiveness of relief efforts and also assess the subjects' overall attitudes and values regarding social policies undertaken to help with the reconstruction of their villages. Both complementarity and triangulation are useful "for cross-validation when multiple methods produce comparable data" (Yauch & Steudel, 2003, p. 466).

A third reason to conduct a mixed methods study is that of **development**, whereby "results from one method help develop or inform the other method" (Greene et al., 1989, p. 259). In the tsunami example study, the researcher will be able to use the findings from an exploratory qualitative study to *develop* a survey questionnaire for the quantitative study. Having realized certain data from the first study, qualitative in this case, the second study is constructed on the foundations provided from this. A fourth reason cited for using mixed methods is that of **initiation**, whereby a given research study's findings raise questions or contain contradictions that require clarification. A new study is then initiated to add new insights to understanding the phenomenon under investigation (Greene et al., 1989, p. 260). In the case of the tsunami disaster study example, it may turn out that there are contradictory qualitative findings concerning how men and women view natural disasters, and attitudes toward coping post-disaster may differ by gender and national origin. Such divergent findings may lead to a more nuanced interpretation of research results by gender and nationality.

Such findings may serve to launch a whole new investigation, which leads us to a fifth reason for performing mixed methods research, **expansion**. Expansion is initiated to "extend the breadth and range of the study" (Greene et al., 1989, p. 259). In the case of the tsunami study, researchers may want to expand their study to include comparisons of gender differences in coping across different types of disasters. For example, a researcher might decide to expand the study to include interviews with survivors of the 9/11 terrorist attack with the intent of examining similarities and differences in coping mechanisms by gender, nationality, and type of disaster. Here the goal is not to increase the validity of one's study but to broaden the study to encompass a broader range of purposes.

The Research Nexus

Research questions are rooted in both objective and subjective epistemologies concerning the nature of the social world. An objective epistemology makes certain assumptions regarding the nature of the social world—that there is a singular social reality "out there," able to be discovered by a researcher who remains objective and does not allow feelings, values, or attitudes to enter into the research process (see Tashakkori & Teddlie, 1998, for a fuller discussion of these issues). A subjective epistemology assumes that there are multiple truths regarding the social world and that knowledge gathering is always partial; the researcher is encouraged to be on the same plane as the researched in an effort to promote a co-construction of meaning. We noted in Chapter 1 that *epistemology, methodology,* and *methods* are linked together to make up what we term the *research nexus.* A *methodology* is the type of theoretical perspective researchers bring to their research; it impacts the types of research problems they tend to address (see Chapters 2 and 3 for further elaboration). Different *epistemologies* lend themselves to a variety of *methodological* (theoretical) perspectives. *Critical theoretical perspectives* are rooted in a subjective epistemology that asks questions about power and control of knowledge-building within a society. *Interpretative theoretical perspectives* ask questions about subjective experience. A *positivistic theoretical perspective* seeks to test out specific hypotheses with the goal of making predictions about the nature of the social world.

There is often a tendency to equate method with methodology. Methods are the tools researchers use to get at their research problem. Objective methodologies such as positivism can employ qualitative methods in addition to quantitative ones. A decision on what specific method or set of methods to employ in a research project is dependent on your particular research question or set of questions. Our research questions, in turn, are tied to our methodological or theoretical perspectives. Different epistemologies lend themselves to a variety of theoretical perspectives. Interpretative methodologies, for example, often ask about individuals' lived experiences. Questions rooted in a positivistic theoretical approach often ask questions that seek to test out specific hypotheses with the goal of making predictions about the nature of the social world. Knowing where your research question lies along a subjective-objective view of reality continuum can help you decide what method or set of methods to use; what method(s) may be primary, secondary, or equal; and whether or not you want to do sequential (one study, then the other) or concurrent (at the same time) studies.

How Do You Design a Mixed Methods Research Project?

David Morgan (1998) provides some practical strategies for designing a mixed methods study. He suggests four mixed methods research designs based on the sequencing (time ordering) as well as relative importance (priority) of each method. In designing a mixed methods project, several decisions need to be made in setting up the particular mixed methods design. You can do this by asking yourself the following two questions:

- What is the primary research method, and what is the secondary (complementary) method?

- What method will come first and which second (i.e., will you begin with a qualitative study followed by a quantitative study, or vice versa)?

Morgan (1998) notes that the researcher's answers to these questions will provide four possible mixed methods research designs; his distinction considers only **sequential (time ordered) mixed methods designs,** one after the other. However, it is important to note that there are a multitude of other mixed methods designs that combine qualitative and quantitative methods using different criteria. In a **concurrent mixed methods design,** methods are combined in a parallel fashion and carried out at the same time. Some researchers maintain the primary/secondary distinction (Creswell, 2003), whereas others place both methods on **equal footing,** without distinguishing between a primary and a secondary method (Creswell, Fetters, & Ivankova, 2004; Creswell, 1999, 2003). Still others talk about the issues of one method (qualitative or quantitative) as nested or "embedded" in the other, with the nested method given a lower priority (Figure 11.1).

In a **nested mixed methods design,** the nested method may even answer a different research question, yet both methods are used to analyze the data (Creswell, 2003, pp. 229–230). There is also the possibility of mixing two qualitative and two quantitative studies; Teddlie and Tashakkori (2003) refer to this as "multiple method" design.

Figure 11.1   Nested Mixed Methods Design: A Quantitative Study Embedded Within a Qualitative Study

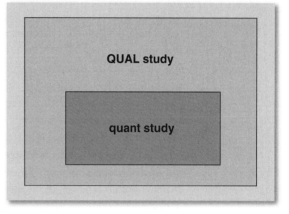

We present David Morgan's (1998) typology for mixing methods (Table 11.1) with the above caveats in mind. We can see in Table 11.1 the four research design possibilities.

The first design (qual—QUANT) consists of having the qualitative component of the research project first, but secondary to the project's goals. The quantitative method is primary but administered as a follow-up to the qualitative study. Using a qualitative study before a quantitative one provides researchers who are unfamiliar with a given topic the opportunity to generate specific ideas or hypotheses that they might address more specifically in the quantitative part of the project. An illustrative example of this form of mixed methods study design comes from a research project conducted by Kutner, Steiner, Corbett, Jahnigen, and Barton (1999) on terminally ill patients.

Table 11.1   Combining Qualitative and Quantitative

Design 1	qual followed by QUANT
Design 2	quant followed by QUAL
Design 3	QUANT followed by qual
Design 4	QUAL followed by quant

Note: All lowercase means secondary method and all uppercase denotes primary method (adapted from David Morgan, 1998).

The researchers were interested in understanding the lived experiences of those who are terminally ill. At this stage of illness, health care often means taking into account more of the patient's mental, physical, and spiritual needs, relying less on medical intervention. It is important to understand the lived experiences of the terminally ill and to convey their needs directly to those who provide care to them, especially their doctors. The researchers also wanted to be able to generalize the results of their study to the wider terminally ill population.

The research design begins with a qualitative exploratory interview study (qual) of 22 terminally ill patients, using open-ended interviews with the goal of understanding the concerns of the terminally ill. The qualitative information the researchers gather enables them to create a set of closed- and open-ended questions and scales based not on hypothetical scenarios but directly on the experiences of the terminally ill population. In other words, the survey component of the study (QUANT) was "grounded" in the direct experiences of the terminally ill population. The quantitative study was the primary study and consisted of a structured survey of 56 terminally ill patients. The goal of the survey was to assess how patient characteristics were related to the gap between patient and physician expectations of terminal care. What the researchers found was that doctors and patients can often have different values concerning what it means to have a terminal illness. Whereas doctors concentrate on the medical aspects of their illness, patients' needs concerning social and personal issues are often ignored and outweighed by medically related issues. The qualitative data show that the terminally ill hold valuable information concerning what specific care and interventions they need to feel empowered in their daily lives, but doctors do not often elicit this valuable information.

In the second design (quant—QUAL), the quantitative study is used secondarily (quant) with the qualitative study primarily used (QUAL). In this case, the quantitative study is used to first *identify specific populations or issues* that need to be further explored in more depth. An example of this type of research comes from a study done on general practitioners' (GP's) attitudes concerning the issue of patients' smoking. The authors wanted to identify a diverse pool of GPs who held a range of attitudes. The quantitative study (quant), a short attitudinal survey of 327 GPs, assisted with the selection of an attitudinally diverse pool of respondents, ensuring an in-depth understanding of smoking concerns across different types of GPs (Coleman, Williams, & Wilson, 1996).

The third design (QUANT—qual), as Morgan (1998) notes, is designed to have the quantitative study as the primary mode of inquiry, conducted before the qualitative study. This type of design is often used when there is a need to provide clarification or elaboration of research results from quantitative findings. The qualitative study assists in understanding such things as negative results or outliers, findings that do not appear to fit the overall hypothesis or theoretical pespective. In essence, qualitative data can be used to supplement quantitative data and help the quantitative researcher salvage his or her data by understanding apparently "erroneous results" from his or her survey (Weinholtz, Kacer, & Rocklin, 1995). An example of this design comes from a research project on the integration of immigrant families into Swedish society (Bjeren, 2004). The primary data for this study are based on two social surveys (QUANT) whose purpose was to gather demographic information on immigrant and native-born Swedes from available data (a previous large-scale study on the welfare of immigrants) and to survey 3,408 adults (native and foreign born) concerning their work and family lives. The researchers wanted to compare the economic and social conditions of Polish and Turkish young adult immigrants with that of their native-born counterparts. The qualitative study (qual) was employed as a secondary method to clarify some of issues of family dynamics and community relationships among Turkish and Polish immigrants. A convenience sample of interviews, as well as formal and informal observations of young immigrants and some of their parents, was also conducted. The authors note that the qualitative study

> [points] to inconsistencies, areas that should be given more attention and possible consequences of the non-response to the social surveys. In the other direction, analysis of survey data [has] indicated that some of the conclusions drawn from the intensive studies seem to have limited validity, maybe reflecting the restrictions under which those studies were made or more profound issues around difference between the self-images people present and what they actually do. (Bjeren, 2004, p. 6)

An important finding that the survey data appears to lack is an understanding of the importance of religion in the lives of immigrants. The authors note that Sweden is a secular society that does not place much emphasis on "religious sentiments which are likely to be regarded as throwbacks to distant times," while religious identification is far more salient among the immigrant groups studied (Bjeren, 2004, p. 7). It is interesting to note here that the quantitative study was conducted by demographers while the qualitative study was done by anthropologists. This raises the question of the training required to engage in a mixed methods design. A mixed methods approach often requires interdisciplinary engagement, which may also raise issues of communication between researchers who do not share the same philosophical and methods perspectives.

The fourth research design (QUAL—quant) begins with a qualitative research study (QUAL) primarily, followed by a smaller quantitative study (quant). The quantitative study is used to test results on different populations to ascertain whether or not the qualitative findings "transfer" to other populations (Morgan, 1998, p. 370). Gioia and Thomas's (1996) multimethods study was interested in how academic administrators identify the important issues that impact universities undergoing "strategic change." In an example of the fourth and final mixed methods design, the researchers used a qualitative method—a single case study of one university's management team—to get at the lived experiences of high-level administrators in higher education. The qualitative case study enabled the researchers to identify "image" and "identity" as two key themes that are particularly important in helping administrators sort out what strategic changes universities will require as they continue to undergo dramatic organizational changes. In the minds of administrators, fostering a desired university image was very much related to how their insitutions were to be envisioned in the future. These two factors were also important in understanding how top officials labeled university concerns as either *strategic* (those that would move the university forward) or *political* (often viewed as internal and promoting the "status quo"). The qualitative findings were phrased in terms of a set of propositions concerning the relationships among identity, image, and interpretations (strategic versus political concerns). These propositions were then tested out in a quantitative survey of a sample of 611 high-level college administrators drawn from 372 colleges and universities across the United States.

In this mixed methods research design, the qualitative data becomes a critical element in understanding the research problem, and the quantitative study serves to assist the researchers in "testing out" the findings from the qualitative study to generalize its results to a wider population of university administrators. In general, the survey findings supported the importance of the relationship between image and identity held by key administrators. These findings become an important lens through which administrators make interpretations about what key concerns they should be tending to in a climate of dramatic change.

What Are the Problems and Prospects of Mixed Methods Designs?

A range of concerns have arisen regarding the practice of mixing methods. Some researchers are not clear about what to do when findings from one method are not in agreement with findings from the other, or if one type of study (qualitative or quantitative) gets short shrift. Hesse-Biber (2010) notes,

> A plethora of mixed methods studies assume the standpoint of a positivist interpretation fueled by a growing movement in the social sciences toward more "evidence-based" research practice. Qualitative approaches to mixed methods remain marginalized in mainstream books and articles on the topic. If this point of view appears in a discussion of this method, it often takes on the standpoint of "second best." (p. vi)

Brannen (1992) suggests that even in studies where the qualitative component is primary, there may be a tendency for the quantitative findings to overpower the qualitative (p. 27). She cites a study conducted on home workers (Cragg & Dawson, 1981), noting that the qualitative component of this study was not praised for its theoretical insights but for its size.

Significant financial costs are incurred in performing this type of research, given the amount of time and energy needed to complete any given project. Furthermore, there is the added issue of whether or not individual researchers can acquire the range of skills needed to do both qualitative and quantitative research (Brannen, 1992, p. 20). Zeller (1993) notes that "most researchers have a research method loyalty. Researchers are comfortable operating in their own area of methodological expertise; they are vulnerable operating outside that area" (p. 110). O'Cathain, Murphy, and Nicholl (2008) note that often, in the name of saving money or time or simply in an effort to keep the study more contained, "if quantitative research is a small part of a mainly qualitative study, then qualitative researchers tend to undertake it" (p. 1575). However, qualitative methods are less likely to be undertaken by quantitative researchers, and team members may be acquired that have experience in using both methods (p. 1575).

Some mixed methods studies are conducted by teams of researchers, combined groups consisting of both quantitative and qualitative researchers. Some of these studies may be conducted by two different research teams, which may or may not integrate their research findings. The consumers of this type of research may also not be knowledgeable about both methods. Therefore, it is important for the researcher to take the time to introduce concepts that may be foreign to individuals not versed in a particular paradigm. Given that these studies straddle two different paradigms and methods, there is the added concern that such research will fall through the cracks of academic journals, many of which may be hostile to the mixing of methods (Brannen, 1992). However, the past decade has shown the development of mixed methods-specific journals and publications, signs that mixed methods is increasingly validated in its usage.

How Do I Analyze Data From a Mixed Methods Study Using Computer-Assisted Software Programs?

A major reason for the recent successes of mixed methods is the development of research technologies, specifically computer-assisted software programs that gather, organize, transcribe, and link quantitative and qualitative data. With the advent of computer-assisted qualitative data analysis software, known as CAQDAS (see Fielding & Lee, 1998; Hesse-Biber & Crofts, 2008), new directions in analysis have blurred the boundaries between qualitative and quantitative methods. It is now possible for researchers to take their qualitative data, such as interview material, which is also textual data, and create variables from this data in a process known as quantizing. CAQDAS programs assist the researcher in creating variable data (codes) based on qualitative material and to export this information for statistical analysis. Some qualitative software programs also permit researchers to import quantitative data, such as data gathered from a survey, directly into their computer software programs, allowing them to work simultaneously with both a qualitative and a quantitative database (see Sandelowski, Volis, & Kraft, 2009).

As qualitative data analysis programs continue to advance toward quantizing, there are new software techniques that allow researchers to generate and test their theories on qualitative material. Some programs employ artificial intelligence, knowledge-based expert systems. One CAQDAS program, HyperRESEARCH (www.researchware.com), includes a hypothesis tester component that provides for the creation of "if/then" propositions or hypotheses. HyperRESEARCH supports the use of production rules to help researchers create relationships between coded text segments and to formulate and test hypotheses about the nature of these relationships (Hesse-Biber & Dupuis, 1995). Another program, ETHNO (Heise, 1991; Heise & Lewis, 1988), is a software program that performs an *event structure analysis*, which examines the timing of specific events and analyzes the logical temporal sequence of relationships between events, based on causal narratives within data. In addition to HyperRESEARCH and ETHNO, there are a variety of other commercial software products you can choose from such as QDA Miner, MAXQDA, ATLAS.ti, and NVivo (see Bazeley, 2007; Lewins & Silver, 2007, for an overview of these commercial software packages). There are also noncommercial products, such as CDC EZ-Text, produced by the U.S. Centers for Disease Control and Prevention.

The Process of Quantizing: An Example

Qualitative data *codes* are labels given to segments of data from text that have been transcribed from an interview or other narrative source (magazines, newspapers, etc.). Through **quantizing**, these codes can be transformed into numbers—quantitative (variable) data—that allow for the application of statistical analytical techniques on previously qualitative material (Miles & Huberman, 1994), were the first researchers to use this term; see also Sandelowski, 2000, p. 253; Sandelowski et al., 2009). The application example of this technique comes from Hesse-Biber and Carter's (2004) analysis of 55 young women 2 years after college, who were interviewed about their eating patterns and body image concerns (see Hesse-Biber, 1996). The authors were interested in exploring this data to understand the following question:

- Is there a relationship between critical remarks from family and friends and the development of eating-disorder symptoms among young women?

The qualitative data revealed that while some families and peers were supportive of young women's weight and body image, others were quite critical. The following are excerpts from several of the interviews conducted by Hesse-Biber (1996, as cited in Hesse-Biber & Carter, 2004). In this first excerpt, we can note how Joanna's mother is supportive of her body image:

Joanna: My mother, all she wants is that I'm happy. I can weigh 500 pounds as long as I'm happy. Her focus was always on my health, not so much with my appearance. So her comments were more towards always that positive support. Very rarely do I remember her giving like negative comments about how I looked. It was mostly encouraging. My mother would stay stuff like "You have a beautiful face, you have beautiful hands." She'd focus on individual qualities about me.

On the other hand, Joan and Becky relay stories about how critical their families are concerning their weight and body image.

Joan: My brothers and sisters would go around and make pig noises. . . . My dad would say, "You need to lose weight." And I'd try and I'd be successful.

Becky: My brothers would mention to my mother, and she would say, "Rob thinks you are getting fat," and then she'd say, "Maybe you should stop eating so much." He [father] commented a lot. Never bad. Always good. He'd say, "You look good, you lost weight." He was always commenting on pretty young girls. So I knew it was important to him that I look good too. I wanted him to see that I could be as pretty as all the girls he was commenting on. I wanted him to be proud of me for that, and I knew he was.

With 55 interviews, however, it quickly becomes difficult for the researchers to establish clear relationships among the data. In fact, using qualitative analysis to answer a quantitative question becomes difficult as the number of interviews increases. As we mentioned earlier, qualitative data is good at getting at experience, but this question is asking about causality: Is there a relationship between X (critical remarks) and Y (eating disorders)? In this question *critical remarks* becomes the independent variable (cause) and *eating disorders* becomes the dependent variable (effect).

The *quantizing process* allows us to look at the qualitative data (code) more quantitatively by transforming them into quantitative data (variables). Let's see how this process works.

Step 1: Coding the Text

To aid in identifying the key patterns in these 55 interviews, Hesse-Biber and Carter (2004) coded them with a qualitative data analysis software package, HyperRESEARCH (Hesse-Biber, Dupuis, & Kinder, 1991). For example, Joan's comment concerning her family, "My dad would say, 'You need to lose weight,'" was given the qualitative code "Parents-or-peers-or-siblings critical" (PPSC) (see Chapter 12 for a more detailed description of the qualitative coding process). A similar coding procedure was used to create codes for eating disorders and so on.

Step 2: Converting Codes Into Variables (qual to quant)

Qualitative codes were then transformed into quantitative variables. The researchers note that 16 of the interviews reported that a parent, peer, or sibling was critical of the respondent's eating habits and body and were assigned the PPSC code. A computer software program for qualitative analysis then transformed the variable PPSC by giving these 16 interviews the value of yes and the other 39 a value of no. The same type of procedure was done to provide variables such as eating disorders (EATDIS) a value of yes or no (see Hesse-Biber & Carter, 2004, p. 89, for a more detailed account).

Step 3: Quantizing Analysis

For analysis, the quantized codes (now transformed into variables) were exported to a statistical software package, HyperRESEARCH, to obtain quantitative summaries of key relationships identified in the research question. We can see some of the results of this process in Table 11.2.

Table 11.2 The Relationship Between Having an Eating Disorder (EATDIS) and Growing Up With Parents, Peers, or Siblings Being "Critical" of One's Body and Eating Habits (PPSC)

		PPSC		
		No	**Yes**	
EATDIS	**Yes**	12.8	56.3	
		(5)	(9)	
	No	87.2	43.8	
		(34)	(7)	
		100%	100%	
		(39)	(16)	$N = 55$

Source: Adapted from Hesse-Biber and Carter, 2004, p. 89.

More specifically, Table 11.2 shows a strong relationship between (PPSC) and reported eating disorder symptoms such as bulimia and anorexia (EATDIS). In fact, the authors went on to further validate and elaborate on this relationship by looking at other quantized variables they theorized might be related to this finding; they looked for other factors that might weaken or strengthen the relationship between the degree of criticism and the development of eating-disorder symptoms. Interestingly, the researchers found that when a parent is overweight and is critical of the daughter's body, the parent's words have less power than if a parent is not overweight.

The quantizing process enabled the researchers to fully articulate the conditions under which the original relationship between critical remarks and eating disorders becomes stronger (when mother is not overweight) or weaker (when mother is overweight). The authors note:

[We find] interaction between PPSC and having an overweight parent (or not) in determining the likelihood of an interviewee developing an eating disorder. More specifically, we find that PPSC only really matters in the context of a family where the parents are *not* overweight. In sum, having a critical parent who is at the same time overweight seems to have little impact on a daughter developing an eating disorder, whereas a daughter with parents who are both "thinnish" and *critical* has a strong likelihood of developing bulimia or anorexia. (Hesse-Biber & Carter, 2004, pp. 89–90)

The Process of Qualitizing: Using Quantitative Variables to Directly Enhance Qualitative Analysis

How can researchers use quantitative information directly in the qualitative analysis of their data? This is the situation of directly incorporating insights of quantitative data into a qualitative analysis. The term **qualitizing** is used to refer to the process of transforming quantitative data into qualitative data (see Tashakkori & Teddlie, 1998, who first coined this term; see also Sandelowski, 2000, pp. 253–254). Qualitizing quantitative data serves to (1) enhance the researchers' understanding of the quantitative data by placing it in a qualitative context, creating a hybrid analysis; and (2) provide researchers with a set of variables with which to sort their qualitative data into quantitative categories to enhance the generalizability of their findings. Researchers who qualitize their data may want to enhance their understanding of quantitative variables by nesting these variables in a qualitative context.

Hesse-Biber's (1996) study on women's body image and eating disorders contained both qualitative and quantitative data. She conducted intensive interviews with a sample of women 2 years post-college and followed up these interviews by having her respondents fill out a self-administered questionnaire regarding women's attitudes toward eating as well as a range of quantitative eating-disorder scales. The interviews and questionnaires were matched for each respondent in her study. Hesse-Biber created an "eating typology" based on the quantitative data. The qualitative data from the intensive interviews provided a more detailed "grounding" of the meaning of the eating typology she had made. In addition, the quantitative typology provided her with quantitative categories with which to differentiate her qualitative sample and enhance the generalizability of her findings regarding women's eating patterns. Hesse-Biber used insights from the quantitative study to make inferences about the qualitative data.

One of the important advantages of using a *mixed data analysis design* is that it enables researchers to see complex relationships in their qualitative data. The ability to quantify the qualitative data and incorporate quantitative data into qualitative analysis provides a different analytical window into finding patterns within qualitative data and coming up with precise numbers on which to use statistical techniques. It also provides a context within which to understand quantitatively derived variables. Use of these quantizing and qualitizing techniques for transforming and analyzing data, however, creates a range of issues that stem from crossing the boundary between quantitative and qualitative *analytical* realms.

There are conceptual issues (epistemological and methodological concerns) as well as more practical issues (such as how to choose an appropriate statistical analysis of qualitative variables or how to interpret research results) to consider as the researcher applies these new techniques. Transforming qualitative codes and treating them as variables violates some important measurement assumptions regarding how quantitative variables are gathered (i.e., statistical issues regarding random sampling), especially when the research data digresses from standardized question format, as is the case with open-ended interviews and most other qualitative research. For example, in the eating disorder study cited above, Hesse-Biber and Carter (2004) note that while many interviewees discussed how their parents, peers, and siblings were critical of their bodies—and the researchers transformed this code into a variable called PPSC—not all interviewees were asked about this issue in a standardized way, as is done in a quantitative survey. Nor did the interviewer strive to bring up this particular issue in every single interview. Thus, measurement error is a real concern for anyone following the path that we are suggesting in this chapter.

There are counter points of view to these criticisms. First, many would argue that interviewees will tend to bring up those issues most salient in their lives—and thus the research need not be overly concerned about not having directed every interviewee's attention to every particular code (Hesse-Biber & Carter, 2004). There is also the added concern about how to analyze this type of data.

Each of these issues needs to be addressed by going back to the basic goals of the mixed methods research project; in addition, the researcher needs to consistently practice self-reflexivity concerning his or her own epistemological stance. What is a limitation for one researcher is an opportunity for another, depending on researcher goals and epistemological standpoints. A positivist might cringe at the idea of turning codes into variables and would definitely view this as a major violation of positivist measurement standards. On the other hand, a qualitative researcher who has also received quantitative training might be open to positivistic analyses, using quantized variables as an important **heuristic device**, that is, as an aid to analysis, one that reveals potential relationships that can be explored more fully in more refined studies taken from both qualitative and quantitative approaches. In fact, such an analysis could enhance the positivistic scientific underpinnings by repeating studies and, in a repeated study, ensure that the codes the researcher found most important in the previous study are introduced to all interviewees. In addition, by quantizing variables from our qualitative study, we are pinpointing important codes that can be, for example, recast as fixed-choice survey items or incorporated into qualitative studies using more directed and focused interviewing. Quantizing or qualitizing should be considered "means of making available techniques which add power and sensitivity to individual judgment when one attempts to detect and describe patterning in a set of observations" (Weinstein & Tamur, 1978, as quoted in Miles & Huberman, 1994, p. 41).

Conclusion

Mixed methods designs are not intended to be a magic elixir that one pours onto a research project to make it work. Mixed methods constitute a technique for getting at knowledge-building. In some cases, more is not necessarily better; the sum may not be greater than its parts. In fact, in our "behind the scenes" interview, Janice Morse, a leading qualitative researcher, warns about embracing mixed methods as a substitute for sharp conceptual thinking and insightful analyses. She raises again the important issues we addressed earlier in this chapter that have to do with the cost of carrying out a mixed methods project and the training required to do so. How well-versed can any researcher be in both methods? Can more harm than good be done when researchers are not adequately trained in both methods? In addition, Morse raises issues stemming from the expectations of funding agencies and the pressure some researchers may feel to do a mixed methods design at the behest of the funding agency, independent of the research problem (see also

Brannen, 1992, p. 20). Morse is unequivocal about the importance of not losing sight of the contribution qualitative methods continue to make, in their *pure* form, to our understanding of the nature of social reality (see also Morse, 1996). Keeping vigilant on the essence of this insight is what is needed to avoid losing our way in the quest for knowledge-building.

BEHIND THE SCENES WITH JANICE MORSE: MIXED METHODS AND "THEORETICAL DRIVE"

Cisneros: In what ways do you see multi methods evolving? How will qualitative researchers deal with such diversity?

Morse: I think it is going to get into a terrible mess but it will sort itself out in the end.

Cisneros: What kind of "terrible mess" are you talking about?

Morse: I think people lack analytic skills to handle both qualitative and quantitative data. I don't think there has been enough work done on theory development, I think that not enough people even want to do theoretical development and are content with their descriptions. I think the pressure to do mixed methods, in order to get funding, overwhelms or overrides the goals of qualitative inquiry. I think the funding agencies say they fund qualitative inquiry, meaning that they really do fund mixed methods. This still places qualitative inquiry in an inferior position.

Cisneros: What are the empirical implications of using mixed methods? I mean, facing the complexity of the actual world every one of us for sure will be more in need of mixed and multiple methods.

Morse: I do not think we all have to give in to these pressures. I feel I use multi methods if it is required in the design, not simply to please funding agencies.

Cisneros: Because we need this kind of multi method research to produce knowledge?

Morse: Nonsense. Fiddlesticks. Basic knowledge also comes from doing qualitative research alone.

Cisneros: But qualitative research needs multi methods?

Morse: No, it does not need multi methods; the funding agencies need multi-methods and some questions need multi-methods.

Source: This is an excerpt from a two-part interview which was conducted by Mexican sociologist Cesar Cisneros in January and May 2004 and can be found online (Cisneros-Puebla, 2004; used by permission).

Another issue researchers should contemplate is the issue of crossing research paradigms. Mixed methods may blur the line between research paradigms, and it is unclear how concerned researchers should react to this. There are those pragmatists who advocate for whatever methods work, sometimes with little regard for issues of epistemology and methodology, whereas others, known as purists, see such boundary crossings as violating the very foundations of scientific thought. Still others take positions between what we see as a continuum of opinions on this matter.

With these caveats in mind, mixed methods designs hold a great deal of promise for the researcher who wants to tackle complex issues that reside at multiple levels—the individual level as well as the societal level. They can enhance the type of information gathered and serve to increase the validity of both qualitative and quantitative projects. There is the idea that by using both approaches, the researcher can bring out the best in each method (increasing the validity of a given study through triangulation, for example), while offsetting the weaknesses of the other. The idea, as we have noted earlier, is that "the whole is greater than the sum of its parts."

Tips for Student Researchers: Embarking on a Mixed Methods Project

Student researchers who choose to embark on a mixed methods project should consider the following sensitizing questions in developing a workable research question or situation (adapted in part from *Mixed Methods Research: Merging Theory With Practice* [Hesse-Biber, 2010]):

- How do I come up with a research problem?

- Are there other stakeholders involved in the development of this research problem? What considerations do they bring to the table?

- Do I have the skills to complete the project? If not, whom should I consider adding to my team in order to complete this project?

- How and to what extent will I incorporate different methodological and method approaches to this issue?

- Do I have the resources to complete this study? What type of support (monetary, emotional, etc.) will I require in the course of this study?

- Do I have the time and skills to accurately and faithfully complete this study?

- Am I open and flexible to design change?

- What will be my primary and secondary methods?

- In what sequence will I conduct my studies?

- At what stage in the research process will I mix methods?

In addition to these questions, it is, as always, important to consider ethical guidelines as well. The ethics issues we've discussed in Chapter 4 remain relevant throughout the mixed methods research process, with responsibility toward respondents and data remaining of utmost importance.

Glossary

Complementarity: One reason for employing a mixed methods design; the researcher seeks to gain a fuller understanding of the research problem or to clarify a given research result.

Concurrent mixed methods design: When methods (quantitative and qualitative) run parallel to one another and are carried out. One method may be primary and the other secondary or both may be on equal footing.

Data triangulation: Different data sources or data types, using the same method. For example, you might look at the same data longitudinally or compare data on a specific issue from a single state versus the nation as a whole.

Development: A reason given for using mixed methods; it occurs when results from one method help to develop or inform the other method.

Equal footing: The mixed methods design does not distinguish between a "primary" or "secondary" methods component. Both mixed methods components are equally important.

Expansion: A motive to employ mixed methods in order to extend the range of a study.

Heuristic device: An aid to analysis that reveals potential relationships that can be explored more fully in more refined studies taken from both qualitative and quantitative approaches, for example when a qualitative researcher who also received quantitative training is open to positivistic analyses and uses quantized variables.

Initiation: One reason for using mixed methods is that of *initiation*, whereby a research study's findings raise questions or contain contradictions that require clarification.

Methods triangulation: The use of multiple (different) methods of collecting data to examine how consistent the research findings are from each different method used to study the same phenomenon.

Nested mixed methods design: A *nested* design consists of one method (qualitative or quantitative) nested or "embedded" in the other, with the nested method being given a lower priority. The nested method may even answer a different research question, yet both methods are used to analyze the data.

Qualitizing: The *qualitizing process* provides a way to examine quantitative data more qualitatively by transforming quantitative data (variables) into qualitative data (codes).

Quantizing: The *quantizing process* allows us to look at the qualitative data more quantitatively by transforming our qualitative data (codes) into quantitative data (variables).

Sequential (time ordered) mixed methods designs: Designs in which quantitative and qualitative components are related at the data collection stage and/or the data analysis and data interpretation stage. One method component follows the other in time (qualitative followed by quantitative or quantitative followed by qualitative) with the goals of exploration or explanation.

Synergistic: The combination of two different methods can create a *synergistic* research project whereby one method enables the other to be more effective, and together, both methods provide a fuller understanding of the research problem.

Theoretical triangulation: Using different theoretical perspectives in one study. For example, you might apply both a feminist and a postmodern perspective to study a single problem. One of the advantages in doing so is that the researcher can examine the efficacy of several theoretical perspectives in one study.

Triangulation: This strategy involves using more than one method to study the same research question. The researcher is looking for a convergence of research findings to enhance the credibility or validity of research findings.

Discussion Questions

1. What are some of the reasons why a researcher might employ a mixed methods approach?

2. How do methods "speak to each other"?

3. How should researchers reconcile their varied (qualitative or quantitative) data? What are some of the programs or techniques used for mixing methods?

4. What is triangulation, and why is it important to a mixed methods discussion?

5. What are some of the drawbacks or potential problems in using a mixed methods design?

Resources

Suggested Web Sites

Glossary of Mixed Methods Terms and Concepts

http://www.fiu.edu/~bridges/glossary.htm

This Web site is a resource for terms and concepts related to mixed methods research. The terms found on this site are adopted from Tashakkori and Teddlie's *Handbook of Mixed Methods in Social and Behavioral Research* (2003).

Research Design and Mixed Method Approach: A Hands-on Experience

http://www.socialresearchmethods.net/tutorial/Sydenstricker/bolsa.html

This site is helpful for seeing mixed methods put to actual use in a study.

CAQDAS: Computer-Assisted Qualitative Data Analysis Software

http://caqdas.soc.surrey.ac.uk/

This Web site lists the range of commercial and noncommercial computer-assisted qualitative data analysis software packages on the market with a description and contact information for each software product.

Noncommercial Qualitative Software Package EZ-Text

http://www.cdc.gov/hiv/topics/surveillance/resources/software/ez-text/index.htm

Read a description and download a noncommercial qualitative research software product produced by the U.S. Centers for Disease Control and Prevention.

Employing Multiple Methods

http://writing.colostate.edu/guides/research/observe/pop4b.cfm

This Web site offers a writing guide for using multiple methods.

Mixed Methods for Novice Researchers

http://mra.e-contentmanagement.com/archives/vol/3/issue/1/mixed-methods-for-novice-researchers

This is a special issue from the *Journal of Multiple Research Approaches* that is devoted to mixed methods theory and practice for novice researchers. This Web site lists the table of contents for the special issue, which you might want to check out.

Relevant Journals

Journal of Mixed Methods Research

Evaluation

International Journal of Multiple Research Approaches

Qualitative Inquiry

Qualitative Health Research

PART III

Analysis and Interpretation

CHAPTER 12

Analysis and Interpretation of Qualitative Data

Data analysis and interpretation are interrelated. You will find yourself analyzing and interpreting your data as your qualitative project proceeds. This process requires that you be open to new ideas in your data, visiting and revising your analysis and interpretation as your study proceeds.

In the following passage, ethnographer Michael Agar (1980) distinguishes between analysis and interpretation:

> In ethnography . . . you learn something ("collect some data"), then you try to make sense out of it ("analysis"), then you go back and see if the interpretation makes sense in light of new experience ("collect more data"), then you refine your interpretation ("more analysis"), and so on. The process is dialectic, not linear. (p. 9)

The process of turning your observations into what Harry Wolcott (1994, p. 1) terms *intelligible accounts* calls forth reflection on how you might answer the following questions (Hesse-Biber & Leavy, 2004, p. 409):

- How do you know if you have focused on the major themes contained in your interview material or ethnographic fieldwork account?

- Do the categories of analysis you gathered make sense?

AUTHORS' NOTE: Parts of this chapter are adapted from "Analysis, Interpretation, and the Writing of Qualitative Data," in Sharlene Nagy Hesse-Biber & Patricia Leavy (Eds.), *Approaches to Qualitative Research: A Reader on Theory and Practice,* New York: Oxford University Press, 2004.

- What type of analysis should you proceed with?

- Should you conduct a descriptive study or venture beyond descriptive findings with your own interpretation?

- How much interpretation should you conduct? To what endpoint?

What Are the Steps Involved in Qualitative Data Analysis and Interpretation?

While we are providing you with some steps to consider as you proceed with your analysis, you should not get the idea that qualitative analysis proceeds in a cookbook fashion. There is no one right way to go about analysis. C. Wright Mills noted that qualitative analysis is, after all, "intellectual craftsmanship" (Mills, 1959, cited in Tesch, 1990, p. 96). As Renata Tesch (1990) states, "qualitative analysis can and should be done artfully, even 'playfully,' but it also requires a great amount of methodological knowledge and intellectual competence" (p. 97). Norman K. Denzin (2000) posits that there is an "art of interpretation":

> This may also be described as moving from the field to the text to the reader. The practice of this art allows the field-worker-as-bricoleur . . . to translate what has been learned into a body of textual work that communicates these understandings to the reader. (p. 313)

With these caveats in mind, we break down data analysis and interpretation as a series of steps, beginning with data preparation.

Step 1: Data Preparation Phase

It is important to think about *what* data you are going to analyze and whether or not these data are going to provide you with an understanding of your research question. If you are conducting interviews or focus groups, for example, you might want to make a transcript of your data. You will probably need to enter and store these data into a database of some type. You can print out copies of what you have entered in your database and carefully begin to read through and perhaps correct any data entry errors.

Transcribing Your Data

The transcription process is not passive. How we collect our data is crucial to analysis and interpretation. If you are conducting an interview or focus group, for example, several key issues arise in terms of how you will collect this data:

- Will you videotape or audiotape your interview session or use some other recording device?

- Will you transcribe the entire data session? Will you only summarize key passages or quotes? Will you select only those passages you perceive to be related to key research issues?

- Will you transcribe all types of data you collect (i.e., all verbal data including laughter, pauses, emotions such as sadness or anger, and nonverbal data such as hand gestures)?

- Who will transcribe your data?

- What transcription format will you use? How will you represent a respondent's voice, nonverbal information, and so on?

How researchers answer these questions is often dictated by their research question as well as the type of theoretical framework they hold regarding the interview as a process of meaning making. A positivist might in fact dispense with some of these questions, opting to view the transcription process as a simple translation from the oral to the written language, something that can be done by almost anyone who can listen to the tape and has good typing skills, for example. What they transcribe is regarded as "the truth," and each transcription is considered to contain a one-to-one correspondence between what is said orally and the printed word.

Those with a more interpretative viewpoint might not view the transcription process as so transparent (see Mishler, 1991). In fact, they would stress the importance of the researcher's point of view and the researcher's influence on the transcription process itself. Those researchers with a more discourse-analytic or linguistic-theoretical framework will be especially aware of the lack of transparency in the translation process by noting the importance of multiple levels of meaning within the transcription process, which include such things as pauses, the way in which something is said, and the nonverbal cues used by a respondent.

Feminist researchers such as Marjorie Devault (2004) are especially aware of the importance of listening to the data when transcribing interviews, especially from those groups whose everyday lives are rendered "invisible" by the dominant society. Devault notes the significance of listening to those moments in the interview where the interviewee is tentative or says "You know what I mean?" She suggests that these are the very moments where the researcher is able to unearth hidden meanings of interviewees whose lives and language are often overshadowed by the dominant discourse. She has garnered the following in conducting interviews with women regarding the daily activities they perform in their homes, especially the work they perform in feeding their families:

The words available often do not fit, women learn to "translate" when they talk about their experiences. As they do so, part of their lives "disappears" because [it is] not included in the language of the account. In order to "recover" these parts of women's lives, researchers must develop methods for listening around and beyond words. I use the term "listening" . . . in a broad sense, to refer to what we do while interviewing, but also to the hours we spend later listening to tapes or studying transcripts, and even more broadly, to the ways we work at interpreting respondents' accounts. . . . As the interviews progressed, I became increasingly fascinated with some characteristic features of my respondents' talk. They spoke very concretely, about the mundane details of everyday life, but they often said things in ways that seemed oddly incomplete; . . . they assumed certain kinds of knowledge on my part ("like, you know, the Thursday section of the newspaper," an implicit reference to the fact that many U.S. newspapers include recipes and features on food and diet in their Thursday editions). . . . I began to pay more and more attention to the ways things were said. (Devault, 2004, pp. 233–234)

Devault notes that tentative words like "you know?" might in fact be discarded in transcribing one's data but in fact are the very moments where standard vocabulary is inadequate and where a respondent tries to speak from experience and finds language wanting (p. 235). Devault comments that her own transcripts of interviews with women regarding the work they do to feed their families were

filled with notations of women saying, "you know?" in sentences like "I'm more careful about feeding her, you know, kind of a breakfast." This seems an incidental feature of their speech, but perhaps the phrase is not so empty as it seems. In fact, I did know what she meant. I did not use these phrases systematically in my analyses, but I think now that I could have. Studying these transcripts now, I see that these words often occur in places where they are consequential for the joint production of our talk in the interviews. In many instances, "you know" seems to mean something like "Ok, this next bit is going to be a little tricky. I can't say it quite right, but help me out a little; meet me halfway and you'll understand what I mean." (Devault, 2004, p. 235)

Transcribing research data is interactive and engages the researcher in the process of deep listening, analysis, and interpretation. Transcription is not a passive act but instead provides the researcher with a valuable opportunity to actively engage with his or her research material from the beginning of data collection. It also ensures that researchers are aware of their own impact on the data early in the gathering process and that they have an opportunity to connect with this data in a grounded manner that provides for the possibility of enhancing the trustworthiness and validity of their data-gathering techniques.

Transcription Software for Qualitative Data Analysis

An increasing number of researchers have started using computer-assisted transcription software such as HyperTranscribe (www.researchware.com) and Transana (www.transana.org) to access the analysis possibilities contained within the process of transcription, as we have already noted above. So, for example, these programs will allow you to transcribe both audio and video data. The features of these programs (such as being able to set the controls of the program to meet your own typing skill level and providing you with a variety of ways to loop back the audio and video segments) allows you to listen intently to your respondents' words and also to note and record nonverbal behaviors if you are working with digitized video data. Both these programs provide you with a time stamp, which means that as you are transcribing, every now and then you can time-stamp the point where you are in the transcription process so that you can retrieve specific segments of your transcript without having to rewind and restart the original transcription of audio or video data. The transcription process is often delegated to a junior member of a research team or an outside company that specializes in doing transcriptions. Transcription software has begun to provide a way for researchers to cut down on their transcription time as well as to take advantage of the analysis possibilities contained within the process of transcribing one's own data, as we have noted above.

Steps 2 and 3: Data Exploration Phase and Data Reduction Phase

These two phases work hand in hand. In the exploration phase, you read your textual or visual or audio data and *think about it.* In the process of thinking about it, you might begin to mark up your text by highlighting what you feel is important. Perhaps you may write down these ideas in the form of a memo. We want to emphasize the importance of *description* during this phase. Try summarizing the data you have collected thus far; write down (memo) any ideas that come to you as you are reading your notes, interviews, and so on. What things fit together? What is problematic? Using visual aids—such as diagrams—might help you think about ideas. What are the most telling quotes in your data? Researchers who want to get a closer picture of their data to build theory and to potentially draw out some findings engage in all of these "first run through the data" techniques.

The following is a "first run through the data" of a study on African American women who attend predominantly white schools (Hesse-Biber et al., 2009). This memo is both descriptive and analytical. Note how the memo describes the early background of the interviewee and some information about her family background and her early family life. The memo also is linked to the text of the interview by noting the line numbers on which this information was gathered from the interview. When you are taking a memo, you might also begin to line-number your interview transcript so that you can have an easy cross-reference to the actual text in the interview to which the memo relates. We also note that this memo goes beyond description and begins to move into analysis. The analytical moments of this memo are about putting information together that relates to the larger goals of the study, which deals with issues of racial identity and body image as well as what impact, if any, attending a predominantly white school has on those issues for African American women. You will notice that this memo links issues of racial pride, self-esteem, and self-confidence as important factors that appear to "protect" women of color from white Western norms of beauty that have been shown in the research literature to be an important factor in the development of body image issues among Caucasian women. While the linking of the factors in this memo is still very tentative, we can see that we have the beginnings of an important set of linkages that the researcher needs to explore in more detail in other interview material.

MEMO: INITIAL IMPRESSION OF YOUR INTERVIEW

This participant was born and raised in Alabama by her mother and her brother. Her father and mother separated when she was two. She grew up in a house with her mother's parents (her grandparents), her aunt and uncle, her brother, and her mother living in the basement. [lines 55–60]

She had no interest in going to a school that had fraternities or sororities because she does not like how cliquey they get, how much they control your life, and how shallow and materialistic they are. She is not into cliques and being elitist about your group and she is not from money and not materialistic, so that was a no. Part of the appeal of her current college is that it has no fraternities or sororities.

This participant comes from a very close-knit family, who all live close together or did in Alabama before she and her brother and mother moved to Illinois so that her mother could go back to school. But they used to spend every Sunday together: the traditional Southern picnic she called it. [lines 69–80]

When her mother went back to school, she had to take on a more parental role when she was only seven and eight. She cooked, cleaned, and watched her little brother. [lines 129–131] This could explain her confidence, good work ethic, maturity, responsibility, et cetera.

Her father has been in jail. [lines 155–160]

This participant really respects her mother for going back to school to get her bachelor's degree in order to make a better life for herself and her children, so that her children could have more opportunities than she had. [lines 167–170] I feel that having such a strong, positive, optimistic female role model helped mold this participant's attitudes towards life.

This participant and her mother have both been diagnosed with clinical depression.

Her mother was on disability for it, and the participant is on medication for depression. [lines 196–201]

This participant feels the need to persevere, despite all the hardships in her life, like her depression for example. She says that she draws a lot of inspiration to "never give up" from her family: both from seeing that they never give up and from feeling that if she does give up, she will be letting her family down which she cannot do after all they have done for her to have a better life. "Everything I do is for my family." [lines 265–280]

This participant identifies herself as Black American, and refuses to call herself African American because she feels that this just "simplifies" what she is. She says she is part African, plus other ethnic backgrounds as well. [lines 283–297]

This participant had a great sense of racial identity and self-worth, and a high degree of self-confidence. I feel these three things are the reasons why she never got drawn into the idea that she had to "be whiter" or into issues such obsession with her body image that more white women appear to face in her predominately Caucasian college. Her identity, as she notes, is "Black American." (Hesse-Biber et al., 2009)

After gaining more familiarity with your data by simply reading it over several times and perhaps writing up a brief memo of your impressions about the respondent and any ideas you may want to jot down about what you think is going on in this interview, you might begin to *code* your data. The coding process can start as soon as you begin to collect some data; you do not need to nor should you wait for all your data to be collected. A little bit of data collection and data analysis can reveal some important patterns, as we shall see in the excerpt of an interview with a black adolescent in the next section. Data collection and data analysis are iterative processes—the two work interactively, as depicted in Figure 12.1.

Figure 12.1   Diagram of the Iterative Process in the Analysis of Data

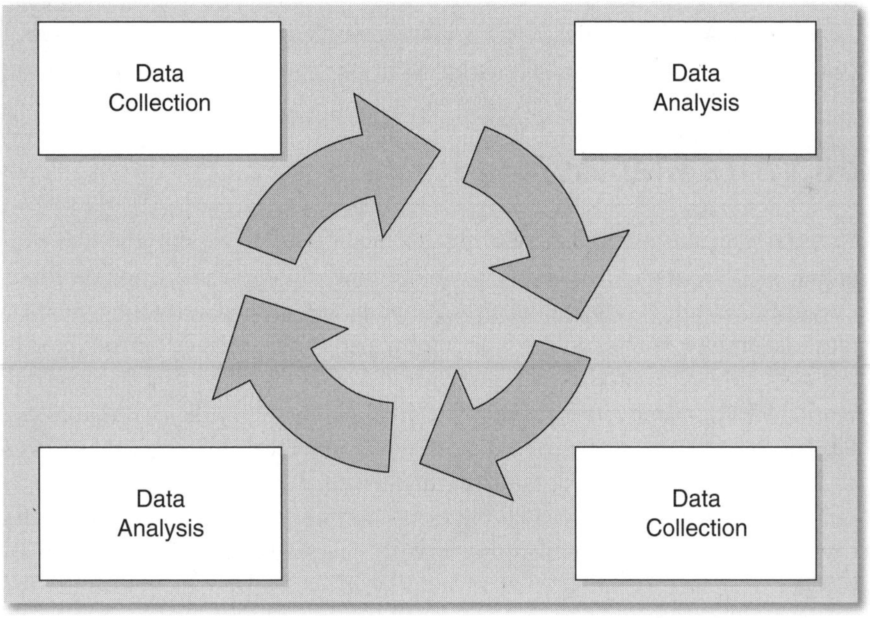

What Is a Grounded Theory Approach to Data Coding and Analysis?

The process of **coding** and analysis we describe below is modeled after a grounded theory approach to the analysis of qualitative data, which we have discussed in previous chapters (see also Glaser & Strauss, 1967). This analysis perspective starts from an engagement with the data and ends with a theory that is generated from or grounded in the data. Kathy Charmaz's (2004; Bryant & Charmaz, 2007) work with **grounded theory** provides us with one important strategy for extracting meaning from qualitative data. Charmaz refines the ideas of grounded theory into a concise set of step-by-step analysis instructions. She takes the reader through the process of collecting data, analyzing, and writing memos. All of these parts of the analysis work iteratively. As one collects the data, one is analyzing the data. One begins the process, says Charmaz, by doing "open coding." This consists of literally reading *line by line* and carefully coding each line, sentence, and paragraph. Charmaz (2004) suggests the following questions to ask during this process to assist with coding:

- What is going on?

- What are people doing?

- What is the person saying?

- What do these actions and statements take for granted?

- How do structure and context serve to support, maintain, impede, or change these actions and statements? (Charmaz, 2004, p. 507; see also Morse et al., 2009)

As the process continues, the researcher may begin to see more developed codes—focused codes—especially through the process of writing memos.

How Do You Write Memos?

By writing memos one can raise a code to the level of a *category*. The idea of a grounded theory approach is to read carefully through the data and uncover the major categories and concepts and, ultimately, the properties of these categories and their interrelationships. Memo writing is an integral part of the grounded theory process and assists researchers in elaborating on their ideas regarding their data and code categories. Ideally, memo writing takes place at all points within the analysis process. Reading through and sorting memos can also help researchers to integrate their ideas and may even serve to bring up new ideas and relationships within the data.

The grounded theory approach represents only one of many analysis strategies (such as narrative analysis or discourse analysis) one might employ to analyze qualitative data. There is no right or wrong way to synthesize data, and often the researcher jumps back and forth between collection, analysis, and writing. We have also suggested some specific analysis strategies at the end of each research method we present in our book. However, a grounded theory approach is a widely used analytical technique that spans several research method approaches, from the analysis of interviews and field observations to the analysis of unobtrusive data, that is, data the researcher gathers that already exist and are valuable for the research project. These data are "nonreactive" in that the researcher's own biases and agenda did not intervene in the original collection of these data. An example of this type of data might be recording the specific type of clothing a respondent wears during an interview as a measure of the respondent's "fashion consciousness."

Coding is a central part of a grounded theory approach and involves extracting meaning from nonnumerical data such as text, audio, video, and multimedia. If we were to describe how the coding process is actually done with text materials such as interviews, for example, it would sound something like this: Coding usually consists of identifying meaningful "chunks" or "segments" in your textual data (the interview) and giving each of these a label (code). Coding is the analysis strategy many qualitative researchers employ to help them locate key themes, patterns, ideas, and concepts that may exist within their data. Analyzing qualitative data presents a distinct challenge for the qualitative researcher. Perhaps the best way to approach this topic is to say that there are a multitude of different forms of analysis with many different goals, depending on the stated research question.

What Is an Example of the Coding Process?

Let's return to our guiding example of body image. Hesse-Biber (1996) collected interviews and participant observations from research on how black American teens view their bodies (Hesse-Biber, Howling, Leavy, & Lovejoy, 2004). She did not have any specific hypothesis she wanted to test out on the data, but instead, she was interested in discovering the following:

- How do adolescent black American girls view their bodies?

Hesse-Biber spent many hours observing and interviewing black American teenagers at a variety of local community centers in an inner city in the Northeast. She obtained hours of interviews with and observations of black American teens and recorded fieldnote observations of the goings-on at each of the community centers for several years. As you read these data, remember that data collection and data analysis should proceed together—as soon you begin to gather the first bit of data from the field, it is important to begin to make sense of it. In conducting such a study, you might begin the process of analysis by reading over and becoming familiar with the data that are collected after each visit to the community center. You may also consider marking up or highlighting anything you think is relevant to your understanding of how black American women perceive their identity and body image. The marking up of the text is used to locate those segments that you believe are important. You might then apply a name or code to each of these segments, such as "positive body image." Some segments of text may contain more than one code. Your coding procedure is open-ended and holistic. Your goal is to gain insight and understanding. You do not have a predefined set of coding categories; the analysis procedure is primarily inductive and requires an immersion of yourself in the text until themes, concepts, or dimensions of concepts arise from the data. You would especially look for the common ways or patterns of behavior whereby individuals come to terms with their body image and identity.

How Do You Code Data?

When we talk about analysis, you may get the feeling that the discussion is progressing in terms that are somewhat technical and procedural, and you are right. Analysis usually begins with looking for **descriptive codes** within one's data, eventually hoping to generate a set of key *concepts* (categories), which are much more analytical, concerning black American girls' body image and identity. In the following example, Hesse-Biber has read through an interview with an adolescent black teenager and has jotted down some initial codes.

EXCERPT OF AN INTERVIEW WITH AN AFRICAN AMERICAN TEENAGER WITH SOME INITIAL CODES (SEE HESSE-BIBER ET AL., 2004)

Excerpt:	Initial Code:
I don't think that the ideal woman has to	Ideal woman
look like anything personally. I think the ideal woman	Importance of personality
has personality and character, it's how you act.	
My looks don't bother me, it's just my personality.	Physical appearance is secondary
I wanna have a good personality.	Importance of personality
and have people like me, if they don't like me for	Importance of personality
my personality, or just because of my looks, then	
they must be missing out on something	Missing out on noticing
Um, when you have it [self-esteem]	Self-esteem
so much that you don't care what people	Don't care what others say
think about you. I mean, I flaunt my self-esteem	Flaunting myself

Excerpt:	Initial Code:
not like "Oh yeah, dahdadada," I just sit up real	Sits straight
straight and that shows self-esteem right there.	
I'm a woman, I'll wear stuff to school that's	
like . . . wacked	Wears what she wants
I have earrings that are about this big, and that	Wears big earrings
shows my self-esteem, I don't care what you say	Doesn't care what others say
about them	
Oh well, that's what I think,	
I don't care, I don't fit in anywhere anyway,	
I'm my own self so why can't I act like that	Internal self-assessment: own person
why can't I dress like that?	Internal self-assessment: wears what she wants

As you can see from the above example of coding, some codes listed above are **literal codes**—these words appear within the text and are usually descriptive codes. Others listed are more *interpretative* **analytical codes** (i.e., *internal self-assessment*). These codes are not tied as tightly to the text itself; rather, they begin to rely on the researcher's insights for drawing out interpretation. This type of coding relies on more **focused coding.** A focused coding procedure allows for the building and clarifying of concepts: a researcher examines all the data in a category, compares each piece of data with every other piece, and finally builds a clear working definition of each concept, which is then named. This name becomes the code (Charmaz, 1983, p. 117). Focused coding also requires that a researcher develop a set of **analytical categories** rather than just labeling data in a topical fashion. Modifying code categories becomes important to develop more abstract code categories from which one can generate theoretical constructs. For instance, in the above example, we identify the category *internal self-assessment*, but we can also see some additional codes that might help us clarify the meaning of this concept from the respondent's perspective.

GOING FROM INITIAL CODES TO MORE FOCUSED CODES

Initial Code (literal code)	evolves into	Analytical (more focused) Code
don't care what others say		internal self-assessment: ignores external
flaunting self		supercharged identity: belief in abilities
sitting straight		supercharged identity: being proud
wears what she wants		internal self-assessment: ignores external
wears big earrings		internal self-assessment: ignores external

As your coding progresses, you will have an opportunity to expand on the varied ways in which respondents talk about internal self-assessment as a process. To get from the more literal to the conceptual level of analysis, you might mark up what you see as the different and similar ways the respondent talks about the idea of internal self-assessment. In fact, you might begin to memo about this idea (see the memo on internal self-assessment below). As more and more interviews are analyzed and you continue to memo about what is going on in your data, you may come up with several **analytical dimensions** or subcodes to the concept of internal self-assessment (such as the subcode entitled "ignores external").

By memo-ing on the idea of internal self-assessment, the researcher is encouraged to theorize about the meaning of this concept and the ways in which it may be related to other factors. In fact, internal self-assessment was found to be related to the code categories *cultural pressures to be thin* and *racism*. The researchers who conducted this study (see Hesse-Biber et al., 2004) found that black American girls often protect themselves from the cultural pressures of white Western norms of beauty by adopting a stance of internal self-assessment. The process of internal self-assessment was found to be an early coping strategy young children learn within their communities to cope with racial discrimination from the wider society (Hesse-Biber et al., 2004). Let's go "behind the scenes" and look at a memo that was written for this project by coauthor Meg Lovejoy.

MEMO ON INTERNAL SELF-ASSESSMENT

An interesting and significant pattern of responses emerged in the interviews that we captured with the code *internal self-assessment.* This code category describes an orientation in which the self assesses itself according to a set of internal standards rather than by the (external) judgments of others. Typically, this type of response emerged in relation to questions about whether the respondent was worried about her weight or appearance or felt pressured to look or act a certain way by peers or the media. Respondents answered this kind of question with an assertion that they didn't care about what others thought about them (*Ignores External*) or that they were only concerned about how good they feel about themselves (*Listens to Internal*), or some combination of the two (*Ignores External Listens Internal*)—for instance: "I don't care what others say, as long as I look good to myself, it doesn't matter what people say"). Nineteen respondents made statements that could be characterized as demonstrating the orientation of *internal self-assessment.*

Often, these kinds of statements included the assertion that the respondents loved or felt good about the way they were and that they were not willing to change in order to please others. Some respondents said they learned this attitude from their mother and/or father. One respondent said she had learned it from Bill Cosby, her role model: "I watched this show where he told his daughter that she shouldn't worry about what boys say to her. She should just worry about what she thinks about herself."

Significantly, this strategy or attitude protects these girls from the judgments of others and may make them less susceptible to white Western norms of beauty and the propensity to lose themselves in their efforts to please and attract men. In fact, several respondents said that they did not feel pressured to please men (in terms of skin color, body size, and other aspects of appearance) because it is more important in their view to feel good about themselves. It is unclear from the interviews to what extent this strategy is based on a kind of defensive denial or on genuine self-acceptance and maturity. This attitude may be a coping strategy developed in the black community in response to racism and societal devaluation. For instance, when asked what it means for her to be a black female, one girl said that it meant "to be strong with what I'm doing and you know I can't really worry about what other people think." This strategy may also develop in response to often fierce teasing by peers that many of these girls describe.

Subcodes for Internal Self-Assessment

Several subcodes were arrived at for further reflection on the overall meaning of the concept of internal self-assessment:

Ignores External—Respondent indicates that she doesn't care or is not worried about others' judgments about her. Not willing to change in order to please others.

(Continued)

(Continued)

Listens to Internal—Respondent indicates that what matters to her is how she feels about herself or what's on the inside. Often the respondent asserts that the important thing is that she likes/loves/feels good about herself.

Ignores External Listens Internal—Respondent indicates that she doesn't care what others think of her because she feels good about herself, or it only matters what she thinks about herself. (written by coauthor Meg Lovejoy; see Hesse-Biber et al., 2004)

We've seen that the qualitative coding process consists of cycles of coding and **memo-ing**; Figure 12.2 illustrates the dynamic process between these two techniques. (For additional examples of coding with specific examples provided, see Saldana, 2009.)

Figure 12.2 Coding and Memo-ing: A Dynamic Process

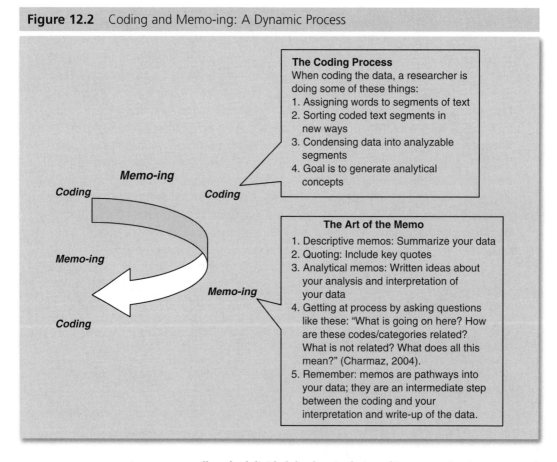

As you can recall, we had divided the data analysis and interpretation into steps, and the last step we worked on, discussing coding and memo-ing, was the data exploration and reduction phase. Next, we look at the phase of interpretation in this process.

Step 4: Interpretation

It is important to note that analysis and interpretation are not necessarily two distinct phases in the qualitative research process, as we have seen in the case of grounded theory analysis. The process is much more fluid, as the researcher often engages simultaneously in the processes of data collection, data analysis, and interpretation of research findings. Memo writing is an important link between analysis and interpretation. With early observations in the field or with the first interviews conducted, early memo writing will allow researchers to look at what ideas seem plausible and which ones they ought to revise. David Karp notes the following concerning memo writing:

> Especially at the beginning you will hear people say things that you just hadn't thought about. Look carefully for major directions that it just had not occurred to you to take. The pace of short memo writing ought to be especially great toward the beginning of your work. I would advocate the "idea" or "concept" memos that introduce an emerging idea. Such memos typically run 2 to 3 pages.
>
> By this [a data memo] I mean a memo that integrates the theme with data and any available literature that fits. By a data memo I mean something that begins to look like a paper. In a data memo always array more data on a point than you would actually use in a research paper. If you make a broad point and feel that you have 10 good pieces of data that fit that point, lay them all out for inspection and later use. Also, make sure to lay out the words of people who do *not fit the pattern*. (Karp, personal correspondence, 2004)

Working with qualitative data, whether those data are collected from fieldwork observations or intensive interviewing, the task of the researcher is one of involvement with the data at an intimate level. As we transition from problems with data collection and coding to issues of writing up research results, other questions begin to emerge concerning the interpretation of qualitative data. At the heart of this questioning are issues of power and control over the interpretation process.

As we mention in many chapters, some qualitative researchers follow a scientific model of research, using patterned research procedures along the lines of the natural sciences and following the tenets of positivism. Under this framework, it is imperative that the researcher be objective, that is, not allow his or her values to enter into the research process. In this model of research, the scientist remains objective in order to gain a "true" understanding of reality. It is as if "reality" or the "true" picture will emerge only if the researcher is true to the scientific tenet of objectivity.

Much of qualitative research, however, deals with observation and interviewing, methods that require constant interaction between the researcher and the researched. The researcher can impact the research process at multiple points along the research path—from the choice of research project and problem to the analysis and interpretation of findings. There are important **power dynamics** within the interviewer/interviewee relationship that can affect the interpretation of research results, a topic covered heavily in our discussion of oral history interviews. In the chapter on in-depth interviewing, we noted that certain social attributes of researcher and researched can impact issues of power and authority in the research process. We also saw in Chapter 8 (Ethnography) how these attributes can guide one's entire research project, from gaining access to the setting, to the social relations in the setting, to how one exits the setting.

We now turn to another important way in which the researcher's social attributes can impact the research by looking at issues of interpretation. One of the central issues to examine in this discussion of the interpretation of findings is the extent to which power differences between the researcher and researched impact the research findings and the researcher's assessment of what they mean (the interpretation process).

- What power does the researcher have in determining whose voice will be heard in the interpretation of research findings?

This question is of central importance in the work of Katherine Borland (1991). She explores the range of interpretive conflicts in the oral narrative she conducts with her grandmother, Beatrice Hanson. She asks her grandmother to relay the story about when she accompanied her father to the racetrack at the fairgrounds in Bangor, Maine, an event that happened more than 42 years earlier. Borland is interested in understanding the different levels of meaning making that take place in the telling and interpretation of oral narratives. She recognizes that there are multiple levels of interpreting narratives. A first-level narrative story—that is, the story her grandmother tells her—conveys the particular way her grandmother constitutes the meaning of the event (pp. 63–64). There is, however, a second level of meaning to the narrative, the meaning the researcher constructs, filtered through the personal experience and expertise of the researcher. Borland listens to her grandmother's story and reshapes it by filtering the story through her own personal life experiences and outward experiences—keeping in mind the expectations of her scholarly peers, to whom, she notes, "we must display a degree of scholarly competence" (p. 73).

Borland (1991) uses a gender-specific theoretical lens to interpret her grandmother's story as a feminist account. However, her grandmother does not agree with her interpretation. In dealing with these issues of authority or ownership of the narrative, Borland raises issues about who has the authority to interpret narrative accounts. For Borland, the answer lies in a type of delicate balancing act. Borland shows her interpretation to her grandmother, and the process of exchanging ideas and interpretations begins. It is clear that no story should remain unmediated. In other words, the storyteller's viewpoint ought to be present within the interpretation. While not all conflicts can be resolved, it is important that the researcher be challenged by the narrator's point of view. The exchange of points of view might provide new ways of understanding the data.

Figure 12.3 sums up what we talked about concerning the four phases of the data analysis and interpretation process. We can observe that as we move from one step to another, we begin to reduce and collapse our data. Coding helps to reduce our data, and memo-ing assists with thinking about how to organize our data into meaningful categories and patterns.

Figure 12.3 Steps in Data Analysis and Interpretation: A Visual Model

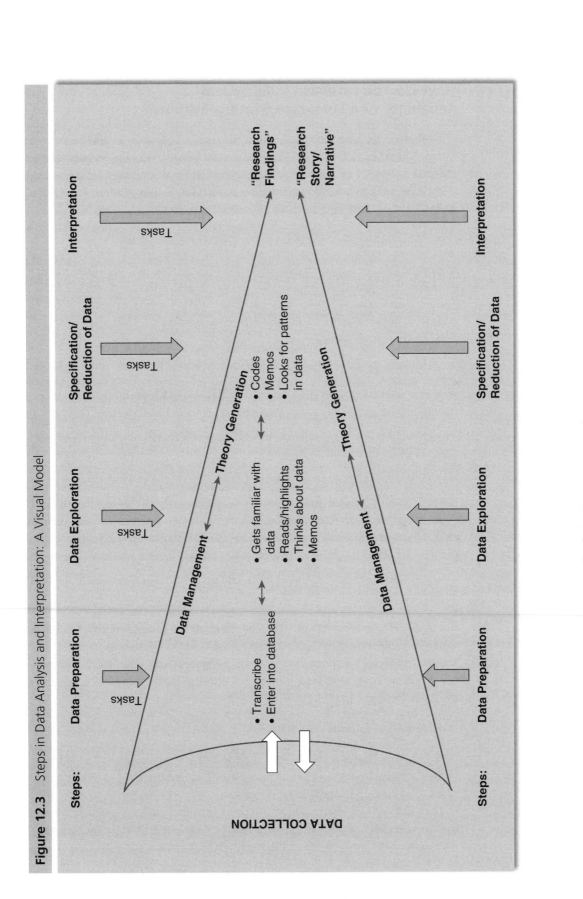

How Do You Establish Validity and Reliability of a Qualitative Interpretation?

Now that you have interpreted your qualitative data, how do you know your interpretation is valid and reliable? When thinking about the validity of the research findings, you can put your interpretations against competing knowledge claims and see how your findings stand up. You should also provide strong arguments for any knowledge claims you draw from your data. Ask yourself:

- What factors make the research findings resonate for you?

Beyond this, we suggest following Kvale's (1996) three-part model for judging the validity of qualitative data: validity as craftsmanship, communicative validity, and pragmatic validity. These dimensions of validity were discussed in detail in Chapter 3, but at this point in the research, we suggest the following steps and questions (derived from Kvale):

- Are you telling a convincing story?

- Try theorizing from your data interpretations. What are some of the major themes in your data? How are they related? What ideas link these themes together?

- Have you reached your findings with integrity? Are all your procedures valid and ethically conducted?

- Look for and address negative cases. Do these outliers change your interpretation?

- Make your interpretations available for discussion (agreement and debate) among *legitimate knowers* (others in the social scientific community). This may require that you go back to the literature to explore new ideas that emerge from this process.

- How do your findings impact those who participated in the research, and how do your findings impact the wider social context in which the research occurred?

Once you have gone through this checklist and the research findings resonate with you, validity has been appropriately considered. As we saw in Chapter 3, reliability is different in qualitative research compared with quantitative research, which is more easily replicated. With this in mind, in terms of reliability, ask yourself the following:

- Is the data internally consistent?

If your data makes sense, your method was suited to your question, and your procedures were implemented systematically, you can proceed from the interpretive phase to writing up your findings.

Data analysis and interpretation can be highly developed and aided by the use of computer-assisted software and other technological advances. In the following section, we will discuss some of the ways in which computer programs could be used for data analysis.

What Computer-Assisted Software Exists for Qualitative Data Analysis?

As researchers collect many pages of text, they may want to use a computerized software program to analyze their data. Computer-analysis software available these days can be highly effective, especially when organizing, storing, and analyzing a significant amount of data. However, important analysis and interpretation issues may arise when using such an analysis tool (Hesse-Biber & Leavy, 2004, p. 410):

- Should a researcher employ a computer software program at all? After all, isn't analysis more of an art form?

- Will the software program interfere with the creative process of analysis?

- Will using a computer software program make the researcher more distant from the data?

As researchers begin the process of turning their research data into a finished product, they may find that their analysis is highly complex. They can be overwhelmed by the mounds of research data consisting of unanalyzed textual data that may often number in the thousands of pages. Miles and Huberman (1984) note:

> A chronic problem of qualitative research is that it is done chiefly with words, not with numbers. Words are fatter than numbers and usually have multiple meanings. This makes them harder to move around and work with. Worse still, most words are meaningless unless you look backward or forward to *other* words. . . . Numbers, by contrast, are usually less ambiguous and may be processed with more economy. . . . Small wonder, then, that most researchers prefer working with numbers alone, or getting the words they collect translated into numbers as quickly as possible. . . . [However,] converting words into numbers, then tossing away the words gets a researcher into all kinds of mischief. . . . Focusing solely on numbers shifts our attention from substance to arithmetic, and thereby throws out the whole notion of qualitativeness; one would have done better to have started with numbers in the first place. (p. 546)

The use of computer software packages can enhance a researcher's analysis. As Fielding and Lee (1998) note, the work of researchers in the past two decades has been transformed by computerized software programs. Software programs can be categorized into two main types. The first consists of *generic software,* which is not specifically designed for qualitative research. There are three types of software in this category: (1) *Word processors* assist the researcher with the typing and organizing of fieldnotes and interviews, as well as developing an organizing scheme for these data; (2) *text retrievers* can quickly sort through a range of data to find a specific pattern or "string" of characters to enable the researcher to identify themes or topics within a large body of data; and (3) *textbase managers* are large database systems that allow for the retrieval of semistructured information, which is entered into *records* and *fields.*

A second type of software is specifically designed for qualitative data analysis. These packages fall into four types: (1) code and retrieve programs; (2) code-based theory-building programs; (3) conceptual network-building programs; and (4) textual mapping software. Code and retrieve programs allow codes to be assigned to particular segments of text and make for easy retrieval of code categories using sophisticated Boolean search functions (i.e., using *and, or,* and *not* to filter your data). Code-based theory-building programs allow the researcher to analyze the systematic relationships among the data, codes, and code categories. Some programs provide a rule-based systems approach that allows for the testing of hypotheses in the data, while others allow for a visual representation of the data. Conceptual network-building and textual-mapping software programs allow researchers to draw links between code categories in their data. Researchers see these last two as "add-on" features to their code-based theory-building programs. Miles and Huberman (1994) note the following uses of computer-assisted software in analyzing qualitative data.

USES OF COMPUTER SOFTWARE IN QUALITATIVE STUDIES

Making notes in the field

Writing up or transcribing fieldnotes

Editing: correcting, extending, or revising fieldnotes

Coding: attaching keywords or tags to segments of text to permit later retrieval

Storage: keeping text in an organized database

Search and retrieval: locating relevant segments of text and making them available for inspection

Data "linking": connecting relevant data segments to each other, forming categories, clusters, or networks of information

Memo-ing: writing reflective commentaries on some aspect of the data as a basis for deeper analysis

Content analysis: counting frequencies, sequence, or locations of words and phrases

Data display: placing selected or reduced data in a condensed, organized format, such as a matrix or network, for inspection

Conclusion-drawing and verification: aiding the analyst to interpret displayed data and to test or confirm findings

Theory building: developing systematic, conceptually coherent explanations of findings; testing hypotheses

Graphic mapping: creating diagrams that depict findings or theories

Preparing interim and final reports

Source: Miles & Huberman, 1994, p. 44.

Fielding and Lee (1998) note that the field of qualitative software development has grown over time, and there is a growing and extensive international community of software users. The growing usage of computer software programs as tools in qualitative analysis raises a number of methodological and theoretical concerns regarding data analysis and interpretation of qualitative data. Sharlene Hesse-Biber (1995) discusses five fears that critics frequently express in discussing the use of computer software. The first of these fears is that computer programs will separate the qualitative researcher from the creative process. Some analysts liken the experience of doing qualitative work to "artistic work," and the use of computer technology is often seen as incompatible with art. There is a strong fear that the use of computer programs will turn the researcher into an "unthinking and unfeeling human being."

Another fear is that the line between quantitative and qualitative analysis will be blurred by imposing the logic of survey research onto qualitative research and by sacrificing in-depth analysis for a larger sample. These concerns stem from the fact that computer software programs now permit the easy coding and retrieval of large numbers of documents. The volume of data now collected for some qualitative studies is comparable to the volume collected in quantitative research, and there is the fear that qualitative research will be reduced to quantitative research.

Another fear that is common for computer-assisted research is that the software may dictate the definition of a particular field of study. Computer software program structures often set requirements for how a research project should proceed. This raises concerns among some critics that computer software programs will determine the types of questions asked and specific data analysis plans. Furthermore, another concern that researchers have is that they will now have to be more accountable for their analysis as computer-assisted software programs provide the capability of counting the number of code instances rather than just using the terms *few, some,* or *many.* It is in this sense that programs for analyzing qualitative data require researchers to be more explicit in the procedures and analytical processes they went through to produce their data and their interpretations. Asking qualitative researchers to be more explicit about their method and holding their interpretations accountable to tests of validity and reliability will raise some controversies: Should there be strict tests of validity and reliability for qualitative data? Last, there is also the fear of the loss of confidentiality through the use of multimedia data.

What Computer Software Programs Are Out There, and Which One Should I Choose?

A range of both commercial and noncommercial software products are on the market. Student researchers should take advantage of a number of Web sites that describe what programs are available and include information on how to download them and give them a test run. Probably the most comprehensive of these is the CAQDAS networking site (http://caqdas.soc.surrey.ac.uk/links.html; see also di Gregorio & Davidson, 2008; Lewins & Silver, 2007). Hesse-Biber, for example, used HyperRESEARCH (www.researchware.com) to code her data from her study of anorexia and black adolescent body image, which we talked about earlier in this chapter. However, in selecting a software program that meets your own unique study requirements and general work style, Hesse-Biber and Crofts (2008) suggest the following set of reflective questions to consider. This checklist is partly derived from the wisdom of Renata Tesch (1990), Eben Weitzman and Matthew Miles (1995; Weitzman, 2000), and John Creswell and Ray Maietta's (2003) work on computer software usage and the evaluation of specific computer software programs.

The perspective taken by Hesse-Biber and Crofts (2008, p. 665) is grounded in a user's perspective. It is important for users to prioritize which questions are most relevant for their research agendas.

1. What type of computer system do you prefer to work on or feel most comfortable working on? Does your operating system support the program? Do you need to upgrade your system or perhaps purchase a new computer to meet the requirements of a specific program? Do you like the look and feel of a program's interface? What excites you about this program at a visceral level?

2. Does the look and feel of the program resonate with your own research style? What is your analysis style? How do you plan to conduct your analysis, and how might computers fit into that style? How might each program enhance (or detract from) your analysis? In what sense? For example, do you plan on coding most of your data? If so, what type of coding do you want to do? How do you prefer to retrieve your data, and how important is it to you to be able to look at the full context from which the data were taken? Are you a visual person? Do you like to see relationships and concepts selected in some type of diagram or network? Do you anticipate quantifying any of your data?

3. On what research project or set of projects do you anticipate using a computer software program? For example, what type of data does your project consist of? Textual? Multimedia?

4. How do you want a computer program to assist you? What tasks do you want to mechanize? What specific tasks do you want computerized? You may not want all the features espoused by these programs. What are your expectations of what the program will be able to assist you in doing? Are your expectations realistic?

5. What resources are available to you? Which programs can your computer support? Which programs can you afford? What resources (time, personnel, material) necessary for learning how to use this program are available to you?

6. What are your preconceptions about these programs? How have other users' opinions, product marketing, or other sources of information about qualitative data analysis software programs influenced your preferences? Are your assumptions about programs accurate? What more would you like to learn about particular programs?

7. Which of the above questions or concerns are most important to you? How would you rank-order what are your most important factors in considering a software purchase? What questions have been left out? (Hesse-Biber & Crofts, 2008, p. 665)

Reflecting on these types of user concerns before attempting to select a qualitative data analysis program puts users in the position to critically evaluate for themselves how each program might integrate into their unique research projects. By trying out free demonstration versions and reading through each program's features, as well as looking at examples of how their colleagues use these programs, researchers can get a feel for how each of these programs may be of use to them. Going through this checklist serves to enhance user empowerment and program accountability. It is important to also note that there is no technological tool, regardless of its features, that can independently "perform" your analysis (Hesse-Biber & Crofts, 2008).

Computers hold the promise of revolutionizing the way researchers conduct their analysis, but they also come with a set of caveats for the qualitative analyst. Researchers who use these programs should assess their own strengths and weaknesses as well as the implications of using computer software programs to analyze qualitative data. We recommend that you try these programs when appropriate and see how they work for you.

How Can I Use a Computer-Assisted Program to Analyze My Qualitative Data?[1]

Sharlene Hesse-Biber offers a look behind the scenes into what computer-assisted programs have done for her research projects and what changes have occurred in qualitative research with the advent of these technologies.

BEHIND THE SCENES WITH SHARLENE HESSE-BIBER: A DATA ANALYSIS TALE

Dissertation data had been occupying one room of my apartment, often spread out over the floor, organized into neat and sometimes not-so-neat piles. Many months had been spent in this room devoted to managing and analyzing a set of almost eighty in-depth intensive interviews. With scissors in hand, I would read over a set of new interviews and proceed to "cut up" all relevant chunks of textual data from each interview and paste similarly coded data bites into a separate file folder. However, each time my analytical/conceptual scheme changed, categories would have to be completely altered. If I wanted to apply a different code to the same chunk of text,

(Continued)

(Continued)

I needed to recopy the segment. As my data analysis proceeded, I found myself revising and deleting some previously coded category. This also required me to photocopy interviews again and repeat part of the coding process. My ability to assign multiple codes to text and to recode different segments was often thwarted by the "cut and paste" procedure. While I liked the idea of seeing and handling all of my data in its entirety, as the interviews increased, it became more and more difficult to see the "big picture."

Creating memos on different aspects of my analysis and coding procedure was a critical step in assisting with the discovery of some major code categories and themes in my data as well as relationships between code categories. It was during this time that I discovered a set of "key sort" data cards or "edge-punched cards." These cards were the new technological rage at the time, especially among anthropologists working in the late 70's and early 80's. They were 8" × 3" cards ringed with holes that were numbered across the edge of the card. I placed all my interview material on these cards and proceeded to code the data on each card by punching open the numbered ring corresponding to that code. You could conceivably have up to one hundred codes for any given card, but usually I had between five or twenty codes per card, given the information contained on any given hole card.

Periodically, I would assemble or "stack up" all the cards and begin to retrieve my code categories from the deck of cards using a rod, or what I called my "knitting needle," which was inserted through the circular holes in my stack of cards. If I was interested in retrieving a particular code or set of codes for my study, I would put my knitting needle through those relevant code numbered holes, shake the pile, and out would drop all the data chunks for that code. In fact, I would sometimes have a great time shaking the deck, and I can remember curious onlookers asking me if I was "ok" as all my coded cards came tumbling out of the pile so I could retrieve my data bounty to analyze. I would repeat this process of coding and retrieving as my analysis process proceeded by hand until I felt I had sufficiently captured the meaning of a specific code by comparing and contrasting different chunks of similarly coded data or latched onto a significant pattern in my data.

Source: Hesse-Biber & Crofts, 2008, pp. 655–656.

Hesse-Biber's analysis tale is not that unfamiliar to those who have struggled with the mounting textual data they collect from interviewing and/or audio and video materials, as well as still images such as photographs that make up their qualitative data collection materials. The analysis process itself generates many memos, fieldnotes, and additional nonnumeric data. Until several decades ago, as Hesse-Biber notes, most of this manipulation of data was done manually (Hesse-Biber & Crofts, 2008). Qualitative research consisted of amassing and manipulating data by hand, using these types of manual procedures. These procedures often consisted of copying and retrieving segments of text, cutting up textual data and pasting them onto note cards as a means of developing categorization systems, and sometimes color-coding these data as a means of sorting and sifting through materials more easily. The use of a computer-assisted software program can definitely provide a quicker way to code and retrieve your qualitative data.

Pfaffenberger (1988) notes that qualitative data analysis breaks down qualitative material into its "constituent elements that need to be 'compared,' named, and classified so that their nature and interaction becomes clear" (p. 26). Comparing aspects of your qualitative data analysis requires the researcher to decontextualize and recontextualize these data (Tesch, 1990). Decontextualization means that segments of your data are first looked at in isolation from their particular contexts. These segments are linked to other decontextualized segments that appear to contain the same meanings and ideas. Assembling like segments into groupings or categories, a process known as recontextualizing, provides a mechanism for discovering larger themes and patterns in your data that reveal a new level of understanding of your data as a whole. Researchers often repeat the process of decontextualizing and recontextualizing their data, and this is where a computer software program can help with the coding and retrieval of text segments. A computer software program's ability to assist with these basic analytical procedures also allows researchers to test and question the themes and ideas they have discovered, by searching for negative cases to question the original thematic groupings of their data.

It is important to remember that there are a variety of analytical procedures available, which range from taking a grounded theory approach to your data to taking a narrative approach, for example. As Hesse-Biber and Crofts (2008) note,

> not all qualitative research approaches and traditions use the inductive analytic methods (such as a "grounded theory approach" to analysis). Narrative analysts are interested in stories and want to code and retrieve narratives looking at their inherent structure, such things as the chronological sequence of events in a narrative. Other researchers prefer to analyze their data utilizing theories prior to their collection of data. Burawoy (1991) suggests an *extended case method* of data analysis that begins with explicit theorizing about what the researcher hopes to find in conducting a given research project. This method then uses the specific research study to test out critical components of the researcher's theoretical framework with the idea data are collected in order to reconfigure existing theory by subjecting them to empirical verification. The researcher's theory drives all aspects of the data project. (p. 658)

We will provide a general grounded theory approach to analyzing qualitative data and understanding how a computer-assisted software program can facilitate the analysis and interpretation process. We cover four analytical and interpretative aspects of the research project: (1) the preparation of data; (2) the exploration phase; (3) the specification/reduction stage; and (4) the reporting of results (see Table 12.1).

Table 12.1 Using Computer Programs to Analyze Qualitative Data

Step 1	Preparation of data
Step 2	Exploration of data
Step 3	Specification/reduction (developing an organizing system)
Step 4	Reporting

Source: All steps adapted from Miles and Huberman, 1994, p. 44, and Kelle, 1995.

The Preparation Phase

Using CAQDAS in the Preparation Phase

Step in Analysis	Computer Program Function
• Make notes in the field. • Make a transcript of data, edit, revise. • Enter and file material. • Store data in a database. • Scan data. • Work out theoretical frame by becoming familiar with the data.	• Type notes into preferred word processing program. Edit and revise transcript. Store and save files. Print out a copy and carefully read through data.

Many qualitative researchers already use some form of computer program, such as Microsoft Word or another word processing program, to accomplish many of the tasks listed here. What is important to note, however, is that these seemingly clerical tasks may seem mechanical but often provide opportunities to begin the analysis of your data. Let's take as an example the task of transcribing data. The act of transcription requires researchers to make some judgments about what they will transcribe, which often amounts to making some important analytical decisions: What type of transcription (a summary or an intact transcription)? Will you transcribe every word and note all situations (both verbal and nonverbal interactions)? How will you transcribe them? Will you take account of what is not said? How do you deal with what is absent in your transcript?

The Exploration Phase

At the data exploration stage, the researcher's goal is often to decontextualize the data into meaningful segments, often labeled with a code. A computer program is useful in attaching a category name to basic units of data (chunks of text) and easily retrieving similarly coded chunks of text for comparison. In this sense, the data are analyzed while they are being collected, and such analysis can lead researchers to change or refine their research questions or approaches to data collection. Contained in these processes are memo writing and rewriting, as well as coding and recoding of data, looking for patterns and relationships between categories or themes, and querying and retrieving code categories. Qualitative analysis also includes a variety of ways to display data, especially by depicting conceptual thinking in terms of a matrix, network diagram, or outline. Computers are useful to many of these analysis and interpretative functions.

Remember that coding is a process, not just a single step of isolating and naming codes. As Strauss (1987) states, we need to learn "how to dimensionalize [codes] and discover their conditions, consequences, and associated interactions and strategies" (p. 154). The coding process consists of the formation of code categories that are driven by the data. Categories are linked and structured through the method of theorizing about the data.

Using CAQDAS in the Exploration and Decontextualizing Phase

Step in Analysis	Computer Program Function
• Read text and think of codes (called indexing or tagging)	• Assign codes
• Assign codes to segments	• Attach codes to text segments; automatic coding of words and phrases
• Clarify codes (if necessary)	• Assign and change codes, create theory memos and attach to text/codes
• Write memos about codes, their interrelations, new directions in research, etc; link codes to research questions	• Memo-ing, theory memos, formulate new questions and hypotheses

A researcher following the grounded theory approach (see Glaser & Strauss, 1967; Glaser, 1978; Strauss, 1987; Strauss & Corbin, 1990) reads carefully and analyzes a small unit of data codes. A computer program allows the researcher to continually ask questions of the data by constantly comparing data; collecting new data on the basis of theoretical sampling; writing memos about codes and their interrelations and new directions; and drawing diagrams. Coding, collecting data, and memo-ing are all interrelated with the goal of generating theory.

The Specification/Data Reduction Phase

Using CAQDAS in the Specification/Data Reduction Phase	
Step in Analysis	**Computer Program Function**
• Link text segments that have the same meaning	• Retrieve text segments by codes or combinations of codes
• Relate concepts to an emerging theory; draw conclusions and test hypotheses	• Retrieve data that meet or fail to meet a range of conditions; display data in a variety of ways to assist with theory building and drawing conclusions. Display data in a matrix or network; test hypotheses.

The Reporting Phase

A large part of the reporting stage consists of retrieving your recontextualized data to begin the process of interpreting meaning. You can think of the reporting state as iterative, in that the researcher gathers data that have been recontextualized and looks again for ways to make meaning of the data that have been reconfigured with the goal of theorizing about what is going on in the data.

Using CAQDAS in the Reporting Phase	
Steps in Reporting	**Computer Program Function**
• Prepare interim and final reports	• Print out reports on codes or combinations of codes; display code segments or send to printer or file
	• Provide frequency counts on codes
	• Display networks or graphs of data
	• Export code counts to statistical program for further analysis

Conclusion

As we end this chapter, we provide you with a list of questions you might consider in undertaking your own evaluation of the *analysis and interpretation* section of your research project. This evaluation checklist is not exhaustive but is meant to highlight some of the important factors you might take into account.

• Overall research question: Is my research question clearly stated? Is the question too broad? Too narrow?

- Data collection: Do the data fit the research question?

- Method: Is the method compatible with the purpose (research question)? How thoroughly and well are your data collection strategies described?

- Sample: How did you choose respondents? Are these respondents a valid choice for your research?

- Analysis: How did you arrive at your specific findings? Are specific analysis strategies talked about? Have you done what you said you would do? Are data analysis approaches compatible with your research question?

- Interpretation: Can readers get a sense (gestalt) of the meaning of your data from your written findings? Are your research findings placed in the context of the literature on the topic? Does the evidence fit your data? Are the data congruent with your research question?

- Validity (issues of credibility and trustworthiness): Why should the reader buy into the validity of the analysis and interpretation? What are some criteria for assessing the validity of your research study? Do participants recognize their own experiences in your analysis and interpretation of the data? Why or why not? Do you provide an audit trail of your work—the analytical steps you provide as evidence of credibility? The more transparent you are about these issues, the higher the probability that your reader will find your findings trustworthy and credible.

- Conclusion: Does your conclusion reflect your research findings? Have you overstated what you have found (i.e., gone beyond your research findings)?

Qualitative data analysis and interpretation proceed as an iterative—back and forth—process, keeping in mind the metaphor we suggested in Chapter 8 of putting together the pieces of a puzzle, and the spiral metaphor discussed in the Chapter 9. (We end with a little advice from Sharlene Hesse-Biber, 2010, pp. 201–202.)

BEHIND THE SCENES WITH SHARLENE HESSE-BIBER

A few pieces of data can go a long way in gathering meaning, but one should not be tempted to gather too much data while failing to reflect on or analyze the information bit by bit. A creative spirit and a set of analytical and interpretative skills are imperative to this process. *Coding* and *memo*-ing are two powerful techniques we might employ in the process of understanding and interpreting our data, practicing reflexivity is also incredibly important. We may encounter false starts, as well as moments of great discovery and generation of theoretical insight into the analysis and interpretation of our data. This type of work is not for the fainthearted. It often requires attention to detail, perseverance in the face of chaos, as well, and a knack for tolerating ambiguity. The writing up of our research also requires that we, the researchers, be reflective of our own positionality—the set of social and economic attributes we bring to bear in analyzing and interpreting our data. It is a journey well worth taking, for it ultimately leads to a better understanding of the lived reality of those whom we research. (Hesse-Biber, 2010, pp. 201–202)

Glossary

Analytical categories: Analytical categories are developed to classify the more focused analytical codes. They take into account the meaning of concepts from the respondent's perspective.

Analytical codes: Analytical codes, developed from literal codes, are not tied as tightly to the text itself but begin to rely on the researcher's insights for drawing out interpretation.

Analytical dimensions: As more and more interviews are analyzed, you may come up with several analytical dimensions, which can be viewed as subcodes of analytical categories.

Coding: Coding generally consists of identifying "chunks" or "segments" in your textual data and giving each of these a label (code). Coding is the analytical strategy that many qualitative researchers employ to help them locate key themes, patterns, ideas, and concepts that may exist within their data.

Descriptive codes: Descriptive codes within data are discovered during the analysis process and eventually can be used to generate a set of key *concepts* (categories), which are much more analytical.

Focused coding: A focused coding procedure allows for the building and clarifying of concepts. In focused coding, a researcher examines all the data in a category, compares each piece of data with every other piece, and finally builds a clear working definition of each concept, which is then named.

Grounded theory: This is a form of analysis that starts from an engagement with the data and ends with a theory that is generated from or "grounded" in the data.

Literal codes: Literal codes are codes consisting of words that appear within the text itself. They are usually descriptive codes.

Memo-ing: Memo-ing, or memo writing, is the writing of documents that track any ideas the researcher comes up with when reading notes, interviews, and other data. Memo-ing should be done at all points in the analysis process.

Power dynamics: There are important power dynamics within the interviewer/interviewee relationship that can affect the interpretation of research results. In Chapter 5 (In-Depth Interview), we noted that certain social attributes between researcher and researched can impact issues of power and authority in the research process.

Discussion Questions

1. Discuss the pros and cons of using computerized analysis tools.

2. How can coding be best used when analyzing data? Are there any drawbacks to using coding? Is there such a thing as too many codes? Can this become problematic?

3. What accord does the researcher owe the researched during the analysis phase—should the researched have a say in how he or she is represented?

4. How does the relationship between researcher and researched affect the interpretation process?

5. Explain the grounded theory approach to data analysis. How is this process inductive?

6. What is the relationship between analysis, interpretation, and writing?

7. How can a qualitative researcher check the validity of his or her findings?

Resources

Suggested Web Sites

Computer-Assisted Qualitative Data Analysis Software

http://caqdas.soc.surrey.ac.uk/

This Web site offers workshops and training sessions (as well as general information) about using computer-assisted analysis programs to analyze qualitative data. This is a great Web site for those interested in exploring computer-assisted analysis.

http://onlineqda.hud.ac.uk/Introduction/index.php

A comprehensive Web site that covers different types of qualitative data analysis procedures.

http://onlineqda.hud.ac.uk/Which_software/index.php

A Web site that describes the range of software programs to analyze qualitative data.

Relevant Journals

Acta Sociologica

Critical Sociology

Evaluation

Qualitative Inquiry

Sociological Methods and Research

Note

1. This section is adapted from Hesse-Biber and Crofts (2008).

CHAPTER 13

The Writing and Representation of Qualitative Research

The writing up of your research is the final phase in a qualitative research project. Presenting research findings effectively is vital to ensuring that our research endeavors contribute to the larger knowledge base on our topics. In the last chapter, we reviewed how data are prepared, coded and analyzed, and interpreted. Once we have analyzed our data and systematically "made sense" of the findings, those findings need to be communicated to an audience. Before writing up our findings, it is important to assess the audience for whom we are writing.

Who Is Your Audience?

While this may seem like a trivial question, it is critical to the way you decide how to write up your findings. Is your audience already knowledgeable about your topic? Knowing this information will enable you to determine how specific you need to be in explaining terms, concepts, and so on. It will also let you know how much explicit detail and preparation are required in the text as opposed to more general referencing of ideas and going directly into the research aspect of the paper. Knowing your audience also means placing your paper in a social context. You should think about the extent to which audience demographics play a role in the reception of your ideas. For example, how might the age, race, gender, or class of your audience affect your conveyance of the specific ideas of your paper? If you are writing this paper for a course, to what extent are you writing this paper for your instructor? If your research is being funded by a particular organization with a specific stake in what you find out, do they have a given set of expectations for this research project? To what extent are you obligated to report certain research findings? Are you free to report what you feel is important as opposed to what a specific stakeholder deems important (or unimportant—they perhaps may even want certain findings suppressed)? To what extent do you take into account these various audience factors? How do you feel about targeting your findings to a specific audience? What are the ethical implications of how you choose to represent your findings? To what extent do you feel you have compromised your ability to report your research findings in a way that you feel is true to your data? All these questions are key implications of your research writing, and it is important to take time to consider them carefully before embarking on the writing and publication of your work.

Of note to researchers writing up their projects is the degree of formality in tone taken with their readers. This highly personal choice is dependent on the researcher and the audience, as well as the relationship the researcher chooses to have with the reader. Writing in a more informal tone may in fact serve to include the reader on the journey of the research process. Researchers should be conscious that the degree of formality may change with the chapter topic, or even with subtopics of a particular text.

Now, let's turn to the writing up of the project itself. Your research can be presented in numerous ways. A standard model for a research article generally follows the initial research design plan. Table 13.1 shows the standard model.

Table 13.1   Template for Write-up

1. Title Page and Abstract
2. Introduction:
   (a) Research Topic
   (b) Research Purpose
   (c) Guiding Research Questions
3. Literature Review
4. Research Design
   (a) Method(s) of Data Collection
   (b) Sampling Procedure(s)
   (c) Ethical Considerations
5. Data Analysis and Interpretation Procedures
6. Conclusion and Implications
7. References and Appendices

Writing Up a Qualitative Research Project: Steps for Getting It Done

We break down the process of writing a paper into a series of steps that encompass the template provided in Table 13.1. Writing up a research project is not always linear; you may not follow the exact sequence we gave you in the template. Writing is largely a "two steps forward and one step back" process. Nevertheless, it is important to remember that writing qualitative papers is iterative in that you collect data, analyze it, and go back, collect more, and so on. Max Van Manen (2006) describes the particular situation of qualitative writing as follows:

> Qualitative writing may be seen as an active struggle for understanding and recognition of the lived meanings of the lifeworld, and this writing also possesses passive and receptive rhetoric dimensions. It requires that we be attentive to other voices, to subtle significations in the way that things and others speak to us. In part, this is achieved through contact with the words of others. These words need to touch us, guide us, stir us. (p. 713)

We must note that this chapter deals specifically with writing up a qualitative project. For those interested in quantitative research reporting, or who seek more information on writing up a quantitative project, we refer you to the following Web site from Carleton College, which offers advice and resources: http://serc .carleton.edu/sp/carl_ltc/quantitative_writing/index.html.

Title Page and Abstract

The title of your work needs to be as clear and explicit as is possible. Use key words to describe your title; the key words will most likely alert researchers to your work, so choose them carefully and make sure that your title accurately describes your paper. For example, if your study is an ethnographic study of college-age students, you may want to prominently use the words *ethnography* and *college/ university students* in your title. It may be useful to have a shorter title and then a slightly longer subtitle. Be sure to include your full name and affiliation on the title page, including the date and any pertinent contact information. The abstract should contain the title of your paper as well as your name and the name of any coauthors, with appropriate affiliations. An abstract is a self-contained summary of your paper (about 150 to 250 words), which should give your reader a sense of what your paper will reveal. The first two sentences of your abstract should convince the reader about the importance of your paper. Next, state your specific research problem or purpose. Note the methods you employ and, finally, what you found out or what conclusion you came to through the research project. Be sure to highlight only your most important findings; don't try to get everything into an abstract. Finally, remember that your abstract functions as a self-contained overview of your study. It should alert readers to what you are doing and your main point without requiring them to read the body of your work.

Introduction

Setting up your problem by introducing it in the first set of paragraphs is a chance to market your paper to your audience. Consider the following questions as issues to answer within the first few pages of your paper: Why should anyone read it? What do you intend to show that they should care about? You need to be sure that you grab readers with your first sentence and then quickly tell them what you intend to do in the paper. That is, you must alert your readers to the goals of your paper. The following is a list of questions you might want to ask yourself as you finish your introduction and statement of your research problem:

- Does your introduction place your research problem in a broader research context?

- Does this placement contribute to the significance of your project?

- Do you state the research problem early in your introductory section?

- Is your research problem stated clearly?

- Are you asking any subquestions?

Literature Review

The literature review serves several important functions. First, it informs the reader that you are knowledgeable about your research problem and that you have a good grasp of the major theoretical and empirical research related to your research problem. The literature review is a summary of a body of work that is related to your problem; moreover, it is a critical evaluation of what you see as the relevant issues and questions that need to be addressed in other research (primarily yours). It also shows the audience that you can integrate and synthesize a range of different but interrelated studies that deal with your research issues. Reading your literature review, the reader needs to be left with a sense that you have developed some unique insights, theories, or ideas about the research topic and that your specific research problem(s) will in fact contribute substantially to ongoing discussion in the area of inquiry you have chosen for your research.

Remember that in a qualitative project, the literature review is often not collected all at once in the beginning of your project. As a qualitative project seeks to discover theories, an iterative process is more useful, whereas a quantitative project demands a literature review that is conducted up front because the priority is to test out hypotheses. Figure 13.1 depicts the iterative process and role of the literature review in qualitative research projects.

The following is both a checklist and a short self-evaluation to apply to your literature review:

- How well does your literature review frame the context of your specific research problem?

- Have you referred to the most relevant literature regarding your research problem?

• Is your literature review current? Have you made sure to include the most recent research conducted in the given inquiry area?

• Have you identified the key readings and authors in this area?

• Does your literature review bring out the significance of your research problem?

Figure 13.1 Iterative Model of a Qualitative Literature Review

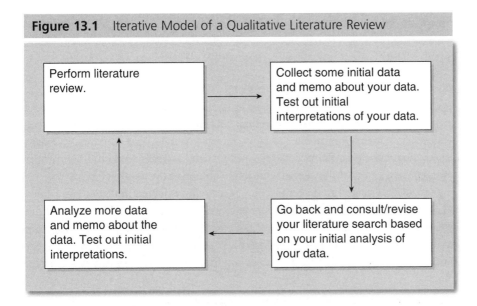

Research Design

Your research design section is very important because it tells the reader specifically how you plan to tackle your research problem. This section describes the details of your research design. Let's look at the parts of this design you need to describe.

Specific method(s). You should make a convincing case that your specific qualitative methods approach is the most appropriate for answering your research question. Make an argument that this data collection method fits your research question. Is the method compatible with the purpose? How thoroughly and well are your data collection strategies described? The length of your methods section depends on the particular set of expectations of your audience. If you plan to have your research report as part of a student project in a research methods class, your instructor would probably want you to devote some space to specifically outlining your methods procedures. If you plan to send this report to a journal, look at the set of expectations the particular journal has in terms of how much detail you need to give to this section and other sections as well.

Sampling procedure. You should specify how you collected your data. Describe your sampling procedure (i.e., convenience sample, snowball sample, etc.). Provide details about your specific sample: How many subjects are there in your sample? Are there any demographic characteristics of your sample that are relevant to your research questions? You might also talk about some of the limitations of your particular sampling procedure. How were the respondents chosen and how many were used? Are they a valid choice for this research project's goals? As Ponterotto and Grieger (2007) wrote in their study on communicating qualitative research, in writing up the sampling procedure, researchers need to describe "the research participants in sufficient detail to allow readers to get a clear picture of the salient characteristics" without giving away any identifying information (p. 413).

Ethical considerations. You need to explain in detail how you have protected the confidentiality of your respondents. Be as specific as you can in talking about the steps you have taken to ensure respondent confidentiality. You may want to include your consent form letter in the appendix of your research paper. You may also want to talk about the specific procedures you took into account to ensure that proper ethics protocols were followed. In addition to obtaining the consent of your respondents, did you make sure to remove any identifying information from your interview materials? Was your project approved by an institutional review board, or did you need to make adjustments to your research design based on specifications from a supervising ethics committee? This may also be a good place to address researcher positionality and reflexivity as processes and foundations that frame your research.

Data Analysis and Interpretation Procedures

The analysis and interpretation procedure should be mentioned in the methods section of your writing. You should address the specific procedures and techniques you employed for data analysis. For example, in Chapter 12, we discussed a variety of data analysis techniques you might apply to qualitative data. One of the techniques described was a grounded theory analysis. If you applied such an analysis, you would need to talk about this technique and how you used it to analyze your data. You need to convince the reader that your data analysis procedure(s) will allow you to answer your research question. How will you go about interpreting your data (making sense of what you found in your analysis)?

Sometimes in the writing process, we give data analysis a backstage role, once it has been completed. While the data are often brought out of their context, it is important to be reflexive on how we want to use the data we have collected. Before going on to discuss the various choices on how we can use our data, I want to stress what Ron Chenail (1995) calls the "star role" our data plays in the writing-up process.

> I believe that the data, which have been painfully collected, should "be the star" in the relationship. By this, I mean the main focus in qualitative research is the data itself, in all its richness, breadth, and depth. When all is said and done, the "quality" in a qualitative research project is based upon how well you have done at collecting quality data. So, it only seems natural that when it comes time to present "the fruits of your labor," you should make every effort to feature the data in your presentations.

It is important to decide how you will present your data. For example, you can provide visuals of your data in the form of charts and diagrams. Of course, this will depend on the original format of your data. If you have done qualitative interviews, you might want to present excerpts of your interview transcripts to illustrate a specific finding from your analysis. Some forms of qualitative data can be transformed into numbers. For example, you might provide a demographic table that lists the characteristics of your research sample in terms of their age, race/ethnicity, gender, and so on. Part of what you choose to present as important depends on the specific research problem and the type of sample you have collected.

The bulk of qualitative data, however, often consists of text from interviews or focus groups as well as observations. Your specific analytical technique (i.e., grounded theory) will stress what types of data you will present and how you might present it. Yet, a researcher is often left with lingering questions as to *how much data to present* and *what specific evidence to select from the apparent mounds of data.* Here is where your analysis of the data will lead you to making sense of your data. Very often in the process of analysis, a theory or perspective on the data will emerge. This theoretical perspective will often be tested out along the way, even modified, and your analysis will require data to speak to the efficacy of this given explanation. Go out of your way to look for negative instances that might upend your interpretation.

The process of presenting the findings from your analysis is often to show the reader the analytical steps you have taken to "make sense of your data" and to present *a credible case* that you have well-constructed ideas about what is going on (i.e., your theoretical frame). Choose your data examples wisely because it is through these detailed examples that readers can "logically understand the process from initial coding to theme generation" (Ponterotto & Grieger, 2007, p. 413). The more *transparent* you are with your reader as to how you did your analysis, the more *trustworthiness* and *credibility* you will have with your reader. These steps are important for establishing the validity of your findings.

There are different ways to structure your analysis presentation. What analysis styles might you employ in the presentation of your findings? We can think of different levels of analysis styles as lying along a continuum, depicted in Figure 13.2.

Figure 13.2   Continuum of Data Analysis and Interpretation Presentation Styles

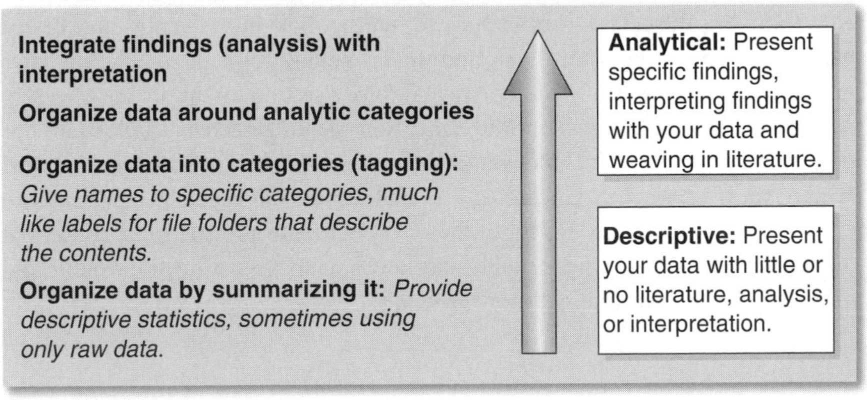

Integrate findings (analysis) with interpretation

Organize data around analytic categories

Organize data into categories (tagging): *Give names to specific categories, much like labels for file folders that describe the contents.*

Organize data by summarizing it: *Provide descriptive statistics, sometimes using only raw data.*

Analytical: Present specific findings, interpreting findings with your data and weaving in literature.

Descriptive: Present your data with little or no literature, analysis, or interpretation.

The simplest level of looking at your data is to present the "raw findings." That is, you report what you found, with no commentary or interpretation. You might do a bit of analysis that would take the form of summarizing the data into descriptive categories and presenting an illustration from your data that describes each of the categories you created. The next level of analysis would also address the question of what the data mean. This level crosses the line between analysis and interpretation of data.

When you interpret your data, you are asking yourself several questions: What theoretical understanding did I generate from my research? Does my analysis back this idea (theory) up and how so? Where does it not support my idea? When writing up your interpretation of your data, it is critical that you explain to your reader how you arrived at your specific interpretation of the data. Can the reader get a sense of the meaning of your interpretation? If you are working with a diverse sample, it is important to include a diversity of voices in both the analysis and interpretation of your data.

It is also important to let the reader know that you have been *reflexive* about your analysis and interpretation and that you have dealt with issues of your own research bias on this specific topic. How did you choose excerpts from the interviews? When presenting your research findings, it is important to show the audience some of the data. Showing the data lends credibility to your interpretive claims, allowing readers to see on what basis you have reached your conclusions. In addition, when the study involves human participants, as in the case of ethnography or any of the interview methods covered in this book, including selections of data allows the voices of the participants to come through. As the process of data analysis greatly reduces the volume of data, and a typical research article allows for minimal inclusion of data (through word or page limits), the selection of *representative quotes* or examples of data should be carefully considered.

Ethically, it is important to provide readers with representative pieces of data or to contextualize anomalous data. As transcript excerpts and the like are selected, it is important to avoid the kind of editing one might expect on "reality television," where videotape is reduced to create the most myopic and sensationalistic portrayals. When working with human subjects, we must attend to the voices of our participants and take care to provide rich, nuanced, and multidimensional portrayals of individual participants and aggregated participant data. For example, let's say we have conducted in-depth interviews with 40 college students regarding their use of social networking Web sites such as MySpace and Facebook. One theme that emerges out of the data during analysis is "Internet bullying." Twenty-three of our participants spoke about this issue, and we have many pages of coded transcripts on this theme. In our final write-up, we may have a section on this theme where we recount the overall findings on this dimension of our research. To illustrate our points, we would likely include two to five representative quotes from our coded transcripts. If we were also including a quote that was not generally representative of the overall findings on this topic, then we would also provide some contextual information so that the reader could better understand the nature of the quote and how it fits in with our findings more generally.

We mentioned earlier the importance of validity. Do readers resonate with your specific analysis and interpretation? This is a type of validity check based on their overall assessment of how valid they feel your analysis is. Let's return to Ron Chenail for advice on writing up your qualitative findings. He suggests that a good way to present qualitative data is a process that looks something like this: data presentation → talk about data presented → more data presented → more talk about data, and so on. The term he employs for this type of presentation is *juxtaposition* (Chenail, 1995). He suggests that in addition to this, we should think about "weaving in" some research literature to support our point of view along the way.

BEHIND THE SCENES WITH RON CHENAIL

In qualitative research, juxtaposition is also the key to producing a quality presentation or paper. To do so, you have to juxtapose data excerpts with your talk about the data. Be it in the presentation of categories, themes, taxonomies, typologies, pictures, or drawings, the essence of presenting qualitative research comes down to how well you are able to juxtapose the data with your descriptions, explanations, analysis, or commentaries.

Also involved in this juxtaposition of data and talk about the data is how you choose to use "the literature" in this weave. Do you annotate the data by citing relevant previous studies or theoretical pieces? Do you contrast the data you have collected with what has been previously said in the literature about similar data? Do you use the data to guide you to areas in the literature you had not previously considered? Do you triangulate your data with the literature as a way of validating your observations? In all of these choices, juxtaposition is still the central concern!

In this process of juxtaposition, your emphasis should be on staying close to the data. The true art of presenting qualitative research is to be restrained by your data. Don't overstate the data and don't understate it as well. Keep the whole process as simple as possible: Look at the data and record that what you see—Report nothing more and nothing less! If you keep to that aesthetic, your data will help to support the validity of your analysis and your analysis will help to feature the richness of your data.

An important concept to keep in mind as you juxtapose your data and your talk about the data is that of rhythm. By rhythm, I mean for you to create a template for representing your data so that there is a recognizable pattern throughout the Analysis or Findings section of your paper. In this way, the readers can begin to read in a rhythm.

To accomplish this rhythm, you need to structure each phase of your data representation in a similar pattern. For example, the following is a common way in which your findings can be displayed:

Section Heading

Present the Distinction or Finding

(Continued)

(Continued)

Introduce the First Data Exemplar of this Distinction

Display the First Data Exemplar of this Distinction

Comment Further on the First Data Exemplar of this Distinction

Make Transition to Second Data Exemplar of this Distinction

Display the Second Data Exemplar of this Distinction

Comment Further on the Second Data Exemplar of this Distinction

Make Transition to the Next Data Exemplar of this Distinction and Repeat the Pattern Until the Closing of this Section

Source: R. J. Chenail, "Presenting Qualitative Data," *The Qualitative Report,* Volume 2, Number 3, December 1995. Used by permission.

Chenail emphasizes that throughout the analysis writing-up process, using a pattern to present data will provide a beneficially structured layout that allows for both data presentation and commentary.

Conclusions and Implications

The conclusion generally includes a summary of the major research interpretations (findings and what they mean) that are directly linked to answering your research question and subquestions. It should be clear to the reader that your research questions support the answering of your particular problem or particular contributions of the study. Conclusions may also include a brief review of the limitations of the study and suggestions for future research. Finally, your conclusion should tie together the major research findings. Your concluding section might include a restatement of your thesis in light of the evidence you have supplied to the reader; it is yet another opportunity to convince your reader of the trustworthiness and credibility of your research project. The conclusion is your final chance to make a lasting impression on your reader. It is also important to remember that this is only one research paper; try not to claim that you have done more than you have. Don't paper over issues that remain, and be careful not to give the impression that your work has solved all aspects of your research problem. Harry Wolcott's (2001) advice to students is to be modest and practice restraint, especially when giving your personal opinion as to what your findings mean, and be sure to stick close to your data. In concluding a qualitative study, Wolcott (2001) suggests practicing some of the following techniques:

Qualitative researchers seem particularly vulnerable to the tendency—and urge—to go beyond reporting what is and to use their studies as platforms for making pronouncements of what ought to be. A critical divide separates the realm of the observable from the realm of judgments as to what is good and better. . . . There is nothing wrong with offering personal opinion or professional judgment. But it is vitally important to label them as such, and to search out and acknowledge their origins in your thinking. While you're at it, you might give some thought to why we feel so duty-bound to come up with conclusions, and why the conclusions are supposed to be filled with cheery optimism. . . . My suggestions for anyone new to academic writing is to work toward a conservative closing statement that reviews succinctly what has been attempted, what has been learned, and what new questions have been raised. (pp. 121–122)

The conclusion section can also be a place where you suggest how your research can be taken in new directions for exploring your research problem. What are the new questions this project brings up that may be worth exploring in the future? What implications does this have for existing research? Furthermore, the conclusion can also be where you as an author and researcher can look outside the immediate space of the research and suggest not just the academic but also social consequences or benefits of your research. Are there any social policy implications that are derived directly from your study? Are there particular voices or experiences that your study uncovered that are not frequently discussed in research or in mainstream media?

References and Appendices

The references and appendices are not to be overlooked in writing up a research project. Here is where you offer additional information and even proof that what you have written in the paper can be corroborated against other sources and where you perhaps give room to detailed data you could not provide within the main text. Be sure that your references are in proper format. If your paper is part of a course assignment, your course instructor may dictate the format. If you are submitting your paper for publication, you would need to look up the required article format for that particular publisher. Note also that some journals require a template different from the one we propose here, so you may need to modify this template organization and adapt your writing to fit the specific requirements of the journal or publisher.

Appendices are often used to place more specific and detailed information such as a questionnaire or interview schedule you used in your study. Not all papers require an appendix, but it is important to ask yourself if an appendix would be beneficial to the reader's understanding of your paper, or whether you might better summarize some of the appendices and place them in the body of your paper. If the former is the better option, make sure your appendices are similarly formatted and readable in relation to the rest of the paper. Appendices can be extremely useful in instructing other researchers of your specific forms and data collection techniques and as such can be critiqued just as heavily as other parts of the paper.

Editing and Revising Your Research Paper

Very often, students find that they are strapped for time in getting out their final research paper and forgo a thorough reading of their paper for editorial changes and then for substantive revisions of the paper. The following are some basic editorial tips for going over your paper, even when you are short on time.

- Look for repetition. You may find that you tend to repeat your ideas and even words or phrases.

- See where you can say something in one word instead of two or three.

- Stick to the active voice because it conveys action. Avoid the passive voice.

- Does your writing assume too much? It is important to ask whether or not your audience is expected to have some prior knowledge of a term or idea that you mention but do not elaborate on in your paper. You may need to spell things out in more detail if your audience is unfamiliar with your research topic. If your audience is familiar with the topic, make sure that the level of knowledge assumed is pitched to your audience.

- Structure of your paper: Did you answer your overall research question? Go over the basic outline of your paper. Do the parts fit together? Do you have transitions from one idea or point to the next? Are you consistent in the usage of terms?

- Grammar and basic formatting: Have you proofread your paper, looking for grammatical errors and spelling errors? Check the format of citations and references. Are your major headings and subheadings consistent?

- What is the tone of your paper? Here again your audience is key. What are their expectations for how formal or informal the writing needs to be?

- Seek perspective and feedback on your paper: Perhaps it might be good to wait a few days before going back to your original paper. You might want to save your paper as a PDF file and use the read-aloud feature to listen to your paper. Also useful is asking a colleague to read your paper and provide feedback.

How Do I Represent the Voices of My Respondents?

It is important to consider the issue of representation: From whose perspective do we write our research paper? For example, the ethnographer John Van Maanen (1995) conveys the sense of early ethnography's attitude toward the researched, which often resulted in a point of view that one should always "let the ethnographer speak for the data," with minimum interpretation from the researched. He notes the following:

> There once was a time—some might say a dreamtime—when ethnography was read as a straight-ahead cultural description based on the firsthand experience an author had with a strange (to both author and reader) group of

people. Those who wrote ethnographies may have had their doubt about what the adventure of field work taught them and just how "being there" results in an ethnography, but few doubts surfaced in their written products. It seemed as if ethnography emerged more or less naturally from a simple stay in the field. One simply staked out a group, lived with them for a while, took notes on what they said and did, and went home to write it all up. If anything, ethnography looked like a rather pleasant, peaceful, and instructive form of travel writing. (Van Maanen, 1995, p. 1)

Yet little by little, Van Maanen (1995) notes, this important premise of ethnography in particular and qualitative research in general—the authority of the researcher to represent the subject—was itself the target of severe scrutiny. As he notes, "new understandings are gradually altering the way we think about cultural representation practices both past and present" (p. 17). Van Maanen notes that new questions are being raised, including the following:

- What role does the researcher play in the process of interpreting his or her data?

- Should the qualitative researcher allow his or her feelings to enter into the interpretation process?

- Whose point of view is the ethnographer really representing with his or her data? (Van Maanen, 1995, pp. 16–17)

Much of qualitative research entails observation as well as participation between the researcher and the researched. The power of the researcher resides along all points of the research process—deciding on the research question(s), the type of research method, and the method of data analysis and interpretation of research findings. Some critics of traditional qualitative research analyses are concerned about representing the life stories of those researched, especially the lived experiences of those oppressed in terms of their race, gender, class, age, and so on (see Wolf, 1996). Emerson (2001) traces the breakdown of the "colonial" model of representing respondents toward a more "reflexive" turn, which breaks down the division between the researcher and the researched:

With the decline of colonialism, conditions that had been taken for granted became uncertain and problematic. Researchers had to obtain more direct approval of the people to be studied, without implicit or explicit reliance upon colonial power. . . . As access and the day-to-day process of fieldwork became more problematic, more dependent on actively establishing working relations with particular people, personal and relational self-consciousness inevitably increased. (p. 23)

Qualitative research itself is becoming more reflective of the power imbalances and issues of authority and representation in the analysis and interpretation of findings (see Hesse-Biber & Leavy, 2004, pp. 409–425). Contemporary qualitative researchers are turning toward a more "interpretative" model of writing, one that acknowledges the existence of multiple realities. There is no one-to-one correspondence between the researcher's understanding and the experiences of "the other." Denzin (1997) notes, "There can never be a final, accurate representation of what was meant or said—only different textual representations of different experiences" (p. 5, as cited in Emerson, 2001, p. 50).

We now turn to a few of ways qualitative researchers can represent the voices of their respondents.

Qualitative Approaches to Representations

The Postmodern Turn Toward Representation

Carol Bailey (1996) contrasts two modes of writing up a research project: One is a **realist tale** and the other a nonrealist tale. In writing a realist tale, the author works within a traditional writing genre that often takes the form of a scholarly publication for a journal, a research paper or report, or a book-length monograph. The presentation of respondents' voices is assumed to be a true reflection of their point of view. The researcher dispenses a realistic tale as the disembodied voice of authority. The writing approach is formal and follows the norms of conventional writing that one may see in a standard book on writing up research results. The realist tale represents a writing paradigm whose very epistemological foundations assume that there is "truth" out there waiting to be captured by the researcher. Bailey (1996) explains the "realist tale" writing style in a bit more detail:

> First, the members in the setting are written about, but any details about the author are absent from the body of the text. The text is written as if anyone who was there would have experienced the same thing, so characteristics of the author, even his or her presence, are irrelevant to the tale. Second, realist tales contain concrete details of what is done, how often, in what order, and by whom. The goal is not to document everything that occurred, but rather to identify the typical activities and patterns of behavior in the setting. Third, realist tales present the members' points of view. The author includes quotations, interpretations by members, summaries of informal interviews, and members' accounts and interpretations of events. Finally, realist tales include interpretations of the setting. The field research is written as if the meaning of the setting is now understood from the perspectives of the members of the setting. (p. 106)

The postmodern turn in writing goes against the positivist model of research writing and strives to push on the boundaries of what is considered "real" and "unreal," often leaving researchers to struggle with exactly how to write up their research findings. This perspective argues that a researcher's power and authority are ever present within the research process and impact how a tale is framed. Postmodern researchers have launched a "crisis of representation" that has in effect changed the very ways that some researchers choose to represent their research findings. The postmodern turn in writing sees all research results as mediated through the researcher's personal values, style, and ethical perspective (Shapiro, 1985–1986, in Richardson, 1995, p. 199). Richardson (1995) talks about several writing styles that strive to take into account the power dynamics in the researcher/researched relationship in order to let the voices of the respondents be heard and to create space for a multitude of tales to be told, each of which is considered to provide, at best, only a partial understanding of the nature of the social world under investigation. An important goal of this type of writing is to allow for the voices of subjugated individuals and peoples to be heard and to provide space for researchers to reflect on their own role within the research process.

Several nontraditional genres of writing style have come out of reflections on the postmodern turn. Laurel Richardson (1995, p. 200) sees a narrative form of writing as a particularly useful mode of "reasoning and representation." The narrative form "reflect[s] the universal human experience of time and link[s] the past, present, and future" (p. 218). A narrative form makes "individuals, cultures, societies, and historical epochs comprehensible as wholes" as it allows people to see themselves as part of a larger system (p. 200). In this way, the narrative fosters dialogue; it "reveal[s] personal problems as public issues, to make possible collective identity and collective solutions" (p. 216). Norman Denzin suggests that a new "moment" of writing is emerging in the postmodern era. Researchers are turning their findings into various "performative" styles, borrowing from the arts and the humanities to create a writing genre not unlike that of theater performance (Denzin, 2000). Postmodern and post-structural perspectives in particular question the belief in the authority of the researcher's gaze. These perspectives stress researchers' accounts as no more than a tale told through a specific set of differences in terms of race, class, gender, and so on. As Denzin and Lincoln (2000) note,

> Poststructuralists and postmodernists have contributed to the understanding that there is no clear window into the inner life of an individual. Any gaze is always filtered through the lenses of language, gender, social class, race and ethnicity. There are no objective observations, only observations socially situated in the worlds of—and between—the observer and the observed. (p. 19)

Experimental writing and traditional writing are not dichotomous choices. Researchers may decide to move to an experimental model in some parts of their research while retaining a more traditional model in other aspects of their writing. We can think of the analysis, interpretation, and writing up of research as an iterative process, as we showed in Figure 13.1. Moving from a traditional to an experimental model can take place at different points during the research process. Switching to a more experimental model of research may require time to retool one's research and writing skills. Some researchers working within a more experimental genre may have to contend with some publishers of journals and monographs who do not embrace this form of scholarship (even though more experimental works are published by mainstream journals and publishing houses).

The student who is writing a paper in a course or writing a dissertation thesis may find that his or her professor or thesis adviser is wedded to a more standard writing style (see Bailey, 1996, p. 108).

The postmodern turn toward representation has, overall, encouraged many researchers, even those who embrace a standard writing format, to write with a more *reflexive* style. A reflexive writing style asks questions such as these: How will I represent myself in the research process? To what extent have my own biases, values, and points of view entered into my selection of the questions I ask, the data I collect and analyze, and what I do and do not see? How much of my own voice is represented? In what sense have I not let others speak for themselves? To write reflectively means to have a good sense of your own positionality on the research you are conducting.

Rhodes (2000) provides qualitative researchers a new way to conceptualize their place within the representation. Rhodes uses the term *ghostwriting* as a metaphor for how researchers can understand their role within the representation of their research findings. With respect to traditional qualitative writing, Rhodes (2000) writes, "I am, therefore, in the text, but rather than being explicit, I am hidden; I am like a ghost" (p. 511). Qualitative researchers are co-creators of knowledge with research participants. The metaphor of ghostwriting suggests a critique of traditional uses of transcripts in the writing up of research reports. Issues of reflexivity and voice are central to this process. Rhodes argues that the traditional approach to writing up interview studies, for example, actually may obscure the role of the researcher in the process. Conventional qualitative writing relies on quoted transcript excerpts, implying that the text represents what the participants have said and may consequently render invisible the role of the researcher in the process.

Alternative Arts-Based Approaches to Writing: Beyond Prose

As a result of theoretical advancements such as postmodernism as well as an increase in interdisciplinarity, the last two decades have seen a surge in alternative approaches to traditional academic prose. **Arts-based research practices** have been particularly robust for producing innovations in the representation of qualitative research. Arts-based practices are

> a set of methodological tools used by qualitative researchers across the disciplines during all phases of social research including data collection, analysis, interpretation, and representation. These emerging tools adapt the tenets of the creative arts in order to address social research questions in holistic and engaged ways in which theory and practice are intertwined. (Leavy, 2009b, pp. 2–3)

Arts-based forms of writing include short stories, poems, novels, and performance scripts. Additional arts-based forms of representation beyond the written word include dance and movement, music, visual art, photography, film and video, and performance. With technological advances such as the Internet, which allow for the storing and dissemination of varied media, these alternative representational forms are more easily done than ever before. With respect to arts-based approaches to writing, we offer the example of poetic work (for a full discussion of arts-based practices, see Leavy, 2009b).

Poetic Approaches to Representation

Poetic approaches to the representation of qualitative research findings are also increasing. Poetic forms can be particularly fruitful for unsettling stereotypes, opening up multiple meanings, expressing complex identity research, and representing subjugated perspectives. There are numerous approaches to research poems, including using participants' precise words, creating composites out of multiple transcripts, and merging theory and literature with researcher and participant voices (Leavy, 2009a). Poetic works are accessible to a diverse audience and are meant to present the complexities of shifting identities within the structural and personal contexts in which they emerge.

Whatever method of representation you choose, it is important to bear in mind that you are a storyteller charged with telling the story of another. You need to find a way to make sense of large amounts of qualitative data in a way that is congruent to the data you have collected and helped create. Let's join David Karp for a final look behind the scenes.

BEHIND THE SCENES WITH DAVID KARP

What you might now imagine is, a big, thick folder that looks like this [shows a folder with several hundreds of pages]. I'm writing now about obligations, so I'm writing a chapter on obligations. This is a folder that has all the data from my current work on obligations. Well, I would produce such a thing. And I would then spend maybe a month sitting and reading these pages. And if I opened this up, you would see that I scribble on every page almost, making comments. Because what I'm trying to do is have a dialogue with this material. I'm trying to envelop myself in this material. I'm trying to live with it, to be with it, you know, for maybe a month. I mean, the insistent question as I'm scribbling in what are now several hundred pages of material is, "What kind of story can I tell from this data? What are the uniformities that I'm seeing in this material?"

You see, everything we write is, in fact, a story we are telling. We are trying to tell a compelling story, but it must be a story that is disciplined by your data. I mean, you just can't tell *any* story. And the reason that I'm spending a month reading all this stuff and having this dialogue, in effect, with the data, is to try to see my way to what are the underlying forms, the underlying dimensions, of an interesting story, a truthful story, that I can tell about the experience of having depression.

(Continued)

(Continued)

I do things like I create a book index. After I've read this whole thing, making marginal notations, I literally create the equivalent of a book index. So, I might have 25 to 30 categories and the pages where I find the data for each one of them. What you're trying to do throughout this whole thing is to gain clarity, continue to gain clarity, on what's there. And at some point you stop and say, "This is what I think is a reasonable story that is consistent with this data, a story to tell about the experience of living with depression." I then create a kind of scenario, a vision, an outline of where the chapter might go. Finally, then, I begin to do the writing.

That's another whole thing, because you learn through the process of writing. You might have a scenario about how this thing is going to go, but once you get into the writing and actually begin to use the data to tell the story, you see that maybe the story is going to be slightly different, or it doesn't quite work the way you first thought about it. And I really believe what Howie Becker says in his book on writing: that writing is not the process of putting down what you think; it's the process of *telling* you what you think. So, for me, the actual act of writing tells me what I have to write. You see, what I'm trying to do is to give a picture of qualitative work where you have to continually get as close as you possibly can to the data on the issues that you think are important. It begins with the construction of an interview guide; then you make voluminous notations on the very first interview that you do, and so on. Even transcribing the interviews. I transcribed all these interviews. I have mixed feelings about that. But there is some real value to transcribing them yourself. It's another way to get close.

The key to all of this is to stay close, you know? Which means writing memos all the time. It means writing one-sentence memos. Sometimes you think you've got an idea and it means writing five pages, sometimes a paragraph, sometimes doing a broader assessment—"What do I have here now?" Let me write a memo about some of the themes. The great strength of qualitative analysis, I think, is that the processes of data collection and data analysis go on simultaneously. And if you don't constantly make efforts to analyze the stuff, right from the git-go. . . . If you just collect your data and wait till the end to do the analysis, you are abusing the great strength of this method. And so even with all of that close work, you still get to the point where you have to create the data books—at least that's how I do it—and work intensively with them. By the time you get to that point, you really know what's in these interviews.

As you can see from Karp's discussion, the ongoing process of writing in qualitative research helps the researcher to figure out what story or stories he or she seeks to tell.

Conclusion

During the writing and representation phase of research, we allow a story to emerge from our research. After all the labor-intensive work of conducting qualitative research, it is the final write-up that comes to represent the study. As we try to effectively communicate our research findings, we must keep our intended audience(s) at the forefront.

Writing well is a skill that can be developed. Good writing takes practice and planning of your time. It is important to set aside some time to write each day, even if only for an hour or so, especially those times when you really don't want to do it. Creating writing goals for your entire research project would be one way to ensure you do not wait to write up your research in a short span of time. It is hard to come up with a fully formed and well-edited research report at the last minute. Taking time to reflect on what you have written often requires that you set aside your work to allow a fresh perspective on your work to take hold. It might even be a good idea to buddy up with a writing partner, someone you meet with on a regular basis to provide each other mutual support and feedback on your writing projects and goals. Providing constructive feedback to others on their writing projects also helps you to become a better researcher and writer.

Glossary

Arts-based research practices: A set of methodological tools that adapt the tenets of the creative arts and are used by qualitative researchers during all phases of social research including data collection, analysis, interpretation, and representation.

Realist tale: A traditional writing format that often takes the form of a scholarly publication for a journal, a research paper or report, or a book-length monograph.

Discussion Questions

1. What is the relationship between analysis, interpretation, and writing?

2. What are the different ways that theory can be used during the interpretation and representation phases? How can a literature review be incorporated into the final write-up?

3. What are the differences between "realist tales" and "nonrealist tales"?

Resources

Suggested Web Sites

Advice on Writing Up Qualitative Research: Des Moines University

http://www.psy.dmu.ac.uk/michael/qual_writing.htm

This Web site, from the Des Moines University Psychology Department, offers useful advice for writing up a qualitative research project in a way that extends beyond use in psychology to sociology and so forth. In addition, it also offers a series of links to online resources for research, writing, and editing.

Relevant Journals

Qualitative Inquiry

Qualitative Research

Sociology

Critical Sociology

Current Sociology

Journal of Sociology

Convergence: The International Journal of Research Into New Media Technologies

Journal of Mixed Methods Research

Sociological Methods and Research

Theory and Research in Education

CHAPTER 14

The Research Nexus

The Future of Qualitative Research

Qualitative research is unique in content, focus, and form. We began this book by explaining that qualitative research is a *holistic process* that explicitly integrates epistemology, methodology, and method in order to develop unique approaches to the study of the social world. The relationship between ontology, epistemology, theory, and method can be thought of as a nexus—the research nexus. As previously explained, by a holistic process we mean that from topic selection to final representation, research involves a series of interrelated choices that all influence one another. A prime consideration in qualitative research is the research nexus and how the methodological and epistemological positions brought to bear on the research process deeply impact the knowledge-building process, including the selection and use of appropriate research tools or methods. By conceptualizing research as a holistic process, we are able to attend to a range of influential factors, including

- Our own topical interests

- Assumptions about what can be known and who can be a knower

- Ethical considerations

- The kinds of research questions we want to ask and to whom

- The kind of data we want to produce

- The tools available for gathering the data

- Practical considerations such as time, money, career, physical safety, and emotional well-being

What Have We Learned About Traditional Qualitative Methods?

Methods are but one part of the research endeavor. The research question and method should always work well together and have a "tight fit." From the vast range of options available to qualitative researchers, from perspectives to methods to representational forms, the qualitative research process truly requires creativity and is accordingly often viewed as a craft. Through the metaphors of dancing with data and spiral approaches to research, we have illustrated the process by which qualitative researchers build knowledge and generate theory by getting to know the data, jumping in and out of the data, and often engaging in inductive and reflexive practice.

This book has focused on the qualitative approach to knowledge-building: the qualitative paradigm. Specifically, we have examined the relationship between ontology, epistemology, methodology, and method—the research nexus—in the knowledge-building process. What we have learned throughout the book is that qualitative approaches to knowledge-building are an important part of creating new knowledge, expanding or contesting old knowledge, and accounting for perspectives that had previously been invisible. Beyond the causal explanations that typically characterize quantitative research, qualitative research yields exploratory, descriptive, and explanatory data and is often used to generate theory.

What's New in Qualitative Research Practice?

The field of qualitative methods is ever changing as new theoretical perspectives such as postmodernism, as well as large-scale trends toward an increasingly globalized and digitized society, challenge researchers to ask new questions that traditional research methods may not adequately address. Methods are not fixed entities, as we have noted; they are flexible and fluid. There are new *emergent qualitative methods* under construction that are interspersed throughout the disciplines, and we have touched on a few of these.

As we near the end of this journey into qualitative research practice, let's take a brief look at the field. Specifically, let's consider the following questions:

- How is the qualitative paradigm changing?
- What cutting-edge practices are reshaping qualitative practice?
- What is the future of qualitative research?

In this book, we have focused on the emergence of the qualitative paradigm and the major research methods and approaches qualitative researchers employ. The past two decades, however, have fostered tremendous methodological innovation, which has strengthened and expanded the boundaries of qualitative practice. We label these new practices *emergent methods* (see Hesse-Biber & Leavy, 2006, 2008). We define emergent methods as arising in order to answer research questions that traditional methods may not adequately address. Evolving theoretical paradigms in the disciplines have opened up the possibilities of the development of innovative methods to get at new theoretical perspectives. . . . Emergent methods are conscious of the link between epistemology (a view on how knowledge is constructed), methodology (the theoretical question/s that informs our research and how it is carried out) and method (the specific tools used to carry out research). Emergent methods are particularly useful in getting at issues of *power and authority* in the research process, from question formulation to carrying out and writing up research findings. We can think of these methods as "hybrid" in the sense that they often borrow and adapt methods from their own disciplines or can cross disciplinary boundaries to create new tools and concepts or re-fashion tools or concepts that exist in order to answer complex and often novel questions. (Hesse-Biber & Leavy, 2006, p. xii)

With respect to qualitative research, we briefly review four categories of emergent qualitative methods: (1) new variations on the traditional qualitative methods reviewed in this book, (2) new or underutilized qualitative methods, (3) arts-based research practices, and (4) emergent technological practices.

Emergent Methods: New Approaches to Old Methods

Emergent research methods can include modifying a traditional method to address new questions from different theoretical perspectives. One of the important things to note about any method is that methods are not fixed entities. Even standard methods can bend and be combined to create tools for newly emerging issues and to unearth previously subjugated knowledge.

For example, some researchers have tweaked ethnographic methods toward the practice of feminist ethnography, which draws on postmodern and feminist approaches to anthropology as well as cultural studies. This form of ethnography differs from traditional ethnography in that it centers on the concerns of women, whose experiences have often been left out of traditional ethnographic research. Also, in the very practice of ethnography, researchers are highly reflexive of the multiple roles they occupy vis-à-vis their informants. The feminist practice of ethnography challenges binary role conceptualizations in that researchers do not adhere to the traditional insider-outsider dualism of traditional ethnographic practice but are aware of the multiple roles which they occupy and the fact that these roles are fluid throughout the research process such that one becomes both insider and outsider, to varying degrees, at the same and different times within the research process.

Emergent Methods: New and Underutilized Methods

Emergent research methods have been developed within and across academic disciplines to yield new kinds of data about the social world. The development of new approaches to research has not, however, occurred in a vacuum; it has developed in relation to emergent theory. Emergent research methods are the logical conclusion to paradigm shifts, major developments in theory, and new conceptions of knowledge and the knowledge-building process. As researchers continue to explore new ways of thinking about and framing knowledge construction, so too do they develop new ways of building knowledge, accessing data, and generating theory. In this sense, new methods and methodologies are theory driven and question driven.

For example, embodiment theory has led to methodological emergence. In a general sense, embodiment theory posits that social actors are embodied (located within bodies), and experience is therefore embodied (occurs within bodies that are relevant to experience). Researchers might consider how bodies become raced, gendered, and sexualized (Leavy, 2009b, p. 183), which is linked to social power (Grosz, 1994). Elizabeth Grosz (1994) notes two main strands of embodiment theory. The inscriptive approach suggests the body is produced within historical contexts and becomes a site where social meanings are created and resisted. The "lived body" approach notes that the mind and body are interconnected, and experience is bodily in a holistic sense. Experience has an integral physical component.

Pillow (2000) developed a *body-centered methodology* in direct response to her research question and research needs (in a project about pregnancy). A body-centered methodology attends to bodily experience as a valuable knowledge source. So, for example, in Pillow's project, she viewed changing physicality as an inextricable aspect of the experience of pregnancy. Therefore, she accounted for the experience of the changing pregnant body in her data collection process. She developed a new approach to her ethnographic work based on the failure of traditional methodologies to access the information she was seeking. In her work, she writes about her research process and how a shift to the body allowed her to ask and answer research questions that would otherwise be impossible to address. Likewise, she was able to access knowledge that would otherwise remain invisible. Pillow's example indicates how, as we have suggested in our emergent methods books, theoretical advancements propel methodological innovation.

This is just one example of a new emergent method. Other examples include daily diary research (see Hyers, Swim, & Mallett, 2006), friendship methods (see Tillmann-Healy, 2003), and many other methods practices.

Emergent Methods: Arts-Based Research Practices

One genre of qualitative research that has been exploding over the past couple of decades is *arts-based research* (ABR). ABR is an umbrella term for diverse research practices. Other commonly used terms are *a/r/tography*, which developed in educational research and refers to the merging of artist-researcher-teacher identities and *arts-based educational research*. Some evidence of the increase in ABR across the disciplines is the increase in dissertations using ABR (see Sinner, Leggo, Irwin, Gouzouasis, & Grauer, 2006), the development of ABR research committees and professional special interest groups, the sharp increase in research articles using ABR published in peer-reviewed qualitative research journals, increased conference presentations and conference themes, journal special issues (for example, LEARNing Landscapes, Feb. 2009), and books devoted to ABR (see Knowles & Cole, 2008; Leavy, 2009b).

ABR constitutes a significant expansion of the qualitative paradigm and can be defined as follows:

Arts-based research practices are a set of methodological tools used by qualitative researchers across the disciplines during all phases of social research including data collection, analysis, interpretation, and representation. These emerging tools adapt the tenets of the creative arts in order to address social research questions in *holistic* and *engaged* ways in which *theory and practice are intertwined*. Arts-based methods draw on literary writing, music, performance, dance, visual art, film and other mediums. Representational forms include but are not limited to short narratives, novels, experimental writing forms, poems, collages, paintings, drawings, performance scripts, theatre performances, dances, documentaries, and songs. Although a set of methodological tools, this genre of methods also comprises new theoretical and epistemological groundings that are expanding the qualitative paradigm. (Leavy, 2009b, pp. 2–3)

Researchers across the disciplines are employing ABR as a stand-alone method, in multimethod research, or as a representational vehicle (that has the potential to reach diverse and public audiences). Arts-based research practices are typically social justice-oriented. These methodological tools, useful for data collection, analysis, and representation, adapt the tenets of the creative arts to address social research questions in engaged ways. In qualitative research, ABR offers the following possibilities: unsettling stereotypes, building coalitions across difference, promoting dialogue, cutting through jargon and other prohibitive barriers, extending public scholarship, building critical consciousness, raising awareness, and expressing feeling-based dimensions of social life (such as love, loss, and grief). To better understand how ABR can access and represent dimensions of social life differently than traditional qualitative methods, let's join Patricia Leavy for a final look behind the scenes.

BEHIND THE SCENES WITH PATRICIA LEAVY

Quite unexpectedly, arts-based research has transformed both my research and teaching practices, which thanks to ABR, are becoming more and more integrated, allowing the facets of my work life to feel connected. As I noted in the opening of my book *Method Meets Art: Arts-Based Research Practice* (2009b), I, like many graduate students, entered the academy full of chutzpah. I was passionate about my work and I wanted to make a contribution. At some point, however, during the transition from graduate school to my tenure-track professional life, I started to experience my "work" differently. Quite simply, it started to feel like *work*. At that point I was working with Sharlene Hesse-Biber on innovative approaches to research methodology. This work led me to arts-based research practices (ABR) and, as it turns out, also to a whole new set of pedagogical tools.

In addition to research methodology, I had been researching body image across gender and sexual orientation for several years. I received a summer grant to work with two of my students full-time over one summer. We conducted in-depth interviews

(Continued)

(Continued)

about the relationship between female body image and sexuality for lesbian, bisexual, and heterosexual college-age women. Although a traditional interpretive and writing process produced a series of papers, the project somehow felt unfinished. I felt that the academic writing did not fully communicate the narratives we had heard, the voices of the women we had interviewed. Furthermore, the traditional academic form was starting to feel very limited. Let's face it, most academic scholarship never reaches the publics it claims to study, nor could it due to language and other prohibitive barriers. Given my work with ABR, I decided to turn to a poetic method of interpretation and representation. I constructed a poetic installation of 12 poems titled "Fractured Femininities/Massacred Masculinities" (Leavy, 2009b). These poetic works "got at" different dimensions of the data—the feeling tones, the tensions, the biography-society linkages. I presented a sampling of the poems at an interdisciplinary women's studies conference in Spain. The poems captured the attention of the session participants in a way that earlier readings of the traditional prose never had. In these ways, I felt that the poetic form allowed a heightened critical consciousness to emerge in the audience. Based on these experiences, and others, I anticipate continuing to use ABR as a part of my research practice. What I hadn't intended was the extent to which ABR would also become a part of my teaching.

As a sociology professor at an undergraduate Catholic college, I wondered if ABR could somehow benefit my students. I incorporated ABR into three courses, a 200-level required survey of research methods course, a 400-level qualitative research seminar, and a sociology and gender studies elective on popular culture, called "Images & Power." In each course, I added an arts-based component to students' final papers. So, in research methods, the students' final course project required them to conduct a small-scale content analysis, either quantitatively or qualitatively. In addition to their conventional research paper, they were required to represent their findings using an arts-based approach (collage, poem, script), with a brief artist-researcher statement explaining their project. The resulting work was *outstanding*. Significantly, although some were initially apprehensive about doing something "arty," the result was a much higher performance level on *the traditional paper*. I believe this is because students became more invested in their projects and immersed themselves more fully in their data. I had similar results in the qualitative methods seminar, where students added an ABR component to their final interview projects, for which they collected, transcribed, and analyzed two in-depth interviews. Not only did students "bring culture" into their write-ups via ABR, they also immersed themselves more fully into their data, allowing their participants' voices to emerge. Images & Power views pop culture through the lenses of gendered, raced, classed, and sexualized social power. ABR was a natural complement to course material. Students added an ABR component to their final critical mass media research paper. The results were again astounding. After teaching this course for about a decade, I can say without hesitation that this produced the strongest group of traditional research papers that I have received.

As you can see from this behind the scenes box, ABR is expanding the possibilities of qualitative practice as well as our teaching of it. Arts-based research practices are an evocative set of methodological tools that are pushing the borders of research parameters. These practices offer resonance, something that perhaps is not always captured in traditional academic prose.

Emergent Methods: Technological Practices

Emergent technologies have pushed against the boundaries of how both qualitative and quantitative researchers practice their craft (for an overview of newly emergent technologies and their application to social research, see Hesse-Biber, 2011). The application of new technologies raises issues regarding how to effectively apply technological innovations, including the application of the Internet and new digital technologies such as mobile technologies and geospatial technologies (GPS) for studying human interaction (see Cope & Elwood, 2009). For example, Mei Po Kwan (2008), a feminist geographer, has used spatial technologies to study how geographical space is gendered, classed, raced, and sexualized. The new developments in computer-assisted qualitative data analysis software programs (CAQDAS) can be used to enhance the integration of mixed methods and multimedia research. In addition, the development of grid and high-performance computing tools holds the promise of providing new ways for researchers to share and analyze large qualitative databases (Fielding, 2008).

The application of new technologies to social research inquiry also raises ethical and moral issues, especially with regard to the privacy of information and the confidentiality of participants. When more and more personal information is accessible over the Internet, for example, on such social networking sites as Facebook, new ethical issues emerge: Who should have access to this data? Who owns the data? Should this type of personal data be used by third parties for purposes of marketing, research, and so on? Let's look at one of these innovations—the rise of Internet technology—and some of its impact on how qualitative researchers practice their craft.

The Internet originated in the early 1960s and has mushroomed into a venue to which individuals turn for a variety of information. Individuals around the world spend an average of 27 hours on the Internet each month. Sudweeks and Simoff (1999) observe,

> The Internet has given birth to new research fields, or has diversified existing research fields, connected with human activities, including computer mediated communication (CMC), computer-supported cooperative work (CSCW), electronic commerce, virtual communities, virtual architecture, various virtual environments and information design. (p. 29)

The Internet challenges some basic philosophical assumptions researchers have maintained about the nature of social reality. To what extent is the Internet an extension of social reality, or a new entity, with its own set of rules for behavior? To what extent do positivist assumptions about the nature of social reality hold up within an Internet environment? To what extent do subjective models of experience correspond to Internet culture? Compounding these issues is the changing technological Internet environment, which is infused with ever new ways of accessing information in a multimedia format. Blackberries, iPhones, and other devices that link the individual to a virtual environment provide a multitude of ways to view and access information (Mulder & Kort, 2008). The ability of users to hyperlink their information provides the delivery of data in a nonlinear format as well.

Internet technology has spawned new qualitative data collection methods as well as new areas of research inquiry (Hewson, 2008; Hine, 2008). For example, the rise of Internet-mediated interviewing (IMI) provided qualitative researchers with a new technology for collecting data as well as spawning new areas of social inquiry. Qualitative researchers are now studying the lived experiences of individuals who use Internet technologies such as instant messaging or e-mail discussions. Qualitative researchers are also using the Internet as a new interviewing tool by conducting online interviewing (James & Busher, 2009; Salmons, 2010). However, this form of data collection also poses challenges for social researchers. For example, when a researcher employs the Internet as a medium for interviewing participants, their interaction may sometimes entail a time lag whereby the interview is not conducted in "real time"; instead, the interviewer often waits for the participant to comment later in time. There is also the concern that meaning may be lost in the interview situation because nonverbal cues are missing from the interaction. Ways of establishing rapport with the participant must take place differently, especially with the lack of face-to-face interviewing and verbal communication (except for some emotions that can be expressed linguistically—such as a smile notation in instant messaging, for example). The use of in-depth observational techniques like participant observation in chat rooms and discussion groups, along with Web cam technology, can now allow for the analysis of multimedia data.

The advent of Internet technologies has created ethnographic hypermedia environments (EHEs). These are experimental environments that demonstrate how the researcher can link together various forms of media data like textual and video data. Hyper-mediated data allows for the possibility of multiple representations of the data. Hypermedia data allows the researcher to create an audit trail that guides the reader through the set of connections the researcher makes with these varied data. One is, therefore, able to convey to the reader the complexity of one's analysis and interpretation (Dicks & Mason, 2008).

The continued development of digitized technological analysis tools also offers researchers the ability to collect, analyze, and integrate a wealth of multimedia data including still images, sound, and moving images into their research projects. Hypermedia technologies now provide the researcher with the ability to collect and represent new data that will change the nature of the research process. Computer-assisted software programs (CAQDAS) have the ability to hyperlink data, allowing researchers to move from one type of meaning to another in a nonlinear process, for example, linking text with images and sound (Hesse-Biber & Crofts, 2008). Some researchers look to artificial intelligence to move the analysis of qualitative data to a new generation of software tools that will incorporate expert systems that will be able to do some of the human tasks involved in analyzing data—for example, the coding of research data (Hesse-Biber & Dupuis, 1995). An idea of what might transpire comes from Evans (2002) as he projects the future of CAQDAS programs:

> Ultimately, we can expect a system that will monitor, process, and code texts and images with little human intervention. This system may be able to retrieve and manage great quantities of material and may actively identify opportunities for content analysis, devise and test content analytic hypotheses, and even learn as it does so. In other words, it is now feasible to begin working toward a kind of magic in content analysis. Furthermore, this magic is appropriate and even necessary if content analysts are to take full advantage of opportunities afforded by the emerging era of electronic databases and interactive media.

What is clear is that new technologies are dramatically changing the face of qualitative research design from the way in which social researchers collect data; what they consider data; and the techniques they use to analyze and represent meaning.

Ethical Conundrums of Emergent Technologies

New technologies are also changing the face of ethics practice (see Winston & Edelbach, 2009). As we mentioned throughout this book, researchers are now in a position to gather a range of very personal data via the Internet from social networking sites like Facebook, Myspace, and Twitter. An individual's day-to-day movements can now be tracked via new mobile technologies that contain GPS such that an individual's whereabouts can be traced through real time. Internet users who post very detailed information about their lives may find that they are at risk for a range of unintended consequences such as becoming targets for market researchers who track their consumption behaviors including their specific online purchases. They may also become subjects for research projects they know nothing about. For example, their social behaviors in cyberspace may be monitored by some researchers who may be lurking on Web sites or taking what they feel is "public" information for their own research projects without obtaining permission.

- Is collecting and analyzing "public" data that is personal ethical?

Emergent technologies trouble the waters between public and private information. Sometimes, the information taken from Web sites consists not only of textual data, but also of multimedia information, which may give clues to a user's identity— for example, YouTube videos, still images taken from a Web site, and so on. Increasingly, the identity of individuals is under scrutiny. Surveillance technologies (such as data gathered from GPS devices or the tracking of mobile phone activities) have become part of a new social order. Student researchers, many of whom have grown up with many of these emergent technologies, may acquire a new set of values that in fact normalizes the use of these new types of data. After all, checking one's Facebook or other social networking site is incorporated in the average college student's normal day-to-day activities. In addition, college students today have grown up in the age of reality TV where the public display of one's personal life in general has become more normalized, making it seem more natural to display one's own personal information on the Internet and in turn to gather the personal information of others as part of one's own student research project. Through the use of these social networks, the line between public and private information is increasingly blurred.

In addition, emergent technologies are also challenging institutional review boards (IRBs).

- How do new technologies impact an IRB's decision on the ethics of a research project?

To what extent do IRBs have the resources and expertise to evaluate the ethical impact of emergent technologies involved in any given research project? For example, to what extent are those making ethical decisions regarding the viability of a particular project aware of the range of ethical consequences that may be embedded, especially in surveillance technologies?

Conclusion: Staying Centered and Building Ethical Knowledge

The development of qualitative approaches to research and specific qualitative methods allows for the asking and answering of research questions in ways not possible within the quantitative paradigm. As noted earlier, different tools—different methods—allow us to access, interpret, and represent diverse and complex dimensions of social life. Therefore, the emergence of innovation within the qualitative paradigm brings forth exciting possibilities. As qualitative practice evolves, we must generate new ways of validating our knowledge-building practices. We must also be vigilant that as new practices emerge, so too are safety guards put in place to ensure ethical practice.

Discussion Questions

1. What is the importance of the research nexus for qualitative research?

2. What ethical issues are raised by the use of emergent technologies?

Resources

Suggested Web Sites

http://caqdas.soc.surrey.ac.uk

The CAQDAS (Computer Assisted Qualitative Data AnalysiS) Networking Project provides information, advice, training, and ongoing support in the use of a range of CAQDAS applications.

http://www.cf.ac.uk/socsi/hyper/ht99/EHE.html

A guide to ethnographic hypermedia environments using a graphically intensive and self-guided presentation with hyperlink structuring.

3TU. Centre for Ethics and Technology

http://www.ethicsandtechnology.eu/

This center based in the Netherlands is devoted to information on the link between technology and ethical values. The Web site notes: "We feel that already during the development and design phase of innovation, attention should be paid to social and ethical conditions and consequences. Responsible innovation requires ethical parallel research and value-sensitive design. We thus not only do excellent philosophical research, but also collaborate with technical centres of excellence." (Taken from mission statement on Web site's homepage)

UNESCO Web Site for Ethics of Science and Technology Program

www.unesco.org/shs/est

UNESCO's Ethics of Science and Technology Programme aims to promote consideration of science and technology in an ethical framework by initiating and supporting the process of democratic norm building. This approach is founded upon UNESCO's ideal of "true dialogue, based upon respect for commonly shared values and the dignity of each civilization and culture." Awareness raising, capacity building, and standard setting are therefore the key thrusts of UNESCO's strategy in this and all other areas. (Taken from mission statement on Web site's homepage)

Relevant Journals

ACME: An International E-Journal for Critical Geographers

Canadian Journal of Education

Gender, Place, and Culture

International Journal of Education and the Arts

International Journal of Qualitative Research in Education

International Journal of Internet Science

Journal of Mixed Methods Research

LEARNing Landscapes

The Professional Geographer

References

Addams, J. (1910). *Twenty years at Hull-House*. New York: Macmillan.

Adler, P., & Adler, P. (2002). Do university lawyers and the police define research values? In W. C. van den Hoonaard (Ed.), *Walking the tightrope: Ethical issues for qualitative researchers* (pp. 34–42). Toronto, ON: University of Toronto Press.

Agar, M. (1980). *The professional stranger: An informal introduction to ethnography.* New York: Academic Press.

Agar, M. (1996). *The professional stranger: An informal introduction to ethnography* (2nd ed.). New York: Academic Press.

Altheide, D. L. (2009). Moral panic: From sociological concept to public discourse. *Crime, Media, Culture, 5*(1), 79–99.

Alvino, L. A. (2003). Who's watching the watchdogs? Responding to the erosion of research ethics by enforcing promises. *Columbia Law Review, 103*, 893–924.

Anderson, E. (1976). *A place on the corner.* Chicago: University of Chicago Press.

Anderson, K., & Jack, D. C. (1991). Learning to listen: Interview techniques and analysis. In S. B. Gluck & D. Patai (Eds.), *Women's words: The feminist practice of oral history* (pp. 7–26). New York: Routledge.

Anderson, N. (1923). *The hobo.* Chicago: University of Chicago Press.

Anderson, R. A., Crabtree, B. F., Steele, D. J., & McDaniel, R. R., Jr. (2005). Case study research: The view from complexity science. *Qualitative Health Research, 15*(5), 669–685.

Appelbaum, P. S., Roth, L. H., Lidz, C. W., Benson, P., & Winslade, W. (1987). False hopes and best data: Consent to research and the therapeutic misconception. *Hastings Center Report, 17*, 20–24.

Baez, B. (2002). Confidentiality in qualitative research: Reflections on secrets, power, and agency. *Qualitative Research, 2*(1), 35–58.

Bailey, C. A. (1996). *A guide to field research.* Thousand Oaks, CA: Pine Forge Press.

Banks, J. A. (1976). Comment on "A Content Analysis of the Black American in Textbooks." In M. P. Golden (Ed.), *The research experience* (pp. 383–389). Itasca, IL: F. E. Peacock.

Barndt, D. (2008). Touching hearts and minds: Community arts as collaborative research. In J. G. Knowles & A. L. Cole (Eds.), *Handbook of the arts in qualitative research: Perspectives, methodologies, examples, and issues* (pp. 351–362). Thousand Oaks, CA: Sage.

Barthes, R. (1998). Myth today. In S. Sontag (Ed.), *A Barthes reader* (pp. 93–149). New York: Hill & Wang.

Bauer, M. (2000). Classical content analysis: A review. In M. Bauer & G. Gaskell (Eds.), *Qualitative researching with text, image, and sound* (pp. 131–151). London: Sage.

Bazeley, P. (2007). *Qualitative data analysis with NVivo.* London: Sage.

Becker, H. S. (1967). Whose side are we on? *Social Problems, 14,* 239–247.

Beecher, H. K. (1966). Ethics and clinical research. *New England Journal of Medicine, 13,* 54–60.

Bell, L., & Nutt, L. (2002). Divided loyalties, divided expectations: Research ethics, professional and occupational responsibilities. In M. Mauthner, M. Birch, J. Jessop, & T. Miller (Eds.), *Ethics in qualitative research* (pp. 70–90). London: Sage.

Beoku-Betts, J. (1994). When black is not enough: Doing field research among Gullah women. *NWSA Journal, 6*(3), 413–433.

Bergman, M. A. (Ed.). (2008). *Advances in mixed methods research.* London: Sage.

Betts, N., Baranowski, T., & Hoerr, S. (1996). Recommendations for planning and reporting focus groups research. *Society for Nutrition Education, 8*(5), 279–281.

Beyrer, C., & Kass, N. (2002). Human rights, politics, and reviews of research ethics. *Lancet, 359*(9328), 246–251.

Bjeren, G. (2004). *Combining social survey and ethnography integration research: An example.* Paper presented at the 2nd conference of the EAPS Working Group on International Migration in Europe, Rome, Italy.

Blumer, H. (1969). *Symbolic interactionism: Perspective and method.* Englewood Cliffs, NJ: Prentice Hall.

Booth, C. (1902). *Life and labour of the people in London.* London: Macmillan.

Borland, K. (1991). That's not what I said! Interpretive conflict in oral narrative research. In S. Berger Gluck & D. Patai (Eds.), *Women's worlds: The feminist practice of oral history.* New York: Routledge.

Botting, I. (2000). Understanding domestic service through oral history and the census: The case of Grand Falls, Newfoundland. *Feminist Qualitative Research, 28*(1–2), 99–120.

Bourgois, P. (2007). Confronting the ethics of ethnography: Lessons from fieldwork in Central America. In A.C.G.M. Robben & J. A. Sluka (Eds.), *Ethnographic fieldwork: An anthropological reader* (pp. 288–297). Oxford, UK: Blackwell.

Brannen, J. (1992). Combining qualitative and quantitative approaches: An overview. In J. Brannen (Ed.), *Mixing methods: Qualitative and quantitative research* (pp. 3–36). Aldershot, UK: Avebury Press.

Bristol, T., & Fern, E. (1996). Exploring the atmosphere created by focus group interviews: Comparing consumers' feelings across qualitative techniques. *Journal of the Market Research Society, 38*(2), 185–195.

Brotherson, M. (1994). Interactive focus group interviewing: A qualitative research method in early intervention. *Topics in Early Childhood Special Education, 14*(1), 101–118.

Bryant, A., & Charmaz, K. (Eds.). (2007). *The SAGE handbook of grounded theory.* London: Sage.

Bryman, A. (1988). *Quantity and quality in social research.* London: Routledge.

Burawoy, M. (1991). *Ethnography unbound: Power and resistance in the modern metropolis.* Berkeley: University of California Press.

Burger, J. (2009). Replicating Milgram: Would people still obey today? *American Psychologist, 64*(1), 1–11.

Byers, P. (1964). Still photography in the systematic recording and analysis of behavioural data. *Human Organization, 23,* 78–84.

Byman, A. (1988). *Quantity and quality in social research.* London: Unwin & Hyman.

Calvey, D. (2008). The art and politics of covert research: Doing "situated ethics" in the field. *Sociology, 42,* 905–918.

Candida Smith, R. (2001). Analytic strategies for oral history interviews. In J. Gubrium & J. Holstein (Eds.), *Handbook of interviews research: Context & method* (pp. 711–733). Thousand Oaks, CA: Sage.

Carey, M. (1994). Forms of interviewing. *Qualitative Health Research, 5*(4), 413–416.

Cassileth, B. R., Zupkis, R. V., Sutton-Smith, K., & March, V. (1980). Informed consent: Why are its goals imperfectly realized? *New England Journal of Medicine, 302,* 896–900.

Charmaz, K. (1983). The grounded theory method: An explication and interpretation. In R. M. Emerson (Ed.), *Contemporary field research: A collection of readings* (pp. 109–126). Prospect Heights, IL: Waveland Press.

Charmaz, K. (2000). Grounded theory: Objectivist and constructivist methods. In N. K. Denzin & Y. S. Lincoln (Eds.), *Handbook of qualitative research* (2nd ed., pp. 509–535). Thousand Oaks, CA: Sage.

Charmaz, K. (2004). Grounded theory. In S. Hesse-Biber & P. Leavy (Eds.), *Approaches to qualitative research: A reader on theory and practice* (pp. 496–521). New York: Oxford University Press.

Charmaz, K. (2006). *Constructing grounded theory: A practical guide through qualitative analysis.* London: Sage.

Chenail, R. J. (1995, December). Presenting qualitative data. *The Qualitative Report, 2*(3). Retrieved March 3, 2009, from http://www.nova.edu/ssss/QR/QR2-3/presenting.html

Cisneros-Puebla, C. A. (2004, September). Let's do more theoretical work . . . : Janice Morse in conversation with César A. Cisneros-Puebla. *Forum Qualitative Sozial-forschung/ Forum: Qualitative Social Research* [On-line Journal], *5*(3), Art. 33. Retrieved from http://www.qualitative-research.net/fqs-texte/3-04/04-3-33-e.htm

Clough, P. T. (2009). The new empiricism: Affect and sociological method. *European Journal of Social Theory, 12*(1), 43–61.

Coleman, T., Williams, M., & Wilson, A. (1996). Sampling for qualitative research using quantitative methods: Measuring GP's attitudes towards discussing smoking with patients. *Family Practice, 13,* 526–530.

Collier, P. (2007, June). *Students first: Improving first generation students' performance and retention in higher education.* Address presented at the Peer Mentoring Initiative and Retention Summit, Minneapolis, MN.

Comte, A. (2003). *Positive philosophy of Auguste Comte, Part I* (H. Martineau, Trans.). London: Kessinger. (Original work published 1856)

Cooper, N., & Burnett, S. (2006). Using discourse reflexivity to enhance the qualitative research process: An example from accounts of teenage conception. *Qualitative Social Work, 5*(1), 111–129.

Cope, M., & Elwood, S. (Eds.) (2009). *Qualitative GIS: A mixed methods approach.* London: Sage.

Corbin, J., & Strauss, A. (2007). *Basics of qualitative research: Techniques and procedures for developing grounded theory* (3rd ed.). Thousand Oaks, CA: Sage.

Costigan Lederman, L. (1990). Assessing educational effectiveness: The focus group interview as a technique for data collection. *Communication Education, 38,* 117–127.

Covert, J. J., & Dixon, T. L. (2008). A changing view: Representation and effects of the portrayal of women of color in mainstream women's magazines. *Communication Research, 35*(2), 232–256.

Cox, A., & Brown, A. (2005, January 10). *Treating children's emotional wounds.* CNN. Retrieved from http://www.cnn.com/2005/WORLD/asiapcf/01/05/tsunami.children.cope/

Crabtree, B. F., & Miller, W. L. (Eds.). (1999). *Doing qualitative research* (2nd ed.). Thousand Oaks, CA: Sage.

Cragg, A., & Dawson, T. (1981, May). *Qualitative research among homeworkers* (Research Paper No. 21). London: Department of Employment.

Cressey, P. G. (1932). *The taxi-dance hall.* Chicago: University of Chicago Press.

Creswell, J. W. (1999). Mixed-method research: Introduction and application. In G. J. Cizek (Ed.), *Handbook of educational policy* (pp. 455–472). San Diego, CA: Academic Press.

Creswell, J. W. (2003). *Research design: Qualitative and quantitative approaches* (2nd ed.). Thousand Oaks, CA: Sage.

Creswell, J. W. (2008). *Research design: Qualitative, quantitative, and mixed methods approaches* (3rd ed.). Thousand Oaks, CA: Sage.

Creswell, J. W., Fetters, M. D., & Ivankova, N. V. (2004, January/February). Designing a mixed methods study in primary care. *Annals of Family Medicine, 2*(1), 7–12.

Creswell, J. W., & Maietta, R. C. (2003). Qualitative research. In D. C. Miller & N. J. Salkind (Eds.), *Handbook of design & social measurement.* Thousand Oaks, CA: Sage.

Creswell, J. W., & Plano Clark, V. (2008). *Designing and conducting mixed methods research.* Thousand Oaks, CA: Sage.

Cronbach, L. (1975). Beyond the two disciplines of scientific psychology. *American Psychologist, 30*(2), 116–127.

Crothers, A. G. (2002, March). Bringing history to life: Oral history, community research, and multiple levels of learning. *The Journal of American History, 88*(4). Retrieved May 27, 2003, from http://www.historycooperative.org

Cutler, A. (2004). Methodological failure: The use of case study method by public relations researchers. *Public Relations Review 30,* 365–375.

Daniels, A. K. (1967). The low-caste stranger in social research. In G. Sjoberg (Ed.), *Ethics, politics, and social research* (pp. 267–296). Cambridge, MA: Schenkman.

Dattalo, P. (2008). *Determining sample size: Balancing power, precision, and practicality.* New York: Oxford University Press.

Deegan, M. J. (2001). The Chicago School of ethnography. In P. Atkinson, A. Coffey, S. Delamont, J. Lofland, & L. Lofland (Eds.), *Handbook of ethnography* (pp. 11–25). Thousand Oaks, CA: Sage.

Delgado, R., & Stefancic, J. (2001). *Critical race theory: An introduction.* New York: New York University Press.

Denzin, N. K. (1978). *The research act: A theoretical introduction to sociological methods.* New York: McGraw-Hill.

Denzin, N. K. (1989). *The research act: A theoretical introduction to sociological methods* (3rd ed.). Englewood Cliffs, NJ: Prentice Hall.

Denzin, N. K. (1997). *Interpretive ethnography: Ethnographic practices for the 21st century.* Thousand Oaks, CA: Sage.

Denzin, N. K. (2000). The practices and politics of interpretation. In N. K. Denzin & Y. S. Lincoln (Eds.), *Handbook of qualitative research.* Thousand Oaks, CA: Sage.

Denzin, N. K., & Lincoln, Y. S. (2000). The discipline and practice of qualitative research. In N. K. Denzin & Y. S. Lincoln (Eds.), *Handbook of qualitative research* (2nd ed., pp. 1–28). Thousand Oaks, CA: Sage.

Denzin, N. K., & Lincoln, Y. S. (2007). *The landscape of qualitative research* (3rd ed.). Thousand Oaks, CA: Sage.

Department of Health and Human Services. (1989). *Code of federal regulations (45 CFR 46): Protection of human subjects.* Washington, DC: National Institutes of Health, Office for the Protection from Research Risks.

Derrida, J. (1966). The decentering event in social thought. In A. Bass (Trans.), *Writing the difference* (pp. 278–282). Chicago: University of Chicago Press.

Devault, M. (2004). Talking and listening from women's standpoint: Feminist strategies for interviewing and analysis. In S. Hesse-Biber & M. Yaiser (Eds.), *Feminist perspectives on social research.* New York: Oxford University Press.

Diaz, J. (1999). Blood money: Life, death, and plasma on the Las Vegas Strip. *Electronic Journal of Sociology, 4*(2). Retrieved from http://www.sociology.org/content/v01004.002/diaz.html

Dicks, B., & Mason, B. (2008). Hypermedia methods for qualitative research. In S. N. Hesse-Biber & P. Leavy (Eds.), *Handbook of emergent methods* (pp. 571–600). Thousand Oaks, CA: Sage.

di Gregorio, S., & Davidson, J. (2008). *Qualitative research design for software users.* Berkshire, UK: Open University Press.

Dodson, L., Piatelli, D., & Schmalzbauer, L. (2007). Researching inequality through interpretive collaborations: Shifting power and the unspoken contract. *Qualitative Inquiry, 13*(6), 821–843.

Douglas, J. (1979). Living morality versus bureaucratic fiat. In C. B. Klockars & F. W. O'Connor (Eds.), *Deviance and decency* (pp. 13–33). Beverly Hills, CA: Sage.

Dumont, J. P. (1978). *The headman and I.* Austin: University of Texas Press.

Duncombe, J., & Jessop, J. (2002). "Doing rapport" and the ethics of "faking friendship." In M. Mauthner, M. Birch, J. Jessop, & T. Miller (Eds.), *Ethics in qualitative research* (pp. 106–122). Thousand Oaks, CA: Sage.

Edwards, R. (1990). Connecting methods and epistemology: A white woman interviewing black women. *Women's Studies International Forum, 13*(5), 477–490.

Elgesem, D. (2002). *What is special about the ethical issues in online research?* Retrieved July 14, 2009, from http://www.nyu.edu/projects/nissenbaum/ethics_elg_full.html

Ellis, C. (1996). Maternal connections. In C. Ellis & A. P. Bochner (Eds.), *Composing ethnography: Alternative forms of qualitative writing* (pp. 140–143). Walnut Creek, CA: AltaMira Press.

Ellis, C. (2004). *The ethnographic I: A methodological novel about autoethnography.* Walnut Creek, CA: Alta Mira Press.

Ellis, C. (2009). Revision: Autoethnographic reflections on life and work. Walnut Creek, CA: Left Coast Press.

Emerson, R. M. (Ed.). (2001). *Contemporary field research: Perspectives and formulations* (2nd ed.). Prospect Heights, IL: Waveland Press.

Emerson, R. M., & Pollner, M. (2001). Constructing participant/observation relations. In R. M. Emerson (Ed.), *Contemporary field research: Perspectives and formulations* (2nd ed., pp. 239–259). Prospect Heights, IL: Waveland Press.

Etter-Lewis, G. (1991). Black women's life stories: Reclaiming self in narrative texts. In S. Gluck & D. Patai (Eds.), *Women's words: The feminist practice of oral history.* New York: Routledge.

Evans, W. (2002). Computer environments for content analysis: Reconceptualizing the roles of humans and computers. In O. V. Burton (Ed.), *Computing in the social sciences and humanities.* Champaign: University of Illinois Press.

Eysenbach, G., & Till, J. (2001). Information in practice: Ethical issues in qualitative research on internet communities. *BMJ, 323,* 1103–1105.

Faden, R. R., & Beauchamp, T. L. (1986). *A history and theory of informed consent.* New York: Oxford University Press.

Famradt, J. (1998). Studying up in educational anthropology. In K. Bennett deMarrais (Ed.), *Inside stories: Qualitative research reflection* (pp. 67–78). London: Lawrence Erlbaum.

Fielding, N. (2008). The role of computer-assisted qualitative data analysis: Impact on emergent methods in qualitative research. In S. N. Hesse-Biber & P. Leavy (Eds.), *Handbook of emergent methods* (pp. 675–695). Thousand Oaks, CA: Sage.

Fielding, N. G., & Lee, R. M. (1998). *Computer Analysis and Qualitative Research.* London: Sage.

Fishman, P. (1990). Interaction: The work women do. In J. McCarl Nielsen (Ed.), *Feminist research methods: Exemplary readings in the social sciences* (pp. 224–238). Boulder, CO: Westview Press.

Fluehr-Lobban, C. (1998). Ethics. In H. R. Bernard (Ed.), *Handbook of methods in cultural anthropology* (pp. 173–201). London: Alta Mira Press.

Flyvbjerg, B. (2006). Five misunderstandings about case-study research. *Qualitative Inquiry, 12*(2), 219–245.

Foucault, M. (1976). *The history of sexuality: Vol. 1. An introduction.* New York: Vintage Books.

Foucault, M. (1978). Power as knowledge. In R. Hurley (Trans.), *The history of sexuality: Vol. 1. An introduction* (pp. 92–102). New York: Vintage Books.

Frazier, E. F. (1932). *The Negro family in Chicago.* Chicago: University of Chicago Press.

Frey, J., & Fontana, A. (1991). The group interview in social research. *Social Science Journal, 28*(2), 175–188.

Frisch, M. (1989). *A shared authority: Essays on the craft and meaning of oral and public history.* New York: State University of New York.

Frisch, M. (2003). Sharing authority: Oral history and the collaborative process (Commentary). *The Oral History Review, 30*(1), 111–113.

Frisch, M. (2008). Three dimension and more: Oral history beyond the paradoxes of method. In S. Hesse-Biber & P. Leavy (Eds.), *Handbook of emergent methods.* New York: Guilford Press.

Galanter, M. (1989). *Cults: Faith, healing, and coercion.* New York: Oxford University Press.

Gans, H. (1982). The participant observer as a human being: Observations on the personal aspects of fieldwork. In R. G. Burgess (Ed.), *Field research: A sourcebook and field manual* (pp. 53–61). London: George Allen & Unwin.

Garfinkel, H. (1967). *Studies in ethnomethodology.* Englewood Cliffs, NJ: Prentice-Hall.

Gay, L. R., & Airasian, P. (2003). *Educational research: Competencies for analysis and application* (7th ed.). Upper Saddle River, NJ: Merrill/Prentice Hall.

Geertz, C. (1973). *The interpretations of cultures.* New York: Basic Books.

Gerkin, P. M. (2009). Participation in victim–offender mediation: Lessons learned from observations. *Criminal Justice Review, 34*(2), 226–247.

Gerring, J. (2006). *Case study research: Principles and practices.* Cambridge, UK: Cambridge University Press.

Gilmore, T., Krantz, J., & Ramirez, R. (1986). Action-based modes of inquiry and the host-researcher relationship. *Consultation, 5*(3), 161.

Gioia, D. A., & Thomas, J. B. (1996). Identity, image, and issue interpretation: Sensemaking during strategic change in academia. *Administrative Science Quarterly, 41,* 370–403.

Glaser, B. G. (1978). *Theoretical sensitivity: Advances in the methodology of grounded theory.* Mill Valley, CA: Sociology Press.

Glaser, B. G., & Strauss, A. L. (1967). *The discovery of grounded theory: Strategies for qualitative research.* Chicago: Aldine.

Goffman, E. (1959). *The presentation of self in everyday life.* New York: Doubleday.

Goffman, E. (1961). *Asylums: Essays on the social situation of mental patients and other inmates.* New York: Anchor.

Goffman, E. (1967). *Interaction ritual: Essays on face-to-face behavior.* Chicago: Aldine.

Gold, R. L. (1958). Roles in sociological field observation. *Social Forces, 36,* 217–223.

Goltz, D. (2009). Investigating queer meanings: Destructive perceptions of "the harder path." *Qualitative Inquiry, 15*(3), 561–586.

Gomm, R., Hammersley, M., & Foster, P. (Eds.). (2000). *Case study method: Key issues, key texts.* London: Sage.

Gooden, A. M., & Gooden, M. A. (2001). Gender representation in notable children's picture books: 1995–1999. *Sex Roles: A Journal of Research, 45*(1–2), 89–101.

Gough, B., Lawton, R., Madill, A., & Stratton, P. (2003). *Guidelines for the supervision of undergraduate qualitative research in psychology* (The Higher Education Academy Psychology Network Report and Evaluation Series, No. 3). York, UK: LTSN Psychology.

Graebner, M. E., & Eisenhardt, K. M. (2004). The seller's side of the story: Acquisition as courtship and governance as syndicate in entrepreneurial firms. *Administrative Science Quarterly, 49,* 366–403.

Gramsci, A. (1929). *Intellectuals and hegemony: Selections from the prison notebooks.* New York: International Publishers.

Greene, J. C. (2007). *Mixed methods in social inquiry.* San Francisco, CA: Jossey-Bass.

Greene, J. C., Benjamin, L., & Goodyear, L. (2001). The merits of mixing methods in evaluation. *Evaluation, 7*(1), 25–44.

Greene, J. C., & Caracelli, V. J. (Eds.). (1997a). *Advances in mixed-method evaluation: The challenges and benefits of integrating diverse paradigms* (New Directions for Evaluation, No. 74). San Francisco: Jossey-Bass.

Greene, J. C., & Caracelli, V. J. (1997b). Defining and describing the paradigm issues in mixed-method evaluation. In J. C. Greene & V. J. Caracelli (Eds.), *Advances in mixed-method evaluation: The challenges and benefits of integrating diverse paradigms* (New Directions for Evaluation, No. 74, pp. 5–17). San Francisco: Jossey-Bass.

Greene, J. C., Caracelli, V. J., & Graham, W. F. (1989). Toward a conceptual framework for mixed-method evaluation designs. *Educational Evaluation and Policy Analysis, 11,* 255–274.

Grosz, E. (1994). *Volatile bodies: Toward a corporeal feminism.* Bloomington: Indiana University Press.

Guba, E. G. (1985). The context of emergent paradigm research. In Y. S. Lincoln (Ed.), *Organizational theory and inquiry* (pp. 79–104). Newbury Park, CA: Sage.

Guba, E. (1990). *The paradigm dialog.* Thousand Oaks, CA: Sage.

Guba, E. G., & Lincoln, Y. S. (1989). *Fourth-generation evaluation.* Newbury Park, CA: Sage.

Guba, E., & Lincoln, Y. (1998). Competing paradigms in qualitative research. In N. K. Denzin & Y. S. Lincoln (Eds.), *The landscape of qualitative research: Theories and issues* (pp. 195–220). Thousand Oaks, CA: Sage.

Gubrium, J. F., & Holstein, J. (1997). *The new language of qualitative method.* New York: Oxford University Press.

Haggerty, K. D. (2004). Ethics creep: Governing social science research in the name of ethics. *Qualitative Sociology, 27*(4), 391–414.

Hall, S. (1981). Notes on deconstructing "the popular." In J. Storey (Ed.), *Cultural studies & the study of popular culture.* Athens: University of Georgia Press.

Halpin, Z. (1989). Scientific objectivity and the concept of "the other." *Women's Studies International Forum, 12*(3), 285–294.

Hammersley, M., & Atkinson, P. (1995). Documents. In *Ethnography: Principles in practice* (2nd ed., pp. 157–174). New York: Routledge.

Hammersley, M., & Atkinson, P. (2007). *Ethnography: Principles in practice* (3rd ed.). New York: Routledge.

Hammersley, M., & Gomm, R. (2000). Introduction. In R. Gomm, M. Hammersley, & P. Foster (Eds.), *Case study method: Key issues, key texts* (pp. 1–17). London: Sage.

Harding, S. (1987). *Feminism & methodology.* Bloomington: Indiana University Press.

Harding, S. (1993). Rethinking standpoint epistemology: What is "strong objectivity"? In L. Alcoff & E. Potter (Eds.), *Feminist epistemologies* (pp. 49–82). New York: Routledge.

Harding, S. (2004). Rethinking standpoint epistemology: What is "strong objectivity"? In S. Harding (Ed.), *The feminist standpoint theory reader: Intellectual and political controversies* (pp. 127–140). New York: Routledge.

Harmon, D., & Boeringer, S. B. (1997). A content analysis of Internet-accessible written pornographic depictions. *Electronic Journal of Sociology, 3*(1). Retrieved from http://www.sociology.org/content/v01003,001/boeringer.html

Hartsock, N. (1983). The feminist standpoint: Developing the ground for a specifically feminist historical materialism. In S. Harding & M. Hintikka (Eds.), *Discovering reality* (pp. 283–305). Dordrecht Holland: Reidel.

Heidegger, M. (1962). *Being and time* (J. Macquarrie & E. Robinson, Trans.). New York: Harper & Row. (Original work published 1927)

Heidegger, M. (1982). *The basic problems of phenomenology* (A. Hofstadter, Trans.). Bloomington: Indiana University Press. (Original work published 1975)

Heintzelman, C. (2001). Human subjects and informed consent: The legacy of the Tuskegee syphilis study. In Dushkin (Ed.), *Research methods, 2001/2002.* Guilford, CT: Dushkin/McGraw Hill.

Heise, D. (1991). Event structure analysis: A qualitative model of quantitative research. In N. Fielding & R. Lee (Eds.), *Using computers in qualitative research* (pp. 136–163). London: Sage.

Heise, D., & Lewis, E. (1988). *Introduction to* ETHNO. Raleigh, NC: National Collegiate Software Clearinghouse.

Hendrix, K. (1998). Student perceptions of the influence of race on professor credibility. *Journal of Black Studies, 28*(6), 738–763.

Hennink, M. M. (2008). Emergent issues in international focus group discussions. In S. Hesse-Biber & P. Leavy (Eds.), *Handbook of emergent methods* (pp. 207–220). New York: Guilford Press.

Hertz, R., & Imber, J. B. (1995). *Studying elites using qualitative methods.* Thousand Oaks, CA: Sage.

Hesse-Biber, S. (1995). Unleashing Frankenstein's monster: The use of computers in qualitative research. In R. G. Burgess (Ed.), *Studies in qualitative methodology: Computing and qualitative research* (Vol. 5). Westport, CT: JAI Press.

Hesse-Biber, S. (1996). *Am I thin enough yet? The cult of thinness and the commercialization of identity.* New York: Oxford University Press.

Hesse-Biber, S. (2007). *The cult of thinness* (2nd ed.). New York: Oxford University Press.

Hesse-Biber, S. (2010). *Mixed methods research: Merging theory with practice.* New York: Guilford.

Hesse-Biber, S. (Ed.). (2011). *Handbook of emergent technologies in social research.* New York: Oxford University Press.

Hesse-Biber, S., & Carter, G. L. (2004). Linking qualitative and quantitative analysis: The example of family socialization and eating disorders. In G. L. Carter (Ed.), *Empirical approaches to sociology: A collection of classic and contemporary readings* (4th ed., pp. 83–97). Boston: Pearson/Allyn & Bacon.

Hesse-Biber, S., & Crofts, C. (2008). User-centered perspectives on qualitative data analysis software: Emergent technologies and future trends. In S. N. Hesse-Biber & P. Leavy (Eds.), *Handbook of emergent methods* (pp. 655–674). Thousand Oaks, CA: Sage.

Hesse-Biber, S., & Dupuis, P. (1995). Hypothesis testing in computer-aided qualitative data analysis. In Udo Kelle (Ed.), *Computer-aided qualitative data analysis.* Thousand Oaks, CA: Sage.

Hesse-Biber, S., Dupuis, P., & Kinder, T. S. (1991). HyperRESEARCH: A computer program for the analysis of qualitative data with an emphasis on hypothesis testing and multimedia analysis. *Qualitative Sociology, 14*(4), 289–306.

Hesse-Biber, S. N., Howling, S. A., Leavy, P., & Lovejoy, M. (2004). Racial identity and the development of body image issues among African American adolescent girls. *The Qualitative Report, 9*(1), 49–79.

Hesse-Biber, S., & Leavy, P. (Eds.). (2004). *Approaches to qualitative research: A reader on theory and practice.* New York: Oxford University Press.

Hesse-Biber, S., & Leavy, P. (2006). *Emergent methods in social research.* Thousand Oaks, CA: Sage.

Hesse-Biber, S., & Leavy, P. (2008). *Handbook of emergent methods.* New York: Guilford Press.

Hesse-Biber, S., Livingston, S., & Raminez, D. (2009). *Racial identity, self-esteem, and the development of body image and disordered eating among African American women at predominately white colleges.* Paper presented at the Annual Meeting of the American Sociological Association, August.

Hesse-Biber, S. N., & Piatelli, D. (2007). Holistic reflexivity: The feminist practice of reflexivity. In S. N. Hesse-Biber (Ed.), *Handbook of feminist research: Theory and praxis* (pp. 493–514). Thousand Oaks, CA: Sage.

Hewson, C. (2008). Internet-mediated research as an emergent method and its potential role in facilitation of mixed methods research. In S. N. Hesse-Biber & P. Leavy (Eds.), *Handbook of emergent methods* (pp. 543–570). Thousand Oaks, CA: Sage.

Hill-Collins, P. (1990). *Black feminist thought: Knowledge, consciousness, and the politics of empowerment.* London: HarperCollins.

Hinchcliffe, V., & Gavin, H. (2009). Social and virtual networks: Evaluating synchronous online interviewing using instant messenger. *The Qualitative Report, 14*(2), 318–340.

Hine, C. (2008). Internet research as emergent practice. In S. N. Hesse-Biber & P. Leavy (Eds.), *Handbook of emergent methods* (pp. 525–542). Thousand Oaks, CA: Sage.

Homan, R. (1992). The ethics of open methods. *The British Journal of Sociology, 43*(3), 321–332.

Honigmann, J. (1982). Sampling in ethnographic fieldwork. In R. Burgess (Ed.), *Field research: A sourcebook and field manual* (pp. 79–90). London: George Allen & Unwin.

Horowitz, R. (1986, January). Remaining an outsider: Membership as a threat to research rapport. *Urban Life, 14*(4), 409–430.

Huber, J., & Clandinin, D. (2002). Ethical dilemmas in relational narrative inquiry with children. *Qualitative Inquiry, 8*(6), 785–803.

Humphries, L. (1976). Methods: The sociologist as voyeur. In P. Golden (Ed.), *The research experience* (pp. 100–114). Itasca, IL: F. E. Peacock.

Husserl, E. (1963). *Ideas: A general introduction to pure phenomenology* (W. R. Boyce Gibson, Trans.). New York: Collier Books. (Original work published 1913)

Hyers, L. L., Swim, J. K., & Mallett, R. M. (2006). The personal is political: Using daily diaries to examine everyday gender-related experiences. In S. N. Hesse-Biber & P. Leavy (Eds.), *Emergent methods in social research.* Thousand Oaks, CA: Sage.

Irigaray, L. (1985). *This sex which is not one.* Ithaca, NY: Cornell University Press.

Jaggar, A. (1989). Love and knowledge: Emotion in feminist epistemology. *Inquiry, 32,* 151–172.

James, N., & Busher, H. (2009). *Online interviewing.* London: Sage.

Johnson, J. M. (2002). In-depth interviewing. In J. F. Gubrium & J. A. Holstein (Eds.), *Handbook of interview research: Context & method.* Thousand Oaks, CA: Sage.

Jones, J. H. (1993). *Bad blood: The Tuskegee syphilis experiment.* New York: Free Press.

Jones, P. J., & Wardle, C. (2008). "No emotion, no sympathy": The visual construction of Maxine Carr. *Crime, Media, Culture, 4*(1), 53–71.

Jones, S. B. (1976a). Geographic mobility as seen by the wife and mother. In M. Golden (Ed.), *The research experience* (pp. 315–326). Itasca, IL: F. E. Peacock.

Jones, S. B. (1976b). Personal reflections on the research process. In M. Golden (Ed.), *The research experience* (pp. 327–339). Itasca, IL: F. E. Peacock.

Kadushin, C. (2005). Who benefits from network analysis: Ethics of social network research. *Social Networks, 27*(2), 139–153.

Karp, D. (1997). *Speaking of sadness: Depression, disconnection, and the meaning of illness.* New York: Oxford University Press.

Kelle, U. (Ed.). (1995). *Computer-aided qualitative analysis.* London: Sage.

Kerr, D. (2003). We know what the problem is: Using oral history to develop a collaborative analysis of homelessness from the bottom up. *The Oral History Review, 30*(1), 27–45.

King, N. M. P., Henderson, G. E., & Stein, J. (1999). Regulations and relationships: Toward a new synthesis. In N. M. P. King, G. E. Henderson, & J. Stein (Eds.), *Beyond regulations: Ethics in human subjects research*. Chapel Hill: University of North Carolina Press.

Kitzinger, J. (1994). The methodology of focus groups: The importance of interaction between research participants. *Sociology of Health & Illness, 16*(1), 103–121.

Knowles, J. G., & Cole, A. L. (Eds.). (2008). *Handbook of the arts in qualitative research: Perspectives, methodologies, examples, and issues*. Thousand Oaks, CA: Sage.

Kohler Riessman, C. (1987). When gender is not enough: Women interviewing women. *Gender and Society, 1*, 172–207.

Kohler Riessman, C. (1988). Worlds of difference: Contrasting experience in marriage and narrative styles. In A. D. Todd & S. Fisher (Eds.), *Gender and discourse: The power of talk* (pp. 151–173). Norwood, NJ: Ablex.

Kondo, D. K. (2001). How the problem of "crafting selves" emerged. In R. M. Emerson (Ed.), *Contemporary field research* (2nd ed., pp. 188–202). Prospect Heights, IL: Waveland.

Korn, J. H. (1997). *Illusions of reality: A history of deception in social psychology*. New York: SUNY.

Krueger, R. (1994). *Focus groups: A practical guide for applied research* (2nd ed.). Thousand Oaks, CA: Sage.

Kübler-Ross, E. (1969). *On death and dying*. New York: Macmillan.

Kutner, J. S., Steiner, J. F., Corbett, K. K., Jahnigen, D. W., & Barton, P. L. (1999). Information needs in terminal illness. *Social Science & Medicine, 48*, 1341–1352.

Kvale, S. (1996). *InterViews: An introduction to qualitative research interviewing*. Thousand Oaks, CA: Sage.

Kvale, S., & Brinkmann, S. (2009). *InterViews: Learning the craft of qualitative research interviewing* (2nd ed.). Thousand Oaks, CA: Sage.

Kwan, M. (2008). Emergent methods in feminist geography. In S. N. Hesse-Biber & P. Leavy (Eds.), *Handbook of emergent methods* (pp. 613–624). Thousand Oaks, CA: Sage.

Ladson-Billings, G., & Donnor, J. (2005). The moral activist role of critical race theory scholarship. In N. K. Denzin & Y. S. Lincoln (Eds.), *The SAGE handbook of qualitative research* (3rd ed., pp. 279–302). Thousand Oaks, CA: Sage.

Lather, P., & Smithies, C. (1997). *Troubling the angles: Women living with HIV/AIDS*. Boulder, CO: Westview Press.

Leavy, P. (2009a). Fractured femininities/massacred masculinities: A poetic installation, Parts 1 and 2. *Qualitative Inquiry*, September.

Leavy, P. (2009b). *Method meets art: Arts-based research practice*. New York: Guilford Press.

Leavy, P., & Maloney, K. (2009). American reporting of school violence and "people like us": A comparison of local and national newspaper coverage of the Columbine and Red Lake school shootings. *Critical Sociology, 35*(2), 273–292.

Lewins, A., & Silver, C. (2007). *Using software in qualitative research: A step-by-step guide*. London: Sage.

Lichtman, M. (2006). *Qualitative research in education: A user's guide*. Thousand Oaks, CA: Sage.

Lincoln, Y., & Guba, E. (1999). Establishing trustworthiness. In A. Bryman & R. G. Burgess (Eds.), *Qualitative research* (Vol. 3, pp. 397–434). Thousand Oaks, CA: Sage.

Lincoln, Y., & Guba, E. (2000a). The only generalization is: There is no generalization. In R. Gomm, M. Hammersley, & P. Foster (Eds.), *Case study method: Key issues, key texts*. London: Sage.

Lincoln, Y. S., & Guba, E. G. (2000b). Paradigmatic controversies, contradictions, and emerging confluences. In N. K. Denzin & Y. S. Lincoln (Eds.), *Handbook of qualitative research* (2nd ed., pp. 163–188). Thousand Oaks, CA: Sage.

Locke, L., Spirduso, W. W., & Silverman, S. (2000). *Proposals that work: A guide for planning dissertations and grant proposals*. Thousand Oaks, CA: Sage.

Lofland, J., & Lofland, L. (1984). *Analyzing social settings: A guide to qualitative observation and analysis* (2nd ed.). Belmont, CA: Wadsworth.

Loizos, P. (2000). Video, film, and photographs as research documents. In M. W. Bauer & G. Gaskell (Eds.), *Qualitative researching with text, image, and sound* (pp. 93–107). London: Sage.

Lynoe, N., Sandlund, M., Dahlqvist, G., & Jacobsson, L. (1991). Informed consent: Study of quality information given to participants in a clinical trial. *BMJ, 303,* 610–613.

Malinowski, B. (1922). *Argonauts of the western Pacific.* Prospect Heights, IL: Waveland Press.

Mann, C., & Stewart, F. (2000). *Internet communication and qualitative research: A handbook for researching online.* London: Sage.

Mann, S. A., & Kelley, L. R. (1997). Standing at the crossroads of modernist thought. *Gender & Society, 11*(4), 391–408.

Markham, T., & Couldry, N. (2007). Tracking the reflexivity of the (dis)engaged citizen: Some methodological reflections. *Qualitative Inquiry, 13*(5), 675–695.

Marshall Clark, M. (2002). The September 11, 2001, oral history narrative and memory project: A first report. *The Journal of American History, 89*(2), 1–9.

Marx, G. T. (1988). *Undercover: Police surveillance in America.* Berkeley: University of California Press.

Matoesian, G., & Coldren, J. (2002). Language and bodily conduct in focus group evaluations of legal policy. *Discourse & Society, 13*(4), 469–493.

Maxwell, J. A. (1992). Understanding and validity in qualitative research. *Harvard Educational Review, 62,* 279–300.

McArthur, L. Z., & Resko, B. G. (1975). The portrayal of men and women in American television commercials. *The Journal of Social Psychology, 97,* 209–220.

McDermott, P., & Rothenberg, J. (2000). Why urban parents resist involvement in their children's elementary education. *The Qualitative Report, 5*(3–4).

McGowan, K. (2005, January 10). *Thai village struggles to rebuild.* CNN. Retrieved from http://news.bbc.co.uk/go/pr/fr/-/1/hi/world/asia-pacific/4160753.stm

McKinney, J. C. (1966). *Constructive typology and social theory.* New York: Appleton-Century-Crofts.

Mead, G. H. (1967). *Mind, self, and society from the standpoint of a social behaviorist.* Chicago: University of Chicago Press. (Original work published 1934)

Mears, C. L. (2008). A Columbine study: Giving voice, hearing meaning. *Oral History Review, 35*(2), 159–175.

Merleau-Ponty, M. (1996). *Phenomenology of perception* (C. Smith, Trans.). London and New York: Routledge. (Original work published 1945)

Merton, R. K., & Kendall, P. L. (1946). The focused interview. *American Journal of Sociology, 51,* 541–557.

Miles, M. B., & Huberman, A. M. (1984). *Qualitative data analysis: A sourcebook for new methods.* Newbury Park, CA: Sage.

Miles, M. B., & Huberman, A. M. (1994). *Qualitative data analysis: An expanded sourcebook* (2nd ed.). Thousand Oaks, CA: Sage

Milgram, S. (1963). Behavioral study of obedience. *Journal of Abnormal and Social Psychology, 67,* 371–378.

Mills, C. W. (1959). *The sociological imagination.* New York: Oxford University Press.

Minister, K. (1991). A feminist frame for the oral history interview. In S. Gluck & D. Patai (Eds.), *Women's words: The feminist practice of oral history.* New York: Routledge.

Mishler, E. G. (1991). Representing discourse: The rhetoric of transcription. *Journal of Narrative and Life History, 1*(4), 225–280.

Montell, F. (1999). Focus group interviews: A new feminist method. *NWSA Journal, 11*(1), 44–70.

Moreno, M., Fost, N., & Christakis, D. (2008). Research ethics in the MySpace era. *Pediatrics, 121,* 157–161.

Morgan, D. (1993). Future directions for focus groups. In D. Morgan (Ed.), *Successful focus groups: Advancing the state of the art.* Thousand Oaks, CA: Sage.

Morgan, D. (1995). Why things (sometimes) go wrong in focus groups. *Qualitative Health Research, 5*(4), 516–523.

Morgan, D. (1996). Focus groups. *Annual Review of Sociology, 22,* 129–152.

Morgan, D. (1998). Practical strategies for combining qualitative and quantitative methods: Applications to health research. *Qualitative Health Research, 8,* 362–376.

Morgan, D. (2002). Focus group interviewing. In J. Gubrium & J. Holstein (Eds.), *Handbook of interview research: Context & method* (pp. 141–161). Thousand Oaks, CA: Sage.

Morgan, D. (2007). Paradigms lost and pragmatism regained: Methodological implication of combining qualitative and quantitative methods. *Journal of Mixed Methods Research, 1*(1), 48–76.

Morgan, D. (2008). *Designing for emergence in focus groups.* Unpublished manuscript.

Morgan, D., Fellows, C., & Guevara, H. (2008). Emergent approaches to focus group research. In S. Hesse-Biber & P. Leavy (Eds.), *Handbook of emergent methods* (pp. 189–205). New York: Guilford Press.

Morgan, D., & Krueger, R. (1993). When to use focus groups and why. In D. Morgan (Ed.), *Successful focus groups: Advancing the state of the art* (pp. 3–19). Thousand Oaks, CA: Sage.

Morse, J. (1996). Is qualitative research complete? *Qualitative Health Research, 6,* 3–5.

Morse, J. (2003). Principles of mixed methods and multimethod research design. In A. Tashakkori & C. Teddlie (Eds.), *Handbook of mixed methods in social and behavioral research* (pp. 189–208). Thousand Oaks, CA: Sage.

Morse, J. M., Stern, P. N., Corbin, J., Bowers, B., Charma, K., & Clarke, A. E. (2009). *Developing grounded theory: The second generation.* Walnut Creek, CA: Left Coast Press.

Mulder, I., & Kort, J. (2008). Mixed emotions, mixed methods: The role of emergent technologies in studying user experience in context. In S. N. Hesse-Biber & P. Leavy (Eds.), *Handbook of emergent methods* (pp. 601–612). Thousand Oaks, CA: Sage.

Myerhoff, B. (1978). *Number our days.* New York: Simon & Schuster.

Myers, G. (1998). Displaying opinions: Topics and disagreement in focus groups. *Language in Society, 27,* 85–111.

Nassar-McMillan, S., & Borders, D. (2002). Use of focus groups in survey item development. *The Qualitative Report, 7*(1), 1–11.

Neuman, W. (2003). *Social research methods: Qualitative and quantitative methods* (5th ed.). Boston: Allyn & Bacon.

Nikolaev, A. G. (2009). Images of war: Content analysis of the photo coverage of the war in Kosovo. *Critical Sociology, 35*(1), 105–130.

Oakley, A. (1981). Interviewing women: A contradiction in terms. In H. Roberts (Ed.), *Doing feminist research* (pp. 30–61). London: Routledge & Kegan Paul.

O'Cathain, A., Murphy, E., & Nicholl, J. (2008). Multidisciplinary, interdisciplinary, or dysfunctional? Team working in mixed-methods research. *Qualitative Health Research, 18,* 1574–1585.

O'Connor, K. M., Netting, F. E., & Thomas, M. L. (2008). Grounded theory: Managing the challenge for those facing institutional review board oversight. *Qualitative Inquiry, 14*(1), 28–45.

Opdenakker, R. (2006). Advantages and disadvantages of four interview techniques in qualitative research. *Forum: Qualitative Social Research, 7*(4). [Online]. Retrieved June 5, 2009, from, http://www.qualitative-research.net/fqs-texte/4-06/06-4-11-e.htm

Patton, M. (2002). *Qualitative research and evaluation methods* (3rd ed.). Thousand Oaks, CA: Sage.

Pfaffenberger, B. (1988). *Microcomputer applications in qualitative research.* Thousand Oaks, CA: Sage.

Phillips, N. D., & Strobl, S. (2006). Cultural criminology and kryptonite: Apocalyptic and retributive constructions of crime and justice in comic books. *Crime, Media, Culture, 2*(3), 304–331.

Pillow, W. S. (2000). *Exposed methodology: The body as a deconstructive practice.* New York: Routledge.

Platt, J. (1992). Case study in American methodological thought. *Current Sociology, 40,* 17–48.

Ponterotto, J. G., & Grieger, I. (2007). Effectively communicating qualitative research. *The Counseling Psychologist, 35*(3), 404–430. Retrieved June 16, 2009, from http://tcp.sagepub .com/cgi/content/abstract/35/3/404

Popay, J., Rogers, A., & Williams, G. (1998). Rationale and standards for the systematic review of qualitative research in health services and research. *Qualitative Health Research, 8,* 341–351.

Prior, L. (1997). Following in Foucault's footsteps: Text and context in qualitative research. In D. Silverman (Ed.), *Qualitative research: Theory, method, and practice* (pp. 63–79). Thousand Oaks, CA: Sage.

Prior, L. (2004). Following in Foucault's footsteps: Text and context in qualitative research. In S. Hesse-Biber & P. Leavy (Eds.), *Approaches to qualitative research: A reader on theory and practice* (pp. 317–333). New York: Oxford University Press.

Prosser, J., & Schwartz, D. (1998). Photographs within the sociological research process. In J. Prosser (Ed.), *Image-based research: A sourcebook for qualitative researchers* (pp. 115–130). London: Falmer.

Puchta, C., & Potter, J. (1999). Asking elaborate questions: Focus groups and the management of spontaneity. *Journal of Sociolinguistics, 3*(3), 314–335.

Ramasubramanian, S., & Oliver, M. B. (2003). Portrayals of sexual violence in popular Hindi films, 1997–99. *Sex Roles: A Journal of Research, 10,* 327–336.

Reinharz, S. (1992). *Feminist methods in social research.* New York: Oxford University Press.

Rhodes, C. (2000). Ghostwriting research: Positioning the researcher in the interview text. *Qualitative Inquiry, 6*(4), 511–525.

Riach, K. (2009). Exploring participant-centred reflexivity in the research interview. *Sociology, 43,* 356–370.

Richardson, L. (1995). Narrative and sociology. In J. Van Maanen (Ed.), *Representation in ethnography* (pp. 198–221). Thousand Oaks, CA: Sage.

Rickard, W. (2003). Collaborating with sex workers in oral history. *The Oral History Review, 30*(1), 47–59.

Ritzer, G. (2008). *Modern sociological theory* (7th ed.). New York: McGraw-Hill.

Rollins, J. (1987). *Between women: Domestics and their employers.* Philadelphia: Temple University Press.

Rose, D. (2000). Analysis of moving images. In M. W. Bauer & G. Gaskell (Eds.), *Qualitative researching with text, image, and sound* (pp. 246–262). London: Sage.

Rothe, D. L., & Ross, J. I. (2008). The marginalization of state crime in introductory textbooks on criminology. *Critical Sociology, 34*(5), 741–752.

Rubin, H., & Rubin, I. (1995). *Qualitative interviewing: The art of hearing data.* Thousand Oaks, CA: Sage.

Ryan, K. M. (2009). "I didn't do anything important": A pragmatist analysis of the oral history interview. *The Oral History Review, 36*(1), 25–44.

Safa, H. I. (1981). Runaway shops and female employment: The search for cheap labor. *Signs, 7*(2), 418–433.

Saldana, J. (2009). *The coding manual for qualitative researchers.* London: Sage

Salmons, J. (2010). *Online interviews in real time.* Thousand Oaks, CA: Sage.

Sandelowski, M. (2000). Combining qualitative and quantitative sampling, data collection and analysis techniques in mixed-methods studies. *Research in Nursing and Health, 23,* 246–255.

Sandelowski, M., Volis, C. I., & Knafl, G. (2009). On quantitizing. *Journal of Mixed Methods Research, 3*(3), 208–222.

Schensul, S. L., Schensul, J. J., & LeCompte, M. D. (1999). Essential ethnographic methods: Observations, interviews, and questionnaires. In S. L. Schensul, J. J. Schensul, & M. D. LeCompte (Eds.), *Ethnographer's handbook* (Vol. 2, pp. 278–289). Lanham, MD: Alta Mira/Rowman & Littlefield.

Schofield, J. (2000). Increasing the generalizability in qualitative research. In R. Gomm, M. Hammersley, & P. Foster (Eds.), *Case study method: Key issues, key texts* (pp. 69–97). London: Sage.

Schutz, A. (1967). *Phenomenology of the social world.* Evanston, IL: Northwestern University Press.

Seale, C., & Silverman, D. (1997). Ensuring rigour in qualitative research. *European Journal of Public Health, 7,* 379–384.

Shapiro, M. (1985–1986). Metaphor in the philosophy of the social sciences. *Cultural Critique, 2,* 191–194.

Shopes, L. (1994). When women interview women—and then publish it: Reflections on oral history, women's history, and public history. *Journal of Women's History, 6*(1), 98–108.

Shopes, L. (2003). Sharing authority. *The Oral History Review, 30*(1), 103–110.

Sieber, S. D. (1973). The integration of field work and survey methods. *American Journal of Sociology, 78*(6), 1335–1359.

Simons, H. (2009). *Case study research in practice.* London: Sage.

Sinner, A., Leggo, C., Irwin, R., Gouzouasis, P., & Grauer, K. (2006). Arts-based education research dissertations: Reviewing the practices of new scholars. *Canadian Journal of Education, 29*(4), 1223–1270.

Sitzia, L. (2003). A shared authority: An impossible goal? *The Oral History Review, 30*(1), 87–101.

Slater, R. (2000). Using life histories to explore change: Women's urban struggles in Cape Town, South Africa. *Gender and Development, 8*(2), 38–46.

Sleeter, C. E. (1992). *Keepers of the American dream.* London: Falmer.

Sloan, S. (2008). Oral history and Hurricane Katrina: Reflections on shouts and silences. *The Oral History Review, 35*(2), 176–186.

Smith, D. (1974). Knowing a society from within: A woman's standpoint. *The conceptual practices of power: A feminist sociology of knowledge* (pp. 21–24). Boston: Northeastern University Press.

Smith, R. Q. (1998). Revisiting Juanita's beauty salon: An ethnographic study of an African-American beauty shop. In K. Bennett deMarrais (Ed.), *Inside stories: Qualitative research reflections* (pp. 79–85). London: Lawrence Erlbaum.

Sparkes, A. (1994). Self, silence, and invisibility as a beginning teacher: A life history of lesbian experience. *British Journal of Sociology of Education, 15*(1), 93–119.

Spencer, L., Ritchie, U., Lewis, J., & Dillon, L. (2003). *Quality in qualitative evaluation: A framework for assessing research evidence.* London: Government Chief Social Researcher's Office.

Sprague, J., & Zimmerman, M. (1993). Overcoming dualisms: A feminist agenda for sociological method. In P. England (Ed.), *Theory on gender/feminism on theory* (pp. 255–279). New York: Aldine.

Stacey, J. (1991). Can there be a feminist ethnography? In S. Gluck & D. Patai (Eds.), *Women's words: The feminist practice of oral history* (pp. 111–119). New York: Routledge.

Stake, R. (1995). *The art of case study research.* Thousand Oaks, CA: Sage.

Stake, R. (2000). The case study method in social inquiry. In R. Gomm, M. Hammersley, & P. Foster (Eds.), *Case study method: Key issues, key texts* (pp. 19–26). London: Sage.

Stake, R. (2005a). *Multiple case study analysis.* New York: Guilford Press.

Stake, R. (2005b). Qualitative studies. In N. K. Denzin & Y. S. Lincoln (Eds.), *The SAGE handbook of qualitative research* (3rd ed., pp. 443–465). Thousand Oaks, CA: Sage.

Stein, A., & Plummer, K. (1994). I can't even think straight: Queer theory and the missing sexual revolution in sociology. *Sociological Theory, 12*(2), 178–187.

Strauss, A. (1987). *Qualitative analysis for social scientists.* Cambridge, UK: Cambridge University Press.

Strauss, A., & Corbin, J. (1990). *Basics of qualitative research.* Newbury Park, CA: Sage.

Sudweeks, F., & Simoff, S. J. (1999). Complementary explorative data analysis: Reconciliation of quantitative and qualitative principles. In S. Jones (Ed.), *Doing Internet research: Critical issues and methods for examining the net* (pp. 29–56). Thousand Oaks, CA: Sage.

Sullivan, P., & Elifson, K. (1996). In the field with snake handlers. In C. D. Smith & W. Kornblum (Eds.), *In the field: Readings on the field research experience* (2nd ed., pp. 33–38). Westport, CT: Praeger.

Tashakkori, A., & Teddlie, C. (1998). *Mixed methodology: Combining qualitative and quantitative approaches.* Thousand Oaks, CA: Sage.

Tashakkori, A., & Teddlie, C. (Eds.). (2003). *Handbook of mixed methods in social and behavioural research.* Thousand Oaks, CA: Sage.

Taylor, C. (1987). Interpretation and the sciences of man. In P. Rabinow & M. W. Sullivan (Eds.), *Interpretive social sciences: A second look* (pp. 33–81). London: University of California Press.

Teddlie, C., & Tashakkori, A. (2003). Major issues and controversies in the use of mixed methods in the social and behavioral sciences. In A. Tashakkori & C. Teddlie (Eds.), *Handbook of mixed methods in social and behavioral research* (pp. 3–50). Thousand Oaks, CA: Sage.

Teddlie, C., & Tashakkori, A. (2008). *Foundations of mixed methods research: Integrating quantitative and qualitative approaches in the behavioral and social sciences.* Thousand Oaks, CA: Sage.

Tenni, C., Smith, A., & Boucher, C. (2003). The researcher as autobiographer: Analyzing data written about oneself. *Qualitative Report, 8*(1), 1–12.

Tesch, R. (1990). *Qualitative research: Analysis types and software tools.* London: Falmer Press.

Thomas, M. E., & Treiber, L. A. (2000). Race, gender, and status: A content analysis of print advertisements in four popular magazines. *Sociological Spectrum, 20,* 357–371.

Thomson, A. (1998). Fifty years on: An international perspective on oral history. *The Journal of American History, 85*(2), 581–595.

Thomson, A. (2003). Introduction: Sharing authority: Oral history and the collaborative process. *The Oral History Review, 30*(1), 23–26.

Thrasher, F. M. (1927). *The gang.* Chicago: University of Chicago Press.

Tillmann-Healy, L. (2003). Friendship as method. *Qualitative Inquiry, 9*(5), 729–749.

Van Maanen, J. (1995). An end to innocence: The ethnography of ethnography. In J. Van Maanen (Ed.), *Representation in ethnography* (pp. 1–35). Thousand Oaks, CA: Sage.

Van Manen, M. (2006). Writing qualitatively, or the demands of writing. *Qualitative Health Inquiry, 16*(5), 713–722.

Van Wynsberghe, R., & Khan, S. (2007). Redefining case study. *International Journal of Qualitative Methods, 6*(2), 80–94.

Warren, C. A. B. (2002). Qualitative interviewing. In J. F. Gubrium & J. A. Holstein (Eds.), *Handbook of interview research: Context & method.* Thousand Oaks, CA: Sage.

Wax, R. (1971). *Doing fieldwork: Warnings and advice.* Chicago: University of Chicago Press.

Weinholtz, D., Kacer, B., & Rocklin, T. (1995). Salvaging qualitative research with qualitative data. *Qualitative Health Research, 5,* 388–397.

Weinstein, E. A., & Tamur, J. M. (1978). Meanings, purposes, and structural resources in social interaction. In J. G. Manis & B. N. Meltzer (Eds.), *Symbolic interaction* (3rd ed., pp. 138–140). Boston: Allyn & Bacon.

Weiss, R. S. (1994). *Learning from strangers: The art and methods of qualitative interview studies.* New York: The Free Press.

Weitzman, E. A. (2000). Software and qualitative research. In N. K. Denzin & Y. S. Lincoln (Eds.), *Handbook of qualitative research* (2nd ed., pp. 803–820). Thousand Oaks, CA: Sage.

Weitzman, E., & Miles, M. (1995). *Computer programs for qualitative data analysis: A software sourcebook.* London: Sage.

Weston, K. (2004). Fieldwork in lesbian and gay communities. In S. Hesse-Biber & M. Yaiser (Eds.), *Feminist perspectives on social research* (pp. 198–205). New York: Oxford University Press.

Whyte, W. F. (1943). *Street corner society: The social structure of an Italian slum.* Chicago: University of Chicago Press.

Whyte, W. F. (1996). On the evolution of street corner society. In A. Laureau & F. Schultz (Eds.), *Journeys through ethnography: Realistic accounts of fieldwork* (pp. 9–74). Boulder, CO: Westview Press. (Originally published as an appendix in W. F. Whyte's second edition of *Street Corner Society,* University of Chicago Press, 1955)

Wickham, G., & Freemantle, H. (2008). Some additional knowledge conditions for sociology. *Current Sociology, 56,* 922–939.

Williams, R. (2001). "I'm a keeper of information": History-telling and voice. *Oral History Review, 28*(1), 41–63.

Williams, T. (1996). Exploring the cocaine culture. In C. D. Smith & W. Kornblum (Eds.), *In the field: Readings on the field research experience* (2nd ed., pp. 27–32). Westport, CT: Praeger.

Wilmsen, C. (2001). For the record: Editing and the production of meaning in oral history. *Oral History Review, 28*(1), 65–85.

Wilson, A. (1996). Grandmother to granddaughter: Generations of oral history in a Dakota family. *American Indian Quarterly, 20*(1), 7–14.

Winston, M., & Edelbach, R. (2009). *Society, ethics, and technology* (4th ed.). Belmont, CA: Wadsworth-Cengage.

Wolcott, H. (1994). *Transforming qualitative data: Description, analysis, and interpretation.* Thousand Oaks, CA: Sage.

Wolcott, H. (2001). *Writing up qualitative research* (2nd ed.). Thousand Oaks, CA: Sage.

Wolf, D. L. (Ed.). (1996). *Feminist dilemmas in field work.* Boulder, CO: Westview Press.

Yauch, C. A., & Steudel, H. J. (2003). Complementary use of qualitative and quantitative cultural assessment methods. *Organizational Research Methods, 6*(4), 465–481.

Yin, R. K. (2008). *Case study research: Design and methods* (4th ed.). Thousand Oaks, CA: Sage.

Yoon, Y. (2005). Legitimacy, public relations, and media access: Proposing and testing a media access model. *Communication Research, 32*(6), 762–793.

Zeller, R. A. (1993). Combining qualitative and quantitative techniques to develop culturally sensitive measures. In D. G. Ostrow & R. C. Kessler (Eds.), *Methodological issues in AIDS behavioral research* (pp. 95–116). New York: Plenum Press.

Zucker, D. (2001). Using case study methodology in nursing research. *The Qualitative Report, 6*(2). Retrieved from http:///www.nova.edu/ssss/QR/QR6-2/zucker.html

Index

Supporting researchers for more than 40 years

Research methods have always been at the core of SAGE's publishing program. Founder Sara Miller McCune published SAGE's first methods book, *Public Policy Evaluation*, in 1970. Soon after, she launched the *Quantitative Applications in the Social Sciences* series—affectionately known as the "little green books."

Always at the forefront of developing and supporting new approaches in methods, SAGE published early groundbreaking texts and journals in the fields of qualitative methods and evaluation.

Today, more than 40 years and two million little green books later, SAGE continues to push the boundaries with a growing list of more than 1,200 research methods books, journals, and reference works across the social, behavioral, and health sciences. Its imprints—Pine Forge Press, home of innovative textbooks in sociology, and Corwin, publisher of PreK–12 resources for teachers and administrators—broaden SAGE's range of offerings in methods. SAGE further extended its impact in 2008 when it acquired CQ Press and its best-selling and highly respected political science research methods list.

From qualitative, quantitative, and mixed methods to evaluation, SAGE is the essential resource for academics and practitioners looking for the latest methods by leading scholars.

For more information, visit **www.sagepub.com**.